MAD FRANK'S
UNDERWORLD
HISTORY OF BRITAIN

Frankie Fraser
with James Morton

*To all my pals, they'll know who they are,
and to all my family. To Debbie Oakes,
a true pal. God bless them all.*

This omnibus edition first published in Great Britain in 2007 by
Virgin Books Ltd
Thames Wharf Studios
Rainville Road
London
W6 9HA

Mad Frank's London first published in 2001 by Virgin Books Ltd
Mad Frank's Britain first published in 2002 by Virgin Books Ltd

ISBN 978 0 7535 1275 3

Typeset by TW Typesetting, Plymouth, Devon
Printed and bound in Great Britain by Mackays of Chatham PLC

CONTENTS

PICTURE CREDITS

Illustrated section:

The author and publishers are grateful to the following sources for pictures reproduced in this book:

Draughtsman Ltd, London W10 (Based on mapping generated by ERA-Maptec Ltd)	Maps, p. 1 and p. 2
Hulton Getty	Jack 'Spot', p. 3; George Blake, p. 4; Ruth Ellis, p. 5; The Messina brothers, p. 6; Flower sellers, p. 6; Harold Davidson, p. 6
Topham Picturepoint	The Krays, p. 3; Mandy Rice-Davies, p. 4; Billy Hill, p. 5
James Morton	Hampton Court Palace pub, p. 7; Jimmy Robson, p. 7; The Castle Hotel, p. 8;
Dock Bateson	Marilyn/Frank/Renee and Tommy Wisbey, p. 8

FOREWORD

The first contact I had with Frank Fraser was through his slightly older sister Eva Brindle, to whom he was devoted, as was she to him. He had been arrested in what would become known as the Richardson Torture Trial in 1966 and she was accused of attempting to pervert the course of justice by trying to get a witness to change his statement. I don't know why she chose me as her solicitor. I had only been qualified three years and I had my own firm in Holborn. Generally speaking my clients came from North London and Clerkenwell and I very rarely ventured to South London from where Eva Brindle and Fraser came. Curiously his regular solicitor was also from North London, the almost legendary Jimmy Fellowes from Walthamstow. I have no idea why she didn't go to him.

Hers was a funny old case. The witness Bennie Coulston alleged he had been badly beaten on 18 January 1967 and Fraser had pulled out one of his teeth with a pair of pliers. Fraser denied this and Eva Brindle set about trying to prove her brother's innocence. Coulston was persuaded to make an affidavit changing his story and he was taken to a solicitor and, if I remember correctly, to the organisation Liberty to swear it was true. Somehow the police found out. Coulston said he had been paid; she denied this. The allegation was that the exact amount of money to be paid to Coulston was in a cupboard at her home. When, however, it was counted at court it was substantially more. I arranged for her to have the rogue but brilliant barrister and MP Billy Rees-Davies appear for her and, despite turning up late and claiming the court clock was fast, he did a good job. Even so she received three years. A young girl who had worked for Charlie Richardson was sentenced to six months and the man who had driven Eva around something in between. Later I was offered a defence in the Richardson trial but, when it came to it, the prosecution offered no evidence against the man.

Fraser went down in the case proper and received a ten to go with the five he was already serving for an affray at Mr Smith's nightclub in Catford. In 1969 I saw in the papers he was involved in a riot in Parkhurst prison on the Isle of Wight. I thought nothing of it. Then Eva Brindle rang me up. Defendants, as a rule, have a low expectation of an acquittal. Provided their lawyers try, in the main they are satisfied and I had tried. That was recommendation enough. Now her brother was going to be summoned with incitement to murder. Given his record he would almost certainly receive a life sentence were he to be found guilty. Would I defend him?

Today, Fraser is a small man; then getting on for forty years ago he was bigger but certainly not the bruiser I expected. The prison officers were, however, keen to point out how dangerous he was. 'Sit with your back to the door so's you can get out if he comes at you'. And one day, ' He's bad today. We've put you in the doctor's room where there's a bell you can press with your knee. We'll try and get him before he gets you'. It was all very reassuring but when it came to it we got on well. The only trouble I had was when I saw a witness before I interviewed him one afternoon. To be kept waiting did not fit in with his prison status which was on a par with that of Noel Coward in *The Italian Job*. There was also some trouble in that the tyres of my car seemed to be let down from time to time when I went to see him or other prisoners, and no I could not borrow a jack. But that was not Fraser. The trial went as well as could be expected. Fraser was acquitted of the incitement to murder but received five years for assaulting one or more of the warders.

I heard no more of him until after I gave up practice and started writing and editing a law magazine. I published *Gangland* in which I upset some London identities. That was smoothed over and then I received a call on my answering machine. A Mr Fraser wanted to speak with me urgently. I thought this was just about all I needed. He was perfectly polite, as indeed he had been twenty years earlier. 'I've read your book. I haven't bought it. Someone nicked it for me. I'm writing my life story and I want you to do it for me'. I told him I had something on the stocks. That was all right. He would wait until I finished it. Although my agent was dead against the idea it was an offer which, in *Godfather* terms, I couldn't refuse. Here was an opportunity to discover what life in London's underworld was really like. We arranged to meet and he arrived a little late full of apologies. He had broken his arm and had to go to hospital. I told him he could have cancelled. No, an appointment was an appointment. In all the times we met I do not think he was ever late again. If I appeared five minutes late there he would be looking at his watch, 'I thought maybe we'd made it for tomorrow, James'.

Mad Frank was the first book in a series. Fraser was an incredibly easy man with whom to deal. He had amazing recall of events even if they did not concern him. I remember him telling me of a murder in Waterloo in the 1940s. February it was, he said. When I came to look it up he was a month out. *Mad Frank* was well received and indeed thirteen years later is still in print. One book led to another.

By then Fraser had converted himself into an entertainer. He tells a good story and has a line in repartee. He appeared in cabaret first in Hackney and then in the West End, there were appearances on the radio and television, at literary festivals, a web site, television commercials, two films. There were book signings at which he took great care to speak and joke with everyone, whilst carefully signing their books in his spidery handwriting. People wanted a photograph taken of him pretending to pull out their teeth. Would he mind? 'Have you bought the book, son?' Yes, he had. 'Of course, then'. He set up a tour of London's crime spots with, for a time, his then girlfriend Marilyn Wisbey, the daughter of a Great Train Robber, sometimes doing the driving. I went on one. The punters had come from Northampton and Brighton for a tour which began at nine on a Saturday morning. When we stopped the customers crowded around him. Those who could not get near spoke with me. I asked one elderly couple from where they had come. Bath. Didn't that mean it was a really early start? Five o'clock. They hadn't minded at all. They had enjoyed the tour so much when they came a fortnight earlier they felt they had to do it again.

Writing *Mad Frank's London* we walked around his old haunts and some new ones. Wherever we went people in the street greeted him, wanted to shake his hand, have an autograph on a paper napkin; taxi-drivers hooted at him and gave him a thumbs-up. He was a genuinely popular figure.

When Virgin Books asked me to contribute to this new edition I hadn't seen Frank for a couple of years. I telephoned him and we arranged to meet at Holborn tube station at 10.30 a.m. the next day. When I arrived at ten past ten I could not see him and went out on to the pavement. There he was, dapper as ever, talking to a man in a yellow jacket. 'Who's your friend?' I asked. 'I dunno', he replied, 'Fellow'd seen one of the repeats on telly and recognised me. Happens all the time'.

James Morton, October 2006

MAD FRANK'S LONDON

SOUTH LONDON

1

You don't often find three stiffs when you do a screwing but that's what happened when Jimmy Essex, Dido Frett and me did a tailor's in Lower Marsh off the Waterloo Road in the war. They were the first dead people I ever saw. Dido and me had just got Jimmy out of Feltham Borstal. The wall wasn't that high, and we'd been to visit him so we knew exactly where he'd be working. After that it was just a question of up, over, out and away.

We'd done the downstairs of the tailor's and we'd gone up to see what more there was. The bodies was in an upstairs room. They'd been killed in a bomb blast a couple of days earlier and no one had discovered them yet. They didn't seem to have any injuries on them. I remember one had his eyes still open. We had a look to see if there was any more gear we could nick and when we was out Dido made a phone call. The good thing was there was no question of the stiffs ID-ing us or giving evidence.

I was born at home, which was a minute from Waterloo Station; fifteen seconds if you hurried. All five of us was.

There was the Lying In Hospital just down York Road – it's derelict now – but to get in there in those days cost money which my parents didn't have. To get to our house you came out the Waterloo Road entrance to the station just where Dartmoor Annie and later Buster Edwards from the Train had their flower stalls, down the steps and across the street right into Cornwall Road, and our place was just about opposite Roupell Street. It was still standing until about eight years ago when they knocked it down to make way for the extension to the Jubilee Line. Opposite us on the corner was a newsagent's. Now it's a smart baker's, Konditori & Cook, but on the other corner was a barber's shop and there's still one there. Valentino's it's called now.

If you walked a few yards towards the river, on the same side of the street as us was St Patrick's Church and the school with its green shamrocks on the wall, It's a nursery school now. Opposite was the Cornwall Club, which was a snooker club, and upstairs they'd sometimes have dances. Me and Billy Murray and another boy did it when we was about ten. We got over the roof and come in round the back, but next door was a police hostel named after Edward Henry, who had a lot to do with fingerprinting in its early days and who became a commissioner, I think. There was a copper leaning out the window and he saw us.

Billy and me went off to Olympia and the circus there, where we picked up some more dough saying we'd mind cars. We got to see the circus as well but when we got back to his place the coppers was waiting. The club was very good though, they wouldn't pros us at all. Billy and his family lived about two minutes away in Doon Street opposite where Bowaters, the paper people, used to put their lorries. They had a dock there. The City of London Corporation used to have their dust carts tip the rubbish onto barges to be taken out to the North Sea. Every year they'd give a party for the locals as a sweetener because the smell was something awful. We always used to be told not to swim near Waterloo Bridge because of the currents, but of course, we did.

Another time Billy and me screwed a billiards' hall and took away a set of balls. They were very valuable and we took them to a youth club just opposite the Lying In Hospital, said we'd found them. We were very popular. That was a place chosen to have girls do some dance before Princess Alice at the Albert Hall. My sister Eva was one of the girls. I remember my Mum doing her best to make Eva look smart for that night. Of course they only wore their uniforms. There wasn't any money for anything else.

When I was about five my parents moved a couple of hundred yards away to Howley Place. It has gone now but it's just where the *Chez Gerard* restaurant is as you go up the steps to the station. That's where I ran out into the road and got knocked down asking drivers for cigarette cards. They put me on the back of a lorry and took me to St Thomas' Hospital; I had a fractured skull and then I got meningitis. Howley Place took a fair beating in the war. We was number 6 and the first five all got bombed. On one side of the road running up to the bridge there was little hotels, not much more than case joints really, and on the other there was shops. There was also a pub, the Feathers, which was really two pubs. One on the corner of Belvedere Road and Commercial Road, and the other up in Waterloo Road. On the river side of York Road where the Festival Hall site is now there was hotels for commercial travellers.

I tried a bit of hotel creeping as a kid, nothing much just the cheaper hotels around Waterloo, like those in York Road, and sometimes over into the Strand, but it wasn't really my game. If you was stopped it would be either 'Have you got a job?' or 'I'm looking for Uncle Harry and I think he's in room whatever'. Of course, a scruffy little kid like me couldn't expect to have his Uncle Harry staying in the Savoy. I did a couple of jobs later but only when they was put up by a very good source, otherwise it was a dot in the dark. You could come a real tumble hotel creeping if you weren't careful. Just like me and Jimmy Brindle and Jimmy Humphries nearly did in the Howard Hotel over off the

Embankment, when we was trying to raise funds for Jack Rosa's appeal. The police tried to let the jury know we'd got form, and if it hadn't been for the juror who knew what was what we'd have been onto a seven.

Walk on down past the Lying In Hospital in York Road and you come to Leake Street. That's where me and Dido Frett, Gerry Newman and Danny Swain had a really good tickle at the end of the war. There was all arches with lock-up warehouses in them with stuff like Scotch inside. They had double doors with padlocks on them almost as it looks now. If the doors was open they'd be well guarded, but by chance when we was having a look round we saw in the first arch on the left that there was Scotch being kept there. It's amazing how there really wasn't any security, not belled up or anything. Just a man who acted as caretaker who lived in a house at the end of the road and kept an eye on things. We were back that night with the Stillsons and we was away. We went back three months later but this time the man seen us and we had to be on our toes. There wasn't any problem; we was in a hooky van.

As a kid, I earned a fortune out of the station. There wasn't that number of porters and there wasn't any parking attendants so it was a question of 'Look after your car, sir?' again. Or 'Carry your bags, sir?' You could do it all day long and some people was in such a hurry they'd give you a white fiver to go and buy cigarettes and papers and things and that's the last they'd see of me. It didn't happen too often but when I got home with it and told my mother I'd found it, she'd be exclaiming what a lucky child I was to her. She was sensible enough not to tell my father. I'm sure he'd have realised what was going on.

Another place I did well at was The Ring at Blackfriars, where there was boxing twice a week. Joe Reeder had a cafe almost literally right opposite and I'd mind cars there. My uncle was in the army with him in the First World War and Joe would tell me what cars I shouldn't be looking in. Then suddenly all-in wrestling seemed to take over in the mid

1930s. Not that that did me any harm. There was still cars to be minded even though people didn't come from so far away. People was much more gullible in those days. The man and the woman in the street wouldn't believe you if you said it was hooky.

I think it was because there was talk of plans to knock down Howley Place to make more room for Waterloo Station that, before we were kicked out, my parents decided to move to the Walworth Road. The little place where we'd lived in Howley Place backed on to much bigger houses in Tennyson Street. Ours were two up and two down with a privy in the back yard, but these were on four floors with a few rooms on each floor. As kids we'd keep a look out for which houses were standing empty. There was no question of squatters moving in. Instead we'd steam in and strip the place of lead. The new house had an inside toilet but it still didn't have a bathroom. People kept themselves clean, of course, but a bath wasn't so much of a priority as it is now. If you wanted a bath it was down to Manor Place. It didn't matter you was going in straight after someone else. They had an attendant there whose job it was to clean them; but you had to give him a tip if you wanted him to clean the bath for you. Think how recent it is comparatively that hotels, even quite good ones, have put in private baths.

Every time I go down Waterloo way I see the IMAX there. If my father was still alive he'd never believe it. The Royal Children's Hospital is about the only thing standing from my day let alone his. I got taken into it when I ran my bike into the kerb and fell over. Blood all over the place there was. I've still got the scars. My grandmother stayed on in Howley Place, where we lived, until she died. I think the actor Charlie Drake's father had a place at the end of the street. I've bumped into Charlie in my travels once or twice and I've meant to ask him but I've never got round to it.

As you know I live off the Walworth Road and the gentrification that's going on there is amazing. You've got what I call Beehives all over the place. They're young people, not working class, you see in the Beehive pub round the back of the Elephant. There's Sutherland Square and now it's out of this world. The houses used to be in flats but they're mostly single dwelling units, as the estate agents say. Maybe there's one or two that's not been done up but they're the exception. There's no noise, no traffic. There's a little square in the middle and that's got a locked gate now to keep out the druggies. It's enlightening, it really is.

When I was young, if you had a car you was looked at askance and it was a good way of attracting the coppers. That was the way to get nicked or have to hand over a few quid. The Campbells, who also lived in Howley Place, had a little baby Austin 7. It stood out like a sore thumb in the Cut but they had two pie shops, Harris near the Windmill Pub down by the Blackfriars Road and Woods was the other, so they could account for how they'd got it. People stood with their mouths open watching them drive around on a Sunday. Tom Thumb Brindle could have had a car and be left alone because he was a street bookmaker and was paying up anyway. But little Frank having a car – not a good idea.

When there was talk of legalising bookmakers the police was some of the biggest opponents. Their pensions was going to come to an end. There must have been five street bookmakers between Waterloo and Blackfriars they could tap. I'd run errands for the bookies or be a lookout. The bets were tiny, 3d or 6d, and for the day's running about I'd get 2d or 3d.

When I look back I don't think there was much in the way of what you call domestic burglaries when I was young. For a start there wasn't much to burgle. If you'd done our place there was only my father's blue serge suit and you'd have to do the drum at the weekend because it was the only time it was out of hock. There wasn't any cash even though my parents never had a bank account, either one of them. And we wasn't any different from most of the families round us. Of course those with shops was more vulnerable because they'd have cash. Even people like them didn't trust banks. I think they was afraid they'd be shopped to the tax people. I know now there's a theory that burglaries happen within a mile of the screwer's home but it wasn't like that when I was young. There was more a spirit between people. If my father had thought I was doing someone's home he'd have beaten me blue and then died of shame. But it wouldn't have occurred to me.

There was one good man who did a lot of work just before I was born. Charles White was known as the Clapham Climber because that's where he did a lot of his work. Don't forget that would be half country in those days. He'd started his life as a blue-flyer stealing lead. He picked up a ten from Darling in 1923. Darling said he wished he could have had him flogged but Charlie was in poor shape.

Country houses and rich people's drums in Mayfair was a different thing and there was some fine burglars. For a start there was my friend Ruby Sparks. That's how he got his nickname. He did some Maharajah's drum and come away with a whole lot of rubies. He didn't know what they was and he more-or-less give them away to the fence who conned him they was worthless.

As far as the country houses was concerned George Smithson, known as Gentleman George, was about the finest when I was growing up. He looked a bit like a vicar, which was a help, and he'd often have a sort of college scarf round his neck which give him this air of respectability. He was another who had a double life. He'd been well educated and he lived with his wife and kids in Kensington and until the first time he goes down they didn't know what he was up to. What was good was he was fearless and he didn't cause damage for the sake of it. In them days everyone had dogs and he was good with them. There's a story when he did a job in Upton Magna there's a big black Labrador or Retriever in the chair by the desk. Smithson's so good the dog doesn't really wake up except to be patted when he's leaving.

9

Mostly Smithson worked alone, which is really the best way to do things, but for a time he worked with George Ingram who wasn't his class of thief. Ingram's real name was Alfred Tragheim. What you want to be if you're a creeper is to be soft on your feet. A good creeper like that Welshman Raymond Jones could stay in someone's room half an hour and they'd never wake up. I think they liked the challenge and the danger. That sort of thing was never for me. George Ingram was clumsy, and like me he never settled to his bird. On and off he did a two-and-a-half-year hunger strike in Dartmoor. Smithson copped three long sentences even so, despite how good he was, including a six in Scotland in 1923 and a week later he got another two added at the Bailey. After that he give it all up and wrote a book. Ingram drew a six at the same time and he wrote a book and all.

When they come a cropper in Scotland the bogeys up there thought it was the biggest capture they'd made in years and, in a way, I suppose it was. It come about because they hadn't got their escape laid on. They was relying on trains and in them days the porters as well as the railway police watched the passengers. They'd screwed a big house in North Berwick and was trying to get themselves back to Edinburgh and they was seen waiting for a train. In fact they had a pull from a copper and he'd let them go, so it looked like they'd got away with it. It seems like it was the first time George used the name Ingram. But a couple of phone calls was all it needed. They thought they'd get off before the train arrived in Edinburgh and they jumped off in Portobello and picked up a tram, but the bogeys had found out they wasn't on the original train and they was watching for them to get to the station. In a briefcase they had all the stuff and a burglar's kit as well as a couple of horseshoes for luck.

I never carried horseshoes or wore green or things like that but I never liked the 13th. I was born on that day and the times I've been nicked over the years outside or in prison on the 13th is remarkable. When Dodger Davies and me was nicked when the car wouldn't start in Oxford Street that was a 13th. I've always planned to keep quiet that day but the times I've come out the punishment block, think I'll take it easy, get the day over with and I've been swagged straight down again is almost countless. I still don't like it.

Another good thief, much nearer my time, was Ernie Watts. He was top class and I think he only did a couple of years in the nick early in his career. He'd had a good education but there wasn't enough money to send him to Christ's Hospital, even though he'd got a scholarship, and it was after that he took up thieving in a big way. There was plenty of stories about him, like how he once had a challenge over how many smash and grabs he could do in a night and he got up to twelve. Then there was another how he had the police, who was following him, neck-deep in a pond before he could get away. He was a funny devil though. He was a diabetic and he topped himself – I don't know if it was an accident or not because he'd tried twice already – when he come back from a job just out of London. He give himself an overdose of insulin. By then he'd already met up with Bruce Reynolds who was top notch himself and really took over Ernie's organisation. I had a drink with Bruce not too long ago. He come down my nephew Jimmy's Tin Pan Club in Denmark Street.

But even smash and grab, which was one my games, wasn't that easy. You had to do it right otherwise if you threw the brick it more or less bounced back off the glass, and if you didn't hold it right when you smashed against the glass then you ended up getting a shower of glass on you and a load of splinters. That happened to Ruby at first. He had to use those Bulldog clips to keep the cuts together until someone could sew him up.

INTERNMENT AND THE SABINIS

Before the War I saw Oswald Mosley but I never really went and watched his marches. It was nothing to do with me and there wasn't any money in it. There wasn't any anti-Jewish feeling around the Elephant like there was in the East End. I don't recall ever seeing any Jewish boys my age at all. There certainly wasn't any at St Patrick's, which of course was a Catholic School, and I don't think there'd be many at St John's which was C of E, nor St Andrew's in Joanna Street in Lower Marsh. In fact the only Jewish people I knew was Max Cohen, the tailor, when I went down the East End to get my suits, and Hymie Harris who was the South London tailor we used. There was a man, Levy, at the Elephant and there'd be one or two who'd buy crooked gear but generally they kept themselves to themselves. I think I was thirteen when one of the Chaps took me over to Max Cohen's. A suit probably cost 30/– and you had to put down £1 as a deposit. That was about two years after I saw the first black person in my life. He was in the Boy's Brigade. He was a terrific guy.

I suppose the Jews controlled the pawnbrokers but there was never one behind the counter. Harvey and Thompson were the biggest round us. In went Dad's blue serge suit, with a waistcoat of course, on a Monday and out it came on a Friday. I'm sure he never knew. His pride wouldn't have stood for it. It was the same with the tallymen. The men who owned the firms may have been Jewish but the people who come round knocking for the weekly money wasn't. You hardly knew their names. If you paid up regular then they was just John or Jim. It's funny to write it now but in South London when I was growing up you didn't know what Jewish people looked like. There was no illustrated magazines like today. I think *Picture Post* was the first and that only come out just before the war. There was things like the *Illustrated London News* but that wasn't for the likes of us. We weren't going to be interested in what Lady Muck had said when she opened the flower show.

It all ended in tears for the Mosleys and a lot of others when the War came. Lady Mosley was in Holloway with my sister when Eva was doing a shoplifting sentence. She'd been locked up at the beginning of the War so she couldn't be a go-between between her husband, who was in Brixton, and the British Union. She was let out around the same time as Eva who always spoke highly of her. Of course there was privileges for the Mosleys. They let him come and visit her in Holloway and there was a ruckus. At that time Eva's eldest daughter, Beverley, was a bit under a year old and when our mother got a visiting order they wouldn't let us take the kid in to see Eva. Me and Dido Frett was on the run at the time but I took my chance and went in and Dido had to stay outside at the gate holding Beverley. There were visiting boxes, about a foot by two foot, with thick glass with wire netting. You only got twenty minutes visiting in those days anyway. How could they be so cruel and not even think they was being cruel?

Once Italy joined in the War with the Nazis then there was arrests of Italians and half Italians all round. In all something like 600 people was detained. There was the Quaglino brothers who had the famous restaurant in Bury Street, and there was the head chef at the Cafe Royal and a couple of clowns from Bertram Mills' Circus. They'd been with the circus for fifteen years but they was thought to be dangerous people who'd attack cabinet ministers and people like that. Of course it was a load of nonsense and they was released after a few months. Naturally the Sabinis was among them and they and Bert Marsh got sent down to internment at Ascot racecourse, which I suppose was at least appropriate. They didn't even speak Italian. It was a way of breaking up the gang. A sort of reprisal for the gold Bert Marsh got out of Croydon airport before the War.

Some of the Italian boys I was at school with was detained under those section 18B regulations. Mario Florentini was one and he ended up in Walton. He was only about seventeen when he was locked up. I don't know what danger they thought he could be. He would go to Italy every summer to a camp and I suppose they thought he was bringing back messages. He was a very talented musician

13

and he was on BBC radio for years after the War. The last time I saw him was in an Italian restaurant in Frith Street. Bobby Warren and Italian Albert were with me. Mario was playing the violin and came over to see us.

The Italians still had cell tasks just like the rest of us. Protocol went out the window. If they complained it was, 'Yes, but there's a War on. Rules don't apply.' The Jewish mobs took over then but it wasn't personal, it was business, as they say. They just took advantage of anti-Italian feeling. Albert Dimes went in the air force but he soon walked out. Tony Mancini was one of the few big Italians left outside to rally the flag and he soon got topped for the murder of Hubby Distleman in the Palm Beach.

I remember talking to an Italian kid, Tony Nappi; he was with me and Jimmy Brindle when we went to see Albert Dimes after the Spot fight. He'd been in Chelmsford in 1941 and he was saying how he thought it looked like him and the others was going to be badly done up. Not just by the Jewish prisoners but everyone was in on the war effort. Thankfully, nothing come of it.

When I think of the trouble there's been in Glasgow between the Protestants and the Catholics it's surprising there was never anything like it in London. I think we was the only Catholics in Howley Place but no one ever said a word out of turn to us. There was no bigotry at all. St John's was the big Protestant school and they had a very good boxing team. St Patrick's was always having bouts against them and playing them at football but there was no religious quarrels. Our teachers were Irish or Italian and they encouraged us to support Celtic, which is what our school's football colours were, but that was about all. Of course we had fights on the streets but there was nothing religious in it. Eva and I used to go to the Protestant Youth Club and no one said we shouldn't. I suppose it was because London was more sophisticated, being a bigger city than Glasgow.

* * *

I didn't drive then. I'd had my brief taken away from me when I was seventeen out working with Patsy Lyons down King's Cross way. I wasn't even driving but I lost it for ten years and after that I never bothered. There used to be a juvenile court in the Euston Road at the old Friends' Meeting House. We'd all go for our cases and wait in the hall discussing what we'd been up to. I remember there was one kid was going to get probation and he was asked if he was willing to do it. 'Yes,' he pipes, 'but I don't want to have Mr Smith supervise me.' 'Why ever not, Tommy?' says the beak. 'Because he makes me take me clothes off and dance on the table with only me boots on,' says the kid. In those days people would think he was just a little liar but they'd take more notice now. Back then he probably lost his chance of probation and got detention.

I've never ever had a licence since, incredible though it may seem, and now I'll never have one. It wasn't until after I come out from the Spot slashing that I got a car, an automatic it was. Until then Jimmy, Eva's husband, used to drive me. Once I'd got the car I drove all over the country with the gaming machines, and I must have been a good driver because I never got a pull and I never had even the smallest accident. I was never a wheelman though.

I think you've really got to be born a wheelman. People like Roy James, who was on the Train and one or two other top class jobs, or Danny Allpress were just naturals. Probably wheelmen's fathers were often van drivers and they'd want a car of their own to go out with the family. That's where the kids would learn. They'd probably nick Dad's car and give it a spin round the block a few times. Don't forget the streets was empty compared with today.

A top wheelman would work for up to five teams during his career. He'd have a reputation and firms would approach him. There weren't a lot about. Even though the driver usually got a bit less than the others who actually did the job a lot of people was frightened of getting a five or a ten back then, prison was so hard. So a wheelman could pick and choose.

MRS VIOLET VAN DER ELST

Mrs Violet Van der Elst was the woman who did so much to try and stop topping. She was the first person to try and really kick up a fuss. I'm not sure she was all she said she was but she did wonders. She'd made some money out of her second husband and she was a good businesswoman in her own right, selling cosmetics. She reckoned she could stop hanging inside six months. That was in 1935 and it took nearer thirty years. The first one she tried to do something about was a bloke in the navy, a fellow called Brigstock who'd done a Chief Petty Officer on their ship. She got a petition with 80,000 signatures, and when that didn't work she got another 100,000. It didn't do any good. The authorities said they wasn't on the right bit of paper and only her signature counted.

Then she tried to stop Reggie Woolmington being hanged. He was a funny man. In fact when it come to it he didn't need her because the House of Lords said he wasn't guilty of murder. He'd written a note to his boss something like, 'I'm not coming to work today. I've shot my wife.'

She was quite willing to put herself in the firing line. When Brigstock got topped she had aeroplanes flying black banners over Wandsworth with STOP THE DEATH PENALTY on them and sandwich board men parading. That's when the coppers did her for obstruction.

Next thing she's down in Brighton in April protesting over Percy Anderson who'd done his girlfriend on the local golf course. She'd said he'd been going out with other girls and he'd lost his rag and strangled her with a shoelace. It's amazing how many people do others with shoelaces. I suppose sometimes it's the only thing that comes to hand easy enough. Anyway, once he's strangled the kid he goes off paddling for half an hour. Usually in that sort of case the bloke's tried to rape the girl, but there wasn't anything like it in Percy's case and as a result there was a big petition for him to be reprieved. Violet had 'Abide With Me' played over the loudspeakers in vans she'd hired. People must have thought it was the Cup Final. That was when she got done for assaulting a copper.

In all she got arrested seven times and summonsed seventeen. Most of them were dismissed and when they wasn't the magistrates give her things like conditional discharges. The biggest pros against her was at the start of the War when she got done under the Official Secrets Act. What happened was when Wandsworth got a hit in the bombing one of the cons managed to get hold of the medical records of the fellows who'd been topped there with things like how long they'd actually lived after the drop and what drugs they'd been given to keep them quiet before it went off. Anyway she realises it's dynamite. She'd got a sort of butler-companion and she got him to give the bloke a tenner or something like that, which was all she had in the house. Tells him to come back at the end of the week when there'll be more. Next, she takes the pages to a photographer – no copier you can use yourself in them days – and tells him to guard them with his life whilst he's photoing them. What does he do? Goes to his boss and what does his boss do? Goes to the coppers. Next thing she's at Bow Street. She was fined a tenner and ten quid costs and she undertook not to publish what had been in the documents.

She may have been an exhibitionist but the cons worshipped her. Funny thing, she was just as keen to pros people as she was to save them from topping. One of the people she prossed was Lord Edward Montagu who worked for her for a bit. She'd won a few quid from her bookmaker and she said he'd been and taken a cheque of hers and cashed it for himself. He said she'd endorsed it to him but he went down. He doesn't seem to have held it against her though because they seem to have become quite friendly later on.

Lord Edward Montagu was involved in a funny way in a murder case himself. It was one of those unsolved ones. A good one too – just like an Agatha Christie play. It was a few years before he became involved with Mrs Elst. What he was in them days was a film extra and he'd put up $200 along with a lot of people to go and film a travel documentary in the South Seas. The whole thing was being run by a man who calls himself Captain Walter Wanderwell and he was scamming them all. He'd been an enemy alien in the First World War when he'd had another name altogether. I can't think right now what it was. Anyway in early December 1932 his Lordship and the Captain and the others are all on the boat which is moored at Los Angeles when a man puts his head through a porthole and asks where Wanderwell is. He's told he's in the saloon and the next thing there's a shot and that's the last of his wanderings.

Who did it? At this stage you can never say for certain but the chances are it was a fellow who'd been taken for his money by Wanderwell and dumped in Panama. He was identified as being the man who asked where the Captain was and he'd got a gun of the type that shot him but that was about it. He got a not guilty but when it come to it he was deported to Australia and was killed in the Second World War.

Another member of the family, Lord Montagu of Beaulieu, was involved in a case which started off a campaign to stop homosexuality being a crime. It was in 1953 it was. He and a couple of friends were charged with indecency. It had all come about when Montagu reported the loss of his camera and it somehow got turned around and he was in the dock. Then a couple of RAF servicemen said they'd been involved as well. The servicemen had been well at it with each other but the pros said Lord Montagu and his friends had lavished hospitality to seduce them. When it come to it the lavish hospitality seemed to be some cider and a meal cooked on a gas stove, which don't seem that lavish to me. Anyway the jury convicted but when Lord Montagu and the others were being driven away to the nick the public gathered round the car and cheered them and booed the pros's witnesses.

DOUBLE JEOPARDY

There was another fellow I remember. This was a fellow, Leonard Thomas, who'd been convicted of trying to kill his wife in 1949 and he got a seven. He'd stabbed her at their home in Chelsea. In them days you couldn't be done for murder if the person you'd tried to do lived for more than a year and a day. That's how Harry Roberts, who did the policemen in Shepherd's Bush, was lucky. Previously he'd done a man who lasted the year and then died so Harry couldn't swing for it. This fellow Thomas's wife died inside the year and so he got put up for the murder. He said they couldn't try him because he'd already been convicted of the same offence. Same circumstances but a different offence, said the judge, who was Devlin who tried that doctor Bodkin Adams and wrote a book about it. Made himself very unpopular over it he did – the book that is, not Thomas. Thomas was sentenced to death but he got reprieved and funnily he only served about five years. Not bad.

When it comes to it not a lot of Chaps were topped over work. Well before my time was Joseph Jones who was topped in 1918. He and his mates, a couple of Aussies, Ernie Sharp and Tom Maguire. They used to meet up with soldiers, say they'll take them to a brothel and then roll them in an alley. They did it once too often near Waterloo station and one of the men Oliver Imlay, Canadian he was, died from the beating. Sharp went K.E. as it was then and he got seven, Maguire got a ten and Jones who'd actually killed Imlay swung. Funnily enough he'd used a copper's truncheon.

Babe Mancini was the next to swing and that was nearly twenty-five years later. I knew him a bit from being with the Sabinis. Then after the war Harryboy Jenkins and Flossie Forsyth were a couple more. Funnily, it was much more usual for straight people to swing but there was one of us in 1928 when Frederick Stewart, who was a burglar, was hung. His game was sounding the drum, knocking on people's doors of an afternoon and if there was a reply putting up a moody saying he was looking for so-and-so. It was going all right until a fellow in Pembridge Square come back and surprised him and Stewart shot the man with a gun he'd bought for an oxford. The man was looking through the glass panel of the front door and Stewart fired from the other side. He come a tumble because a copper remembered that he come from Warwick Mews and that afternoon when a woman had answered the door at another drum he'd said he was looking for Warwick Garage. The copper put two and two together and thought it was worth a spin and it was. Stewart said it was an accident but he drew that judge Avory and he might just as well have put his hands up, saved time.

2

Back then to get a girl into trouble, as it was called, was a major offence and a shame. For her and you and the family. That's why there were abortionists. They were almost always women, sturdy, a bit school-mistressy. You'd never sus them out, a bit severe. An ordinary woman would be too squeamish. Remember if it went wrong they was risking a murder charge and a certain five years for manslaughter. No home leaves then, no nothing.

Brasses in Waterloo were really the bottom end of the market. They'd fallen a long way even in their world, down from Mayfair to Soho to Kings Cross and then across the river. They were mostly from up North and I don't remember ever seeing a local girl. Half a crown was what they charged for what they call hand-relief nowadays and five shillings for a knee trembler. Remember, they were making their money off the soldiers who were staying in the Union Jack Club and they wouldn't have much money to lash out. What did a Mickey Bolger get a week before the war? A quid? We'd shout at them as kids 'Fucking old brass' and they'd give us sixpence to go away. The brasses lived in them little hotels, well they weren't much better than dosshouses, along the arches by Howley Place. My Gran used to cook and clean in one. The brasses would toss their rubbish out into our street. No wonder there was rats. You couldn't leave your door open in case they run in.

With the brasses about and the disgrace of a decent girl getting knocked up there was always work for the local abortionists. In fact, that was one of those crimes like bigamy which increased in wartime. With people not knowing what was going to happen the next day they took more chances. Of course, abortion was a crime which didn't get reported unless something went wrong. Before the war there was something like 150 prosecutions a year, but by the end of the war there was nearer 650 and God knows what the real abortion figure was.

The abortionists was really a part of the neighbourhood. Everyone knew who they were but people didn't look down on them. Mind you, it could be a risky business. As I say, usually it only came on top if something happened and the girl had to go to hospital or even died, but at the end of the war there was one old woman, Miriam Palmer her name was, come from Penfold Street, Camberwell, who was done at the Bailey. She was a bit unlucky. She'd scraped a girl and so far as I know it had turned out all right. Then the girl suddenly decided she wanted her money back; reckoned it was too much. She went round and said if the old woman didn't give her back the £50 she paid she'd go to the police. Miriam says she's not going to be blackmailed and tells her to go and do just that and that's what she did. The Pros made a big fuss, saying that what was so serious about the case was the high price Miriam was charging. She got three years. She was 69 at the time. That was a hard sentence for a woman then.

The other thing people got away with more was doing wives who'd been unfaithful during the war whilst they was overseas. There was one case, in Fulham it was, when the fellow came home bringing his rifle with him and laid in wait for his wife and her boyfriend and shot her in the bedroom. The jury brought in manslaughter and the judge just gave him fifteen months. Then there was another case down in Poplar where the husband stabbed his wife in the lung. She'd been having it off whilst he was away. The brief, Birkett, who'd defended Bert Marsh and Bert Wilkins over the dog track killing at Wandsworth and was now a judge, was really sympathetic and give him just two days.

One of the brasses from the Waterloo Road copped it in 1942. Peggy Richards' body was found just by Waterloo Bridge. Someone had tried to strangle her and there were bruises all over her body. Then a funny thing happened. A Canadian soldier called McKinstry went to the police and handed in her handbag. Of course, that was just asking to be arrested. He said they'd been together and quarrelled, then she'd hit him with her handbag and run off leaving him holding it. No one in the cops believed him and he got charged with murder. But, when it came to it, no one could say he wasn't telling the truth and I'm glad to say he got chucked.

Well before my time, but a man who definitely murdered some brasses round here was also said to have made a remark, when he was swinging for the murder of Matilda Clover, about his being Jack the Ripper. Though with the hood over his head I don't know how they could have heard. He was Neville Cream, and he lived in the Lambeth Road.

Cream had been born in Scotland in 1850 to a big family who went to Canada when he was a boy. He'd gone to McGill College at Montreal to study medicine and he did well and graduated. That was when he became involved with a Flora Brooks, whose father owned a hotel. Good start for a young man you might think, but he went and put her in the family way, which was a disgrace in them days. Then he applied his medical skills and aborted her. She nearly died as a result. That was when her father found out and Cream was forced to marry. The marriage didn't last long because he walked out the following day, sailed to England and enrolled at St Thomas' Hospital. After that he went up to Edinburgh and got another qualification there.

He then went back to Canada to continue his career as an abortionist, but either he was unlucky or he wasn't very good or he was doing so many that the law of averages caught up with him, because he was nearly nicked after Kate Gardener, a young chambermaid, was found dead in a lavatory near his rooms. Wisely, he moved to Chicago where he opened a surgery on Madison Avenue, and again was fortunate to avoid a conviction when a girl called Julia Faulkener died. By now he was also peddling pills as a remedy for epilepsy.

From the pictures he wasn't what you'd call a good-looking man – for a start he'd got a very nasty squint – but he could certainly pull the women. A railway agent and epileptic Daniel Stott sent his young wife, who was also called Julia, to Cream to collect his pills and it wasn't that long before Stott himself had to go – poisoned. I don't know what Cream was thinking. He'd got away with it until he sent a message to the coroner blaming the pharmacist for supplying the wrong pills. The man wasn't having it and the end result was that Cream got life in Joliet.

Again he had a bit of luck. His father died and left him $16,000 which wasn't a bad sum in them days. He was released for good behaviour in July 1891, went to Canada to collect his dough and sailed for England. At the beginning of October he took up lodgings at 103 Lambeth Palace Road. Two days after settling in he met a young brass, Matilda Clover, and then purchased a quantity of poison. She wasn't his first victim.

On 13 October Ellen Donworth collapsed outside the Wellington Public House in the Waterloo Road. She was taken to hospital but she died before she ever got there. She'd managed to say she had met 'a tall gentleman with cross eyes, a silk hat and bushy whiskers'. He'd been carrying a bottle of white stuff from which he had persuaded her to drink.

Poor Matilda Clover met up with him a week later. She knew him as Fred, took him back to her lodgings at 27 Lambeth Road and died in agony there. This time Cream had a bit more luck with the coroner because her death was put down to delirium tremens as a result of alcoholism.

Cream really was on a roll because within the week he picked up a Louise Harvey at the Alhambra Theatre and spent the night with her in a hotel in Berwick Street in the West End. The next evening he met her again and give her some pills to take, but she threw these over the Embankment into the river.

He never seemed to learn from his mistakes because he started writing letters again. One was to a Dr Broadbent who practised in Portman Square, near where Charlie Richardson had a tame doctor in the 1960s, accusing him of doing Matilda and asking for £2,500. He also sent a letter to the Countess Russell, who was staying at the Savoy, accusing her husband of the same thing. I don't know how he picked him out. It's funny but no one seems to have taken any notice.

It wasn't until the next spring that he was at it again. He'd been to Canada and within ten days of getting back he poisoned a pair of young brasses from Brighton who were then lodging at 118 Stamford Street, Waterloo.

He must have really been off his rocker because firstly, he suggested to his landlady that another of the tenants at 103 Lambeth Palace Road, a medical student called Walter Harper, was the murderer of the two girls. She thought he must be mad and so she did nothing. Then Cream wrote to Harper's father claiming that he had proof that his son had murdered the two girls. If, however, Dr Harper cared to send him £1,500 he'd keep stumm. You'd think Harper would have done something but he didn't. He just took no notice and Cream did not persist.

Next, Cream took an acquaintance, John Haynes, on a tour of the murder spots, rather like I do with my tour, and discussed the cases in some detail. He really did want to do for himself because he also talked to another man, McIntyre, who turned out to be a copper. That was it.

He was arrested on 3 June 1892 and told the police 'You have got the wrong man, but fire away'. They dug up the body of Matilda Clover and a jury brought in a verdict that she had been killed by Cream. In them days a jury could name an actual person as the murderer. I think Lord Lucan was the last person named before they decided the law was unfair and changed it. Cream was up at the Old Bailey before the hanging judge Hawkins and was sentenced to death on 20 October. He was topped at Newgate on 15 November which is when he called out 'I'm Jack . . .' which at the time people thought meant he was saying he was Jack the Ripper. Now, people think that he was ejaculating. Some men, like that Tory MP a few years ago, like to strangle themselves when they're flogging themselves and maybe it was a question of his coming as he went, so to speak.

Talking of Stamford Street where the last two girls died, the first man I ever knew who was killed lived there. When I heard I can't say I was sorry. Thomas Meaney his name was. He was one of them Holy Joes you come across. He also thought of himself as a great practical joker. He worked for Scotland Yard driving the Black Maria, although he wasn't a copper himself, and he knew my family. In fact he took me up boxing at Scotland Yard and was very friendly with my family. Then the day I got nicked for stealing cigarettes from a little shop in Stamford Street he was the driver of the van I was put in. You'd think he'd be properly sympathetic or have the decency to say nothing but no. There he was upsetting my mother with his false words of advice. That was in the 30s of course.

Anyway he was a great boozer and when he was living in the flats in Peabody Buildings in December 1950 he went out drinking with an Irish mate, Billy Donoghue. When they got back to Billy's flat, Billy collapsed on the sofa and

Meaney got on the bed. When Billy woke up, still half boozed, he saw what he thought was a dummy under the covers left by Meaney and he went and stabbed it. Then, of course, he discovered his mistake. I'm glad to say they dropped the murder and he only got three years for manslaughter.

3

In some ways Walworth hasn't changed that much since I was a boy. When I was about twelve my parents moved from Waterloo to a flat over some shops just opposite and a bit down from what was the Reform Club. That was where Charlie and Eddie did Jack Rosa after Eva's husband had been given a bashing, and is now the Castle Hotel at the beginning of the Walworth Road. I don't think the move was anything to do with the council. They just moved. There was only Eva and me left at home now. All the others were gone, either married or living with someone.

The place where they moved to went up in the war but the arches where the Elephant Snooker Club was situated still stand. My sister Eva and her mates used to sleep on and under the snooker tables in the bombing. They thought it was safer but it was a daring thing for a young girl to go into a snooker club, let alone sleep in one in them days. I don't know about it being that much safer either. A load of slate coming down on you wouldn't do you much good.

The pub, the Hampton Court Palace, hasn't changed a bit. That's just round the corner in Hamilton Place. It was where my old friend Jimmy Robson saw off Lennie Garrett who'd kicked a pregnant woman. Lennie and his brothers lived just down from the Hampton Court and Jim went round to his home and when Lennie pulled a knife Jim did him with a dustbin lid. Of course there were reprisals.

Before he got married Jim had lived with his parents about quarter of a mile down at No 1 Manor Place. There's a doctor's surgery there now. Once he got married he moved to Brixton. Lennie and some others came round looking for Jim. The night they did him, a bit after eleven, I was in a cafe, the Cabin, near the big church in Brixton with Dido Frett and Johnny Carter – I was friends with him then. A couple, George and Mary, owned it and they could often get a steak off the market. It was one of the places the chaps went to after the pubs closed. Lennie came in that night, looked round and went out. I didn't think nothing of it, but so far as he was concerned, once he hadn't seen Jim with us in the cafe then it was odds on where he'd find him.

He went mob-handed to Jim's place and they cut Jim to ribbons and gave his wife Toni a belt for good measure. She was a great friend of Eva – good shoplifter. I went to see Jim in hospital and I put together a little team of people and we sorted them out. December 1944 it was. It took a bit of time to do it but we caught up with them one by one. One of the men with me was Danny Swain, just about the best driver you could ever have. In the war if he was being chased he'd make a turn into a side street, get up on the pavement and wiggle his way between the rubble and the lamp posts. You wouldn't have thought you could get a car down the street but Danny could. He'd got cat's eyes. The coppers would simply continue on down the main road. All they'd see was a concrete block closing off the road. Poor Danny, he had Alzheimer's but I believe he's dead now.

Jim and Lennie finally sorted out their problem down Aggie Hill's club in Soho. Jim was going in there when a fellow said 'You know Lennie and the firm are in there'. That wasn't going to stop Jim but he borrowed a knife off the bloke. Lennie just came over to Jim and said 'Isn't it about time we buried the hatchet?' And Jim agreed. Strangely enough they bumped into each other in the Walworth Road the very next day.

Oddly enough, Jim had always been friends with Lennie, who was known as a good thief himself. He'd been a professional boxer before the war and he'd go out breaking with Jim. You could rely on him. Once, when Jim fell through a roof, Lennie came and picked him up and got him to hospital. A less good man would have scarpered. Lennie also got out of Lambeth Magistrate's Court, which was a small place in Renfrew Road just off the Elephant. It's long been closed now – during the war I think it was. He climbed to the ceiling of the prisoners' waiting room and broke through a skylight and got away through the local hospital grounds. At the end of the war he was back yet again, this time charged with doing a copper. The beak was going to give him bail because he said his wife was pregnant. Then it turned out he wasn't married and the stipe changed his mind.

The last I heard of Lennie was when I read in the papers that he'd been given a right seeing to. It must be ten years ago.

Jim's about five years older than me but even so we quickly became friends. He was a good thief and he had a good name to him. He always used to carry a knife with him. In the Blitz when the windows of a shop or office went in there'd be cardboard put up and Jim used to cut holes in it so he could hand the stuff out. In those days we'd wear a tin helmet and an arm band so if anyone saw us they'd think we were the ARP. There was a lot of looting by people in the ARP, let alone us.

Jim got a four in February 1946 with Jerry Callaghan, from the big South London family, who got a 21 months, and then Jim pulled a long stretch in July 1960 when he was done on two separate jelly cases. He got a ten on the first and the judge gave him fourteen consecutive. We had a benefit for Jim just recently, on 2 July, at the Masons Arms pub in East Street, Walworth. It was his 84th birthday – and it was very good. Johnny Foy was with him. He was doing life and the judge tried to make his sentence for the jelly consecutive and all. Johnny Foy had been given life for robbery in Manchester in 1959. There was some talk he'd thrown corrosive fluid in the victim's face, which is why he'd got such a long stretch. Two years into his sentence in January 1961 they were transferring him from Strangeways to Dartmoor when he jumped off a moving train. They didn't pick him up again until the July, when they surrounded the place he was staying in Lord Street in Blackpool.

Johnny was lucky, throwing himself off the train like that. Just about the end of the war another fellow called Fernie, a smash and grab man, wasn't at all. You used to be taken to the Moor by special train from Waterloo once a month. The vans would come onto the platform and you'd be handcuffed, sometimes on a chain, and loaded on the train. Once you were in the carriages things was a bit relaxed and your relatives could come and bring you food, which you could have with you provided it was all eaten by the time you got to the Moor. Anyway Fernie had always sworn he wasn't going back to Dartmoor, and on his way to the lavatory he broke out of his cuffs and got onto the running board of the compartment. Quite a lot of people tried to escape from that train, and usually the screws would pull the communication cord and that was when a man would take his chance and jump as the train slowed, but it didn't happen on this occasion. Fernie jumped and was killed when he landed on his head.

They stopped taking them to Dartmoor by train whilst I was away in the 60s. You could save your visits if you was on the Moor and have them all in your local nick over a couple of weeks. So when Jimmy Andrews from Islington come up and finished his visits whilst he was doing a seven I knew he'd be going back, and I went along to Pentonville to make sure he got his parcel of food. I met a half hooky screw outside and asked when Jimmy would be going to the station and he said, 'He's gone, Frank. They do it by coach now'. I hadn't heard.

It's funny, throwing vitriol was very big up until the war but it died out after that. Eddie Guerin, who got off Devil's Island in the early years of the last century, made a speciality of that. In the early 30s friend Tommy Speedles got ten years for slinging vitriol in the face of a West End brass, Fanny Simmonds, who was known as Polish Fanny, at Wimbledon dog track. She was in a terrible state. They'd been together for years and they'd been high on the hog when he was winning on the dogs, and when he wasn't then he'd had her on the game. As often as not pimps did it a lot to their brasses. I should think that Tommy Speedles was the last I heard of.[1]

But, getting back to Jimmy Robson, he got made a trusty red band whilst he was in Parkhurst, after working in the laundry. It was through him the football team, the Soho Rangers, with me and a load of others, played the prisoners on the island. Jim did lots of good work whilst he was a trusty. He'd got a screw squared and Jim's wife, Toni, and a man would come down to the island and give the screw quite a bit of dough – maybe even up to two grand. It would be marked down to various men: fifty to this one, a hundred to that. The screw would act as a sort of banker so a man could say he'd like two ounces of tobacco that week or five if he was treating someone and the screw would get it for him. It was much better than the man having a whole load in his cell at one time and maybe getting caught and not being able to explain it. Of course there was some risk for the screw and he took half the money. Being that Jim was a trusty working in the laundry he could get round the prison more or less as he liked, seeing people and taking their orders for tobacco.

It wasn't that difficult to have a screw straightened. I had one in Birmingham once. Eva would send registered letters with the money to a con who'd been discharged and the con would deal with the screw. Then the con got nicked and put up the screw's name. Eva got interviewed and said it was ridiculous and a solicitor came down to see me on the Moor where I'd been transferred. It all blew over and as far as I know the screw went on to be a principal officer.

---

[1] For an account of Tommy Speedles and his part in the Dartmoor Mutiny of 1931 see *Mad Frank and Friends*, Chapter 1.

Jim eventually got out in the early 70s through Billy Hill and his friend, Percy Horne, who'd been in Borstal with Bill before the war and was doing good in the contracting business. Bill suggested that Jim write from prison asking Percy for a job. Percy wrote back to the Governor saying he'd like to help but he normally liked to see a man before he took him on. Of course it was just to give Jim a visit because he was always going to take Billy's recommendation. Percy had a contract to pull down Nine Elms at the time before they built the flower market there. All Jim had to do was make the tea (Dido worked there with him, Percy was very good there) and take the copper to the scrap merchant once a week. Percy was clever there. He'd share out the money from the copper with his boys. As soon as all the metal was gone they'd be off to another job. Percy was also a brilliant pianist and there was nothing he liked better of a Friday evening than to have a sing-song in the pub. The landlords loved him. Free entertainment.

I did a pub at the end of Browning Street where I live now on behalf of the landlord of the King's Arms. Cis and Vic Rosati owned it. He'd been the potman in Cis's father's place, the Duke of Clarence at St George's Circus in the London Road. Before that Vic was about a bit with the Sabinis. They took the Kings Arms in 1937 or the year after. It was almost opposite the old Reform Club. It was the place to go of an evening if you were looking for someone because there weren't telephones then, let alone mobiles like there are today. You might go to one or two other places, but the chaps would all end up in the King's Arms before closing time.

Anyway, Vic and Cis were sort of pioneers. They'd have singers and maybe a small band in; they didn't have to pay them, just pass the hat around. Well, the landlord of this pub in Browning Street started doing the same thing and it wasn't good for Vic's trade. The man wouldn't be told so I went round and did his place up – all the windows – and he soon got the message. I think Vic give me £30 for my trouble, which wasn't bad dough. And then if I was ever in with him and I was a bit skint I'd look at him, pat me waistcoat pockets and he'd give a nod saying it was all right, I didn't have to pay, it was on the house. The pub I did is an Irish pub today – The Stroke of Luck. I can't for the life of me think what it was called back then.

During the war at the end of an evening you'd go to someone's house and have a party. Charlie Saye was one of those people who made a bit of money letting people use his flat. His daughter, Gladys, was another of Eva's pals. There was early closing in the war and anyway there wasn't all that much booze in the pubs. So what people did was have chaps round their house at ten bob a head. The punters had to bring their own booze, beer and Scotch they'd nicked off a lorry. If you'd had a lorry of spirits you were in for a nice few quid. Letting people in for these parties was a precarious living because there was always the chance that a fight would break out and all the furniture would get smashed. These parties went on after the war and some time in the 1950s Charlie had a little mob in his place one night and the place got smashed up and him and his wife took a few digs. I'm not sure he didn't nick them over it.

Outside the Duke of Clarence was where some of the Carter family did Hoppy Smith in 1942. Hoppy's sister was once married to 'Tom Thumb' Brindle of the family my sister, Eva, married into. Tom's second wife was the daughter of a policeman, but that was when he was becoming respectable. Hoppy was a big man, well over six foot and with a club foot which is how he got his name. He was a sort of thieves' ponce and a bit of a con man as well. One of his tricks came if you'd done a job. He'd say he could place the tom for you but he never really tried and then you'd have to pay him for his time. It was his way of taking a few quid off of you.

Hoppy was a beast with a razor and he didn't half cut some people in his time. He cut Harry Carter in another pub, the Flowers of the Forest, and cut Johnny Carter's tie off at the same time. They met up with him a week later in the Duke of Clarence, called him out and were giving it to him when he picked up a child out of its pram. At that time people could leave a child out on the street whilst they went and had a drink and it was perfectly safe, no question of anyone stealing it. Anyway Hoppy picks up the kid and holds it as protection and, of course, with that the Carters backed off. They weren't going to hurt a child.

4

One of the local heroes I was told about in my childhood was Gerald Chapman whose mother had been a washer-woman in Camberwell, I never knew quite where. Chapman was big time in America where he was also known as Lord Reginald Francis and Major Leslie Chapman as well as the Monocled Bandit. I must have been four when they topped him, but he was still talked about in my youth.

It's as they say, prison is a breeding ground for crime. That's where you learn your trade. Chapman started off being put in what they called a House of Refuge when he was a kid, and then took up doing burglaries and went on to a reformatory, and then he got three years in Sing Sing. Then when he came out of that he quickly got twelve for trying to shoot a copper who was after him for a domestic burglary. By the time he got out from that one it was the Prohibition era and he teamed up with George 'Dutch' Anderson who he'd met in the nick and who really taught him the trade.

They got over two million dollars in a mail robbery in 1921 and another $70,000 about six weeks later. Then someone shopped him and he got 25 years. He was sent to the penitentiary in Atlanta and in 1923 he escaped and was in a gun battle with the cops about 70 miles away. They captured him and took him back to the nick, and he got out of the hospital with a bullet in his arm and two in his kidney.

Then Dutch Anderson escaped as well. Both of them came back to England and Scotland Yard tried searching around Camberwell but they could not find them. From the stories, Chapman returned to America and lived in New York where he was known as the Count of Gramercy Square. Then in October 1924 he was found blowing a safe and he shot a police officer dead. By then he was living in Muncie in Connecticut with a farmer and his wife. He was spotted, and I don't know how it come about, the people gave evidence against him – probably to save themselves from getting nicked for harbouring him. As a result they were shot dead on his behalf by a man nicknamed One-Armed Wolfe, who got life for his trouble.

Anyway Chapman's execution was fixed for 28 February 1926 but he said he could not be hanged until he had completed 20 out of his 25 year sentence – the one he'd escaped from – a question of life and death consecutively. So Coolidge, who was the President, pardoned him and Chapman went and rejected the pardon. If he hadn't they'd have topped him straight away. Then there was a long legal battle as to whether a man could refuse a pardon, but of course they weren't going to give him the chance of another escape and he got topped in April 1926. Dutch Anderson had already gone down when he shot a copper who managed to get the gun and turn it on Anderson. There was a story that Anderson was the son of a high class Danish family and his real name was Ivan Dahl Von Teller, but that sounds like a German name to me.[2]

5

A man who went down in 1945 was Frank Everitt, known as Duke, a taxi driver. He was found in Lambeth Bridge Pumphouse on Lambeth Bridge Road in the early hours of 18 October. He'd been shot behind the left ear and it was

---

[2] See Chapter 8.

reckoned the shooting had been done in his cab. They found his taxi over in Notting Hill Gate. Everitt was one of those people who led a double life because, after the initial comments about how could anyone do this to such a lovely man, it turned out he was also in the black market. He'd been a copper himself and then he'd turned private detective. For an ex-copper he'd managed to pick up a lot of property, because he had a place in Soho and another in Ealing and he'd just bought a bungalow in Gloucestershire. One of Scotland Yard's so called Big Eight, Walter Chapman, was in charge. When there was an inquest the next year Chapman said they was still looking but there was never any arrests made. In fact when those two Poles, Grondkowski and Malinowski, was in the condemned cell over the killing of Russian Robert, the coppers visited them to see if they would admit to doing Everitt as well but they remained staunch. Maybe they hadn't, because one of them might have worked his ticket and got a reprieve if he'd given the other up.

There was a lot of trouble around the Elephant at that time. There was stories that the Boys were banding together again, particularly when Joseph Hussey's body was found in the Thames around the same time. He was partly crippled and he'd been a theatre queue busker. No one was ever done for his murder to my knowledge.

Just before the war the Elephant Boys had been on the rampage and a local shopkeeper, Mark Selby who ran the State Milk Bar in the Walworth Road, committed suicide over them. There's not much doubt someone had been leaning on him; Billy Howard, I wouldn't be surprised. He was the real Governor. Milk Bars was all the rage from America at the time and for a bit after the war. They was all chrome and brightness. There was another one down at the Bricklayers, I recall.

Billy Howard was a big, big man and tough as nails. During the war he was having a real set-to with Spindles Jackson when a bomb went off in Munton Road in 1941. It had landed the year before and no one noticed. They

35

stopped the fight at once and ran to help out. I don't think they ever started it again. Billy had the Beehive Club, a very good little drinker in Brixton just by the railway bridge, and he also had a spieler in Wyndham Road off the Camberwell Road. Tony Mella, Billy Blythe and me was in there when we got a call from Tommy Falco that the Jack Spot-Albert Dimes fight had gone down.

Another man who'd been in America and who you'd see round the Elephant was a fellow who'd had his face covered in tattoos in the days when it wasn't fashionable. He'd been in Chicago and he used to say he'd been Al Capone's chauffeur. Then he came back here and got done for stabbing a man in Ruislip. Seven years he got. His name was Jacobus Van Dyn. His was a funny case. Within a few months of getting his bird he was released just like that, but he could never get the pardon he wanted. He was still trying 30 years later, saying if they'd just re-open the case he could prove his innocence. In the meantime he'd joined a circus and toured as a sort of freak 'The Worst Man in the World'. He lived in Parkview House, now a hotel, just by the Elephant. If he was alive now he could go to that new Criminal Review Commission, but he'd have to be at least a hundred.

I don't like tattoos myself and I've never had one. My Dad had a couple of small ones but that was natural, his having been in the Navy, but it's not for me.

6

I do a lot of walking about the place and the other day I was down in Wyndham Road in Camberwell where Charlie Richardson's mother had her shop. It was a sort of general grocery store. She was well loved. If people was skint she'd always give them tick. Eva and her husband, Jim, lived just round the corner.

There was a good murder there years ago. Edgar Edwards attacked and killed John William Darby and his wife, Beatrice, on 1 December 1902. They had a small but profitable grocery shop at number 22 when Edwards arrived carrying a five-pound sash-weight wrapped in newspaper.

By the time Edwards had left the shop he had nailed up the premises and attached a note saying the business had closed down but would soon re-open under new management. Over the next week, he gave a few shillings to the locals and got them to help empty the contents of the shop and the living quarters, taking them to his new home at 89 Church Road, Leyton. Amongst the contents were black sacks containing the bodies of the Darbys and their young daughter, Ethel, whom he'd strangled and cut up.

When it came to it he was a bit unlucky. The police were called but it wasn't to investigate any murder. It was thought that the Darbys had run off with the Christmas Loan Club savings, amounting to nearly £200.

For some weeks it looked as though Edwards was going to get away with it but then, with money running out, what he did was go and attack another grocer. This one survived and give the coppers a description. Once they went round to Edwards' home the police found billheads belonging to the Darbys. After that it was into the garden with the spades until they found them.

When he got to the Old Bailey Edwards ran a defence of insanity. He must have been really loopy because his mother and a great-aunt had died insane, his father was an alcoholic, two cousins were mental defectives and there was another in an asylum. He was a bit unlucky but I suppose the jury thought it was just as well to have him out of the way. If you look at the old newspapers he doesn't seem to have minded all that. When the judge put on the black cap Edwards said, 'This is quite like being on the stage'. On his way to the topping shed in Wandsworth he told the prison chaplain 'I've been looking forward to this a lot'. Of course, you can never tell if he was just play-acting.

One thing you saw when I was a boy and you don't any more is people performing in the streets. There used to be a little band, the Luna Brothers, who would come round regularly the same day every week and play. One of them had a sort of piano he put up and there was a trumpet and violin. People would throw coins to them. Then there were others with performing animals. There used to be organ grinders who always had monkeys and I remember a man with a dancing bear, but Animal Rights has put a stop to all that and it's probably just as well.

There was a man called Weatherly with a performing seal who got involved in a murder case our way in West Square just off St George's Road years ago. He'd cart it around with him and it would honk and flap its flippers. He and his missus, Mary, lived in Coraline Buildings in the Square, and she went and fell for a labourer, William Heeley, and went off to live with him. She probably got sick of the smell of the seal. Then she goes and meets her old man in the street and they're back together. It all ended in tragedy because Heeley waited until Weatherly and the seal were out on the streets doing their act and then he went round to Coraline Buildings and cut Mary's throat. Next he barricaded himself in the flat and cut his own. Poor Weatherly was so upset he tried to drown himself in the seal's barrel, but luckily for one of them he made a mess of it and lived.

The war was a good time to commit a murder. With the Blitz and all the bombs falling and so much rubble about it was easy for someone to go missing and no one thought too much about it. The husband or wife could always say they'd gone to relatives in the country or that they went missing in the Blitz. That's what happened with Harry Dobkin and his wife Rachel, whom he buried in the crypt in the Baptist Church in St Oswald's Place off Kennington Lane.

It was a big trial and that Mr Justice Lawton, whose father I hanged all those years ago when he was governor at Wandsworth, and who give me ten years and poor Charlie 25 at the end of the Richardson Trial, always used to say that was how he got his chance as a barrister.

Dobkin and his wife didn't get on at all. Theirs had been one of those Jewish arranged marriages back in 1920 and they'd had a kid but they'd split up within three years. She went to the local Magistrates' Court and got a maintenance order but it didn't do her much good. He didn't want to pay and if you don't want to there's plenty of ways you can string an order like that out. She had him put away a few times for non-payment and when he was out and they met he'd give her a clip now and again. So then she took out assault summonses on four occasions. That didn't do her much good either because the beaks threw them out.

Then they went and met over in a cafe in Dalston for tea on Good Friday 1941 and after they left there in the early evening she was never seen again. The next day her sister reported her missing, blaming Dobkin, but like I say there was plenty of missing people then. In fact he took her handbag to Guildford and left it there on a post office counter to make it look like she'd been in Surrey. When it was opened they found a card of a spiritualist and when the woman was contacted she said that Rachel had been hit over the head and done in.

So then the police got round to having a word with Harry Dobkin a few days later – 16 April it was, the day after a small fire broke out in the cellar of the Baptist Church where he was a firewatcher. That same day 23 people were killed when a landmine was dropped 250 yards from the church. It had already been blitzed in August 1940. The police circulated a description of the missing Rachel Dobkin but no one ever said they'd seen her, which wasn't really surprising.

It wasn't until two years later when they were pulling down the church for safety that they found her body, and when they did a post-mortem it turned out she'd been strangled. When the wife turns up dead, look first at the husband is the golden rule and Dobkin was arrested. At the trial Lawton concentrated on her height. The body was a bit over five foot but he got in evidence that she'd been a couple of inches taller and so it couldn't be her body. There was no question of DNA back then, of course, and since she'd never been arrested there were no fingerprints to compare. Eventually her sister, who said she was the same height, was measured and they found that, in her shoes, she was 5J 1K. That did for Harry. The jury took only twenty minutes to find him guilty. I've often wondered how he persuaded her to come south of the river with him.

7

Tony Reuter was the so-called King of the Teddy Boys who got religion. He was a great cobbles fighter and he took on some of the best. He was with a gang from the Elephant and one of the stories is of a big fight they all had in the Locarno, Streatham. Joey Dunn was the leader of the Brixton boys and Eddie Richardson and Tony and Peter Reuter – with a bit of help – stood up to him and his team.

Peter also faced up to Bobby Ramsey in the Lyceum dance hall off the Strand. Ramsey had once worked with Billy Hill but then got work as a bouncer in that dance hall. I don't know what it was about but Ramsey swallowed it. Peter Reuter took on Eddie Richardson once in the Imperial Billiard Hall at the Elephant and they just about did for each other. They were both standing at the end but they weren't throwing punches. You could fight someone one week and be friends the next day.

Then Billy Graham the Evangelist come over and held all those revival meetings at Earls Court. The idea was that at the end anyone who'd given his life up to Jesus should come forward and the newspapers give Tony Reuter a few quid to join the line. It was all in the papers the next day – what a wonderful convert for the Rev.

Tony was in and out of trouble in the 50s and early 60s. One time he threw a thunderflash at a copper and got five years. Then in 1962 he got off an attempted murder charge. He'd knocked down a Sheila Fraser, no relation. She'd come over the river to a party at a club in Huntley Road, Kennington, with some friends and as she was leaving she remembered she'd left her handbag. She went back and checked to see her dough was still there and people got the hump. Someone threw a glass at her and outside a ruckus started and the coppers said Tony drove the car at her. She was really badly injured and he got a ten. He still lives round the Elephant and I see him quite often. In fact he was round the other day with a copy of Marilyn's *Gangster's Moll* book for her to sign for him.

8

It was in Bagshot Street, Walworth, that Ahmet Abdullah, the fellow known as Turkish Abbi, got shot in March 1991. He was closely related to the Arif family. He was a drug dealer and he'd quarrelled with some other of the South East interests. Abbi got done in the William Hill betting shop. He knew it was on top because he was pleading with his attackers not to kill him. He was shot but he managed to grab one of the other punters as a shield and he got out of the shop before he was shot again. Two brothers, Tony and Patrick Brindle, were done for his murder. It was a funny case. Witnesses were allowed to give evidence from behind screens and they only had to give numbers not their names, and one couple never turned up at all. One went and topped himself. What the Pros maintained was that Abbi had made something like a dying declaration, saying the Brindles had done him.

Tony Brindle said he never knew Abbi from Adam, and when it went down he'd been playing cards and drinking in the Bell in East Street, Walworth. Patrick didn't give evidence. They got chucked in May 1992. Because of the name it was thought that they were related to me through my sister Eva's husband, but they're not. There must be hundreds if not thousands of Brindles over South London. I suppose we may be related but it's fourth cousins twice removed, that sort of thing, if we are. I'm not sure I've ever met them.

Things didn't end there, though. A third brother, David, was killed whilst drinking one evening in the Bell and the man who was just standing next to him got killed as well. Then in 1995 another brother, George, survived being shot from a passing van earlier in the year. No one was nicked for that.

Then in September 1995 Tony was ambushed and shot in Rotherhithe. The story the Pros told the court was that it had been a hit set up by a George Mitchell, a drug dealer in Dublin who is known as The Penguin, on behalf of Peter Daly who'd been financing him. Anyway Michael Boyle got three life sentences for attempted murder and a fellow, David Roads who'd been keeping the guns for him, picked up ten years.

There was some talk Tony Brindle was going to sue the police, because he said they hadn't stepped in quick enough and he'd been hit in the arm, elbow, chest and another couple of places as well. I don't know that anything came of it; I hope something did.

In April this year David Roads got done in an alleyway off Cowper Road in Kingston. He was in Latchmere near Richmond, finishing off his sentence by going out on day release, and he must have been followed on his way back as he tried to get there before the ten o'clock curfew. Shot twice in the head, he was.

9

Brixton was considered quite posh before the war. The ambition of every thief from the Elephant who made it was to buy a house in Brixton. And that lasted up until the 1950s. By then it was falling away but we thought it was posh and Streatham, now that was really posh. Gleneldon Road, Streatham, was where the kid, Tony Baldassare, topped himself. He'd been on the run since he failed to show at the Bailey on a blagging and was surrounded by coppers. He did a magnificent thing. Before he did himself he set fire to all the money he'd nicked so it was never recovered. He used to collect cigarette lighters and he had one in the shape of a coffin. It had his name and date of birth on one side and just 'Died –' on the other. 25 January 1985 it would have been.

Somewhere like Charlton we thought out in the sticks. After all, how many people had cars? Silvertown was just poor. You never went stealing down there; there wasn't nothing to steal. Now with the building going on along the river it might be worth a look.

How things have changed. I remember that police said that one specific day in December 1996 was only the third day there hadn't been a robbery in Brixton in five years. And that was only because they'd been running a big undercover operation.

Charlie Gibbs, he was a good thief. You could touch him for a loan. He was one of them that come from the Elephant and moved to Brixton. I did quite a few jobs with him. The last time I saw him was coming down from Bedford, when we'd been sussed for the snout factory and I got caught. Him and Teddy Gibbs, his brother, were in the car behind and when they could see they couldn't do me no good they peeled off. Then shortly after I went away Charlie got an eight or a ten PD, and whilst he was in the nick he got cancer. It was about that time they brought out the regulation that if you was dying you could be released so you didn't die in the nick. Charlie was one of the very first, if not the first, who was let out. Eva went to his funeral. Charlie's sister, Carrie, was the first wife of Alfie Hinds.

If you went from the Elephant up the New Kent Road and turned into the Old Kent Road then you'd come to an area known as the Bricklayers Arms, which included Bermondsey. It was an old railway depot. People from South London simply called it the Brick, sometimes the Bricklayers. Our world seemed to stop there. It stopped there for a few coppers in the British Transport police back in 1980, when one of them got seven years and another six. They'd been nicking stuff most weekends for eighteen

months and they'd got away with something like ...
364,000 of stuff. Now, even if you know they didn't get the
full whack when they knocked it out, it was still good
money.

It's always a pleasure to see coppers get done and even
better when they turn on each other and start grassing each
other to try and get out of things. It doesn't happen often
enough, but it did a bit after the war in Catford. In 1949
two young coppers and their sergeant got done for theft and
receiving. Mean thing it was too. An old lady had died in
Honley Road and the police were called in to look after the
house. They didn't guard it all that well because stuff from
it turned up in the sergeant's home. There had also been
complaints that things had been going off market stalls and
a special watch was being kept. The young constable got
nicked, and when it all went to the Bailey he said how the
sergeant had taken stuff whilst they were inspecting the
house and had told him to take something for himself. The
second constable had been the one nicking things from the
market. One was a load of cami-knickers, which were well
fancied then. The copper who give evidence got three years
and the one who didn't picked up five. The sergeant copped
for a seven.

I used to do a bit of thieving down the railway yards
mostly during the war and, often enough, Dave Morbin was
with me. In fact he put the idea up. We used to climb onto
the skylight, down a rope ladder we brought with us, and
we'd have things out of the depot. You wouldn't believe the
lax security. Of course, it was blackout and so there weren't
lights by which we could be seen, which helped no end. We
wasn't the only ones, of course, and someone else come a
tumble and that was the end of it. Dave married Lennie
Garrett's sister. He died a few years back.

A man who had a club down there was Toby Noble. I
think he'd been in the ring at one time. He was a
hard-working man but he'd always buy a bit of gear off
you. Then he opened a gym and George Daley's brother

Tommy ran it for him. You could still see Tommy around at the fights until just a few years ago. A corner man, he was, and a good trainer in his day, but by the end he wasn't doing much more than carry the bucket and sponge.

10

I've never understood why people think it's a good idea to cut bodies in half and then just dump them in the river. They're asking for them to be found. The top half of another body washed up in the river at Battersea just last year. This time it was a young girl, Zoe Parker, who sometimes called herself Cathy Dennis, chopped in half. At first they thought she'd been hit by the propeller of a boat but no, someone had taken a saw to her. It seems she was on the fringes of things, a bit of brassing just to get some money to live. It's no way to make a living at that end of the market, particularly nowadays. There was some research recently which showed that 60 per cent of brasses had been seriously assaulted over the previous months, and another survey showed that a brass is murdered every three to four weeks in Britain. The last I read they hadn't caught anybody, but there was a halfway decent reward on offer.

There was a funny case in Battersea a few years back, around May 1961. One afternoon a doctor's daughter in Chelsea got a call from a man who said his wife was a patient and was ill, could the doctor come? Later they thought the man might have had a Turkish accent or maybe it was a disguise. Anyway, late that night a man comes back to Albert Studios, which was a sort of artists' colony at the back of Albert Mansions in the Albert Bridge Road, where he lived and found the doctor stabbed to death. The doctor was in his seventies then, Raymond Castillo he was. They could never prove who did it, but the story was that it was another doctor who'd had some sort of quarrel with him.

There was another really funny case in Battersea years ago, well before my time and again it was never solved.

You'd hear about these cases in the nick. The screws would talk to an old lag and he'd have told them what really happened and it would get passed on down the line. The screws may even have been in the death cell with someone who'd opened up before he was topped. Remember, there was no wireless, no television and no newspapers for prisoners. We lived on stories about past cons we told each other – nowadays they'd call it oral history.

The man who got killed was a small-time actor, Thomas Weldon Atherston, who appeared in those melodramas that were very popular at the time. In fact he'd been in one, Grip of the Law, a couple of weeks before his death. He was found at the back of a house, in Clifton Gardens in Prince of Wales Drive, where his former mistress, Elizabeth Earl, was having supper with Atherston's son Thomas who, just to confuse things, called himself Anderson. A chauffeur heard a couple of shots, saw someone getting over a wall and drove to the police station. When they got back, there was Atherston shot in the face. He had what they called a life-preserver in his hand. A life-preserver could be almost anything provided it was heavy, and you carried it on a loop round your wrist so people couldn't take it away from you and do you with your own weapon. Like coppers and truncheons. The other funny thing was he had his carpet slippers on when he lived miles away.

Elizabeth Earl'd been on the boards herself and was now teaching what they called dramatic art, still do probably. Young Tommy wasn't all that forthcoming, but eventually he said he'd seen his dad die. It was all wonderful for the papers, of course. What was he doing at night with a life-preserver outside his former girlfriend's flat? Everyone had a different theory including one that Elizabeth Earl, Tommy and a younger brother had all conspired to have Dad knocked off. Then there was a theory that he'd come to believe she was having it off with his son and was going to do him, or that there was another lover. The public was well on the side of Miss Earl, and when it came down to it the best theory was that poor old Thomas was simply in the wrong place at the time. He'd gone to see if there was any hanky panky going on but he was shot by a burglar.

People always said that Clapham was pretty free from crime and it certainly was a step up from the Elephant. Mind you, they had a good couple of crimes. In 1953 Michael Davies was done for murder during a gang fight on the Common and it was never really clear he was guilty. Before that I suppose the last really big one was Leon Beron, who was done on the Common on New Year's Eve 1911. Stinie Morrison got sent down for it, but that's a case which has always smelled. No one was ever too clear whether it was just a robbery or whether Leon Beron was a copper's nark, or even if it was something to do with Russian spies. Part of Stinie's trouble was he called a bent alibi and it got shown up. The judge said that foreigners weren't like us and if they told a lie it didn't mean they was guilty, but the jury still put him down. He was reprieved but he did his time the hard way and he died in Parkhurst on hunger strike. He'd had a quarrel with another prisoner and thrown a kitten into a furnace in temper. As a result he'd been given punishment and thought he was being hard done by so he put himself on hunger strike. Of course even that was well before my time, but plenty of people I met in prison had known him in the nick and he was one of the legends.

11

Tony Ash went down in November 1987 when the police shot him at a garage in Sunbury Street, Clapham. I knew him, of course. He was a bouncer at the Frog and Nightgown in the Old Kent Road. He'd once let Charlie Richardson stay at a place he'd had on the coast after Charlie had walked out of the open prison. It was another ready-eye. Tony and Ronnie Easterbrook had give a man £200 to clean and hide a nicked BMW in his garage, but the police give him £1,000 to grass – so there's no prizes which he chose. The job was at a Bejam supermarket in Hare Street, Woolwich. Tony Ash was shot as they went to change cars. Ronnie was shot and all, and got fifteen years as well. He sent a lovely card to the funeral whilst he was on remand 'With sorrow and regard. May your executors and (and he named the man) live long and suffer every day.' What a lovely gesture. There was also a picture of the man on the grave so people could recognise him. It was said there was £35,000 on his head. He got resettled and left his wife to cope with what he'd done. I'm not sure but people say that the whole thing was filmed by Thames Television, since they'd been doing a programme on the squad at the time. Funnily enough, Tony had been involved in the death of two coppers years earlier, when his lorry had jackknifed down in Whitstable and crushed the officers who were in an unmarked car.

There was a whole spate of killings in South London in 1991. That was the year I got shot outside Turnmills in the August. Of course there was the killing of Turkish Abbi in the March, but then there was David Norris who was reckoned to be a supergrass. He was killed at his home in Belvedere in the April. After David Brindle was shot dead in August at the Bell, his friend Perry Donegan was badly injured when he was shot in the leg at the Green Man in the Old Kent Road in November. Meanwhile a fellow called William Walker was shot in the arm and leg when he was walking in Rotherhithe. Then in the early December Kenneth Neal was shot as he left for work with British Telecom from his home off the Old Kent Road. People said that was a mistaken identity. I don't think anyone was ever convicted of any of them.

Another mistaken identity looks like being that of Michael McCormack, who was a director of an indexing firm, and his works manager John Ogden, who were shot on 21 October 1994 in Cavendish Road, Balham. If you looked at it you'd say it was a stone cold contract killing. The fellow who did it was waiting in a sandwich bar and followed the men after they'd had a lunchtime drink in the

Prince of Wales public house. He shot them both in the back of the head with a .45 Colt and then ran to a D-registration Vauxhall Cavalier and got clean away. It was later found burned out in Streatham. The coppers discovered it had been bought in a false name for ... 1,500 cash from some people in Catford, but that was about as near as they ever got. There was talk that whoever did the killing got the wrong pair. Then the next year the coppers had a man on an ID parade. There was talk he'd been in an Open Prison, left for the day, done the shooting and walked back in. Good alibi. He wasn't picked out. Curiously there was another killing in Waterloo a bit before, another drive-by shooting. That car was bought through a newspaper ad and then burned out as well.

Perry Hill, Catford, was where that Andy Birjukove was shot back in September 1993 in the Two Brewers, where he was drinking with his mate Bobby Campbell, the St Mirren footballer. Campbell had once run the Rutland Arms nearby and he got shot as well but he survived. I don't think the locals were too sympathetic about Birjukove. There was stories he'd been dealing in cocaine and ignored people when he was told not to.

12

I suppose one of the oldest cons ever must have been John Day, who was 86 the year I was born. He got fifteen months in the March. He'd been a big burglar in his day and he'd been known as Daylight John because he didn't like working at night, maybe because of the extra bird that would be handed out. He never took any tools with him either; just shoved his shoulder against the door. His speciality was chatting up the housemaid and getting a lie of the land that way, although by the time he last got nicked he was a bit old for that.

This time he just sees a woman leave her house in Ommanney Road, New Cross, and goes and does the front door. He was half away with the jewellery when she comes back because she's forgotten her purse. She grabs hold of him and hollers and some people come to help her. The judge said John was lucky, and if it hadn't been for his age he'd have got longer. He still added in hard labour though and said John was well fit enough for it.

13

When I first read about the Dome robbery I had the utmost admiration even though it didn't work. I thought what a brilliant coup. I didn't know any of the men except Terry Millman, the one who died. They was my sons' and even grandsons' ages. I think Terry was related to the Carters by marriage, a good man. But, no disrespect, the more the story come out and the more I studied it, the more I thought they needed their brains testing. One of them had a brother-in-law for a copper. That's bad enough for a start. Then it looks like they'd already done a run across the Thames in a speedboat as an escape in another blagging. Even if it wasn't them the coppers don't need too much in the way of brains to think that once someone's done it a second team may have a try and they're going to be on the lookout at things beside the Thames which may be targets. Then again did they really think them jewels was real? I wonder if the public can get their entrance money back. They'll never be able to say I saw the Millennium Diamond or whatever. Do you think they can get at the Dome people for false pretences? I mean no one in their right mind's going to go and look at them if they're imitations.

That's the trouble with big jobs. There's too many on them. Billy Hill used to say that you're your own best partner and he's right. There's wives and there's girlfriends and people they've spoken to. It can be accident or it can be a bit of malice if one of the women have found their fellow's having it off round the corner. Then there's people who listen out so they can get a reward. In something like the

Dome there had to be twenty or more knew something really big was going off, and that's a good fifteen too many.

It was like in the Train when Renee Wisbey was knitting balaclavas for them all and Marilyn and her sister found them. They was all staunch, of course, but it only shows how easy it is for things to leak out. That's another thing with the Dome. You don't do jewels or paintings if you can avoid it. You do money. If you do jewels you've got to bring someone else in to sell to and, very likely, if it's a big job they've got to bring in someone as well, and before you know the whole of Hatton Garden's in on it. Think of the rabbit that must be going round. You don't even know who the police is watching which is what seems to have happened. Quite by chance they was watching a man and he went to the Dome. The next day or a bit after they see someone else at the place and from there on it's all on top.

I've often wondered why the Train Robbers needed the farm. Buying it or pretending to they was involving people who weren't full members, probably only half hooky so to speak. If a man's been sent to buy property just near where a big job has gone off he don't need to be the Brains of Britain to know what it was all about. There's always the worry he won't stand up if the police get hold of him. The Train men could have all gone up to the railway in separate vehicles that night and been back in London before anyone knew what had happened.

I still think that the great mistake the Train men made was not to have involved Billy Hill and I think that one or two agree even though their pride won't let them admit it. That, and Billy would have been greedy. He'd have wanted the pickings. But, there again, there was plenty of pickings to go round. No one ever quite knew how much was on the train. It was a robbery where you could let someone be a bit greedy. What I'm sure about is that if Billy had been around there wouldn't have been thirty years all round.

Personally I think it was the same with the London Airport robbery at the end of July 1948 when so many good men was betrayed and picked up a lot of bird. Billy would have done it different. That was one of Spotty's things. He'd picked the job out and it all seemed so sweet then it all come crashing down. Billy Hill and me was in Wandsworth when it went down. There was meant to be over . . . 600 grand in diamonds and money in a bonded warehouse with the prospects of more on the way. The idea was they should dope the coffee of the warehouse staff and it would be a doddle, but instead when they got there they found the man they'd been dealing with on the inside had gone hooky on them and talked to the police. Instead of doped staff there was wide-awake coppers.

Some men got away but Jimmy Woods picked up nine and his brother George an eight. Teddy Machin, who Billy calls Terrible Ted in his book, got away and so did Franny Daniels but Alfie Roome really went off his head whilst he was doing his ten. He was known as Donk and when he come out he attacks his wife who was working on a newspaper stall at the gates of the Ford factory at Dagenham. When people chased him he swallows poison and dies there on the pavement. What a waste of a good man. Billy always reckoned if he'd been running it there wouldn't have been a disaster. He knew so many top coppers, one of them would have got the word to him and he'd have pulled the team out. That was one of Jack's troubles. He didn't have any high-ranking coppers behind him. It took the starch out of Jimmy and Georgie Woods as well. They'd been doing so well out of their blaggings they thought it was too easy. They're both dead now I'm sorry to say. In fact I'm not sure that there's anyone left who was on the job.

Much better was that robbery at London Airport in February this year. Cash, and only two of them involved by all accounts. It had to be an inside job. What was even better is they seem to have gone back and done it again in March. There's a story that the money is for terrorism but I'm not so sure. People have been saying if you've had a £2 million touch why repeat it, but then if you've made £3 million out of a drugs run why do it again? If they've done their homework properly the p.c. of today will get them out. 'The only reason you're looking at us is because we're Asian'. They'll sling that chestnut in if they've any sense. The Asians is the up and coming crime group. Far more slippery and clever than the Jamaicans.

SOHO

1

The first time I went to Soho was when I was a kid. My sister Eva and me and Timmy, our Airedale dog, would go to the baker's just by Gerrard Street to pick up yesterday's bread. If they'd run out we had to walk on through Soho to their other branch the opposite side of Oxford Street. From then on I've been in and out of the West End whenever I've been out of the nick. It's changed over the years, of course. There was no Chinatown like there is today. The old 24-hour Boots in Piccadilly Circus where the druggies used to queue to get their scripts filled after midnight has gone, but the one tucked away on the other side of the Circus, near the Regent Palace Hotel, which was just a small shop when I was a delivery boy for it, has grown and grown. It's huge now.

The hotel's smarter than it was a few years back. When I was young it was always known as an upmarket brasses' hotel or somewhere a woman went without her husband. It went very downmarket. I remember reading of a fellow who was accused of raping a girl on the carpet of the women's lavatory whilst people stood around watching. Her bloke had gone to register and when he came back he found her having it away on the floor. I'll never forget the verbals. This was the Pros's version. The fellow says, 'Hey what are you doing? She's my chick', and the man, who's a soldier in uniform, flicks out his boot at him and says, 'Eff off, can't you see I'm busy?' He got a not guilty, of course, and quite right.

Right on the corner of Shaftesbury Avenue was a newsreel cinema. They were big after the war when there was no television. You didn't pay as much as for a proper cinema and there was the news and a few cartoons and possibly a travelogue. The whole show lasted an hour. They were very popular after something like the Grand National or a big fight because that was the only way people was going to see them. There was one at nearly every large station as well.

In the middle of the Circus on the steps of Eros there was the flower sellers. Not like the gypsies who try and push lavender on you nowadays, and then curse you if you won't buy, but ladies wearing long skirts and straw hats rather like Eliza Doolittles selling violets a lot of the time. Then it seems they just went. They were there before I went into prison one time and then they wasn't. They used to board up Eros on Boat Race night because someone was always trying to climb it. That was such a big thing when I was a kid. You had favours being sold for weeks before the race; little crossed oars painted in light or dark blue. People bought them but I don't suppose half of them knew what it was about until they saw it on the newsreel.

2

There's always silly girls going to run away from home up North, thinking they're going to be actresses. They end up on the streets working for a ponce who they think they're helping to get started in a business or something and then he'll marry them. The only business they're helping get started is his string of tarts. Then, of course, there's a lot of people who buy and sell women and use force to get them on the game.

Being a brass is a risky business. I was reading somewhere that the Albanian gangs who run prostitution along the Italian Riviera simply tip them out of a speeding car when they don't need them any more or if they're being uppity. It hasn't been as bad as that here, but there've been a lot of brasses killed in Soho. And some of their ponces for that matter.

When I was young there was an awful lot of talk about the white slave trade; talk of girls being given injections in the cinema or at a bus stop and next stop it's Argentina. I don't know how true it was. It seems to me it was one of those stories where you knew someone who knew someone whose cousin had been kidnapped, but it was never closer than that. They didn't need to drug these girls, just give them a good time and whoosh.

I suppose one of the first of the big ponces was in the 20s – Juan Antonio Castanar. Before him Eddie Manning, the black man, ran a few girls and some drugs but nothing big. The story is that Castanar had been a great tango dancer who'd danced with Pavlova but he found poncing easier. Who wouldn't? He opened a school for dance in Archer Street but it was just a front. He was what they called white-birding – selling women to dance troupes abroad at £50 a head. That was getting them out of the country. There was also a big market for bringing women in. He was also an arranger of marriages of convenience for foreign women who wanted to get an English passport. His great rival was Casimir Micheletti, an Algerian, who was known as the Assassin because he was so quick with a stiletto. They both ran strings of brasses and were real rivals. When Castanar was slashed across the face in the 43 Club in Old Compton Street it was common knowledge that Micheletti was the one who did it. Give Castanar credit, he stayed game and didn't grass him up.

There were a lot of French gangsters around in the 20s, some of them on the run from Paris where there was a real effort going on to clean out what were called Apaches. And Micheletti was fancied for the murder of another French ponce who went under the name of Martial le Chevalier, when he was found stabbed in Air Street.

There was another killing amongst the Soho foreign ponces in 1926 when Emile Berthier shot an Italian motor car dealer, Charles Ballada, in the Union Club in Frith Street. You can never tell what it was really all about, but one witness said that Berthier believed Ballada owed him money and just went up to him and shot him dead. Doesn't seem a good way of getting your money back to me. That's why money lenders will break your legs if you get behind but they don't often kill you. Unless there's got to be a serious example made of someone.

Berthier got as far as Newhaven, where he was nicked. He came from a family with problems up top. His father was said to have topped himself by throwing himself off a building at the Lyons exhibition in 1904. The jury found Berthier guilty but insane and he was sent back to France. Best place for him.

They slung both Micheletti and Castanar out in April 1929, but it seems like if you want to get back in the authorities can't stop you. It's the same with the Yardies today. Castanar was back within a few weeks but then he got chucked out permanently. The story is he was back being a tango dancer and running a small stable of brasses. Then in February 1930 Castanar met up again with Micheletti and later that night Castanar shot him dead. He tried some fanny about another man doing the shooting and then pushing the gun in his hand, but it was like those stories if you're caught with a bit of gear 'I bought it from a man in a pub. He'd got red hair and his name was Jim'. It didn't wear any better than that kind of story and he got sent to Devil's Island, which is where that American Eddie Guerin escaped from years earlier. Guerin rowed across the sea and was said to have eaten his mates who got out with him. Everyone looked twice at him after that. He was a good man with the vitriol as well. He'd done some big stuff in France at the turn of the century, but he ended up a sneak thief and shoplifter.

All that was when I was a kid, of course, but I was around at the time in January 1936 when another French ponce, Emil Allard, who was known as Max Kessel or Red Max, was found shot to bits under a hedge near St Albans. Only just starting to make my way, I was, of course. Allard was another friend of Micheletti, and whoever killed him took care to make sure he couldn't be identified all that easily.

Allard lived in James Street off Oxford Street and he was meant to be a diamond merchant, just like the Messina brothers were a few years later, but he'd been around over twenty years, selling off girls to the brothels in Buenos Aires. The more they dug up his past the more they found out. They eventually traced back his connection to the murder of a number of Soho prostitutes, including Josephine Martin, known as French Fifi, who'd been strangled with her own silk stockings in her Archer Street flat. She'd been a police informer as well as one of his little helpmates, who looked after the foreign brasses who were smuggled into this country.

Chief Inspector 'Nutty' Sharpe was the copper in charge and he was a right dodgy one for starters. He chased after my friend Ruby Sparks' girl, Lilian Goldstein, the one they called the Bobbed Haired Bandit, looking for Ruby after he got away from the Moor. After Sharpe retired he was mixed up in gambling with the Sabinis. He said he wasn't but he'd got a share in a bookmaking business in Thames Chambers, off Fleet Street. He was also a steward at Wimbledon dogs. The coppers tried to make him get out of it but he wouldn't. Give him credit for that.

Anyway he found out that Allard had been killed in a flat at 36 Little Newport Street just off the Charing Cross Road.

It was one of the matching pieces of glass on the pavement that had led him to it. The tenant was a ponce, George Edward Lacroix alias Marcel Vernon, and the quarrel was all over a brass, Suzanne Bertrand. She was another who'd gone through a marriage with a drunken Englishman and never seen him again. Now she was working Soho streets. As Allard was dying he broke two panes of glass in the window with his forearm in an effort to attract attention and Sharpe matched up the pieces in the street. Lacroix and Suzanne got a car from a garage in Soho Square owned by another Frenchman, Pierre Alexandre, shoved Allard's body in the back and dumped it near St Albans.

By the time Sharpe caught up with them they had fled to France, but for some reason the French government wouldn't send them back. What they did was put them on trial there for Allard's murder. Alexandre gave evidence against Vernon about the car and that did him. He was sentenced to ten years' penal servitude and twenty years' banishment, which is a thing the French have always been keen on. They say you can't come back to the town where you committed the offence for so many years. Suzanne was acquitted but by then she'd spilled the beans about Vernon's partnership with Allard. Apparently they'd first met in Montreal and had worked the white slave trade together for years. The bust up had come over Suzanne. Vernon had left his wife in Paris in 1933 and gone to live with her and while he didn't mind sharing her, he didn't like sharing the profits.

That put an end to the French control of prostitution but from the middle of the 1930s, and with Eddie Manning dead in prison, after that it was the Malts all the way and they was led by the Messina brothers.

There's no doubt the Messinas give Billy Hill and Jack Spot money, but it was done in such a way that Hilly and Spot could pretend it wasn't money from prostitution. It would be money so they'd be allowed to open a club. The club never opened, of course, or if it did it would close just as quickly. With Hill and Spotty it was a question of shutting their eyes, although of course Aggie Hill had been a brass but that was looked on as years before and, although people said Gypsy Hill was a brass before she met Billy, she wasn't really, just a bit wild. The other story I've heard is that it was simply protection in Jack's case. He threatened to cut one of the brothers – who thought he was a pretty boy and a scar would do for him – if he didn't pay him a wage.

3

There was five of the Messinas: Carmelo, Alfredo, Salvatore, Attilio and Eugenio. Their father was really Italian. He went to Malta and helped out in one of the brothels there, learning the trade. He was bright; he made sure all the boys got a good education and, better still, he claimed Maltese citizenship. Then they went to Egypt where he set up a chain of brothels and got kicked out. They started coming to England on the back of the Maltese papers in the middle 1930s. Eugenio was the first and he came with his wife Colette, who was a French brass. He got girls over from the continent and then the rest of the family followed. You can't say they weren't shrewd because they bought up acres of property in the West End. Then it was a question of getting English girls on the game working for them. It was the usual thing – a good time for these inexperienced girls from the sticks then 'I'll marry you if you let me have it' and it worked. Girls didn't put it about then as they do today. The papers reckoned the Messinas were getting £1,000 a week by the end of the war.

It was a real business. The girls were under the control of another French brass, Marthe Watts, who'd had the sense to marry an Englishman. She'd been a working girl herself and she was totally loyal to the brothers. She met Eugenio in the Palm Beach Club in Wardour Street, which is the club where Hubby Distleman got it from Babe Mancini at the beginning of the war. She became his mistress and he had her back on the streets in minutes. They trusted her with everything and they was right to. She must have had chance after chance to turn them over but it never seems to have occurred to her or, more likely, at first, she never dared. And she had a hard time of it if you read her book – threats, beatings with an electric light flex was just part of it. But what does she do? She has herself tattooed over one of her bristols *Man of my life, Gino the Malt*. In French, of course. That's what I was told. I never saw it for myself.

You'd hear from time to time how the girls got treated by Eugenio. They couldn't go out on their own; they couldn't accept American servicemen as clients. I never understood why not. They weren't allowed to smoke, or to wear low cut dresses or even look at film magazines where the male stars were in any sort of undress. They didn't take off their clothes with the customers. There was also a ten minute rule. Punters were only allowed to stay that time before the maid knocked on the door. The other Messina brothers don't seem to have been so severe but they were just as keen on the ten minute rule as well.

They never reported for service during the war and Gino, who was good with his hands and who'd got a flat in Lowndes Square, built himself a hiding place in the form of a bookcase with a removable bottom shelf. Anyone who wanted to see him had to get by a whole series of fronts first.

You can never tell what they let the girls have, but it was meant to be around £50 a week, same as I got a bit later from my club, although they was pulling £100 a night, especially after the war. Of course someone was always going to put in a challenge to them and some other Malts had a go, saying they wanted a pound from each girl a day. A pound a day was good money then, but it was worth not having a bit of acid in your face or a razor scar. Both of them put the punters off. Although Eugenio took off the fingers of one of the other Malts in Winchester Court over in South Kensington, the girls still went to the coppers. Of course they didn't say they were Messina girls, said they only knew of the Messinas as diamond merchants. A jury would laugh today but there was a bit of evidence that the coppers had been on watch in Burlington Gardens, off Piccadilly, when one of them shouted out to the girls, telling her to pay or she'd get a cut. There was a whole lot of stuff in the Malt's car, including a gun and a life-preserver as well as a knife. Three of them got four years apiece. But it was also the start of the end for Eugenio, who was done for GBH over the fingers.

He tried to get someone to smuggle him out of the country and offered £25,000 but there weren't any takers. He picked up three years for wounding. It was whilst he was in the nick doing that bird that I met him. Ponces are another lot you look at twice. Eugenio was all right and he had money, but you don't need to get too close. He got a fearful going over from Flip Hooper in Wandsworth when he tried to get flash. Flip was the younger of two brothers from the Elephant. Flip did a little post office in Rodney Road in 1943 and got three years, along with Spindles Jackson, and then Flip got something like eighteen months, so he was in Wandsworth with me and Eugenio.

Then another Messina brother went down. Just like the Sabinis did for their brother, Joe, when he got three years back in the 1920s. Carmelo tried to bribe a prison officer at Wandsworth for Eugenio. He picked up two months plus a £50 fine. But when he got out he got enough back; something like £700. The girls had been putting his share away for him and he bought himself a Roller. Now they were marked people and there was questions in Parliament about how they were getting their money. No one believed they was diamond merchants any longer. They'd also learned their lesson. No more knives. They just framed the opposition and girls who got out of line.

The man who brought them down was Duncan Webb in the *People* and it took him a while. It was the same Webb who'd go on and cause so much trouble for Jack Spot.

Duncan was a funny man; in Hilly's pocket. He was a big RC and when he got a scoop in the days before there was news stories he'd put an ad on the front page of *The Times* saying thanks to St Jude.

He did it in 1950 – pictures and everything. The Messinas were on their bikes, or into the Rolls more like, over to France. Eugenio and Carmelo that is. They came back on false passports just like today.

Then off went Salvatore, leaving just Attilio and Alfredo. Attilio lived down in Surrey with a Rabina Torrance, a brass from Scotland – I heard her real name was Robina but I suppose Rabina was a bit more exotic. She was one of the girls who was used to frame a kid when the girl had tried to leave the family. As soon as Attilio cleared things up he was off to the continent as well. And then, like in that Agatha Christie story, there was one. Alfredo should have gone as well because he got nicked for poncing and for bribing a copper. He was another 'diamond merchant' and he'd said he'd no idea his 'wife' was on the game even though she'd run up over 100 convictions for tomming.

When she went out in the evening he thought it was to see a relative. It was a great shock to him to learn she was a brass. He had brought his personal fortune, some £30,000, to Britain at the beginning of the war and had dealt in diamonds since then. He'd got both diabetes and high blood pressure, which was why he didn't work. He'd never heard of his brothers living off brasses. He got two years' imprisonment concurrent on each of the charges, and a £500 fine – which wasn't much when you think what he was really worth. In fact Alfredo's 'wife' worked in the next door flat to his real wife, a Spanish woman, who worked under the name Marcelle and who was also on the game.

Marthe Watts took over the control of kids that Eugenio kept on sending over from the continent, where he'd been picking them up at tea-dances. She let them keep their own books and after every grand they earned they had the privilege of going to see to the big boss Eugenio in Paris. But the brothers just couldn't stay away. Attilio got caught next and was charged with living off Rabina Torrance. He had that Judah Binstock, who was later involved with the Victoria Sporting Club, as his brief at Bow Street, but it didn't do him any good at all because he got the maximum of six months.

They still continued. Attilio came out and went back to Rabina in Bourne End. She leased a couple of flats in London in her own name with payments for rent and rates being made through the Messinas' agents. Attilio, who was calling himself Maynard, had another flat in Shepherd's Market and the brothers had another one there as well. Deportation papers were served on him in 1953 but the Italian authorities wouldn't have him and, once the *People* had traced him, he moved to South London.

The brothers kept at it though. Eugenio bought 39 Curzon Street in Mayfair from a woman who ran it as a brothel for him. The coppers found £14,000 in a safe there when they did a raid. Then he decided he was coming back and got himself a couple of fake passports. Things were cracking up, though. Marthe Watts was getting on and her pipes weren't up to what they had been so she called it a day masterminding things and got permission to operate as an independent. After that Carmelo and Eugenio were nicked in a club on the Belgian coast and were charged with being in possession of firearms, having those false passports and procuring women for prostitution. The coppers found the title deeds to four West End properties, along with a report by good old Marthe which showed that one girl had earned £2,400 in six weeks. Eugenio got seven and Carmelo was let out with time served. There were the usual appeals and Carmelo got another ten months. But Carmelo was back over here by October 1958 and was found sitting in a car in Knightsbridge and arrested as an illegal immigrant. He received a six month sentence and was deported at the end. He didn't last long after that and died in Sicily that year.

Attilio had another girl working hard for him. He'd had her for about ten years, taught by that Rabina. Attilio knocked her about continually until she screwed up her courage and went home and to the coppers. He got sentenced to four years' imprisonment. It came out that she had earned between £50 and £150 a week over those ten years and had been allowed to keep £7 a week for herself.

Attilio and Eugenio went back to Italy. Salvatore lived in Switzerland and Alfredo, who by some good luck could claim British citizenship, died in Brentford in 1963. As far as I know the family was still paying rents on flats for tarts well after I went away over the Richardson thing at the end of the 1960s. I heard that Rabina had a son by Attilio who went into the church. She ended up with an antiques shop in Henley and she died in the early 1990s. The rest of them must all be long dead by now. I know their mother is buried in London.

4

As for the Palm Beach Club, like I said, that's where Babe Mancini stabbed Little Hubby Distleman in 1941. Albert was lucky over the case because he was charged with affray when Babe was topped for murder. Babe was one of the last of the Italians who was out and about, because Darby and some of the others including Bert Marsh, whose real name was Papa Pasquale, had all been interned down at Ascot racecourse. Now, what was happening was the Jewish geezers were taking over the Sabinis' clubs. Babe was the doorman at the Palm Beach in Wardour Street and there was trouble over quite a time. He'd thrown a man, Eddie Fleisher (called Fair Hair Eddie, got two years in 1946 and was in Lincoln Prison and Wandsworth with me in 1947), out a few weeks previous and now he was back. Babe went upstairs to see what was going on and he had Albert with him. There was a ruckus and Hubby Distleman, who was a ponce along with his brother, got stabbed. Albert was all for having a go and helping Babe but his elder brother, Victor, who they called Italian Jock, managed to grab him and hold him back. As a result Albert got chucked when the case come up at the Old Bailey. Victor was a likeable guy. He was no mug but he wasn't in the same class as Albert. Mind you he did right by him that day. He died a few years back, having been ill for some time with what I heard was cancer. Poor Babe, the Pros would have taken a plea to manslaughter.

5

Of course there was some smart restaurants in the time I was growing up. Not that I got into many of them, as a punter that is. The smartest must have been the Café Royal in Regent Street. Oscar Wilde used to go there and so did Lily Langtry. Before my time of course. It was about then that a man called Marius Martin got killed there. He was the night porter and it was obvious he was in the way of a robbery. Years later a man give himself up for it and they brought him down from Liverpool to London and charged him, but it soon became clear he was just one of those people that likes confessing. It's amazing how many people do.

Another was in a case down in Oxford after that actor Philip Yale Drew was done for the murder of a shopkeeper. He'd been a sort of Young Buffalo Bill at the Lyceum in the Strand, well before it became a dance hall, and then been in a real good melodrama called *The Monster* which ended up with the villain in the electric chair on stage. I say Drew got done in 1929 but that's not the right word, because although the coppers thought it was him, the jury at the inquest wouldn't name him and he walked free. A few weeks later a man called Dickens just walked into Glasgow Police Station and give himself up. It turned out he'd never even been in Oxford let alone killed the shopkeeper. As for Drew, he toured a bit longer in the play but then he started drinking more and more. No one would have him and he came and lived in Brixton for a time. I think he died in hospital in Lambeth. There was people who thought he killed the shopkeeper when he was drunk and couldn't remember what he done.

The first time I got taken out to a proper restaurant was by the Murrays, whose boy I saved from drowning. The Trocadero it was called, but everyone knew it as the Troc. It was in Shaftesbury Avenue and was a smart restaurant in its day. Smart but not all that expensive. If you was in there you could sometimes hear the fire engines from the fire station a bit further along Shaftesbury Avenue and people would rush out and watch them go the wrong way round Piccadilly Circus. Fat chance of them doing that nowadays.

The Murrays had style. They were before their time, coming out of Waterloo and going to a smart place like that. Tommy Murray, one of the brothers, was a sergeant rear gunner in the war and he was killed. Billy's son, who's also Billy, is still doing life for a murder up in Glasgow in a robbery which went wrong. Like an idiot he didn't come back to prison from home leave one time and that was it. Once they found him they banged him up again.

In the days when they took me out to dinners I used to help take the flowers to their stall on the forecourt of Charing Cross station. Billy and me would walk over Hungerford Bridge and up a little alley off Villiers Street with the boxes. Their mother, Phoebe her name was, had the stall. She'd buy the flowers the night before in Covent Garden and take them home with her for storage. The next day we'd cart them over. She was a wonderful woman, the cream.

It was in 1927, three or four years before I started taking the flowers down to her stall in Charing Cross, that someone went and left a body, or bits of it, in the left luggage office at the station there. I don't understand why they do it and then stay around because the smell's going to attract attention pretty quickly. All right if they've left for

America but not otherwise. But over the years people have left bodies at railway stations up and down the country. There was one in Brighton in the 1940s, and that Tony Mancini kept his girlfriend in a trunk after he'd done her. He was lucky to get chucked and then he goes and tells a paper how he got away with it.

Anyway the body this time was a Minni Bonati, who'd left her husband who was an Italian waiter. She'd gone on the game and had picked up a John Robinson who was some sort of estate agent in Rochester Row – opposite the nick in fact. They found the man who'd sold the trunk, but what did for Robinson was that he'd left a cloth like from a bar in the trunk and a barmaid came forward and said that Robinson, who'd been a regular, hadn't been in to her bar since the time of the murder. Funnily enough they found him over my way at the Elephant. He said Minni had gone back with him to his office and there she'd cut up rough, wanting more money and screaming and shouting. He'd hit her to try and get her to shut up and she'd fallen and knocked her head on a chair. The Pros said he'd strangled her and he swung at Pentonville, which was where they topped anybody who'd killed someone north of the river.

Phoebe Murray's stall wasn't all that far from the Adelphi Theatre where there was a murder back in the 1890s. The very successful actor William Terriss was in a big melodrama, a thing called *Secret Service*, when he was stabbed by another actor who wasn't any good and was just jealous. They called him Mad Archie but his real name was Richard Prince. Just before Christmas 1897 Terriss had been playing poker in the Green Room Club in Maiden Lane where that restaurant Rules is. He was on his way to the stage door when Prince just rushed up out of a doorway and stabbed him. They put him away in Broadmoor where he lived happily ever after, appearing in all the productions. I suppose by their standards he wasn't a bad actor at all.

It was in the Strand that Nathan Goldberg, the guardsman, went mad and shot himself. That was a funny case, just a bit after the war. He lived down the East End and he thought people was after him so he killed a couple and then, when the coppers were closing in, he went and shot himself in a taxi.

At the bottom of Villiers Street there's Embankment Gardens, and one story has it that a woman ran up to a copper there saying a man had tried to rape her. She told him the man was still there and the copper wondered why he hadn't run off. Then when he went and looked he found out why. In them days women wore hats and hat pins and she'd pulled hers out and skewered the man's orchestras to his thigh. Serve him right.

I didn't get into the Savoy for years, although when my Jimmy, my nephew, got married in 1990 we had a good reception there with a lot of the families. In fact the Savoy didn't do poor Dennis Arif too much good in the long run. On 27 November 1990 he and a few others had ambushed a Securicor van with three-quarters of a million on board parked on a garage forecourt in Reigate, Surrey and, in turn, they'd been ambushed by the police. Mehmet Arif and his brother-in-law, Anthony Downer, had thrown down their guns, but when old-timer robber Kenny Baker had shot at the police they returned fire, killing him. Mehmet Arif pleaded guilty and Dennis ran the defence of duress, saying that Baker had threatened to shoot him if he did not repay some £60,000 of gambling debts. It didn't matter to Kenny, he was dead and he'd have been well pleased to help in any way he could. Duress is always difficult. You've got to show you were frightened you or your family was going to get it and, second, and this is the difficult bit, that you couldn't go to the coppers. The coppers found out they'd all been at that wedding together.

I don't suppose there's been a better murder in a hotel than the one in the Savoy in 1923 when that Mrs Fahmy shot her husband, who was some kind of Egyptian prince. Marshall Hall defended her and he made a wonderful job of it. She'd shot him in a thunderstorm in one of the corridors. Here was this poor terrified little Frenchwoman, evilly used because it come out she was waiting for an operation for piles since the prince had been putting it up her deaf and dumb. How could they convict her when all she'd been doing was protecting herself from this foreign beast? French didn't count as foreign. Later it came out she was a high-class Paris brass.

Eva and I used to put out a stall by the Savoy asking for a penny for the Guy before Bonfire Night. That was a place for touches. One of the doormen knew our parents and he wasn't that quick to chase us away. I go quite a bit nowadays. I like the River Room which overlooks the Thames. Of an evening there's a little band or a girl who plays a baby grand piano. You can even dance if you want to and it's not too dear either.

When I was young the papers was always running stories about people who disappeared and had never been seen again, or appealing for help in unsolved murder cases. The MP Victor Grayson was one of those who just disappeared. He was then the Labour MP for Colne Valley, good looking by all accounts and a spellbinding speaker. He'd been wounded in France in the First World War and had a disability pension.

In the autumn of 1920 he had booked himself into the Strand Palace Hotel almost opposite from the Savoy, went into the bar there and ordered a drink. Then said he'd be back in a moment, stepped out and was never seen again. He'd left all his luggage there as well. After his disappearance the pension was never collected. There was all sorts of stories about what happened to him.

The Troc, though, was a big enough stepping stone for the likes of me at the time, but an easier one was Lyons Corner House in Coventry Street. In fact one of the earlier jobs I had was in the Coventry Shoe Shop in Shaver's Place, next to what's now the Prince of Wales Theatre, just opposite the Corner House. That and the job at Boots were about the only two regular jobs I ever had and I was nicking blind from both of them. People were much more trusting in those days; straightlaced but trusting.

The Corner House had a band in a gallery and before the war you'd see every brass under the sun in there. The waitresses all wore smart little black dresses and were called nippys, presumably because they nipped in and out smartish to take the orders and get the food. That vicar from Norfolk, Harold Davidson, the Rector of Stiffkey, got himself into trouble over them back in 1934. A lot of them girls there were half brasses and he used to pop down during the week, when he should have been reading up for his sermon, to do a spot of reforming. Well, that's what he called it. It's like that joke 'Who wants to be saved?' 'I do'. 'Well, I'll save you 'til later'. It caused a great scandal because people complained and the church decided to defrock him. There was a long hearing with everything lovingly laid out in the Sunday papers, where else? Eventually they had him and they threw him out. Poor man, after that he went to do stunts in fairs and was in a bath of ice at Blackpool along with his daughter. He ended up on the seafront at Skegness putting his head in a lion's mouth and one day the lion shut it on him. There was another joke about him. 'What's the registration of the vicar's car?' 'RU 16'. I see his daughter died earlier this year.

The brasses would line up along Coventry Street. They were mostly Messina girls and each had their own bit of pavement and there'd be a real set-to if another girl, particularly a newcomer, took it whilst they were away doing their bit of business. Funny, they all wore hats and there they'd be scrapping it out and trying to keep their hats on so they looked ladylike at the same time.

6

Another really smart joint was the Café de Paris where the bandleader Ambrose used to play. It took a bomb in the war which killed a whole load of people. It re-opened after the war with top class people like Noel Coward and Marlene Dietrich.

Just about on the corner of Wardour Street and Coventry Street was Toliani's Latin Quarter, just where the Odeon cinema stands now. That was another nightclub and it was where Ronnie Knight's brother, David, got stabbed by Italian Tony Zomparelli after they went round to talk about a beating David had taken up in Islington. Zomparelli got four years for it, but when he come out Ronnie had him done by Nicky Gerard, Alf's son, and Maxie Piggott who also went by the name of George Bradshaw. Zomparelli was shot in a pinball arcade, the Golden Goose, up the Wardour Street end of Old Compton Street. The name's been changed now.

Piggott turned out to be a real grass and put up Ronnie and Nicky's names but they got out of it. A few years later Nicky got shot dead by Tommy Hole, who was his cousin, and Tommy himself got done down in Beckton last year. Ronnie did five for receiving some of the money from the Security Express thing and then put it in his book that he'd bought the contract. Piggott was going to be a big supergrass like the others, but when the jury chucked Ronnie and Nicky out the authorities realised no one was going to believe him and they put him back in the nick. I've no idea what happened to him.

Ronnie Knight was one of those who had that A & R Club in Charing Cross Road which all the faces used. I'll never forget seeing Jimmy Logie, the brilliant Arsenal and Scotland forward, working there. He was a sort of potman. Later he managed to get a newspaper pitch just by the church in Piccadilly. Shows what sort of wages footballers got in them days. There was another man worked a pitch outside the big cinema, the London Pavilion, where the rock place is today. He'd got no nose, just a couple of holes in his face, but it didn't seem to put the customers off.

It was on the corner of Frith Street and Old Compton Street that Albert had his famous fight with Spot. He was in

Mrs Bloom's greengrocer's when Spot came in after him. Mrs Bloom banged Spot over the head with the weighing pan and he staggered out into the barber's next door, which was where Albert used to go to get his hair cut. Bert Marsh put a moody knife in the gardens up the top of Frith. Then we let the coppers know where to find it.

If you walk along Old Compton Street towards Wardour Street, at the end on the left was the Two I's Coffee Bar which was famous in the 1950s. It was run by the wrestler Paul Lincoln and his friend Ray Hunter, a couple of Aussies, genuine ones – not like the Yorkshireman Brian Glover who used to wrestle as Leon Arras the Surfboard King from Sydney before he went into films. At one time they had Tommy Steele's contract and he used to sing there in the coffee bar. It was the time when skiffle was all the rage and for half a crown you could sit there all evening and listen to people like the Vipers. When he was wrestling Paul was the real Doctor Death and Ray was one of the White Angels, and they wrestled each other up and down the countryside for years on end. So when they were away they'd leave a doorman in charge. A couple of nights in a row he found he was having trouble with some kids who thought they were being smart, and the next night they turned up they found Ray Hunter was the doorman. That quieted them down quick enough. Ray was very shy, lived in a flat the other side of the street just about over where a Chinese restaurant is now. It's well known that Ray and Paul sold Tommy's contract. Look where they'd be if they'd kept it. I knew Tommy's father, Darbo, well. He was a good man from South London. Not a villain, mind. At the end of the war he had barrows and then for a time he had the cloakroom concession in the Modernairre.

The club leader, Al Burnett, came on the scene during the war and he grew in stature as it was ending. I got on marvellous with him. He was another who liked a good villain. I did a bit of work for him now and then. Nothing in writing, of course, but when he needed help he knew where to go to. We had our machines in his joint. He owned the Pigalle in Piccadilly and you could get through cellars into another of his places, the Society in Jermyn Street. Faces owned or were behind almost all the clubs.

The Pigalle was where I had one of my coming out parties after the Spot slashing and it was where Billy Hill did Tony Mella with a bottle of Scotch when he was getting out of order the night they held a whip for Sully, who was a manager at the Astor. Arthur Helliwell, who had a sort of gossip column in the *People*, wrote it up. At least once a month he would write about Spot and the chaps, mainly Jack Spot. He never named names but everyone who was anyone all knew who he meant. People say there's all this interest today in criminals and there shouldn't be but there always has been.

The Pigalle was also the place where 'Scotch' Jack Buggy did a man called Reeder in 1961. Well, he did him on the pavement outside. They'd had a row when Buggy went to try and invite Shirley Bassey, who was the cabaret that night, to a private party. Reeder hit Jack over the head with a plate, which wasn't the most sensible thing, and they settled it on the pavement. Well Jack did because he shot him point-blank. He got chucked on attempted murder and picked up eight for GBH. Jack was an American really, but he was known as 'Scotch' because he worked for the firms up in Glasgow.

Tony Mella was a man I had a lot of dealings with. He was a game fighter, big man, but probably better on the cobbles than the ring. He fought a few times at the Mile End Arena. Buller Ward says a couple of his fights weren't straight, and when he came up against the Southern Area Champion, Mella got a good hiding. Him and me did a few jobs together. We took him up to Scotland once, more or less as an alibi. If we got stopped we was to say that he was a late substitute at the Kelvin Hall or somewhere like that, but fortunately it never came to it. Then, when the Carter family started quarrelling with Jimmy Brindle, my sister Eva's husband, and I had to take sides, I said to Tony who

knew the brothers very well, that if he met them accidentally well, that was OK, but I wasn't going to stand for him
seeing them on a regular basis. If that was the case him and
me were going to fall out. He went on seeing them and I
went round to his flat in Old Street in 1951 and I cut him
to bits. Just as well he was a big strong man because if he
hadn't been he might not have survived. He was very good
though. He never nicked us nor did his wife and she could
have done. She wasn't there when I did Tony. The police
showed her a photograph of me as one of the likely men,
but she didn't pick me out.

At one time Tony run a spinner at dog tracks. You don't
see them much nowadays. It was a cross between a three
card trick and a roulette wheel. You had to guess which way
cards came, but like all the others it was fixed. There was
what was called a Haley, a stick which was used to stop the
wheel where the dealer wanted. Mella was a bit of a bully
really. Mind you, he didn't always come out best. That little
dwarf Royston Smith, who used to wrestle in dwarf tag
matches as Fuzzy Kaye down the Metropolitan in the
Edgware Road and was in Morton Fraser's Harmonica
Gang, which was very popular in the 1950s, always said
he'd striped Mella – which meant he'd cut him across the
bum like noughts and crosses. At one time Royston had a
club for dwarves in Gerrard Street near where Mella had a
couple of his near beers. Mella went and said something out
of turn and Royston cut him. I suppose his bum was all he
could reach. I don't know if it was true, because I never saw
it, but that was the story. Mind you, in his book Smith says
Georgie Cornell come over to see me the night he was shot
and I was running a North London firm.[1] I never did and I
was in the nick when Georgie went, so Smith's not the most
reliable.

One of the men Mella knocked about with was Big Alf
Melvin, who'd got a good bit of form himself. They'd

---

[1] George Tremlett, *Muscleman of Soho*.

known each other from the days when Mella was boxing for Solomons, but Alf had retired from the game and was running a florist's. I suppose in a way I was partly responsible, because it was after I cut Mella that he got Alf to be his minder. He'd told the papers he'd been held down by six men whilst a psychopath (that was me) cut him a hundred times on the body and he pleaded for me not to touch his face. That was rubbish. There was just me. I didn't need six men to hold him down. Anyway, that's when he got Alf to back him up.

I don't know if he was a partner or what, but Mella treated him rotten in front of the girls and the punters. Mella had the club, the El Alabi, at one time and then he owned the Bus Stop (it was once called the Grill Club), which was a near-beer-cum-strip joint in Dean Street, with Melvin. Either that or Alf thought he should have had a share and Mella wasn't giving it to him. There was a number of different versions. Anyway one afternoon Melvin just pulls out a gun and shoots him. Out Tony staggers on the pavement and dies in the gutter with the girls all around him, whilst Alf sits in the club and turns the gun on himself.

Then a few days after Tony's death a young girl cuts her wrists. She'd been his protégé and he'd been trying to get her acting jobs, but people denied there was anything more in it.

At the inquests there were some letters read which looked as though Alf had just come to the end of his road and Mella had been a right dog to him. One was to his wife saying 'I came into this world with nothing and I'm going out with nothing' and there was another 'This bastard Tony Mella has used me in every shape and form. Sign here. Sign there and everything is down to you. I have been a drunken mug and how he has cashed in on my weakness'. There was talk that the killing was going to cause ructions in Soho but that never happened. In a way most people sided with Alf. He had a much better attended funeral than Tony, whose wife was just a few weeks away from giving birth. Tony's buried in Manor Park Cemetery and Alf in Battersea.

7

The West End was nearly the downfall of my nephew Jimmy, who's now got the Tin Pan in Denmark Street, and it certainly was the downfall of that copper Challenor. He reckoned he was the scourge of criminals in Soho and he simply fitted them up. Eventually he fitted up the wrong man. He'd done well in the war and he was a riser in the police, but he was mad even before he joined the Met.

His finest hour came in September 1962 with his smashing of the 'protection racket' being run by Jimmy, along with Riccardo Pedrini, Joseph Oliva, John Ford and Alan Cheeseman. That's what Challenor said it was anyway. It was based on the evidence of a ponce, Wilfred Gardiner, who ran the two striptease clubs, the Phoenix and the Geisha in Old Compton Street. He said he'd had threats of damage to his car and that he'd be shot and how his car had been slashed. Then Riccardo and Alan were arrested outside the Phoenix Club by two of Challenor's aides. They were taken to Savile Row and told to put their belongings on a table. Alan was slapped and, so he said at the trial, Riccardo was taken into a cell and beaten. Both he and Alan had weapons planted on them. John, who had been involved in a long-standing quarrel with Gardiner, lived in the next block of flats to Pedrini; he got nicked and was charged with demanding money with menaces. The next thing, Joseph was arrested driving along Berwick Street and Challenor and two younger officers dragged him from his car. He was said to have a bottle of turpentine with a piece of torn up towel in the neck and a knife in his pocket. At the trial Challenor said he had information that Oliva intended to attack the Phoenix Club and Oliva was said to have remarked 'If I don't burn him someone else will'. Jimmy was arrested when he was pointed out to police officers by Gardiner and they said he had a knife. I don't think he even knew the others on more than a casual basis. He'd been given a lift by one of them once and after that it was guilt by association.

They were charged with conspiracy and demanding with menaces and went to the Bailey. Jimmy was acquitted of conspiracy but he went down for the knife, and the others were found guilty. Jimmy got fifteen months and the others between three and seven years, which was savage. And it wasn't until 1964 that their convictions was quashed by the Court of Appeal, by which time Challenor was in a spot of trouble himself.

After that Challenor didn't do himself any favours even by the standards of the times. There were a number of complaints, including one by the West Indies cricketer Harold Padmore, whose girlfriend Patricia Hawkins was running a near beer, the Boulevard Club, in Frith Street, when she got done for obtaining by false pretences. Padmore went to the West End Central police station to arrange her bail and, so he said, he was shown into a room with six or seven plain-clothes coppers along, together with Challenor who wanted to know, 'What does a black ponce like you want in a white police station?' Padmore told him, and Challenor replied, 'We'll have some fun with this coon'. The evidence at the inquiry was that Challenor made Padmore turn out his pockets and then hit him repeatedly saying, 'Take that black bastard out of my sight. I wish I was in South Africa. I'd have a nigger for breakfast every morning'. He then began to sing 'Bongo, bongo, bongo, I don't want to leave the Congo', a song which was all the rage at the time.

Padmore was then arrested and charged with obtaining money by false pretences and when he asked to see a solicitor was punched once again. The following day his solicitor applied for a summons for assault against Challenor, but the beak was on the copper's side and turned it down. The case against him, his girlfriend and another girl from the clip joint got thrown out and Padmore picked up damages of £750 for assault and false imprisonment – which I suppose wasn't all that bad, by the standards of the time.

Then Challenor must have totally lost his marbles because next he really picked the wrong man. It's easy to fit up the chaps, but not as easy to do it to political protestors and that's what he tried.

There was a demo outside Claridges in Brook Street when the Queen of Greece came on a visit in 1963 and she was staying there. It was all about the death of some Greek activist. One of the men who was arrested, Donald Roum, turned out to be a member of the National Council for Civil Liberties. Challenor give him a clip and said he'd found a brick in his pocket.

Roum was lucky. He had a good brief and, like I say, he hadn't any form. He was also lucky because he was kept in custody. He claimed the brick had never been in his pocket and because he'd been in the nick overnight he'd still been wearing the same jacket. He got some scientific evidence to show there was no dust and the lining wasn't scratched or anything like that. The beak threw it out but he still didn't get his costs.

But that was the end of Challenor. He was charged but it was found he was too ill to stand trial. Some of the other coppers with him got bits of bird though. Then there was an inquiry by a man who was later the judge at the Train Robbery and it was mostly a whitewash. No one seemed to have worried that Challenor stood and danced on the table or that he walked home to Kent every evening from West End Central. All in a day's work I suppose.

Joe Oliva had made a mess of things for himself. After Albert and Spot had their fight and I was away there was something of a vacancy in the West End and Joe put himself forward. Putting articles in newspapers is always the stupid thing to do but he went and did it, saying he was the new King of Soho and was called King Joe. When it came to the inquiry he said it was just talk and he got rubbished and it didn't help anyone.

8

Apart from spielers and drinkers there was plenty of up-market clubs as well. Bertie Green had the Astor just off Berkeley Square. Jimmy Nash was sometimes the doorman there, around the time there was a quarrel which ended up with Selwyn Cooney dead on the floor of the Pen Club, which was a drinker down in Spitalfields. The Astor opened after the war and you had a decent cabaret. That little fellow Davy Kaye, who was in *Those Magnificent Men in their Flying Machines* – he was one of the French team – was the cabaret a lot of the time. That was a hang-out for the right chaps of a Friday night. Verdi Wright was the compère and he used to sing of a night as well. Bert Wilkins, who's still alive and goes back to the Sabinis and is the uncle of Joe, had the Nightingale which, of course, was right in Berkeley Square. At the top, the Oxford Street end.

Then there was the Colony which faced onto the Square itself. That was one of the ones the Twins used to nip, and where George Raft was meant to be given an interest until he got deported as an undesirable.

Then there was Murray's Cabaret Club, just off Beak Street. Now it's called the Kabaret Klub but it hasn't changed. Marilyn had a party for the launch of her book *Gangster's Moll* there. Tiny little place it is. There was a postage stamp for a dance floor and minute lavatories. You could get a bit of food there. Christine Keeler and Mandy Rice-Davies worked in that club. I didn't go there a lot because it wasn't really for faces. It was considered a classy brasses' drum for punters.

The property man Peter Rachman was very big with Raymond Nash and they owned the El Condor Club together. He had a lot of fashionable clubs in Soho. One of them was La Discotheque in Wardour Street, where Mandy Rice-Davies became the manageress. One night, so the story goes, Ronnie Kray comes in and demands a drink and when she doesn't serve him quick enough he grabs her wrist so she slaps him. Rachman and Ronnie went into an office to sort it out and Rachman had to put up £5,000 so there wasn't any further trouble.

In Bond Street Harry Meadows and his brothers had the Celebrity and Churchill's clubs. Theirs were smart places, real upmarket; decent food, wine, cabaret and top class brasses. For a long time Meadows was a sort of King of the West End. Big man with a handlebar moustache like Jimmy Edwards had; always having his name in the papers about how he'd bought 1,000 ties or 1,000 toy poodles as Christmas presents; always smoking cigars. Mind you he had his ups and downs but, unlike us, when his clubs got done on licensing offences the beaks was on his side, saying things like how good he was in attracting the tourist trade and how it was a benefit to the country. But it was the same as with our clubs but on a larger scale, fashions changed. He had to borrow one and a half million from some Arab in 1975 and two years later the crash finally came in the November when him and his son, Andrew, and another man was done for living off immoral earnings. The Pros suggested that about 40 brasses worked out of the club. The judge, who was a former Pros himself, Sam Morton, said that whilst there might be clubs in London which were little short of brothels Churchill's was certainly not one of them. Not guilty, my Lord, for everyone I'm glad to say. But then a whole lot of waiters were laid off and they had to pay 19,000 quid to them. They'd gone on strike over a dispute about how tips were to be shared out. The club closed down in 1980. I think Harry was also under the cosh from some Malts. He went off to Majorca and his speedboat got blown up out there. I know he was very good in his old age to a brass who'd worked at the club and who had a son; he looked after her like a daughter until he died in the early 1980s.

Bruce Brace ran Winston's and that had the finest cabaret you could ever want to see. Danny La Rue and Barbara Windsor used to appear there when she was hardly out of the chorus, so to speak. Brace wouldn't give them a rise and that's when Danny opened his own club in Hanover Square. Jerry Callaghan, from the big family down our way who was a great pal of Alfie Gerard, had an interest in the Embassy. Another club in Bond Street was the Directors. This was quite a classy afternoon drum also. The girls would take the punters to a hotel since they didn't have flats like they do nowadays. The girls who worked there would know the punters would want something a bit special and they weren't just mugs. Then the Nash family opened the New Bagatelle which was just off Regent Street. That was a classy place too, you got a lot of out of town people coming for the evening, but I was away then.

9

There's not too many people get charged with murder twice. My friend Jimmy Essex was one, and he beat the charges both times. Then there was that fellow Walter Rowland up in Manchester, who killed his daughter and was reprieved and then got done for doing a brass. In his case there was some doubt, but there wasn't none about the man who did another girl near Shaftesbury Avenue.

New Compton Street is across the Charing Cross Road going into Long Acre. That's where she was found dead in October 1931. This time it was nothing to do with the French ponces. She just ran into the wrong person. Funnily the case involved a famous cricketer. The girl was called Norah Upchurch, she was just twenty and she turned up in an empty shop in the street. Her bag was missing. She was found by the manager of the firm of contractors who went to put up a sign on the premises. He got one of his workmen, Frederick Field, to break open the door.

There were a number of suspects in the case and one of them was a former England cricketer, Frank Foster. He'd got a funny story. It was the sort if I told it no one would believe me but he came out smelling like a gent. He'd been the last person to see the girl alive. He said he'd come out of Piccadilly Circus tube station and seen her holding on to the railings. She looked ill and he'd taken pity on her, invited her out for a meal. She'd seemed scared and wouldn't talk about things so he didn't like to leave her but went back to her gaff in Pimlico. There she begged him to stay the night and he'd sat up in an armchair with a couple of sticks handy, ready to give anyone who turned up a good hit over midwicket. Sure enough a man did come into the room, asked the girl if Foster was all right and then went off.

She'd been known to go to Chatham, where she was half-engaged to a sailor, and he was another suspect. Field identified a man who, he said, had borrowed the shop keys and never returned them and the coppers fancied Field as well. The coroner didn't like him one bit but there really wasn't no evidence and so the jury brought in a murder by persons unknown, which was about all they could do.

Then nothing happened for two years when, in the July, Field walked into a newspaper office and confessed. He wasn't the first and he certainly won't be the last. He'd had a deal with the paper at the time of the inquest: they was going to pay for his defence if there'd been a wilful murder against him at the inquest and then he'd give them the full SP for a series if he got a Not Guilty. There was no such thing as legal aid in them days and, unless you had a bit of dough or were one of the chaps and could rely on a whip, selling your story to the papers was about the only way a defendant could get a decent brief on a murder charge.

What Field said now was that he had met Norah Upchurch near where the Hippodrome is on the corner of Leicester Square. It used to be where they had that smart night place, the Talk of the Town. He'd gone with her to the shop but, although she had agreed to give him a plate, she wouldn't lie on the floor with him. He'd lost his temper and he'd strangled her. He said he'd sort of blacked out on the way home after he'd thrown her bag into a ditch near

Sutton. I can't think what he thought he was doing confessing like that. The whole thing had gone quiet, but he said he wanted a bit more money from the paper to send back to his wife who'd gone to her folks in Cardiff.

The other thing is he must have thought he'd got away with the perfect murder and now he wanted everyone to know how clever he'd been. He'd been telling his mates at work but they wouldn't believe him. The newspaper sent a reporter and photographer to the ditch but it was dry and there was no handbag.

Of course, they put him on trial at the Bailey and once he'd thought it over he denied he had killed the girl. His explanation was that he wanted to clear his name as he had been offered a job in Ceylon on a tea plantation and when it had been learned he was involved in the Upchurch murder inquiry the offer had been withdrawn. The judge must have been going soft, because apart from saying that to confess to murder was a funny way of proving his innocence he just about told the jury to acquit. And that's what they did. He never went to Ceylon. He joined the RAF instead and deserted from them pretty quick.

Then in April 1936 they found the body of an old brass, Beatrice Sutton, well in her fifties she was, in her flat at Elmhurst Mansions, Clapham. She'd been suffocated with two pillows.

When the RAF got Field back he was put on a charge of larceny and he decided to have another go at confessing. Back to the Bailey and again he took it all back and ran a moody about hearing a quarrel and seeing a man leaving the flat. His story was that, on the run, he'd been sleeping the past few nights under the stairs in the building and had only gone into the flat when he saw the door was open. This time, though, the coppers had done their homework. They'd got detailed descriptions from him about what was in the flat and the type of injuries she had. The jury took only twenty minutes to convict him and he was topped at the end of June. They didn't hang around in them days.

Of course, if you get a serial killer he might choose any woman, straight or a brass, just like that man Gordon Cummins did in the war. It was in one of three air-raid shelters in Montague Place, a bit behind Oxford Street, that he did a 40-year-old schoolteacher in 1942. In a way she was a bit lucky, really, because after that Cummins started mutilating the girls as well. No one thought her death was anything like that of Evelyn Oatey who was strangled with a pair of silk stockings in her Wardour Street flat, just like Margaret Lowe, another brass, who got done in Gosfield Street just off Tottenham Court Road. Sometimes the papers referred to it as the Silk-Stocking Murders. Evelyn had been a Windmill girl and Cummins had got at her body with a tin-opener. He did another woman, Doris Jouannet, as well. She had a flat in Sussex Gardens in Paddington, which was always an area full of brasses, but she traded round Leicester Square. She must have taken him back to her flat because that was where her body was found. Then he tried to pick up a Greta Haywood near the Trocadero.

Anyway, this Greta Haywood was on her guard. They had a drink in the Troc and were on their way for another in the Captain's Cabin which was off Coventry Street. That's when he attacked her but she fought him off and, what did for him, he left his gas mask in her hands. She was able to describe him as an airman, and it was only a matter of time before the serial number on the gas mask was traced to him.

He'd still got one go left in him though. He picked up a Kathleen King, and took her in a cab back to her flat which was in Sussex Street, Paddington. When they got there he tried to strangle her but she yelled out and his bottle finally went. It wasn't long before they found where he'd been billeted in St John's Wood.

Just after the war a number of brasses got done and the coppers was never sure if their ponces had killed them or they were just unlucky with their choice of punter.

One of them was a girl, Margaret Cook, who was what they called an exotic dancer – which meant she took most of her clothes off behind a fan. She'd served a Borstal sentence and was found shot dead outside the Blue Lagoon Club in Carnaby Street which in 1946, when it happened, wasn't the fashionable place it is today. The police gave a description of who they wanted to interview but they never found anyone. They knew there were stories that her new boyfriend carried a gun but no one was ever nicked. Another girl who was killed around then was Frances Mizzi. She was found strangled in her flat in Poland Street just off Beak Street. After she died her husband got three months for living off her immoral earnings. No one ever got prossed over her death either.

Just about two years later, in September 1948, Rachel Fennick copped it in her flat in Broadwick Street. This time it wasn't a gun but a stiletto. She was found by a punter and she'd been stabbed in her back and chest. She'd married an American who'd gone and died in Paris, and she'd been a brass over twenty years and was getting on to run up 100 convictions of one sort or another. She was known as Red Rae or Ginger Rae. Rachel was a good-looking girl and she was well liked. She'd always hand out a shilling or so to a tramp and sweets to the kids, and she'd been really upset when her dog got run over. Butch it was called. She was quite a decent card player too.

What the coppers did know was that she had a friend who visited her more or less every weekend and he did the cooking for Sunday lunch. Although he denied it there's no real doubt he was her ponce. There's a story that she was a police informer and she was done either as revenge or to shut her mouth. Funnily one of the papers said she'd been done by someone left over from the Micheletti gang. It's difficult to know what that might mean. I suppose that the man and his mates were thinking of having a go at the Messinas, but I doubt it.

Brasses seemed to go on a long time in them days because that same month a sixty-year-old tart, Dora Freeman, who was known as Russian Dora, was stabbed to death in her flat in Long Acre in Covent Garden, which certainly wasn't the upmarket place it is now. If she owned it today she needn't have gone out brassing, she could have just let it out. She'd been on the game since as far back as 1910. There'd been a terrible fight and you'd think the neighbours would have heard but the wireless had been turned up loud by whoever killed her so they didn't hear her screaming. There was also stories that she was both an informer and a blackmailer. There's another story that it was Teddy Machin, who was once a Jack Spot man, who done the three of them. There's no way there was anything to do with sex if Teddy did do it. It would have been purely business.

10

Great Windmill Street has hardly changed except the place is full of strip clubs now. The place for the faces to be seen and be found was at Jack Solomon's gym at No 41. It was over the Nosherie and he had his offices there as well. There was a snooker hall in the same building and people just hung around there. I liked Jack much better than I liked Harry Levine, who really took over boxing from him. I don't know why. Jack liked a good villain and originally he was something of a Spot man but Hilly soon turned him round. I did a few bits of work for him; cut a couple of Americans, nothing too serious.

I was never much cop at snooker, or billiards for that matter, though I used to like to go to Thurston's off the Charing Cross Road of an afternoon when they were playing those long matches: Joe Davis and his brother Fred and John Pulman and Walter Lindrum. You'd get someone leading 64 frames to 43. Scores like that. Posh place it was and I found it very relaxing. That's long gone, of course. Ordinary snooker halls was where people often started their careers in crime. The halls was often over Burton's clothing shops. Out of work, scratching a living, go down to the hall and a bit of work might come to light. Maybe there'd be a lorry to help unload or even to drive. There'd be big betting on the top games in them places. People would bring their local player over and the money could run to a hundred easy, and sometimes up to a monkey. Snooker halls were the life blood of crime.

Then almost opposite Jack's was the Windmill Theatre where they had non-stop revues and the girls used to pose naked except for a few stars. They weren't allowed to move. It had been a cinema, the Palais de Luxe, and then in 1932 it was taken over by Vivian Van Damm who promoted speedway before the war. It opened at noon every weekday and it was so popular that soon there was half a dozen or more rivals. But the Windmill was the one that lasted. The place billed itself as 'We Never Closed', which they didn't all during the Blitz. The week of 7 September in 1940 there was 42 shows in the West End and the next week there was only the Windmill. Wags said it was 'We Never Clothed'. It was very popular with people on leave and more or less all our top comedians of my generation started as the comics there. There used to be a board outside of people who got their start there which was a roll call of honour. Dickie Murdoch, Kenneth More, Jimmy Edwards, and after the war most of the Goons, Harry Secombe, Peter Sellers, Michael Bentine, as well as Arthur English and Leslie West who was one of those memory men who could tell you who won the Boat Race in 1930 and the distance – you don't get them around now. They were just some. Of course there were a lot of others who you don't remember nowadays. There was Afrique, who was very popular when I was young. You see him in some of those old British comedies on the box in the afternoon.

It was good training because the punters weren't there to see them. They wanted to see the girls because your ordinary mug had probably never seen a woman undressed. He might not even have seen his wife without her nightdress on. Things were very different then; different manners.

I remember hearing of a poncing case at Sessions with a young lady barrister cross-examining the copper, who was saying he'd seen a girl take a man back to her room. In those days there wasn't really legal aid even for serious cases but if you'd got something like £2.50 in today's money you could get what they called a Dock Brief. All the old hacks who didn't have any work and the new kids would sit in court, hoping they'd be chosen by the defendant. Anyway the ponce chooses the young girl and the copper had said he had been watching from outside as the brass and her client had it off. Now it's her turn to cross-examine and this young barrister asks the officer how he could see in the dark. 'The light was on,' he says. 'Now, I know you're lying,' she says. And there's instant uproar because the ponce had got form and this sort of thing is going to let the judge put his character to the jury. 'Why do you say that Miss Smith?', or whatever her name was, asks the judge, trying to smooth things down. 'Because people don't do things like that,' she says. There's an uproar, with the defendant saying she's sacked and the judge realises it's hopeless and he says maybe there's a case in another court which she's better suited for. The Windmill's a lap dancing place nowadays.

At the Windmill the show lasted only about an hour and a half and they always had the Can Can, and then it started over again but, once you had a ticket, like the newsreels, you could stay and watch the show a couple of times. The jimmers used to clamber over the seats at the end of the performance to get nearer the front for the next time. It was quite a privilege to be a Windmill girl and you'd often see in the local papers how some young kid had been chosen and this was going to be the start of her stage career and she was going to be the next Vivien Leigh. There'd be some comment from the old woman who'd taught her tap dancing about how she practised since she could walk and how she knew she had a future, but I doubt many of the girls did make it to anything like the top. Not a few of them became brasses. Not all of them, of course, and not street brasses; half brasses more like.

The place all the faces went in those days was in a club on the ground floor in Denman Street, the Mazurka it was called. It was also known as Ginnie's Club after the woman who ran it and who'd been a Windmill girl herself; a lot of the girls from the show would get down there. Everybody used it until Aggie Hill opened her Cabinet Club in Gerrard Street. Halfway along it was, a lovely place. It was there that me and Slip Sullivan's brother-in-law had a straightener. Well, on the pavement outside – no one would think of having a fight in the club itself. Except when Hilly went and cut the man who'd been taking the piss out of Aggie's singing. She kept the club open when she went and opened the Modernairre in Greek Court. She left behind a man in charge, a guy from Southend, who was a very good driver. She had them both going at least until 1955 when I went away. Later the Modernairre got took over by a retired copper; Sandy his name was, and he called it Miranda's.

Great Windmill Street was where Climax Films operated. It was run by Mick Muldoon who had a bodyguard, Gerry Hawley. Gerry was another face who ended up in Epping Forest in May 1969. It was all over blue movies. They'd been making porn films down in a flat in Bedford Hill, Balham, and they did really well for a time. I think the killing was over him trying to muscle in on Muldoon's business. Hawley was a real hard man, one of those who can take a car door off with his hands. He'd been getting a few quid for acting in the films and like so many he wanted a bit more. He wasn't killed there; it was in the Stockwell Road that he copped it. Then one night there'd been a big fight and that was when Hawley got stabbed. The Pros said he'd been stabbed with two weapons a total of 89 times, which was going it some. He'd been put in a car and driven out to the Forest. Funnily one of the films he'd been in was shot in the Forest. It was stuff for perverts; he'd strip off, run through the trees, chase this girl, catch her and then rape her.

Eventually Muldoon and his wife Sandra, who worked at Churchill's, and a kid with the unusual name of Kenneth Eighteen, who was her brother-in-law, got done for his murder. They said it was self-defence and that they was trying to stop Hawley from attacking Sandra but Muldoon got life. Sandra got a discharge but the kid picked up three years.

11

The first club I ever owned was in 1955 in Old Compton Street and I had a Malt front it for me. There was no way I was going to get a licence. It was a good earner. It depended on what it took, what I got out of it, but it was never less than £50 a week. I didn't have to put a penny in it; they was just happy to have me on the payroll.

Then years later Albert Dimes and me had a club with a fellow who owned a very fashionable restaurant. Again I didn't have to do anything, just show up of an evening so people could see who owned it and so they weren't going to cause no trouble. It was a classy joint, the Bonsoir in Gerrard Street, just about where Lee Ho Fook is today. It had a little band, food, everything. The fellow who had the restaurant had wanted Tommy McCarthy from the Log Cabin to go in with him but it hadn't worked. The thing with Albert and me was we was well known. Tommy, good man that he was, wasn't as well known in them days.

That did well for a time but it's the same with everything in Soho, all the clubs, all the restaurants; one day everyone's going there and tomorrow you're yesterday's dinner. That's what happened to ours. Also it was probably the wrong side of Shaftesbury Avenue. That bit hadn't become fashionable as Chinatown then and it was looked on as a bit grubby. Maybe we'd have done better if it was the other side.

Albert simply walked away. He didn't like staying out at night anyway and the place stayed open until half past two. So Joe Wilkins, who was the nephew of Bert, came in with me for a time. But it was no good. We had to have a fire and that's where we was lucky. It took a while to get the place alight. In went the petrol and when we couldn't get a draught going we were smashing bottles of spirits to make what they call an accelerant. Eventually it did go up. It was comical really, but Joe worked hard at it, I'll give him that. Then we were lucky because we had that Bloom who'd done time back in the 30s but who was still working as an insurance assessor. Paid us out double quick. After that I went out of town for a bit. I had some trouble in Brighton and I was on the run, otherwise Joe and I were going to have a very smart little dive in Stratford Place off Oxford Street together.

The last place I had any real interest in was Charlie Chester's Casino in Archer Street when it was owned by a lovely Welshman who had clubs in Cardiff, Port Talbot and Southport. Charlie Chester, the comedian, was just the name. He'd look in at the beginning and shake hands with the punters. But Eddie Richardson and me looked after it for the Welshman after he'd had a bit of trouble with some local villains. He knew Bert Wilkins and he recommended us. We went there, discussed business and they were more than pleased to have our machines in as well. They were new then and they paid a decent weekly wage. At first we'd go in every night; let people know, but then it was just mostly on a Friday night for a drink. It was the presence that mattered. He was a good man, a really smashing fellow; paid me something all the time I was away after the Richardson trial.

Jack the Hat cut Timmy Hayes' son, Jackie, in the club. When we weren't there after the trouble at Mr Smith's Jackie Hayes was minding it for us. Jack came by thinking he might be on a pension but Jackie said it belonged to me and that was when the Hat cut him. Mind you McVitie was going well downhill by then. He wasn't the man he was when he attacked the Governor in Exeter with me, and it was only the fact that I'd been certified that saved us from another flogging in addition to the beating we got. The Home Secretary said it wasn't right to flog a man who'd been certified and it was a question of all of us got the Cat or none of us did. The place in Archer Street is shut now; closed about the end of 2000 and they've gone somewhere else.

12

If we were coming from across the river for a night out what we'd often do is stop and watch Ginger, the strong man who used to perform opposite the Garrick Theatre. I was there again the other day. Ginger's long gone but it seemed to be bigger than I remembered it. It's meant to be the other way around and things are supposed to get smaller as you get older. There were always pavement artists there – real ones not like us – people who did Leonardo's *Mona Lisa* and things. There was all sorts of acts – people who'd have musical spoons and who could play the 'Flight of the Bumble Bee' on a musical saw. You don't see them nowadays. There'd be bands who would keep on the move so they couldn't be done for blocking the pavement. But people liked them. We'd start off of an evening in Tommy McCarthy's Log Cabin which was the best place in the 1960s. You could buy anything in it; it was like a labour exchange for faces. People would come in and ask around if anyone wanted work the next day, and work would mean a pavement job or a bank. You'd think someone would lolly them but it never happened that I knew of. We'd get to the Log Cabin about seven, spend a couple of hours there and go on to Charlie Chester's and then about midnight go to the Astor. That wasn't a place for wives or regular girlfriends, though sometimes I'd take Doreen. She never really liked it because we was living in Hove and by the time we even got to the Astor the last train to Brighton had gone. You got straight people – racehorse trainers and the like – in there as well.

Going up Charing Cross Road from where Ginger used to do his act there's a series of little shops in alleyways and back doubles that lead to St Martin's Lane. It was in one of them, Cecil Court, that the shop assistant got stabbed to death in March 1961 and it was just about the first time they used an Identikit to trace the man who did it. It was one of those shops which sold antiques and curios like bayonets and daggers. They found the woman on the floor with two daggers stuck in her. They'd still got the price tickets on.

They talked to the man who owned the shop and he said there'd been a half Indian fellow in the day before who'd spent a lot of time looking at things but never buying nothing. He looked a bit shabby and came back later with a blonde girl and asked the price of a sword, which at £15 should have been well out of his reach.

Then the man opposite who had a gun shop said that an Indian fellow had been in the day of the murder saying he wanted to sell a sword which he'd paid fifteen quid for but he'd take a tenner. It seems like he had a Cockney voice as well. The fellow had left the sword and never come back for it. Anyway the coppers put together this Identikit of the fellow. A few days later the geezer's picked up walking along Old Compton Street with the blonde girl so they thought. She said she'd never been in the shop and she was telling the truth because it turned out to have been the fellow, Edwin Bush his name was, and his sister who was dark who'd been in the shop. It makes you worry about identification. In fact in his case there was a lot of evidence and he said the reason he'd killed the assistant was she'd called him a 'nigger', complaining that he was like all of them coming in the shop and then never buying anything. The judge said if that was true then it shouldn't have been a case for topping, but the jury reckoned it was just robbery and he swung.

Funnily Cecil Court was where that hooky MP, Mark Hewitson who was on Billy Hill's books, had a flat. Good man he was but foolish. He took a couple of half brasses he'd met in Aggie's back to his flat and they turned it over. Instead of doing the sensible thing and getting Bill or even Aggie to straighten it out he goes to the coppers. Of course the girls lollied him, the papers got hold of it and that was the end of him. He had to stand down at the next election. He just didn't understand that if you mix like that in our world you have to play by our rules.

Just up from Cecil Court in Little Newport Street was another club, the Premier. Any night of the week you could find coppers, chaps and the odd barrister or two, a few film stars on the way down; it was a right mix in there. It was the place where fixes could take place, where money changed hands. The owner was a funny old man who always wore carpet slippers.

There also used to be an escapologist who worked in Leicester Square by the Empire cinema. He'd be handcuffed and tied up in a sack with chains on the outside and he'd wriggle out in about half a minute. The usual way is to be a bit of a contortionist and be able to dislocate your shoulder so one of the chains comes off. Once you've got one off you, then the others just follow. The handcuffs would be those you give a bang to and they come apart. It seems a hard way to earn a living, for all he was getting was pennies and halfpennies and he'd have to have a bottler who'd also act as the barker with him.

His act wasn't far from what was one of the most notorious men's lavatories in London, just by the side of the green bit in the centre. No one who knew anything ever went down those steps. The police would have someone from it in Marlborough Street or Bow Street most weeks and sometimes it could be some straight mug who was down there having a jimmy when one of the poufs comes across and cops his joint. Wouldn't do him any good up before the beak.

There was one from that khazi ended up in Wandsworth with Dave Morbin and me doing half a stretch. What happens is a screw falls in love with him, and tells him when he gets out to go straight round to his quarters and he'll find a key and let himself in. Of course the pouf tells me and Dave and we didn't half have a laugh at the screw over it.

13

The escapologist wasn't really a conman but there was plenty of other cons going around. Really what the Americans call short cons – in and outs; no long-term planning required. There'd be people who'd have blue films – well they said they did – this was well before the porn business took off. It was really the corner game. They'd take a punter's money and send him round the corner to the second floor of some building and be well gone by the time he came down after he'd found there was nothing there. If the workers knew there was an empty room they'd send a whole lot of people, telling them the show would start in about fifteen minutes and they'd better pay now and go straight there so they got a good seat.

Another version of the corner game was the near beer joint. They were usually run by Malts. Girls stood outside getting the mug punters to come in and pay a few quid for lemonade which was worth a few pence in them days. Then a couple of girls would come over and they'd have to be bought drinks and probably given a few quid for their time as well. After that it was the hand on the thigh and a suggestion they'd meet later. Payment up front, of course. There was no question of the girl being allowed to go out with the punter from the club. The owner was 'far too strict' and of course there'd be an appointment at the clock at Charing Cross station or somewhere, and the punter would both do his dough and have a long cold wait before he twigged the girl wasn't coming to meet him. There was a big purge of them just before the World Cup in 1966 when Soho was going to be made safe for tourists. What had happened is that some kids on a night out had been swindled in a club in Lisle Street, which runs parallel with Coventry Street. Full of brasses it used to be. 'You'll always find a smile in Lisle Street' was the joke. Spring of 1966 it was. They'd been thrown out and found some rubbish in the street, poured petrol on it and threw it in the doorway of Number 23. Place went up and a man who'd gone in just to try and find a khazi choked on the smoke. The kids did the brave thing and went and owned up at the nick and they picked up threes and fours.

Nipper Read was in on the clean up before he tried to do the Twins over the Hideaway Club, which is what our Bonsoir had become.

I was in the nick over the Mr Smith's shooting when that fire happened but even before that I never had anything to do with near beers. They'd sprout up and shut down overnight. Most of the punters never went to the police because they'd be ashamed to admit having been in the place and doubly ashamed to admit they'd been conned. That's what the people who ran them relied on.

One of the troubles with going into Soho and going off with girls or boys is that you're open to blackmail. Much more when I was young than today of course, but there's still the worry that your wife isn't going to be too pleased to find you've been putting it about in strange places. One of the big blackmailers of the 1930s worked out of a caff in Lisle Street. He ran a real large racket blackmailing respectable people who'd got involved with a homosexual. Don't forget that in them days buggery was worth life imprisonment, whether the other geezer consented or not, and you could always expect at least a few months for being found plating some other fellow.

This man had it all going for him. One of his young men would form a relationship for a few weeks with a respectable person, in fact the more respectable the better. Someone like a vicar or a retired colonel, well they had more to lose. Then a bit after it had all ended a clergyman would turn up on the doorstep of the victim and explain how the young man in his past had seen the Light and wanted to go to Australia to make a new start in life. How about a small donation to help him forget about them disgusting things the colonel had done to him? And of course it always worked. They'd even have a little pray together when the cheque was handed over. Then down the drive out of sight and the clergyman would take off his dog collar and head back for the caff in Lisle Street. And once there was one cheque that was never going to be the end of it. Cheque after cheque until they'd bled the man dry or he screwed himself up and went to the coppers. The leader got ten years. He'd already done a five and started again within the month. When he wasn't blackmailing bummers he was into the white slave traffic, letting flats out to women. Having it both ways so to speak. The man had been an actor, which explained why he was so good playing the parson.

Much more down the scale of things there was the wallet or the fake ring which someone had found and didn't know the value. The mug is asked to put up a bit of money whilst a third person goes and gets it valued or, in the case of the wallet, puts it in the safe of a nearby hotel. The mug gets to hold the deposit slip, but when he goes to get the wallet then either he finds someone's been there first or that the wallet's stuffed with newspaper. It's all a question of greed. Some punter thinks he's getting something for nothing and he isn't as straight as he pretends or thinks he is. That's the only way the tricks can be worked.

The main racket on the streets then was the three card trick. It's been around for centuries. You think you can find the Queen of Spades and of course, even though you think the card's the one with the bent corner, it isn't. Even if you do choose correctly, and that's like winning the lottery, then one of the team will create a ruckus and the dealer will call the bets off. If you see anyone winning and think how easy it is, well they're just part of the team and the come-on. If you ever think you can beat them or it's a straight game then it's a question of think again. If you was ever in Bow

Street or Marlborough Street where they used to bring them up you'd hear them asking for time to pay. The beaks had a standard reply: 'Yours is a cash business, and so is mine'. They knew the men would always have someone from the team in the public gallery ready to go down the fines office and get them out.

We always really looked down on these conmen and the three card tricksters. They weren't the cream. A lot of them liked to drink too much and weren't reliable and a lot of the others used to blow their dough in Albert's betting shop, A Barnett in Frith Street. Some did both. It's a club now.

From time to time I'd do a bit of work in Albert's shop and sometimes I'd be at the races with him. I've never been a betting man and Albert had to give me clear instructions what to do if I was putting money on for him. If Albert had a big bet you could take it the thing was a boat race. He'd had a top jockey straightened for years. I remember one day at the races Albert sends me to put some money on the nanny and there's a long queue. A chap comes up to me, well known he was. 'Don't you wait, Frank,' he says. 'I'll put the bet on for you'. But I was smart enough to say no. 'Thanks but no'. He knew I was doing a bit of running for Albert and he was just trying to find out the name of the horse.

WEST END

1

When I was young and in prison for the first few times, I heard about people who was legends even though they'd been dead for years. Everyone big, that is. You have to remember that the prison population was around 8,000, maybe 10,000 at the most (sometimes as low as 5 or 6,000) and everyone knew the stories of everyone else. They'd go on being told like you tell children bedtime stories. They love to hear them over and over again. Stinie Morrison was one they told stories about, and so was an American fellow called James Hynes. Hynes had run around with Legs Diamond in New York when they was bodyguards for that man known as Little Augie, Jacob Orgen. When Orgen copped it in New York in 1927 Hynes was shot four times in the stomach. He was taken to hospital and he must have thought that life wasn't going to get any better for him if he stayed, so he smuggled his way on board a cargo boat with a mate of his, Harry Kleintz, and come to London. So what he wants to do is put together a team and do a hold-up in Newcastle. Why he picks that place I don't know, but he couldn't get a team because no one wanted to know about guns. Use them on a robbery which goes wrong and it was a topping matter. Eventually he finds a few people who'll go along on the basis there's no guns. What they really wanted was a safe in a jeweller's shop. They're tunnelling in from next door when a couple of young coppers surprise them and get a beating for their pains. Three people got nicked but Hynes managed to get back to London where he was nicked as well. Then, you've got to hand it to him, he tries to get off the train back to Newcastle and leap from the footboard. It didn't work and both him and Kleintz got five years and deportation, but they got back in from France.

Next time he turns up is in November 1937 when he put together a wrap-up on a woman in Aldford House, Park Lane. Mildred Hesketh-Wright her name was, daughter of a millionaire, so he got that bit right. They tied up the maid and threatened her and then yelled out the house was on fire and kicked the woman's bedroom door in. They threatened her with an electric drill and she anted up the keys to the safe. They got away with £20,000 of jewellery and a bit of cash.

It was funny the way they traced Hynes and it shows how you should keep your gob shut. They found out who sold electric drills and the shopkeeper come out with the fact that the man who bought them had got an American accent and had been complaining about the weather. He also had said he was off to the Turkish baths. Someone put two and two together about how Hynes had been complaining in Parkhurst that there was no Turkish Baths when they had them in Elmina, the nick in New York, and even Sing Sing had steam baths. That was the place to get him – no chance of his having a machine gun under his towel. He came up in front of Goddard and asked for the Cat and a shorter sentence but Goddard wasn't doing no favours. Goddard said that the bullet wounds Hynes'd had when he was shot wouldn't allow it and he give him twelve years. At the time Hynes said he'd die in prison. He was right. He died in

Parkhurst around the middle of April 1943. Couldn't stand English winters, I suppose.

Burlington Arcade was one place I never did. Never even tried; I just didn't fancy it. For a start all you was going to get was tom and that would only go for a third at best. It's the same with buying and selling straight. You want to buy and it's a very rare piece. Many people have fancied it. Probably the Queen herself was looking in last week and she's still thinking about having it. Try and sell the same bit and if you get half what you paid an hour earlier you're doing well. 'No, there's some scratches and it's pretty common really'. Sometimes if it was hooky you'd more or less have to give it away. Then with something like Burlington Arcade you needed quite a bit of muscle. Including drivers, you'd probably really need to be five to eight handed, and where's the profit in that from a load of tom you might or might not get? Then there's the question of getting away. You'd have to run to one end or the other. There's no little alleyways in the middle. So you're either coming out just near Savile Row nick or into Piccadilly and think what the traffic's like there. You'd maybe need three drivers and three motors. If it went sweet you'd get in the first, but if it come to a right stoppo and you couldn't get to him then you'd have to try to make it to one of the others. You couldn't just rely on one. It seemed to me you was volunteering to get nicked.

Over the years some have tried it, though. The best one was when five men did the windows of the Goldsmiths and Silversmiths' Association in June 1954. They'd found a stolen Jaguar and people who saw them thought it was a film stunt. The car was found just round the corner in Carlton Gardens. They cleared something like £40,000 in stones but they'd have got nothing like that for them – at most, a third.

Look at that little George Enright, before my time but he was still being talked about. He'd been a jockey and a stuntman and he was another of those known as the Human

Fly. He played a big part in the robbery of the Werner collection from Bath House on Piccadilly back in 1924, then took it all back because they couldn't find a buyer. It was like that Adam Worth who nicked the *Duchess of Devonshire*, the painting by Gainsborough, from Askew's back in the 1880s. He could never find a buyer and eventually had to negotiate to give it back.

George picked up a lot of bird when he was nicked years later by Greeno when he tried to do an MP's house in Surrey in 1935. Whilst he was out he lived well. He had rooms in Jermyn Street and was a real man about town. I believe he'd done a bit of time in Sing Sing as well.[1]

Another who lived high off the hog was Robert Delaney whom they called Gussie, the burglar of the nobility. He was said to be the original Flannelfoot, but he wasn't. That was a man called Vicars. Delaney lived in Half Moon Street in Mayfair. Fabian of the Yard nicked him in a funny way. Gussie'd go out in rubber-soled evening shoes and the coppers reckoned he'd have to have them made special for him, so they toured the shoemakers in Jermyn Street and round there. According to Fabian he suddenly saw Gussie in the Range Bar, which was a smart joint off Piccadilly, and had him followed to 43 Half Moon Street. They kept on watching him and trailed him to Hatton Garden and then out to Southgate, where they found he'd been selling the jewellery from a series of raids. Gussie got three years and he was in and out of the nick from then on until he died in Parkhurst in December 1948. He was a brilliant climber and he'd got a lot of imitators. A couple of them died in falls, one fell on railings and another fell from a portico in St James'. He crawled about two miles before he died and they found £8,000 worth of tom on him from his final haul. I think it was the writer Edgar Wallace who coined the name Flannelfoot.

---

[1] Edward Greeno, *War on the Underworld*. In the book Greeno uses a number of aliases for the characters and Enright is referred to as Reggie Scott.

Old Johnny Hilton was another one who fancied having a go at Burlington Arcade and it was the end of him – just about literally. I first met him in 1959 in Wandsworth. I was sent there just after Marwood was hanged at Pentonville, and me and some others put buttons in the locks on the cell doors. They changed the rules after that. Up till then everyone had to be out of their cells if there was a topping. Then everyone got locked in their cells until lunchtime.

The atmosphere in a prison was oppressive when there was a hanging. It didn't matter if it was a dog who'd killed a woman or a little child, it was still all over the prison. The screws were generally bouncy when there was a topping, it made them feel more important. The screws in the condemned cell came from another prison but when they went for their breaks screws from the local prison took over for a few minutes to relieve them. You'd know they'd been in from the important way they carried themselves, some would even boast about it to the cleaner. On the morning of a topping people would bang their doors just like they do in those American films and the screws would swallow it.

At Wandsworth the condemned cell was on the ground floor in E2 wing and there was a basement. Pentonville didn't have a basement. When you went outside, though, you could see there was a drop. Visitors to the condemned cell there would come through the double gates, then right and go up some stairs which let you into the man's visiting room.

One of the people who always turned up at a hanging was Mrs Violet Van der Elst. She started in 1935 when George Harvey was topped. He was a punter who had a row with a bookmaker over his winnings. On the day before the execution she tried to see the Home Secretary and claimed to have new evidence that Harvey had suffered brain damage at birth, but in them days she was on a loser. When he was topped at Pentonville in the March she arranged for a brass band to play the 'Death March' and for 60 sandwichmen to parade with placards saying 'Stop Capital Punishment' and 'Mercy is Not Weakness'. From then on she appeared regularly at executions, arriving in her Rolls Royce, yelling at the crowd and throwing leaflets. She'd made her money out of cosmetics and she carried on for the better part of 30 years, being nicked for disorder regular. Some people thought she did more than anyone else to obtain the abolition of capital punishment, but there was others who thought she was turning the whole thing into a circus and they called her VD Elsie.

Anyway, Johnny Hilton was lucky not to get topped. He was doing a five. I knew him from working in the pouch shop and he wasn't a bad guy. Then again in 1966 I bumped into him in the nick when he was done with my friend Gus Thatcher. That's when he got life over the murder of a man in the Royal Arsenal Co-op in Mitcham. Johnny had gone up a league. I've written about Gus and the case before in *Mad Frank's Diary*. Then Johnny Hilton turns out to be a stone killer. He was out on licence in February 1978 and him and a feller, Alan Roberts, have a look at a Hatton Garden jeweller, Leo Grunhut. They fancy the job and follow him home to Golders Green but there it all goes wrong, and not only does Johnny shoot Grunhut but he also goes and shoots Roberts. He did the right thing, bundles him in the car and gets him to a garage in South London where he bleeds to death. It was a good haul, mind. Three grand in cash and near enough 300 grand in diamonds. So Johnny goes and buries Alan on a railway embankment down at Dartford, Kent.

Then in June 1981 he picked up fourteen years for seven robberies and a couple of conspiracies. It took him nine years before he was out this time, when he escaped from Kingston Prison which is now an old folks' nick near Portsmouth, and he did a jeweller's in Brighton. Then he and a friend tried their luck at Burlington Arcade. It worked all right for a minute, and the brothers who owned the shop handed over the better part of half a million in jewels, but when John left the shop the brothers ran out after him. He fired at them a few times, but you have to admit they was game and they got to him. By this time the police was involved and other jewellers was helping so Johnny was a bit outnumbered.

It was when he was waiting trial on the robbery that he confessed to the killing of Alan Roberts and the jeweller. The last I heard of him he was back in Brighton. He'll be in his seventies now. Killed three people, he did. I don't suppose he'll ever come out, I hope he does though.

Alfie Fraser – no relation – was another who didn't have any luck in the West End. He went down a couple of times for the same bank even though it was years apart. He did the Martins Bank in St James' Street in February 1955 and got over £23,000 from tunnelling through from next door. It was a great job, sheer artistry. It took them six hours or more because they come up against an iron grating they couldn't shift. Then they had a go at another wall and there was a place right up the top where they could pickaxe a hole they could squeeze through. They did that right enough and then they packed the safe with jelly and ran some wires into the street and blew it up from outside. That was just about the standard way to do it.

The trouble for Alfie was that there wasn't too many people in the country capable of doing such a skilled job: Eddie Chapman of course; Johnny Ramensky the Scot; Jimmy Boyle and Paddie Meehan; and maybe a few others. You didn't have to be Brain of Britain to work out who was in the nick at the time and look at who was left.

Alfie always said that Ted Greeno, the copper, fitted him up. It was easy in those days, particularly if you had a bit of form since you couldn't really challenge the police evidence. It gave them a licence for villainy. Greeno made out there was brick dust where they tunnelled through and there was the brick dust in Alfie's shoes. It didn't do Alfie no good at all to have a receipt which showed he'd bought the shoes after the robbery. Alfie always said Greeno took out the car carpet, put dust from the cellar on it and said 'That's how you got dust on your shoes'. He got ten years.

Alfie did the tunnel, but that isn't the point is it? Greeno wrote up the case when he retired and published his book.[2] One good thing, though, is they managed to keep their car because the Pros couldn't prove it had been bought with the stolen money. They had to hand back a few grand, though.

When you think of all the successful raids there's been on jewellers it's the failures that stand out. The Aussie, Joe the Bash, whose real name was Leonard Davies, must have been the unluckiest I know of. Before the war he does a shop in the Haymarket and gets clean away, but just as he's getting in the car he spills the tom into the gutter. They didn't have time to pick it up and it's all lost to them. Then, twenty years later, he goes out with Teddy Gibbs, who got away when I picked up three for the stuff in Bedford. Same jeweller's as the one in the 1930s and again he gets clean away but this time a bus pulls in front of the car, passers-by start to have a go and they're nicked. Joe was 70 when that happened. He pulled a four and Teddy got eight years PD. They were giving them out like eyes were winking then.

Teddy Hughes is in Billy Hill's book *Boss of Britain's Underworld*. Bill refers to him as Teddy Oddlegs because he'd got a sort of a limp. Someone was asking me if I'd got a copy of Hilly's book the other day because people are willing to pay good money for it, it's so scarce. So if you ever see one in a second-hand shop you should be on to a few quid.

It was Billy Hill who really started the smash and grab raids pre-war, him and Ruby Sparks. I think the first of Bill's was Carringtons, the big jeweller's in Piccadilly, in March 1940 and a couple of days later he followed up with a raid on Attenboroughs in Wardour Street. His idea was the car should go on to the pavement and so block the shop doorway. After that he did Phillips in Bond Street. He used a decoy car as well on that one. It had the number MUG 999 which, surprise surprise, the coppers discovered to be false plates. Billy did always like a joke.

---

[2] Edward Greeno, *ibid.*

There was another big raid on Carringtons back in 1965 when something like one and a half million worth of diamonds went. It was all a bit peculiar because the man who was done for conspiracy and receiving ten years later was Oliver Kenny, who owned the Horse and Groom, a pub in Brighton. He got bail, which was something, and he ended up involved in the trial of Reggie Dudley and Billy Maynard who were said to have killed Billy Moseley and cut up his body. The Pros said Kenny had nearly died of fright when someone showed him Billy's head in his pub. Bobby and Reggie got life and Kenny had a heart attack just before he was to go on trial for the jewellery. He'd been drinking something like twenty pints a day, so his wife told the inquest. The head eventually turned up in a khazi in Barnsbury.

I've said what a brilliant driver Danny Swain was but I think the best feat he ever pulled was in Jermyn Street at the end of the war. Him, Ginger Randall who was a good man in those days, and Jimmy Robson were trying to do a jeweller's when they come up against some Army officers. Of course a ruckus was meat and drink to the military and they got hold of Jimmy whilst Ginger was trying to hold them off from him with an iron bar. Danny just drove with two wheels on the pavement and somehow managed to catch hold of Jimmy and drag him away from the men. Jimmy scrambled in and in the confusion Ginger Randall got in as well. What a bit of driving.

A few people would steal jewellery and then sell it back to the jeweller, but now it's a dead art and jewellers are much more on their toes nowadays. It used to be very hard for an insurer not to believe jewellers, so if a claim was made there'd be a quick inquiry and then they'd cough up, but these days they go into things a lot more. As for art thefts that's really sold out unless you've got some crank who's going to put it in his cupboard and pull it out every Pancake Day. I've never been lucky enough to meet a millionaire who wants to keep the *Mona Lisa* in his cellar. There may be one or two, but your average thief isn't going to meet them. They're probably abroad as well. No one is going to touch it. The only way you'll get rid of it is at a car boot sale, if you're lucky.

It's much more likely to be an insurance job so you've got to know how to sell the stuff back to the insurance company. That's what Peter Scott, who was a brilliant burglar in his time, tried to do a few years back in 1997 and he came a cropper then. He was trying to help out Russell McVicar, John's son, whose position at the time was just about unhelpable. Russell went into the Lefevre Gallery in Bond Street and produced a gun before he walked off with a Picasso painting. Peter tried to negotiate its return but he ended up with three years. Russell was following in John's footsteps. He broke out of Kilburn Police Station and fell out of a tree, then whilst he was in St George's, Tooting, having his injuries treated, he managed to get past the security guard and he was away again. After that he did a series of robberies and I suppose it was just a matter of time before he got a pull.

Peter Scott's great mate was George 'Taters' Chatham. Taters, who was on Billy Hill's Eastcastle job, also did the Victoria and Albert in 1948 when he nicked the Duke of Wellington's swords, which he'd fancied for a long time. He didn't do anything useful with them though. He took the stones out and gave them to his girlfriends or used them as credit in spielers. Money just poured through his hands. He did the National Maritime Museum in Greenwich where he picked up Lord Nelson's hat. The jewels went the same way. He was still working when he was nearly 80. Poor George, he was a lovely man but he couldn't pick horses and he didn't play cards as well as he thought he did. He died back in 1997 with nothing to show for things.

2

If you walked along Piccadilly and turned right down towards Berkeley Square and then along into Curzon Street and into Shepherd's Market that was where the quality brasses used to work. Messina girls to a man. There was also a fair number of cards in shop windows for the girls who had flats of their own. There wasn't many in the 1950s because it was still difficult to get a telephone but these girls were the class end. The advertisements were discreet, a sort of code, not like the stuff you get in telephone boxes nowadays. Just things like 'Miss Macintosh gives riding lessons', 'Butterfly Needs Careful Mounting', 'Big Chest for Sale' and 'Miss Strict, ex-governess, will accept pupils'. There was a place, 43 Curzon Street, with a red neon sign saying 'French Lessons'. It was there for years and years. Eventually, for some reason, after the girl had left the police went in and found a whole lot of what they called equipment. They said they'd never even dreamed it was a vice girl's flat. They must have been the only ones who didn't.

3

It's funny, I've never been to the zoo in my life. My parents didn't have the money for treats that often. It was one thing to send Eva and me on a tram to Abbey Wood, which was a wood in them days, with a thermos of tea and sandwiches and our elder brother and sisters pleased to be playing mother and father, but it was another spending good money at something like the zoo. I suppose in a way since I've been locked up so much of my life I don't like seeing animals in cages either.

I'd have been coming up for seven, though, when one of the elephant keepers went and killed another. There'd been a lot in the papers when the man who was called Sandy Wee came over as a keeper with a special white elephant from Burma. It was the same later, when a panda came from China and when, after the war, that baby polar bear got born there and the papers ran a competition to name it. Brumas it got called – after its keepers I think. Anyway

Sandy Wee stayed on and looked after the elephants, giving the kids rides whilst the head man who was Indian went home. It was good money because parents would always give the keeper something and he was getting about 30 bob a week. When the head man came back he wanted to take back this little earner and Sandy got sidelined. Of course, he didn't like it at all and he went and did the keeper. Well, that's what the jury found. Sandy said he'd been in the quarters with the keeper when four men had come in and attacked the Indian with a pick axe. He got a guilty, but they reprieved him and he was released and sent back to Burma inside four years so there must have been something which people didn't know about.

There've been a lot of good murders in the Regents Park area. By that I mean not simply straightforward ones. One of the best was that of Alice Hilda Middleton. She was shot by her lover Cecil Maltby in August 1922 and he kept her body for nearly five months in his flat above his tailor's shop in Park Road. Alice had been married to a seaman and she moved in with Maltby whilst her old man was away. Her husband seems to have known about her having it off and after he'd reported his wife missing the police went round to Maltby's shop in January the next year. Maltby called out of the window that she'd left him in the middle of August and he hadn't seen her since. There was also a terrific smell around the place.

The police then started keeping watch day and night and crowds gathered watching them. Finally the coppers got an order allowing the Medical Officer of Health into the flat on the grounds that the premises were insanitary. That was the moment Maltby topped himself, shot himself in the mouth. There she was, wrapped in a sheet in the bath in the kitchen. On her body there was a note, 'In memory of darling Pat, who committed suicide on 24th August 1922, 8.30 a.m.'

All around the flat were other notes he'd written, and there was one nailed to the bedroom door which said she'd killed herself, but no one believed it because she had been shot from behind. What was odd, though, was that the coroner thought Maltby was sane when he did himself.

It's funny how people like keeping bodies. That's what did for a man called Crossman. He was standing smoking a cigar in Kensal Rise, supervising the removal of what was left of his fifth wife, who was in a tin box and wrapped in cement, when the police come after him. He cut his throat as he was being chased down Ladysmith Road. The sixth wife had been living happily with him not knowing that Number 5 was under the same roof. It was the usual story: a neighbour complained about the smell and Crossman said he'd do something about it, but before he got round to it the neighbour went to the coppers. I suppose he was smoking the cigar to hide the smell. Back in 1904, that was.

Just after the war there was a big case when the lightning cartoonist Harry Michaelson was killed at his flat in Marylebone. He used to sleep with his window open and on Boxing Day 1948 a young fellow, Harry Lewis, saw it and jumped over the railings. Once he was in, Michaelson heard him and Lewis bashed him over the head with a metal chair. He'd never bothered to wipe off his prints from the chair and since he'd got form they was on file. The jury recommended mercy but it didn't do him no good. It's funny how some got reprieved and others who did exactly the same thing swung.

There was another funny case in 1956, the year I went down for slashing Spot. Ten years earlier a woman called Olive Nixon had been battered to death near where she lived in Park Village East, a small mews-like place just off the Marylebone Road. No robbery and no rape and no one ever got nicked – although funnily enough they fancied a copper, wrongly as it turned out – until a fellow, Adam Ogilvie, just walks into the nick and puts his hands up. It's like so many of these unsolved cases. Apart from DNA the coppers are just going to have to wait until they get a man for a traffic light and whilst they're taking his particulars he'll say 'I think I ought to tell you . . .' That's more or less what happened with Adam Ogilvie. He just volunteered it all. He said he'd been walking with a girl in the woods near Hampstead the previous Wednesday and he fancied killing her. And he thought he'd better give himself up, before he did another one. The only thing to do at his trial was like so many others – take it all back, and all that shows is you shouldn't open your trap in the first place. He was another who said he'd made his confession to prove his innocence because his wife had started suspecting him. Funnily, after he'd done Mrs Nixon, he'd gone up to a woman in Torquay from behind and bashed her with a brick. He got three years for that but no one had ever put two and two together. He and me were in the nick together. He was lucky. It was one of those times when Parliament was talking about stopping hanging altogether and for the moment no one was being topped.

There were a few more murders up that way about the same time which never got solved. There was Gladys Hanrahan who was found strangled on Cumberland Green. The cops fancied one of her friends she'd been drinking with, as they'd been seen having a row the morning she was done. The man produced an alibi to say he'd gone on impulse to Brighton but some witnesses said that they'd seen him in London. The coroner said that even if he'd been in London there wasn't anything to connect him with her death.

Then there was a brass known as Irish Kit whose real name was Kate Higgins. She was still on the game at the age of 70, so God alone knows what sort of punters she was drawing. She used to hang out in the Princess Alice in Acacia Road and she was found strangled in the grounds of Winfield House where that American heiress Barbara Hutton used to live.

The other case was Emily Armstrong, a lady who had a small dry cleaning business in High Street, St John's Wood. In those days shops closed during the lunchtime and that was when someone took a claw hammer to her. Whoever done it must have been covered in blood but in them days the High Street wasn't busy like it is today. No one ever came forward to identify the man.

A man they half fancied was John Allen, the Mad Parson who'd escaped from Broadmoor. He'd been a chef down in Burford in Gloucestershire and before the war he'd strangled the young daughter of some other people who worked in the hotel. There wasn't anything like sex in it. He was just annoyed that the little girl's mother had been put in charge of making cakes instead of him. He'd been in the nut-house twice before, so there wasn't any question of topping him and he went to Broadmoor. Then in 1947 he simply walked out. He was in the concert party they had and he was wearing a parson's collar, which is how he got the name. He stayed out for some years and got work, so when he finally got nicked and no one had ID'd him for the murders he went back to Broadmoor. That's where I met him. He was released not too long later and after one of Alfie Hinds' escapes the newspapers had him write a piece about how easy it was to stay out. He also wrote a book which was very popular for a bit. He'd be nearly 90 if he was alive now.

Poor Henry Jacoby wasn't as lucky as Ogilvie, or Allen for that matter, and he didn't have any social people to help him like Ronald True who got reprieved around the same time, as he swung the year I was born. Jacoby's mother had been a brass and when she had punters in she used to push the kid under the bed whilst she had it away on the top. Then he became the pantry boy in the Spencer Hotel, which was one of those residential-type hotels where old ladies played bridge, and probably still do for all I know.

It used to be behind Selfridges in Portman Square. Jacoby hadn't been there three weeks when he decided to steal something from one of the rooms in the middle of the night. He opened the door of the room of a Lady White, and when she screamed he hit her with a hammer he'd taken from a toolbag. He washed the hammer and put it back in the bag and went back to bed. He might have got away with it because the police thought it was an outside job but eventually he went and confessed.

His brief suggested that he'd been given the third degree by the coppers – which was about all that he could suggest – but the judge, McCardie, wasn't having it and said 'What is the First Degree?' The jury recommended mercy and there was a campaign for a reprieve because he was only eighteen but it didn't do him any good. He still got topped. Some people also brought up a campaign to have his body buried outside the prison but that didn't work either. It was there when I was in after the war. Just a number in the wall for him: H.J. 382.

As it happened, a few years later in 1932 the judge topped himself. He did it in his flat in St James', shot himself. Just as well he was successful because, if he hadn't, he could have been charged with the offence of attempted suicide. Only crime that I know when the attempt was punished and the crime itself wasn't. There was all sorts of stories about why he did himself, but it seems like he was in the hands of the moneylenders. Big gambler – and you know what happens with them ninety-nine per cent of the time. It was also said he had a Jewish mistress, which wouldn't have gone down too well in society. He was never seen with her in public. She used to go up the back steps to his flat so the porters never saw her. Of course, it was all put down to overwork, service of the country, all that sort of rubbish.

The last time the police came to see me over a murder was when that businessman Donald Urquhart, who had owned the Elstree Golf Club, got himself killed in Marylebone High Street in a drive-by shooting. The guy had been having dinner in this restaurant with his girlfriend and was on his way home with his girlfriend to the block of flats where old Bert Wilkins – who was with the Sabinis and the uncle of my friend Joe – had lived, when he got shot. A man pulled up on a motorbike and did him twice in the nut. Then a bit later that year this fellow, Tommy Roche, who'd been working on the M4 down near Heathrow, was shot in another drive-by. Someone took him out from the back of a motorbike.

Anyone who's been searched regular will know when the coppers are serious. That's when the light fittings get unscrewed, the wallpaper comes off and the floorboards come up. Then there's the ones which are more for show and this was one of them. Marilyn and me were living in Duncan Street in the Angel at the time and they just turned up with a warrant saying they were looking for charlie. Of course there wasn't any and that's when they said they were from the Murder Squad and were wanting to talk about Urquhart. I told them I'd never heard of him and I hadn't.

As for Tommy Roche, apparently he'd done a bit of work for Urquhart and he'd been a hanger-on of the Twins so I suppose there was reason to think at least I knew him but, in fact, I didn't. I'd have been older even than Johnny Hilton if I'd done it. I never fancied motorbikes at all, and getting on the back of them at the age of 71 would have been a bit much. I don't think I've ever been on the back of one in my life and I've certainly never driven one. The coppers were very pleasant; we had a cup of tea but then they went and took my address book – and just on ten years later I've still never had it back.

There was all sorts of stories as to who had done Urquhart. No one ever thought that the shooter was anything but a contract, but it was the why that was interesting. A report in the papers said it had cost £20,000 and that it was all over drugs and, in fairness, that was the way it looked at first. But when it come to it, it wasn't. It was just a simple business deal which had gone wrong and the loser wanted something done about it.

Graeme West was the guy who actually did it and he couldn't have advertised himself much better. As well as telling people, he'd done just about everything else wrong. He'd been seen around the golf club and he'd got Urquhart's ex-directory number on his mobile. Not only that but he'd left his BMW near Urquhart's flat and when he comes back it had been clamped. If that's not enough his van had been given a parking ticket in Marylebone as well. What is it those advertisements say? It pays to advertise.

It seems the figure was £20,000 but no one has ever been prossed for putting out the contract. The story is that it's a solicitor who has been on his toes ever since. If it is, he won't be the only solicitor who's been suspected of organising a killing.

You might think nothing happened in that bit of town but you'd be wrong. Bickenhall Mansions was where those Russians, Ruslan and Nazarbek Outsiev, got done way back in 1993. Ruslan fancied himself as the Prime Minister of Chechnya and the pair was pouring money around the clubs like it was water, spending other people's money on the brasses. Both of them shot in the head. One of the men who did it topped himself in Belmarsh and the other got life.

4

I suppose in my time there's been two really big events in Knightsbridge and one of them was the Spaghetti House siege, which lasted five days in September 1975. Of course in those days it was before terrorism and those embassy sieges. The guys who got done for it claimed it was political, a strike for Black Power, but really I think it was over money. That wrestler, Norbert Rondel, got done for putting up the job and supplying the guns but Norbert denied it all and I'm pleased to say he got chucked.

What the Pros said was that Norbert ran a gambling club, the Apartment in Rupert Street, and he was owed money by a punter, Lino Termine, who'd worked at the Spaghetti House and knew that every Saturday evening the managers from the other branches in London come round with the week's takings. He put the job up to clear his debt. Well, that's what the Pros said anyway. It was going to be a straight blag but one of the managers escaped and rang the police, who was round in a minute. The response time was better in them days. And that's when it all came on top and

Frank Davies, who was leading the whole thing, and the others took the rest hostages. They said they was only coming out in an aeroplane or a coffin but eventually they surrendered. The only one who was hurt was Frankie, who shot himself accidentally when it was nearly all over. It seems that by the end there was one of those situations between the hostages and the men where they congratulated each other that they'd survived. Frank, who'd done a previous ten for a blag in North London, picked up 21 and the others a few years less. As I say, Norbert got chucked and there was a picture of him in the papers standing on his head to celebrate. I think he'd lost his club with the eight months he was in the nick on remand, though. Termine pleaded guilty and got a six.

Norbert went on to have clubs in Bayswater. He's still alive and was dealing in cars in the Borough the last I heard of him. He come over before the war as a refugee so he's got to be my age and more.

The second big thing was the blag organised by Valerio Viccei from the Knightsbridge Safe Deposit Centre. His book said he cleared £60 million, but who can tell? I don't think anybody ever knew how much really went. If it goes from one of the boxes people aren't really in a position to tell the coppers they've had a £100,000 in notes locked away from the taxman are they?

Viccei's father was a lawyer back in Italy but the boy was wild. He was on the run from Italy and he'd already done a blag at Coutts, where he'd got bitten by a cashier, before he thought of the Knightsbridge job. He did a second job and that picked him up nearly £50,000 and then he did £70,000 in travellers' cheques from the American Express in Mayfair, so you could say he was big time.

What he did next was to latch on to a fellow, Parvez Latif, who was the manager of the safe deposit. He took him out to places like Tramps and wined and dined and charlie'd him to persuade him to be part of a phoney tie-up job. The man was to let him and some others into the

Centre and switch off the closed circuit telly. He was also supposed to point out the best boxes. In return he was going to get a fabulous pay out. It would be running down his nose. The guards at the Centre weren't in on it and they had to be overpowered. The first mistake Valerio made was to cut himself whilst he was opening one of the boxes and leave blood and fingerprints all over the place. After that it was just a matter of time. One of the others was staying in White's Hotel in Hyde Park and he was watched. The coppers soon found out that Viccei was visiting him and he got a pull in a traffic jam at Marble Arch. One of the members of the team, Steve Mann, turned grass and got a five whilst poor old Latif drew an eighteen. The others got bits in between. Valerio picked up a 22, but by 1993 he'd been sent back to Italy. He'd always boasted that was what was going to happen. I see he died in a shoot-out with the coppers there a couple of years back. He was game to the last. Him and his mate had some carnival masks and the coppers thought he was going to do another bank.

5

Victoria's never had the happiest memories for me. It's where I had a bull with that judge, Lawton, on the platform when I was with Doreen waiting for the train to go home to Brighton. I was really giving it to him and shouting, telling him what a dog his father had been as a screw, when Doreen pulled me away. Years later in the Torture Trial I wanted my counsel to object to Lawton being the judge, saying that he'd had this row with me and it wouldn't look like he was unbiased. At first Lawton denied he'd ever seen me and then a bit later he swallowed it and said, well yes, there had been an incident with a drunken man, but he'd clear forgot it and it wouldn't prejudice him or me. And everyone said 'Of course not, My Lord' and that was that.

Not that I haven't had some touches in the area. Back in the November of 1944 me and Patsy Lyons and another man did the jeweller's in the courtway from Victoria Street to Caxton Street. It was one of a series of shops. You couldn't get a car up the alleyway. Me and the other man, who got Borstal, we went in the jeweller's and held them up with a bar of iron. I started smashing the display counter and we cleared about £12,000 from the window. All the people came running out and seeing as how it was wartime, with all these soldiers and airmen and sailors about, those were the 'have a go' days. Not like today when that poor woman who got killed at Euston trying to get her handbag back seems to have been blamed for trying. People should shout for help and not have a go themselves, some spokesman said. It wasn't like that in the 1940s.

We were on our toes at once and got clean away in the car back to Bermondsey. It was when we tried to fence it that we found out there wasn't as much as we'd hoped. I know it sounds good money, but £12,000 of tom is going to come down to three for a quick sale and that means a grand each at best. So we decided to do another jeweller's in Bond Street. Stark raving mad we was, using the same car. Someone had obviously taken the number and the coppers were looking for us. We was going through the Rotherhithe Tunnel to work our way through to the West End when the police cars came after us. We got out of the tunnel, which was the main thing, but at the junction of Old Street and City Road we was hemmed in and crashed. We all jumped out and made a run for it. I ran behind a bus, stopped, took off my gloves and scarf and just turned round and walked along back towards the police. The police thought I'd run straight on and I got clean away. Poor Patsy got five years' penal servitude.

Wilton Road just by Victoria Station was where the first conviction in the world came from a glove print. Fingerprints was one thing and later came palm prints, but it wasn't until 1975 that a fellow got caught through a glove. He'd done a surveyor's. The Pros said that police laboratory tests showed that 'the chances of finding matching gloves were the same as one man's fingerprints matching another and that, as is well known, is virtually nil' and he went and pleaded guilty. So that was the end of wearing gloves if you're caught with them on you.

I think it was about that time that the Biograph cinema in Wilton Road next to Victoria Station closed. It was a real gobbler's gulch, a rundown fleapit of a place where the punters never even pretended they was watching the film. There was a constant stream of men going to the lavatories. You'd ruin your trousers rather than go in the khazi there. Of course the coppers kept watch on it and it kept getting raided. You'd have thought men would have learned not to go in.

TOTTENHAM COURT ROAD

1

The best robbery there's been – and that's not knocking them on the Great Train – was Billy Hill's Eastcastle Street Post Office job in 1952. That was where a car was driven across a post office van. Once they got the money out they moved it from place to place in London until it was safe. The reasons I say it was the best is that the coppers never got the money back and no one got done for it. The money, with inflation, must have been about what they got for the Train, certainly what they kept. The other thing was it actually taught the coppers how to do their job. Not that they learned.

What Billy was keen on was security. He didn't want anyone lollying him by mistake or being evil, so when he decided the job was on he had all his team in his flat and locked them up until it was time to go. Yet a few years later when that copper Bert Wickstead, who liked being called the Fox, was doing a raid on the vice haunts in Soho he made the mistake of letting it be known what was on, and as a result all the birds had flown by the time he came looking for them. He didn't make the same mistake twice and neither did Nipper Read when he went for the Twins. I read Wickstead died in March this year. I never knew him, thank the Lord. Even other coppers acknowledged he was a king fit-up merchant.

What I can't emphasise enough is how security-conscious and clever Bill was. The trouble with jobs is that the more people on them the bigger the chance there is of a leak. In a way Bill was lucky. The London Airport job, which Jack Spot organised, must have had about twelve men on it and the chances of a leak just multiply. People are bound to tell their wives or girlfriends something's going off, and they tell their mothers and then it's all over London and someone's going to grass. The best job is if there's only one of you. With the Eastcastle job Bill didn't really have to tell too many people exactly what was going to happen or when. He was lucky in so far as he'd got Billy Benstead, who was one of the men who got away from the airport, on the job. So he could say, 'Look what happened when too many people knew about that job'. And Billy Benstead could back him up and say 'Bill's right'.

One of the men on the raid was Terry Hogan. He was a good man who only ever did a bit of bird and nothing to do with the blaggings he was on. Then he give it all up in the 1960s, married and left crime altogether. He died in the middle 1990s.

A few years later, in March 1961, there was another robbery in Maple Place near Eastcastle Street but this time it wasn't anywhere nearly as successful as Bill's. In fact there was a lot of bird handed out over it. Someone had grassed even before it got underway. It was on a firm of building contractors and the coppers got on to a man, Henry Jeffery, whose van they spotted in the neighbourhood. He'd just finished a six and was looking for work. They knew he was linked up with Tony Terroni from a very good family. When it came to it the whole thing was a ready-eye. The coppers got the driver straight away and they knew where to look for the rest. By today's standards, and given firearms was used, the sentencing wasn't that bad. The seven of them got 46 years between them. It would be about double that today, if not more.

Down just by New Oxford Street there used to be the Horseshoe Hotel and there was a big killing there back in 1913. An Armenian shot and killed the manageress, and newspaper vendor John Starchfield, who had a pitch just on the corner, got in the way and cut off his escape. He got shot in the stomach and was given £50 and a quid a week pension. That year he was the hero. But the next year he was the villain when his seven-year-old boy, Willie, was found dead in a train at Shoreditch. The train had come from Chalk Farm and when another kid got on at Mildmay Park he saw Willie under the seat. He'd been strangled and his teeth had been loosened, which sounds to me as if someone had tried to get him to plate them.

Apparently his mother said she'd sent him out on an errand to a shop a couple of hundred yards away, and it was a mystery how he ended up on the train. Anyway they interviewed Dad and he told them he'd been in bed at the time and a hotel porter confirmed it. Then that hooky man who run *John Bull* and ended up doing time himself, Horatio Bottomley, put up a reward of £500 and of course all the grasses came out looking for it. A man called Moore said he'd seen the Starchfields together in Endell Street in Covent Garden, where they later had the clap hospital, around three-thirty the afternoon the boy was done. John Starchfield then got arrested and things got worse for him when a signalman said he'd seen a pair who looked like the Starchfields as the train went past and the man had been leaning over the boy. That did for him. The inquest jury said it was murder and Starchfield went up to the Bailey.

Things did get better, however. Moore, the man who'd put Starchfield's name in the frame, tried to commit suicide. Then the judge said he didn't think the ID evidence was strong enough and he told the DPP to throw the case out. John Starchfield didn't last long, though, because he died a couple of years later from the injuries he'd received when he'd been a hero. A lot of people always said he had done his son in, but why? I'd go along with his meeting a maniac.

Just behind the old Dominion Cinema – where Tottenham Court Road meets New Oxford Street and the Charing Cross Road – was where Jack Spot did the reporter Duncan Webb. He had him set up with a fake call and started bashing him about in an alleyway, Bainbridge Street. Webb falls to the ground and breaks his arm. He prossed Spot and then sued him in the local county court. He said he'd lost a whole lot of money through not being able to type and he'd had to hire a secretary so he could finish a book. He got a bit over £700. Duncan was a good-looking man, a lot of wavy hair, smoked a pipe like so many did then. I liked him. He come to see me on a visit in Birmingham once and he gave me a gee when I was locked up, awaiting the Cat, when I did the governor in Exeter.

Eddie Richardson and me had Atlantic Machines in Windmill Street. That was just opposite Store Street where they had the Court of Protection which looked after the estates of nutters. It's funny how the law gives protection but when we do it it's an offence. At first we just had one shop but then we took the one next door as well. Leslie McCarthy was really the office manager and he kept things running properly. He was Bert McCarthy, the boxing promoter's, brother. One time Bert had Frank Bruno on his books. There was dozens of McCarthys and they all seemed to be half related to each other in one way or another. Sammy McCarthy, who was also a boxer before he got done for armed robbery, was a cousin of some sort. Those were good days, things was running well and it was being run straight. As I've said, when we was all nicked over the Torture Trial the coppers went round the country trying to find someone who would say we'd been running Atlantic as a long firm, but they never could.

We'd begun at the right time getting the one-armed bandits from America through Hilly and Albert's connections. We were trying to build it up and we just took our exes out of it. We'd have about twenty machines there at any one time. They were always coming in for repairs – people would be giving them a kick or pulling the handle out of alignment and we'd have to have spare ones to take around the countryside. It was a tragedy about Atlantic; a good business. We never needed it to be hooky. When Eddie and me were nicked Leslie carried on as best he could, but then he tried to help us with a juror and he was nicked himself. It was really nothing. We heard that the brother of a juror went into a café down the East End and what we wanted was the truth to come out and get a proper verdict. The owner of the caff introduced the brother to Leslie and Billy Stayton, who used to play with us for Soho Rangers. The man said so far as he was concerned there was no problem and even though the police were all over his brother he'd mention it. After that it was all on top and poor Leslie got eighteen months. And that was the end of Atlantic.

2

Round the corner in Charlotte Street was that famous Italian restaurant, Bertorelli's, and we used to eat in there quite a lot. It's still there but I haven't been in it for years. I was in Chez Gerard though the other night, and that's nearly opposite. The Book Club ran a competition for people who bought their edition of *Mad Frank's Diary* and the prize was a dinner in the restaurant with me. You had to have a tie-breaking answer to the sentence 'I would like to have dinner with Mad Frank because . . .' And the girl that won it – real nice she was, her and her partner – wrote 'Frankly I'd be mad not to'. It was about the only time in my life I've ever been late for anything. I'd had to go and do a show up in the North. It was after the train crash at Hatfield and everything was running at quarter speed, so I was an hour late but she was lovely about it.

Charlotte Street used to be the home of the Scala Theatre which staged Maskelyne and Devant, a children's magic show every Christmas, and it was there in April 1947 that a famous robbery took place. Harry Jenkins from the Elephant, Christopher Geraghty and Terence Rolt did the job on a jeweller's which went all wrong. First of all the jeweller shut the safe door, then one of the employees threw a stool at them and when they went to get their car they found they was blocked in by a lorry. As I've said, in them days passers-by would have a go and one of them, an Alec de Antiquis, tried to block them with his motorcycle and he was shot. They was eventually bubbled by a man who'd been on a job with them in Queensway. Harry and Christopher was hanged, Rolt was detained at Her Majesty's Pleasure. De Antiquis was given a medal named after a man, Binney, who'd tried to stop a raid in the city and had been killed when he'd been dragged under a car. Funnily enough, Harry had been on that raid as well.

If people think that capital punishment stops crime then they'd better think again. Harry and Chris was hanged in December and when he heard about it on the radio a kid named Flossie Forsyth, who'd known them, went out to do a bank raid in Worthing. That went all wrong as well and he killed a guard. Then him and his girlfriend went off to Glasgow and he got caught when he told a taxi driver to keep the change from a ten bob note when the fare was only half a crown. His defence was that he thought he was being controlled by the spirit of that New York gangster 'Legs' Diamond, but the court wasn't wearing it and he got topped about six months after his mates.

3

At the top end of Tottenham Court Road on the left is Warren Street. It used to be full of used car dealers, who'd have cars in showrooms and parked on the pavement. There could be up to 50 cars and other people would just stand on the pavement and pass on the info that there was a car to sell. They was mostly for mug punters. People would come down from as far away as Scotland to buy a car. All polished and shiny with the clock turned back and the insides hanging out. Chaps wouldn't buy one, or if they did the dealer would make sure it was a straight-up one and the engine wasn't going to fall apart within a month. The dealers may have been small time and they may have been ruthless but they weren't that big mugs.

At the lower end of the street they might sell hooky cars, but not the ones who'd been there years. They were hooky in their own way but not that hooky. At the bottom end if you'd sawed the engine number off then they'd be game enough to give you a price; they'd do a trade with anyone but the ringing had to be really good. Remember, there was a premium on cars in them days. If you wanted a new car you had to put your name down on the dealer's list and you might have to wait months. It was no use you saying you wanted a green car either. If a red one came along you took it or if you didn't the next man in the queue would bite the dealer's arm off trying to get it. They was making so much dough they didn't have to take risks.

And if you bought a car and it fell to bits who was you going to complain to? There wasn't these Fair Trading officers and if there was they weren't as powerful as they are now, and there certainly wasn't all these television shows and articles in newspapers. Duncan Webb had his work cut out with vice, not old bangers. Well, in a way they was old bangers I suppose, but Webb's sort sold more papers.

Some of the dealers had Spotty and Billy Hill behind them. It wasn't that either of them had an interest in the cars, it was more that their names were kept buzzing and it was good for the dealers to be able to say that Billy or Spot was with them. And if a firm wanted a hooky motor then Bill could arrange it for them. Mind you there was some good men who worked the pitches there from time to time.

Old Alfie Alpress and his son Danny Teale were a couple. Danny was a top-class getaway driver. He could almost have been a racing driver he was so good. He got put away by that grass Bertie Smalls at the end of the 1960s and wasn't out too many years before he got cancer. He was game to the last. At the time he really took ill he was on bail for taking a mechanical digger to a bank cash machine. Parking wardens and regulations by the Council did for Warren Street in the end.

One of the big dealers in Warren Street was Stanley Setty, him and his brother Max who went on to own the Blue Angel in Berkeley Street – very fashionable that little club was and absolutely straight. Poor old Stanley wasn't straight though.

And that was why he got done by Donald Hume. Now there's one of the few men who've served a life sentence for murder and gone on and done it again. In a way he was another who was lucky he wasn't topped the first time. Stanley's real name was Suleyman Seti and he come from Baghdad. He was a banker for the black market as well as dealing in cars. He'd put up money for a load and take a cut at the end but he wouldn't touch it himself. He was a bit of a pimp as well and he'd got a conviction for fraud, which is how when they came to it they identified him. The Pros said Stanley got stabbed and cut up in Donald's flat at 623 Finchley Road. What was right was that Donald, who was an expert flyer, hired a plane and dropped the bits of the body in parcels over the Essex Marshes back in October 1949. What he never reckoned on was the tides, or maybe he thought he was further out to sea than he was, but anyway the bits floated back. The coppers traced him through the plane he'd hired and he said he was just dropping the bits for a couple of men who really killed Stanley.

Donald had a good story about how he had agreed with two men, 'Mac' and Green, to pilot an aeroplane for them on a smuggling trip. They had called at his home with parcels containing what they said were 'hot' plates used for forging clothing coupons. He agreed, for a fee of £50, to fly them out to sea and drop them. After the first flight, on his return to Golders Green he found them, along with a third fellow called 'Boy', waiting outside his flat and he agreed to drop the third parcel for another £100.

He put this third parcel in the kitchen cupboard and on the way down heard a gurgling from the parcel. He thought it might be a body inside and, possibly, even that of Setty because there was talk the man was missing.

But there was a lot of evidence against Donald. Notes which Setty had drawn from the bank were traced to him. He had taken a carpet to be cleaned on the morning Setty died and Donald had had a knife sharpened locally just before the killing. What he was lucky with was that no one had heard the sound of a quarrel and there wasn't a single fingerprint of his in the flat. Nowadays I suppose there'd have been some DNA evidence, which would have done for Donald, but there was nothing like it then. They got that pathologist Francis Camps, who reckoned that half the neighbourhood would hear if someone was sawing bones. And that was enough for Donald to get a disagreement. Of course, they were easier then, when it had to be all twelve jurors.

The Pros was never keen on topping a man after a retrial so he got offered the chance of a plea to being an accessory after, which meant he couldn't swing. He used to tell me he'd never have taken it if he'd known he was going to get a twelve.

Whilst he was away his wife Cynthia, who'd been a hostess, went and married Duncan Webb. When he was close to Billy and we'd all meet in Peter Mario's restaurant in Gerrard Street – it's a Chinese, the Harbour City, nowadays, best dim sum in London – we used to tease Duncan that Donald was about to be released and would be coming after him. He used to get really scared. Anyway the moment Donald's out he goes to the *Sunday Pictorial* and tells them that it was him killed Stanley all along; a quarrel over money. Don was only out about a year when he goes over to Zurich and robs a bank there. A taxi driver tries to stop him and Donald shoots him dead. The court said that this time life for a man of his kind really did mean life. But it didn't. Eventually he come back to England to serve the rest of his sentence and he was released. That was when he did a bit of electrical work in the flat Marilyn and me had in Duncan Street in Islington. Then he died down in a wood in Gloucestershire. It was days before they found the body and they had to identify him through his teeth.

As for Duncan Webb, when it came to it he died just before Donald was released the first time. He'd been to Liberia on a story for the paper on smuggling out there and he picked up a virus from which he never recovered. He had a big funeral, of course. Bill went to it. He really was the biggest name in reporters of his time. The other journalists on the paper made sure Cynthia got a pension.

Another man who made his dough out of Warren Street was Charlie Mitchell. He was a good thief. He could turn his hand to anything and then he took up horse doping. Unfortunately he turned into a grass in the Kray trial. That was one of the things which took the stuffing out of them, not that they would let it show. There was Mitchell in the dock in Bow Street with them, and next minute he's out and in the witness box so to speak. Later he was badly done over down the Fulham Road and went to live in Spain, where, I'm glad to say, someone topped him.

4

Almost opposite Warren Street on the right was Maples, the furniture store Alfie Hinds done, and Bert Sparks the copper almost certainly fitted him up for it. Alfie used to drive us all barmy in Pentonville telling us how he was going to get out of it – and in the end in a way he did. He was bright, was Alfie. He'd got an IQ of over 150 and he ended up a head of that thing for brainy people, MENSA. He came from round the Elephant and his dad had a flogging over a bank robbery down in Portsmouth. His mother used to wear fur coats from the proceeds of his dad's robberies and it was no wonder Alfie Snr was nicked.

Alfie himself was a class safebreaker but he didn't have all that much luck and for a time he was in and out of Borstal. Then it looked like he was settling down and was working with his brother. When the Maples job went off in 1953 he had a small bungalow at Wraysbury on the Thames. Him and his mates blew the safe and lifted a lot of jewellery. It was another of those cases where he was meant to have had dust in his turn-ups which matched dust from the store and there was some verbals. In the end Alfie received a sentence of twelve years' preventive detention from Lord Goddard.

Alfie never gave up. He complained about the trial year in year out. When he was in the nick that was, because he was a good escaper. He reckoned he hadn't had a proper defence because he'd had a change of brief and, of course, he also reckoned he'd been fitted up.

The first time he got out was from Nottingham Prison in November 1955, using a hacksaw blade and a prison workshop key he'd copied from memory. He stayed out about nine months and that was when Patsy Fleming and me got him an interview with Duncan Webb. Of course the more he got his name in the papers the better people liked him and there was all sorts of people lined up to write about him including that 'Mad Parson' John Allen. Alfie got caught in Dublin in the July, and he did even better when he successfully defended himself on a charge of prison breaking.

The next time he got out was when he locked a screw in the khazi in the Law Courts, but it was more like nine hours this time not nine months. He got out again in 1958 and stayed away for two years. He was a hero. Once they picked him up all he would do was talk about how he was to go to the House of Lords. But when he got there that didn't do him no good either.

Finally, he got a turn up when the copper Herbert Sparks wrote an article saying that Alfie should grow up and take his punishment like a man, so Alfie sued him for libel. He was lucky. People could still remember the Challenor case, and they was beginning to realise that the coppers weren't always on the up. During the case Sparks didn't do well in the box and at one time covered his face and a wag called, 'Watch out! He's doing a Challenor'. Of course the judge was against Alfie but the jury gave him £1,300. Alfie wasn't satisfied. He was a free man to all intents and purposes, but he wanted to clear his name and so he went back to the Court of Appeal but they wasn't being fooled. I saw him from time to time after his release. He died in the Channel Islands. I think by then he was a rich man.

There's a story about Sparks and Billy. The day Sparks become the new Superintendent in 'C' Division there was an article in one of the papers about how Billy was the King of Soho. Sparks had Billy in. Coppers could just summons a man in then, not to charge him or anything, just to talk. Sparks yells at him, 'Hill, I'm the King of Soho, not you, interview finished.' All Billy says is, 'Bloody Hell.' But I know who ended up better off.

HOLBORN, KINGS CROSS, CLERKENWELL AND THE CITY

1

Sometimes I sit in a coffee shop in Kingsway waiting for James Morton so we can discuss the book. I like to get there early and I get a corner seat so I can watch what's going on. It's got big plate glass windows and you can just about see all human life there is passing. One or two people recognise me and they wave or give a thumbs up and sometimes they'll come in and ask me to sign my autograph on a paper napkin. There's two things I think when I'm watching. One is how many people smoke despite being told its bad for their health. I can just about see Holborn Tube station from the coffee shop and the second people are off the forecourt they're lighting up. The second is I rarely see a slim woman. You hardly ever saw a fat woman when I was young. Not unless they was getting on and they were boozers. There was no McDonald's or Kentucky Chicken and all the others. There was Lyon's Corner House and the fish and chip shop and the pie and mash and you couldn't afford to go there very often even though it was cheap. Now it seems like Kingsway's just wall-to-wall restaurants and café's and takeaways. No wonder people's fat. The young ones and all. And you see people eating in the street. When I was young if my mother had seen me eating in the street she'd have taken the food away and smacked me. It's like these young women, and men for that matter, who comb their hair on the tube. If Eva had done that my mother would have thought it a terrible disgrace. Back in my time I remember an old lady turning to one woman and saying, 'Don't do that my dear. You may know what's in your hair but we don't.' She wouldn't have dared now. She'd have had her eye poked out with the comb. I know there aren't so many nits about today but that's not the point.

Down Kingsway towards the Aldwych there used to be the Stoll, big theatre it was. It got pulled down but there's now the Peacock just round the corner. That's been through a few names in its time. People could queue for the gallery and you could rent little stools for about sixpence so you didn't have to stand whilst you waited. As far as I remember the big show at the Stoll was Kismet. Before the War though, Eva and me and another kid used to do a bit of a song and dance and get pennies and ha'pennies from the crowd. I remember one night, there waiting to go in was my eldest sister, Peggy, with her boyfriend who she married later. We saw her and give her a nod, saying she'd have to give us something otherwise we'd shame her by stopping and saying she belonged to us. Her husband joined the army and he stayed in after the War, did well and served his full twenty years. She's still alive.

There used to be trams which ran in a tunnel under Kingsway down to the Embankment. When Jimmy Brindle, who went on to marry Eva, and me went over to see our Italian pals in Clerkenwell we'd often take his car down the tunnel. It was all right if there weren't two trams in it. We'd have a few drinks in us and we'd be hooting and laughing but eventually we realised the authorities would be after us. We never drove through it after we'd been working. You might have to in an emergency but you was far too likely to get blocked because it was several hundred yards long. You can still see where it come up or went down, depending on which way you were going, just over the traffic lights at Holborn Station on the way to Southampton Row.

It's funny thinking back on how things and manners have changed. We wouldn't have thought we was dressed unless we had a trilby on. And if you met some woman you took it off and kept it off until she sort of nodded to say you could put it back on again. I'm amazed sometimes when I watch the racing on the television and some man's won a big trophy. He goes up to collect it and he never even takes his hat off to the woman who's presenting it to him. It was even worse when they had the minute's silence for the Queen Mother, some of the men, not just in the crowd, but those who should have known better didn't take their hats off.

The coppers, detectives that is, was made to wear a hat in them days. You certainly wasn't allowed in the CID without one even after the War. And good publicity it was too. There was a famous photograph of a copper, Beveridge it was, raising his hat before he made an arrest. It was a funny case, that was. Beveridge was the one who put a temporary stop to the war between Bill and Jack Spot and the Whites.

Anyway, the woman he raised his hat to was Florence Ransom and he did it in High Holborn. It was back in July 1940. She'd been the mistress of a man, Lawrence Fisher. He'd got a wife and a nineteen-year-old daughter and they lived in a village called Matfield near Tonbridge, whilst she and Lawrence lived on a farm in Oxfordshire. She kept things in the family because although Lawrence didn't know it, her mother was the housekeeper and her brother Fred was the cowman.

One day she goes visiting the Fisher women and she takes a shotgun wrapped in brown paper with her. Since none of them came out alive except her and she wasn't saying, it never come out how she got them into the orchard where she blew them away. The maid ran out hearing the shots and she got it as well. What Mrs R. didn't realise was she'd dropped one of her white leather gloves and, since these things are usually family, it was only a matter of time before Beveridge took his hat off. She was found guilty, of course, but she got a reprieve and she ended up in Broadmoor.

Once you started going into the city from New Oxford Street, unless you peeled off into Covent Garden things started to get a bit shabby really, compared with Oxford Street itself. I had my first dinner suit from Moss Bros in Covent Garden. I suppose I was about nineteen at the time. I went in and tried on the various jackets and trousers and then when I knew what size I wanted I told Eva and one of her pals went in and nicked it for me.

Just off Covent Garden was Endell Street and in the 1930s there was a famous case over a club there. A cripple called Jack Neame and his partner William Reynolds got prossed over the Caravan Club. It was one of the usual sort of cases, men dancing with men and calling each other Josephine and Henrietta, but there were also women there. I still remember the newspaper report said that Neame told the court a solicitor came in and danced all by himself. It didn't help. He'd no form but he still got twenty months and Reynolds got a year. It may have been because of the blackmail of homos which was going on in the West End at the time. The coppers were still giving evidence about men dancing together and calling each other darling well into the 1960s.

But if you continue down New Oxford Street you come into High Holborn. That's changed beyond recognition. Down the bottom end there used to be a big department store, Gamages, but compared to say Selfridges that was a bit shabby and all. Not that Eva and her mates didn't get a very nice wage out of the place. It wasn't the first place they'd go, more if they'd had a bad day they could always do a bit of business on the way home.

Almost opposite Gamages used to be the Daily Mirror building in New Fetter Lane and that's where there was a payroll raid in June 1978 when a guard was shot and around £200,000 stolen. My boy Frank was said to have been on it, and another job the previous year at Williams & Glyn's Bank in the City, but it all worked out well. Some police went to see George Copley in his cell and offered him a deal that if he pleaded guilty and give evidence against some detectives who was being done for corruption he'd only get five years. George had a tape recorder hidden in a wad of depositions and when the Pros heard what George had recorded the case got dropped against both him and my boy.

The raid on Williams & Glyn's on 27 September 1977 was a smart one. My David was said to have been on that one. It was a Securicor job. Just after 11 a.m. the van arrived at the bank and the robbers struck. The driver was shot in the leg and they snatched just over half a million. They got into a Ford Transit but that got snarled up and then they got to another van and that too got stuck in the traffic. They'd left over half in the first van. There were three getaway cars but the trouble was the traffic. They made it to the third but by this time the alarm was up and another security vehicle rammed theirs. So they held up a Mercedes and got away in that. There was a couple hanging on to the doors trying to get in. Eventually they abandoned the Merc and took a taxi. The police was keen to write it up as a Bungling Gang, but they still got away with nearly a quarter of a million. Funnily enough, it was in Birchin Lane where Ralph Binney was killed in December 1944. He was dragged nearly a mile after he tried to stop a getaway car and they struck a medal for his gallantry.

2

A bit after the war there was a very famous murder, still unsolved, in High Holborn when Daisy Wallis, the woman who ran the Adelphi Secretarial Agency with offices on the top floor of 157, got stabbed to death one evening in August 1949.

Apparently she liked to be called Dorothy and she lived with her parents in London. She'd set up the agency with what she had saved from her earnings and all she had was a couple of second-hand typewriters, chairs and a filing cabinet. Two sisters who lived in the building heard her screams but did nothing about it. One of them said, 'We often hear screaming and shouting, and take no notice of it.' The other one said she thought she'd heard 'Murder' called out. She reckoned it was a fairly rough area and much of the noise could be attributed to the postmen in the Drury Lane sorting office nearby.

She was right in that. It wasn't far from Seven Dials, just off the Charing Cross Road. It's still there now, but that and Drury Lane was a real thieves' kitchen in the old days. Back in the eighteenth century there was some famous names like Jonathan Wild, who worked both sides of the fence, come out from around there. Then there was more modern Jimmy Lockett, a great safebreaker who worked a lot with Cammy Grizzard, the fence. And maybe the best of them all, Billy Hill's family come from there. Big warren of a place.

Dorothy had been stabbed repeatedly with a stiletto-like knife and she'd bled so much that, when a sample was required for the autopsy, that Doctor Camps, who was in so many big cases then, had difficulty in taking one. The only clue the police ever really had was that a man seen running away was dark haired and of Italian appearance. One witness described him as clean-shaven, fairly thick set with dark hair brushed straight back from his forehead. Two witnesses said they had seen her on other occasions with a similar looking man, once in a restaurant in Piccadilly and the other in a pub in New Cavendish Street.

What she'd done was kept a series of diaries in shorthand and when they managed to translate one of them they found she'd cancelled an appointment for the night before. What the coppers did find out is that every day she locked her office for a 90 minute lunch break but they never could find where she went. You'd think it wouldn't be Brain of Britain to reckon she was seeing a bloke but they never found him. Her parents said she didn't have any men friends and only a handful of girlfriends either. There was fingerprints all over the office and all but one set of them were eliminated from the inquiry. It seems the owner of that remaining set did not have a criminal record – which shows that maybe there should be compulsory fingerprinting at birth, like they say.

There'd certainly been a man in the office because one of her clients had rung in about six and spoken to someone they said sounded well educated and who said she'd gone home for the night. Then there was a mysterious Polish man who came looking for work and at the same time offering bigger space in a better class building. He was never traced.

A month before her death her office had been burgled. Funnily, only the older of the typewriters was taken, with the thief disregarding a £20 new radio and a cash box. For a bit the coppers thought that this might have some significance, but eventually they said it hadn't. Eight years later, when the office block was being pulled down, some workmen found a sword hidden behind packing cases filled with rubbish on the second floor. The coppers re-opened the case but no arrests were ever made.

3

If you go into Lincoln's Inn Fields there's Sir John Soane's museum. It's a lovely place with things like Hogarth's Rake's Progress. It's where poor Dennis Bergin was killed back at the beginning of February 1987. It was a ready-eye since the coppers were already in the building. A warning shot was fired but it ricocheted and hit him in the heart. You can see the bullet scar in the wall on the right as you go in. They've got it preserved under a bit of Perspex. His brother

George and a whole lot more got done over it. George got a seven. The coppers say they was after one of the paintings to finance a drugs deal.

If you stand with your back to the museum, Lincoln's Inn where all the barristers work is on the left. That's where the fraudsman Kenneth De Courcey jumped out of a window. He'd got a seven at the Bailey, and when he was having his appeal heard in the Strand he got permission to go back to his lawyers' offices to look at some papers. He said there was other papers in the next room he had to look at and within seconds he was out the window and on his toes. That brief Manny Fryde, who defended the Twins, said if it had been his window Courcey had jumped out of, he'd have been in the nick himself by nightfall.

You can walk on into Carey Street where the bankruptcy court was and where both Jack Spot and Darby Sabini ended up. Then it's into Chancery Lane and Cursitor Street where Freddie Ford had a club. Mind you, Freddie Ford had clubs all over the place. He also had that one in Ham Yard, the New Avenue Club. On a Sunday he used to send his punters over to the Cursitor Club. When they got done in 1925 there was over 200 people on the premises, a lot of them in fancy or evening dress, so it wasn't just a mug's joint. Well, maybe it was a mug's joint but they was high-class mugs. He had that bent brief, the Irishman Edmund O'Connor, defend him. O'Connor was meant to have been very good in his day, but the gambling got to him and he ended up with a seven himself just before the war.

Freddie got some form when he was young; a five at the Bailey in around 1912 and steady form from then on. He got chucked on a manslaughter in 1924 and got a bit more bird when he went down for receiving in 1927. Later he was a good friend to Billy and found him a very decent spieler in Ham Yard again. It was Freddie who thought of buying up hotels around Kings Cross and making sure the brasses had suitcases when they took the punters in. That way the owners of the hotel had a good defence if anyone said they was allowing the place to be used for an immoral purpose. He died a very wealthy man. Argyle Square was the big place for toms round there.

Like the Premier Club, the Albion pub down at Ludgate Circus, just round the corner in Bridge Street, was where deals were struck. It's got a brand new name now. The owner and his wife were great friends with Alf White's son Harry. That was where two coppers fought over a tape recorder in 1980. One of them was wired up against the other who was suspected of being on the take. One was Detective Superintendent John Keane and the other Detective Inspector Bernard Gent, and the fight was started by Keane trying to snatch a tape recorder from Gent's pocket and within seconds they were both rolling round on the floor. The landlady leaned over and said if they didn't stop she'd call the coppers and they said they were the police. Gent had been taping a conversation about a £10,000 bribe for Keane doing what he could to get someone out of a big blagging in South London. It seems that Keane had telephoned Gent, who was the officer in the case, blind, asking 'if anything could be done'. It was as blatant as that. He got a three year sentence. I'm not sure he didn't go on and become a brief.

Blackfriars Bridge was where they found that Italian banker Robert Calvi hanging in May 1982. At first it was said to be suicide because he'd been found with his hand in the till. Later, though, it seems like he may have been hanged by the Mafia for just the same thing. There was all sorts of talk about the bridge being symbolic, with Black Friars having some connection with the Vatican. I don't know if that's right. What I do know is that when that Judge John Maude sentenced a couple of irons for plating each other under the bridge he told them not to do it again, but added that if they felt they really had to they must do it under some other bridge, as that was his favourite one.

If you go down Theobalds Road towards Little Italy, Jockey's Fields is on the right. It's a little mews just by the gardens of Lincoln's Inn and that's where Billy Hill did the second of his big raids. It was on 21 September 1954 and the load was gold bullion being unloaded for the KLM offices. It took all of twenty seconds and the haul was £45,000, which wasn't as much as Billy got for Eastcastle but it wasn't bad at all. No violence, just a straight snatch. Speed was what was wanted and that's what they had. The coppers knew Billy was behind it, of course, but they thought he was in the South of France and so they pulled in everybody else who was anybody. One of the great things to do if you know a job is going off, but you're not on it, is to make sure you've got an A1 alibi and the best of those was to go round to your local nick and report something stolen. Get the sergeant to record your visit and there you are. You can't do that too easily now because there aren't many local nicks. Anyway, that's what one of the chaps who was pulled in had done, said his dog was lost.

There was all sorts of raids to find the gold and there was all sorts of fanny put up too. Someone had the coppers down at Surrey Docks one Sunday because there was a wire the gold was going out through there, but all they got was overtime. In fact Billy hadn't been in the South of France, he'd been with Duncan Webb and that other writer Hannen Swaffer who was writing his story at the time. Then the coppers had another go at Surrey Docks, and finally they thought Billy might have it at a toy warehouse he had in Aldgate. They turned out all the dolls and, so Bill told me later, it seems when you shook them they all went M-a-m-m-m-y. Must have sounded like a whole lot of bleating sheep. Billy went there with his brief because he was dead afraid of being fitted up, he was. That's not to say the coppers who did the searching would do it, but as Billy said photos could get mislaid or mixed up with others. The coppers found what they thought was wood shavings and Billy had them photograph them with a ten shilling note in the picture placed so you could see the serial number clearly. Then he give the note to his brief.

In fact Bill had planned it all within a couple of weeks. What had happend was that a KLM plane had gone down near Shannon airport at the beginning of the month and he had had people watch the salvage operation and report to him where the stuff was taken. That was how he knew it had ended up in Jockey's Fields. After that it was just a question of getting hold of the driver. The next year the coppers did a couple of men: the driver who'd agreed to let his van go and another man who'd worked at KLM. But they never got the gold.

Along the Gray's Inn Road was where the first killing of a copper took place. It happened in August 1830 when the Met hadn't been founded five minutes. He was PC Long and he followed three men all the way along Doughty Street, where that famous brief Geoffrey Robertson's got his offices nowadays, and into Mecklenburgh Square. He went up to them and that was when they turned on him and stabbed him. There was another copper nearby and one of the men, William Sapwell, was caught and topped. Apparently there was a big whip for Long's wife and kids.

It's funny how quick the police became unpopular because a few years after that there was a riot in Coldbath Fields, which was just near Gray's Inn Road, when a PC Pulley got stabbed to death as the police tried to stop a protest march. No one was too sympathetic this time and the jury went and returned a verdict of justifiable homicide.

It was in Red Lion Street that Harry Barham went for tea in a caff on the corner of Princeton Street the day he disappeared. Harry Barham was a good chap but a bit greedy. If I say he was greedy it's only because you can't be a successful businessman if you're not. Once, when it looked like I was going to come unstuck after I'd done a tobacconist's, Harry was the one I got hold of and he came straight down and took the gear off of me. I don't really know that much about his killing. I do know Harry was in some trouble with tax and looked like he was going to get a good bit of bird at the Old Bailey. He'd been told if he pulled up money to pay some of the tax he'd stand half a chance of staying out, so he went round Hatton Garden buying jewellery on tick and then selling it at a loss. A one man LF really. Apparently he'd done quite well and he'd got quite a bit on him when he went to the caff. That was more or less the last anyone see of him until he's found dead in the back of the car. And, of course, there's no cash to go with him.

People said it was Teddy Machin, who was out of West Ham and who'd been one of Jack Spot's men. But since he's dead you can put the blame on him for more or less anything. Like Jimmy Moody who helped carry me after I was shot in Mr Smith's Club. After he escaped from Brixton with Stan Thompson, who'd been with me on the Parkhurst Riot, Jimmy showed up dead years later and if you listened to people he must have murdered half of London whilst he was on the run.

You can work your way through a series of little streets from Red Lion Street to Southampton Row and the Russell Hotel. That's where Harry Roberts stayed the night with a bird after the coppers were shot in Shepherd's Bush and I got hustled out of the Scrubs in double time.

4

If you go down Theobalds Road towards the City, at the corner of Gray's Inn Road there's the pub, the Yorkshire Grey. That used to be the hangout for Darby Sabini and the Italians of the 1920s. There was a big shooting there when the Sabinis were fighting it out with the Brummagen Boys and Fred Gilbert's Camden Town Mob over who controlled the racecourses. That's where Little Italy starts and that was the Sabinis' stronghold. Opposite the Yorkshire Grey was the old Holborn Police Station. The building's still there and you can still see the lettering in the brickwork. It's not surprising the police was on hand when there was that ruckus and a number of people got lifted. People from Little

Italy just about stormed the building when Albert got lifted over some sort of driving insurance offence back in the 40s. They was very hot over insurance in them days and I'm not sure that Albert didn't get a few weeks before it got quashed on appeal.

The Central Club in the Clerkenwell Road was the place. It was known as the Italian Club and it was an official working men's club. There was a little porter's lodge inside the front door, just as they have in West End clubs, and you had to be checked in. That was good, because as a result of having a man on the door no coppers ever got in. Sometimes they'd have a concert upstairs and I used to take Kathleen, the mother of my first three boys, there at the end of the war when we was courting.

Next door was the Griffin. That's still there. It was where Tommy Bennyworth, who was known as Monkey and was from the Elephant, was knocked out by Darby Sabini after he'd deliberately torn an Italian girl's dress. Remember, Darby had been handy with his fists all his life. He'd done a ranked middleweight when he was young but he just wouldn't train. When Monkey's broken jaw had mended he returned with some of the Elephant boys, but Sabini had got word and with the help of Italian lads he drove them out of Little Italy once and for all. That was really when Darby came to the fore, and after that he was the Godfather of the quarter.

Monkey was a bit of a plague to them over the years and there's stories he did some of their men in a club in Maiden Lane off the Strand. He ran for a long time, did Monkey. He got off cutting the fence, Moses Levy, in the Aldgate High Street along with my old friend Dodger Mullins, Johnny Jackson and another couple of people I never knew, in February 1925. They and three others was all nicked and they had the very good brief G. L. Hardy defend them. I used him later in his life, but he was over the hill by then. They got a week's lay down, but it was all squared up the next week because Moses couldn't recognise who did him and the case was slung.

At one time Monkey was in partnership as a bookmaker with Johnny Jackson in South London. He was still around when I was a teenager. I know in August 1935 he was involved in the beating of a pickpocket by the name of Flatman in the Waterloo Road.

Bert Marsh would never go in the Central. Nestor Montecolombo, the brother of the man who got killed in the fight with Bert at the Wandsworth dog track would use it and, out of respect, Bert never went in. I used it a lot. After the Spot troubles that was where the Krays shot Tommy Falco in a dispute over the Point to Point races. Nothing ever came of it but you could mark the Twins' rise almost from that moment. It's been done up now as offices. Very smart it looked when I passed it.

Tommy Falco, who had himself slashed after Spot put all of us away and then said Spotty had done it, always used the Central. He was very good to me over the years I was in prison. He was in Wandsworth with me in 1943, he and Jimmy Essex used to look after me when I was on punishment diet. He'd come and see me, put a bit of money my way, always send cards at Christmas. It may not sound much sending a card at Christmas but there's many who didn't. He'd died by the time I come out from the twenty and I went round to Leather Lane where his wife had a stall to pay my respects and thank her.

The Fratellanza Club was just down the road in Great Bath Street – now Topham Street – and this too was where the Cortesi brothers shot Darby and Harryboy Sabini after they'd fallen out with them in the 1920s. A girl got herself in the way to protect them. She was said to be in love with Harryboy. The Cortesis picked up a good bit of bird over that but they weren't deported. It was the end of them anyhow. Some people say that Enrico Cortesi was really the smartest of the whole bunch and that included Darby.

The Duke of York at the corner of Vine Hill was known as the 11 o'clock house by us in South London. For some reason it was open half an hour later than other pubs and when we left Vic Rosari's place in the Walworth Road we'd pile into cars outside and come over to get the last twenty minutes and an extra drink. Of course, in those days there wasn't no traffic and you could be there in five minutes.

What there was down the bottom of Back Hill was another place, known to us as the Italian pub, the Coach and Horses. There was also the Roma Club in Eyre Hill Street. That was a nice place. It opened some time at the beginning of the 1950s. The thing that made the bottom of Back Hill so special was it was really a series of badly lit alleys and passageways which all ran into one another. Coppers didn't go there too often and if they did there was so many twists you could get away from them easy enough.

When I'd had the really bad run-in with the Carters and I was seriously looking for Johnny, I'd meet with the Raddis down there by the bridge in Warner Street which goes under Rosebery Avenue. There could be up to 40 of us and we'd have a couple of vans and a couple of cars. We'd go off in different directions, asking where they was. Eventually just after Christmas Albert Dimes and I caught up with them.

5

I think the only case when hanging was in force and two juries disagreed was in 1963 when the Pros offered no evidence against Robert Reed in what was called the Holy Lady of Clerkenwell murder.

The Pros said that Reed had robbed and battered an old lady, Annie Mary O'Donnell, to death in her rosary shop in Victoria Dwellings in the Clerkenwell Road, in the early evening in the middle of October 1962. Whoever done it probably got away with less than £5 because the old girl kept nearer £600 in a body belt and that was found on her. She'd been to Mass earlier that evening and had probably been done during the tolling of a church bell at about 7.50 p.m. which the Pros thought had muffled any noise she made.

Reed had been seen near the shop and there was an ID parade when he had been picked out by someone who had known him as a boy. The man said he had seen Reed outside the shop, mopping his face shortly before 8 p.m. There was also his fingerprints on a Catholic newspaper and on a piece of glazed paper in the shop. When questioned Reed said it was nothing to do with him and he told the coppers he had been off work because he'd injured his thumb.

The reason his prints were in the shop, he said, was that he'd been there a few days previous to buy a St Christopher medallion for the baby his seventeen-year-old wife was expecting. He said he'd got no need of money and that when the robbery took place he'd been home with his wife and mum and the rest of the family. Asked if he was short of money he said, 'Not by a long shot'. That wonderful brief Victor Durand defended him. Funnily he was in the nick with Harvey Holford, who was accused of shooting his wife in Brighton, and he give him a Catholic medal for luck. It must have done Harvey some good because he got slung on the murder and only four years for manslaughter.

There've been some good bullion raids down Clerkenwell over the years. One of the earlier ones was in 1936, when four men just drove up to the London North Eastern Depot in Aylesbury Street and drove off with gold dust and bullion worth getting on for £3,000. There had been another just a few years before that in October 1932, but the most interesting one was when a whole lot of gold, something like £700,000, went missing from Bowling Green Lane back in 1967. No one was ever caught but that Wembley speedway rider 'Split' Waterman went down for four years over receiving some of the gold and smuggling, which was big business then. Years later when Alfie Hind's friend, Tony Maffia, got killed the police found a bar of gold which could be traced back to the robbery, but then Tony didn't get the name the Magpie for nothing. He must have handled every sort of stolen jewellery and gold which ever came on the market.

There's rather a sad bit to that story. One of the ways to get gold out of the country was to smuggle it in women's corsets – there were no x-ray machines and things like that then. A fellow called Mickey Kenrick was one of those nicked at Victoria Station on his way to Dover and he picked up a few years. Whilst he was in the nick the Twins was arrested and he was charged over an LF he'd been running for them. He couldn't face any more bird and he topped himself in his cell. What a waste. When it came to it, by the time they'd weighed off the Twins and the others, the Pros decided not to go on against the LF men. He'd have been chucked.

It was in 1976 that my friend Battles Rossi, who hadn't been with me when I did Jack Spot but still got four years (Bob Warren got seven), got chucked over the murder of Beatrice Gold who ran a dress factory down in Clerkenwell. There were all sorts of stories about why she'd been done – including to silence her because it was thought she might be putting the black on some people over the porn business. Bert was seen handing over a parcel just off the Strand to the kid they convicted of the shooting and the Pros said it was the gun. Bert said he thought it was jewellery. I'm not sure if the kid isn't still in and trying to clear his name. There was a story that a solicitor had set the whole thing up, but there's always talk.

I still go over in July to the Italian festival in Clerkenwell with Battles. The festival's really lovely; parades and bands and they carry the church figures from St Peter's. All the churches them days seemed to have a school and St Peter's was where I went. My mother insisted we went to a Catholic school, and so that was where Eva and I used to go before there was room for us at St Patrick's just near where I was born. We'd set off every morning at eight to get there for lessons at nine. And remember I might have been over the river and back even before that to get the stale bread from Soho. Harryboy Sabini went to St Peter's as well, but that was a few years before me. Bert's been a bit unwell these last few years but we still go out and have a few drinks.

It's a shame to see the church all chained up against vandals but that's the way of things nowadays. The last time I was there was for the funeral service for Alfredo who stood bail for Albert Dimes in his Spot case. Never hesitated when he was asked. He had that caff at Islington Green for years. What a lovely man.

6

If you went right where the left split goes to Rosebery Avenue again on your right you'd come to Hatton Garden. That place speaks for itself really; always been the home of jewellery from the days before the First World War when the big fence Cammie Grizzard operated. That was where there was a big pearl robbery in 1913. It was called a robbery but really it was the interception of pearls on their way over from Paris. Grizzard, Jimmy Lockett and some others picked up a lot of bird over it.

Hatton Garden had everything – money, jewellers, diamonds, pearls and not too much security. Someone was always sticking up a big job. In fact you heard of them so often 'looks like it's belled up on the outside but it ain't' that you got frightened and didn't do them in the end. If you listened to people there wasn't an alarm that worked in the whole of the Garden. What you really needed was a good bellman, someone who'd disable the alarm, and they weren't all that easy to come by. I had a couple of little touches, well not so little really, of wholesale tom during the war. You could sell anything then. Get your hands on a lorryload of aspirin and people would be biting your arm off to get to it.

It just shows how quick things could get to the Garden. Within 24 hours of Prince Charles having some jewellery nicked, cufflinks and a tiepin had turned up there. Of course the fellow didn't know where they'd come from and when he learned he contacted Scotland Yard.

The dealers, a lot of them were Hassidic Jews, used to stand on the pavement rather like the car men did in Warren Street. They'd have the ordinary stuff in their pockets and a little rolled up piece of cloth on which they'd display stuff. If there was a special bit then they'd go into the offices. Their word was their bond with each other, but that didn't stop some of them dealing in stolen tom. Funnily, there wasn't a great number of street snatches. If there was a snatch it was because someone had been stuck up but generally they all looked out for one another. It was a community just like the Raddis up the road. And again funnily the Raddis weren't all that keen on going down Hatton Garden. If you were seen people thought you was up to no good and so generally we steered a bit clear. There was at least one Raddi who had a place there though, Silvio Mazzardo, who was known as Shonk. He was the one who went down for receiving some of the gold that Bert Marsh got out of Croydon Airport in 1934. Georgie Shillingford, who was my wife Doreen's uncle, had a place there as well and so did Matty Constantinou who eventually went down for a VAT fraud. He was an ill man by then though, and he got a suspended. George was a good judge of tom, really one of the best.

Before that, in the 1980s when bank robberies became a bit dangerous, there was a run on VAT frauds through the Garden. In a way it was just a version of the LF.

Nowadays the old Jewish dealers are going but there's a lot of Afro-Caribbean and Indian dealers because their people like gold. There's also a lot of drug money being washed there nowadays.

A bit further along you get to Holborn Viaduct where a hotel called the Holborn Viaduct Hotel stood, and it was there back in September 1912 that a company director, called Edward Hopwood, decided to kill his girlfriend Florence Dudley, who was on the stage. It was the usual story. He was married and she was saying either he left his wife or she was calling it a day. She said she wasn't going to stay with him and she was going home on the last train to Essex. On the way to Fenchurch Street station he shot her and turned the gun on himself. He wasn't that lucky with his judge because he picked up Avory. Hopwood said he'd been drunk but there was no question of the judge recommending a reprieve. North of the river it was, so he was hanged at Pentonville.

It was in Fenchurch Street that the coppers had their famous raid on Austin Reed in September 1980, the year the Countryman Inquiry into the police was going on. The coppers got called to a break-in at the shop and whilst they were there helped themselves to clothes, suitcases, squash rackets, just about anything handy. One of them was a DI. It's always good to see a few coppers get a bit of bird. Makes up for the ones who should but don't.

7

After you come over Holborn Viaduct you get to the Old Bailey. I was there three times and totalled 22 years, but I got off the murder charge when Dickie Hart was shot in Mr Smith's Club in 1965.

If you was in custody, and I always was, it was an ordinary start to the day. You'd have your cell opened up about seven in the morning and you'd slop out. In no time you'd have your breakfast and then it was the cell door open and down to reception. I'd always have my own clothes throughout, but some people would wear prison clothing believing theirs was being looked after ready for their day in court. Very often you'd be disappointed and they'd have been slung about any old how. Some screws were dogs – they'd deliberately loosen a button or give a shirt a small tear when they knew you wanted to look your best, particularly in a famous case. It's silly how a thing like that could upset you but it did. Gave you a bad start to the day and then you didn't think carefully, it was always niggling. What would the jurors think seeing you with a button half off your jacket or whatever? What could your brief do? If you complained to him he might not take any notice and if he was a good one and he did, all that would happen is he'd get a letter eventually saying 'all care had been taken' ... 'no evidence to show' ... 'done our best, sir' ... you know the routine. By keeping them myself, I could look after my clothes in a respectable way. How well you was looked after depended on your visitors. You could have clean underclothes every day if someone would bring them and the screws weren't saying they were too busy. And you could have a pint of beer or half a bottle of wine and all. That lasted until the 1980s, I think.

You'd leave from Brixton about half past eight because in them days traffic, though it could be bad, wasn't nothing like it is today. It would take about half an hour. Once I was done in the Mr Smith's affray and I'd been given five years, I was a convict and so I came on my own to the Torture Trial with a special escort, hooters and sirens going, part brainwashing the jury. Sometimes it would be in the evening papers or on telly. It was like you'd see in the papers 'Police ringed the dock when Francis Davidson Fraser appeared before magistrates today charged with causing grievous bodily harm with intent to cause grievous bodily harm'. All that show was to tell the beaks that you was a real danger who'd leap at their throats if you had half a chance and if it wasn't for the boys in blue keeping them safe. So when the Pros said they wanted you kept in custody the beaks would know what to do. I never noticed anything in the papers like 'Criminals ringed the dock when three policemen appeared charged with bribery and conspiracy to pervert the course of justice'.

Then once you was at the Bailey it was down into a little cell, no more than four foot wide with a bed and table concreted into the floor. You'd often have to share it and then you got taken down the passage to a cell which was a bit bigger for your brief to talk to you. If those interview rooms were occupied then they'd turf out the fellow who was in with you and your brief would come in the little four-footer. Mind you it was better than at some Magistrates' Courts like Marylebone, where if you was in custody you was all in a cage and the briefs was pushing each other to get to the bars to talk to their clients and you was pushing to get to your brief. And in those days it wasn't a question of your brief saying 'Can I have a remand to take instructions?' The beaks didn't care. In fairness, I don't suppose half of them knew the conditions in the cells. It was a question of getting on with the case so they could get to their clubs for a good lunch.

What you got for lunch at the Bailey depended on what your family could organise. There was a big cafe opposite and they'd deliver to the cells in time for lunch. You was entitled to that if you was on remand and sometimes, even though I was a serving prisoner, the screws would stand for it and I didn't have to have the filth that was on offer. You were at the most famous court in the land and the screws were proud to be along there. Although they wouldn't admit it there was some kudos for them, so I suppose by their standards they'd be reasonably pleasant.

As for visits, you might see your brief about a quarter to two. Your barrister could come down the steps through the dock in the court quite easy, but solicitors were made to go the long way round and sign in with the screw at the gate. They could use up twenty minutes easy just getting in and out.

After court was over you might or you might not get a visit as a remand prisoner. Years ago you was entitled to it, but later it was what the police said that mattered. Screws were looked down on by the coppers so they would do anything they could to assert their own authority. The police might say they'd like such and such a man they was trying to sweeten to have a visit but the screws might get in the way, and the other way around.

Visits would be over by about a quarter to five and that's when you'd leave if you was special, otherwise it was an hour later, and you'd generally be back at the nick by a quarter to seven. They'd have some grub for you whatever time you got back, but even if you was on the dot it wouldn't be hot. They didn't have things to keep food warm in reception in them days.

In my time I can't remember a successful escape from the Old Bailey. Not those in custody. There was said to be one years back at the beginning of the nineteenth century. Some well-to-do man was done for forgery and that was a swinging offence then. His family had his servant wrap up his face in a scarf so it looked like he'd got toothache and switch places with him on a visit. The man was out into Newgate Street and off to France before he was missed. No one ever said what happened to the servant but at least prison breaking wasn't a topping offence.

Some did try to escape and I remember hearing about how a couple had been standing by the prison van when they suddenly legged it, but they was handcuffed together and they never stood a chance. The screws just lowered the mesh fence and it was bread and water for a bit. People have been off though on the way to court and there was a pair I remember, I can't think of their names, who went to Hampstead Magistrates' Court once and the screw told them to wait by the van whilst he went and found someone to open the gate. Of course, they was on their toes but they was handcuffed together as well and they was heading up the High Street when they come to a Belisha beacon. 'Left' says one, 'Right' says the other, and they just spun round the thing and collided with each other. The screws didn't even have to break into a trot to collect them.

In fact there was another go in April this year. Security isn't what it was in my time because only a few weeks previous some man had got at a judge and blacked her eye before he was hauled off. This time a couple of fellows on trial for robbery got out of the dock in Court Four and had it on their toes. They didn't get far. One got collared in what they call a witness support room, whatever that is, near Court Two and the other only made it as far as outside Court Seven.

I heard there was a hostage taken down in the cells earlier this year. Nothing was in the papers but that's what I heard. You can never guarantee these stories, but maybe it was hushed up because there's been too much bad news over security there recently.

The Twins was once charged with conspiracy to murder a man at the Bailey, at least that's what the coppers said. The idea was that a Scots fellow, Paul Elvey, would carry a case in which there was a hypodermic syringe which he could work by pulling a ring near the handle. It was going to be a bit like that Bulgarian defector who got killed in the Strand when someone stabbed him with a poisoned umbrella. The Pros said the victim at the Bailey was going to be Jimmy Evans who'd given evidence against Jerry Callaghan, Freddie Foreman and Alfie Gerard when they'd all been acquitted over the death of Ginger Marks. Elvey had kept the suitcase in his garage, along with a crossbow which he was meant to use on George Caruana who'd had a run-in with my friend Bernie Silver. Well, that's what the Pros said anyway. The charges got slung at the committal proceedings.

8

If you turned left and crossed the Farringdon Road on your way to Islington you'd come to Turnmill Street which was where I was shot back in 1991 in a nightclub. Marilyn got me to hospital that night but it didn't half shake her nerves up. That was when the Independent said I was dead and it was over a drugs deal. Neither was right but there's no question of suing with my reputation. I've tried before and what did I get? A farthing. Still, they were decent enough to publish my letter.

The Clerkenwell House of Correction is just round the corner. Tiny little prison it was. It's a museum nowadays.

They have a literary festival in Clerkenwell each year and one year they used the prison for an event, with me, Bruce Reynolds and Norman Parker, who got life for murder and now's a good writer, all speaking.

When I was on the run from the Harry Rogers' troubles down in Brighton, and he said I was leaning on him, I was very hot for a bit. I used to get my dough every week from Bill and I'd go and send it down to my wife Doreen from the post office in Mount Pleasant. It used to be open 24 hours a day. That was in the days when there was three deliveries a day.

Bert Marsh had his betting shop almost opposite in Exmouth Market. There's a lovely little caff there, Ayla's. I was in there the other day, quite by chance. I'd never been before but they made such a nice fuss of me. Wouldn't let me pay for my coffee and one of the girls there had me sign a birthday card for her boyfriend. When I think back, a few years ago if I went in a place and didn't pay for my coffee the coppers would have called it protection. I suppose it's one good thing about getting old.

9

Walk left down the Farringdon Road and on down to Kings Cross and that brings you to where the Whites used to hang out after the war. One of their earners was taking money off street bookmakers. Bookmaking except on course was illegal then and there'd always be bookies' runners, very often newspaper sellers, who took bets. Big Alf White would run things from the Bell or from Hennekey's in the Pentonville Road. No swearing or vulgar talk. A warning and then out. He'd grown up with the Sabinis, but he didn't really like the Jewish element who ran with them because Darby really didn't have prejudices. When they sorted out the bookmaking pitches at the racecourses, and who would run them between the wars, Alf got himself made Chief Steward of the Racecourse Bookmakers' Protection Association. He was in and out of the nick for the Sabinis. He got convicted over the shooting of Fred Gilbert of the Camden Town Mob but that got chucked on appeal. Then he tried to organise things for Joe Sabini, who was doing three years, get him letters sent in and better food, but the screw went bent on him and he picked up eighteen months. I think the last time he went inside was in July 1935 when he got twelve months' hard labour for doing the licensee of the Yorkshire Stingo in the Marylebone Road.

Big strong man, Alf was, but maybe not firm enough because he allowed a team of young kids to do him at Harringay dog track before the war and he didn't take any prisoners afterwards.

Jock Wyatt was one of the big men on his team. Before that Jock had been with Billy Hill during the war, when they picked up a four apiece at the Old Bailey in the 1940s. He'd been on the White strength for years. In fact he was living with Margaret White in Swinton Street almost opposite the Magistrates' Court there. Robert Staggs lived in the same street. In April 1951 the three of them got caught up in a very big job, along with Henry John Bryan out of Packington Street at the Angel and a few others.

It was all over keys for post offices around the country and they was eventually pulled down in Hampshire. What the Pros said had happened was that George Allen out of Mildmay Grove had been employed by a big safe firm and he'd made about twenty sets of keys, and the places the team was said to have done was all over London and the South. The Flying Squad had been watching them for some time and it was all on top when a couple of them was nicked in Waterlooville down in Hampshire. Jock did his best to row as many people out as possible but it was never going to be no good. He drew an eight. Funnily enough, the man who was meant to defend me on the Parkhurst Riot but couldn't because of the election, Billy Rees-Davies, was defending a couple of the people and Joe Moloney who did actually pros me was the Pros then. Although they couldn't exactly put it down to Jock and the others, they said that something like 200 post office safes had been done using spare keys and they'd been at it for years.

Eddie Raimo was another from Clerkenwell. He could have a good row and once he put a glass in Billy Hill's face so bad Bill had to have surgery. Eddie was first a Sabini and then a White man. He was as small as me and he did a bit of time with me in the glasshouse during the war. It was about that time he done some bird for slashing George Sewell, the father of the television actor. Eddie was in Wandsworth with me in 1943 when doing his time for Sewell. George Snr had fancied himself as a cobbles fighter and he wrote his memoirs about how he was known as the Cobblestone Kid and fought alongside Darby Sabini. Looking back, I'm not sure he was as great as all that. He was keen to dish it out but he wasn't all that keen to take it.

After the war, when there was a row between Spot and White over the point-to-point pitches, Harry White was hoping Eddie would do the business for him but he was getting old and he copped it himself. Spot did him at Yarmouth Races and that was really the beginning of the end of the Whites.

It was in early 1940 that me and Patsy Fleming did Bravington's, the big jeweller's in Kings Cross on the corner of the Pentonville Road. We got spotted coming out and there was a car chase which ended with Patsy escaping over a wall which had barbed wire on top and me getting caught up. At least he got some of the rings. I ended up losing my brief. I was disqualified from driving for ten years at Stamford House Juvenile Court. They used to hold the hearings in the remand centre itself, just so the magistrates would know what type of a kid you was before they even heard the evidence. What a savage sentence that was. I was just a kid and there hadn't even been a crash. I wasn't driving even. I was given a day's detention and fined a shilling as well.

After that I never bothered to get a licence. I think the first car I had was a Saab in the 1960s. One of the good things about not getting a brief was I could say I couldn't drive and I was banned so I didn't have the aggro of being the one who had to go out and nick a motor.

The Scots Boys ran Kings Cross for a time. That's where they got off the train from Glasgow and that's where they settled in during the 50s and 60s. Some were good thieves, some just copped a quid off the brasses. Andy Anderson was a Kings Cross man. He was the one who escaped quite by chance when Ronnie Biggs got over the wall at Wandsworth and made his way to Atlantic Machines. Later, he was in the Parkhurst Riot with us. When I turned down George Shindler as my QC because he'd prossed one of my boys, Andy had him and, good luck to him, he got an acquittal.

There wasn't half a funny case there in the early '80s. Fellow called John Docherty who been a climber one time who's worked with that fellow Archie Hall, the butler who topped so many people. I've written about him later. Docherty's been running girls and the Pros says that another Scot Alan McCandless is the one who shot him; November 1980 it was.

Eighteen months later there's hardly a witness in sight. One girl, Patricia McClellan, was shot. The body of Pat Malone, who's been cut in pieces, was found in Epping Forest and there's another who's taken a heroin overdose. A fourth seems to have died from natural causes and the fifth drank himself to death. Finally, the case went belly up in July 1982 when just about the last witness 'Big' James Gibson who'd been a bouncer failed to appear. He was meant to have been under surveillance but the coppers couldn't find him in time for the trial. What happened was that the copper who was his minder went abroad on holiday leaving him in the care of two others and Gibson simply walked out of his girlfriend's flat in Leicester in the middle of the night.

There was all sorts of stories that he'd been done away with but, a couple of days after the case is dropped, Gibson telephones the local paper to say he was safe and well and would surrender himself in a short while. I never heard if he did. Another geezer is done for making a false confession in the case and wasting police time but since by then he's doing a life for wounding a shopkeeper in a robbery they don't bother to Pros him when it comes to it. The story was that £500 was the rate for the contract.

By the 1990s though it was a real dump. Most places round railway stations are bad but this was worse than awful. In just nine days in March 1993 seven people died from heroin overdoses within 250 yards of the station, mostly round Argyle Square. There was a big clean up. Dealers had been coming from all over – Naples and Sardinia as well as the usual suppliers. The coppers rounded up over 60 dealers.

I think the area's on its way up again now what with the new terminal for the trains to France – gentrification they call it.

NORTH LONDON

1

Every now and again I do a talk for Gary Mason, who used to be the editor of *Police Review*. It's funny how I'm helping anyone who had anything to do with the law, but he teaches kids journalism and I go down so they can interview me and write it up for one of their classes. We always meet at the Angel and walk down to the City University where he lectures. On the way we pass the Empress of Russia pub, it's a coffee bar now. That was where Ernie Isaacs had a bent screw who worked at Pentonville. It was the same as Jimmy Robson had in Parkhurst. You could get him to buy things for you – at a price of course – and the meets always took place in the pub there. I think the screw got promoted to principal later, which shows how clever he was.

Ernie's death in 1966 was a bit of a locked room mystery really. He was shot in the basement of his home in Penn Street, Hoxton. There's no doubt he was a frightened man because a bit before the shooting he'd been trying to get some ammunition for a Luger he kept in the glove compartment of his car. He went as usual to the pub, the Merry

Monarch in Copley Street, and he must have been shot as soon as he got home. His wife found him when she went downstairs with the baby about five o'clock. There was a story doing the rounds that he was going to grass some people up and that was why he was done. His first conviction had been for stealing pincushions when he was eleven.

Another of the great escapes was by Teddie Rice and his mates out of Strangeways, the Manchester prison, in November 1954. Teddie come from Whitmore Street in Shoreditch. He was a good man, little baby face, you wouldn't think twice to look at him, wore spectacles for a start, but he was a terror in his way. He'd got ten years PD (Preventative Detention) in March 1954 for conspiracy and wounding. Him and Tommy Greenwood, who had also come from round Shoreditch and moved up to Manchester, was the real leaders, along with a number of big names from there. Eddie had copped it after he had broken into a bookmaker's in Levershulme. He'd been a tobacco baron in the nick but he did well because he wasn't even fancied as an escaper.

Tommy was a great escaper. He'd got out of the Manchester Sessions back in 1945, when he and a few others just threw a coat over a screw as they went to the cells, nicked his keys and they was off. That one only lasted a day. Then after he got released in 1947 he got done for breaking and entering and this time he was over the wall at Strangeways, climbing through the prison workshop roof.

That's what they did in 1954. The workshop was very near the wall and the wall wasn't a big one. You might have thought that the screws would have learned something. They may have done but the authorities hadn't. In them days there was really very little security. Prisoners didn't escape because they didn't think it could be so easy. They was sure there was a trick somewhere and the moment they got out there'd be someone come out of a doorway. It's like them fake burglar alarms people have today. You know it's a moody, but you don't want to take the chance.

Anyway they sawed through a bar in the skylight of the mailbag shop and was on to the roof and away. The telly showed their pictures but that didn't do much good. They was old ones from their files at Scotland Yard and didn't look nothing like them.

What baffled the coppers was where they had gone. It was a fair bet that the Manchester fellows would have stayed up north and Tommy Greenwood might make for his mother's, but Eddie Rice was the one they really wanted. In fact what had happened was that Jimmy Robson and Danny Swain went up for him. Obviously if you're going to have a successful break you've got to have it arranged on the outside. It's no use getting over the wall and finding the only way out is on a tram. Jimmy and Danny was very good and they knew exactly what they was doing.

For nearly a week no one knew where they all was and as usual every break-in and nicking was put down to them. There was even some story that they'd been sprung so they could do a really big job. Then one of them did a funny thing. Tommy Greenwood wrote to Duncan Webb saying the reason they'd escaped was to show up the criminal justice system and that the only thing left for men with fourteen years' PD was to try to escape. He put a fingerprint on the letter to show it was genuine. That must be where the Twins got the idea from, when they had Frank Mitchell write letters after they'd sprung him from Dartmoor.

One by one the others got nicked. There's rather a sad story about one of them, George Davis. He hadn't been married long and his wife had left him. He heard there was a reward of £250 going for his arrest and he decided to turn himself in. If he went back home then she could claim the reward. So he goes and breaks into the place where she's living and hides in the attic, but some nosey neighbour sees him and calls the coppers. His poor wife – who never knew he was there – was lucky not to get done for harbouring and it was some other woman who picked up the dough.

The last ones to be found was Tommy Greenwood and Eddie Rice. The coppers got on to Tommy because there was a girl who'd been sent money to come down from Manchester and stay with him. They'd quarrelled and she'd left. She hadn't any money to get back home and so she went to the police. And that left Eddie.

It was only a matter of time before he was grassed up and it was another woman who did it. Now the coppers reckoned he was living in West End Lane, Kilburn, and they started staking out the place and the new milkman and the relief postman were coppers. That sort of caper. The trouble was that the man there didn't look much like Eddie.

They got him at the beginning of February, the day before he was going to hop it. When they did they found a load of tobacco and cash. They dug up the garden and found a load of jelly as well. He got thirteen years' PD at the Old Bailey, concurrent with the ten he was doing, but he never ever said how the escape was planned. I met him in the nick a number of times but when he come out he just sort of faded from the scene.

2

There have been some good people and families come out of Islington. Marilyn and me lived there for years in a little flat in Duncan Street just near the antique market. That wasn't far from where she had a drinker for a short time, before she got run off the patch by some of the other local talent and before she met me. Then there was the City Club not a couple of hundred yards away. That was owned by Georgie Bell at one time. He was a good man. He got shot by a junkie but I'm glad to say he survived.

I was away during the great days of the City Club but I heard all about it. I think it was there that David Knight took a beating from Johnny Isaacs, Ernie's brother, which ended up at the Old Bailey with David's brother, Ronnie Knight, charged with the murder of Tony Zomparelli. I'm pleased to say he was chucked. He was very good to me when I went over to Spain to collect some money on Charlie Richardson's behalf and got nicked at Malaga airport.

One of the other businesses Marilyn had in Islington was a sauna in Upper Street. When she first took me to see it I couldn't believe my eyes: it was in the same building as a tailor's shop I'd screwed in 1943. Everybody around the Angel got measured up in the place. You had half-day closing then and me and two others did it in the afternoon. One of the fellow's sisters was going with Albie Hoy who was a top man at the Angel and he put it up for us. We cleared the place of suits and cloth and had our hands bitten off by other tailors who wanted the stuff. Albie was another who got cut by Hoppy Smith but to his credit he went back and did him. He got a seven after the war, over a security van I think it was. He's long dead now.

3

One of the vice merchants of London after the Messinas was a man called Maurice Conley.[1] He was another who got exposed by Duncan Webb. He had a few clubs, including the Carousel and the Hollywood in Curzon Street, but he also had the Little Club in the Brompton Road. When I was on the run from South London I went and stayed over in Notting Hill and I got quite friendly with the mob there. They used to wander down for a drink in the Little Club and I'd go with them. The place was full of brasses they called hostesses but we wasn't there as punters. We'd say 'Hello, girls' to the brasses who'd be sitting in little cubicles, and they'd say 'Hello, boys' and if things was slack with them we'd send them over a drink sometimes. Ruth Ellis was one of the brasses. It was only when she was in the papers that one of the mob told me who she was. I'd never known her name, she was just someone to say hello to.

---

[1] In 1961 at Marylebone Magistrates' Court Conley admitted running a brothel at the Court Club and was fined £100 and ordered to pay 25 guineas costs.

Hers was a really sad story. If ever there was a woman who had bad luck with men it was Ruth. She'd come down from Rhyl in Wales to make her fortune and she ended up by shooting a man, David Blakely, outside the Magdala pub in Hampstead. Rhyl was an unlucky town. It was there James Hanratty said he'd been on the night he was meant to have shot Michael Gregsten and Valerie Storie. That didn't do him any good at all. I see they've done a DNA and it's come up that after all these years it was him after all. I know the family is challenging it, saying the sample's been contaminated, but it don't look good for him.

Anyway back to Ruth Ellis. She got put in the club by a Canadian who sloped off back home and she had to bring up her little boy, André, and so she went and worked as a photographer's model in places like the Camera Club. That meant posing in her underwear or in the nude for men, half of whom didn't have film in their cameras and got their kicks by saying things like, 'Look as though you'd like to tread on us' and 'I'm a worm'. Then she worked in another place, the Court Club in Duke Street, which later became Carroll's Club. Next she went and married a dentist. She had another daughter by the marriage but it didn't last.

It was the sort of time after the war when them people from the RAF was being demobbed; all of them officers with blazers and moustaches and posh accents, but many of them weren't really gents. All of them had been famous pilots, at least that's what they said. They didn't really settle down either after all the excitement; they didn't want to go back to being clerks. It was as if they was still fighting the war. A lot of them lived in a sort of half-world with the likes of us. Bit of buying and selling cars and other things in pubs and clubs. The really good ones would tell you where a whole load of parachutes was stored and of course we knew who'd make silk underwear out of the 'chutes, or they'd stick up a warehouse which had Scotch and gin for the local officers' mess. Then eventually they faded away, they finally realised that the war was over and it was back to getting ink on their fingers. Funnily, it wasn't the same with people from the army.

Poor Ruth really did tart herself up. She took elocution lessons and had expensive clothes and handmade shoes but when it all come down to it she was still a brass. She did a bit of blue film work as well. Then she met this David Blakely and he treated her rotten. He was halfway well connected and there was certainly money about. The Little Club had top-class punters and she did well. Soon she became the manageress and she moved into the flat over the club and he moved in and all. But he was always two-timing her and giving her a hiding for good measure. He had her Monday to Friday and then it was home to Buckinghamshire and his fiancée. What did it was the announcement of his engagement in *The Times* and it wasn't to Ruth. She was in the club again as well and there was another go with the knitting needles. Then he went off to the motor car races at Le Mans and stayed away and by the time he come back, she was living with another geezer, Desmond Cusson his name was. He had a flat at Goodwood Court in Devonshire Street.

When Blakely did come back it was all hearts and flowers. He broke off his engagement but it didn't last. There was always other women and it was back to this Cusson and soon she was having it off with both. Eventually Blakely won and they set up together in a flat in Egerton Gardens. She was paying the bills and giving him money on the side and then she fell pregnant again. He started building a racing car.

It all came on top over the Easter in 1955. He left her in the flat and promised to call but he never did and she found out he was at some of his friends in Tanza Road, Hampstead. Good Friday she went round but they wouldn't let her in and by the Sunday she'd got hold of a gun and in the evening she went back to Hampstead, found he was in the Magdala pub in South Hill Park and, as he come out, she shot him. The trouble was, and this is what probably did for her, she shot a bystander as well. Didn't kill the woman but injured her. Next thing she did was say to the police that she intended to kill Blakely.

Of course the Pros put it all down to her. She was the one living with two men, she was the one who couldn't bear that Blakely was going off. Melford Stevenson, who put Ronnie and Reggie down, was the brief who defended her then and he didn't put up much of a show. Nowadays as a battered woman who'd just had an abortion she might even have got probation, but then she was a scarlet woman who was having it off with two men. They did call a psychiatrist but the judge said that even on her story there was no defence to murder. She never even bothered to appeal. People said she was just glad to get it over. She was topped; the last woman to hang. The night she swung there was a waxwork of her in Tussauds in Blackpool. The man who give her the gun was Cusson, of course. The story was that provided she wouldn't bubble him, he'd look after her little boy. The boy took an overdose and Cusson died in Australia years ago.

Funnily enough, Marilyn went on a programme about gangsters' molls they had on the television three or four years ago and Ruth Ellis' daughter, Georgie, was one of the other women on the show, but really she was never much around the faces. Georgie'd had an affair with both George Best and Richard Harris and she knew people like Charlie Wilson but she wasn't really one of the chaps, it's said. Some families just have no luck. She and her aunt Muriel Jakubait, Ruth's sister, have been campaigning for years for the case to be reopened, and just when the Court of Appeal says it will hear it Georgie goes and gets cancer. Her aunt's not well either. Life don't seem fair sometimes.

Maybe one of the reasons they topped poor Ruth was because of another woman who did a murder in the same bit of Hampstead just a while before. Anyway, people say that may have played a part. She was an old Cypriot woman, Mrs Styllou Christofi, who was almost certainly a double murderer. She'd done a woman back in Cyprus; now she went and killed her daughter-in-law, Hella, in July

1954. She'd been living for about a year with her son and Hella in South Hill Park and it wasn't working out so they arranged she should go back home. That's when a neighbour out walking his dog saw Mrs Christofi trying to burn Hella's body, setting fire to newspaper in her back yard.

For once the prison doctors thought that she was insane, so she really must have been off her trolley, but she wouldn't let her brief run that defence. The jury recommended mercy and she was examined again. This time three doctors thought she was sane. It was a bit like Straffen. Back in the early 1950s, Straffen got done for killing a young girl in Bath. They found he was insane and put him in Broadmoor. Then one afternoon he escapes and another girl's killed. This time they put him in prison. So what it means is when he walked out of Broadmoor he was insane but by the time he killed the kid – if he did – a couple of hours later he was sane again. The old woman got topped at Holloway. One of the things that did for her was that in 1925 she'd been done for that murder back in Cyprus. They said she'd pushed a burning torch down her mother-in-law's throat whilst the woman had been held down by neighbours, but she had been acquitted. It's likely that's what prevented her reprieve and, when it came to it, it helped to do for Ruth.

Generally, they didn't like topping women. Partly it was the mess. They made them wear rubber knickers when they went on to the scaffold. That was because women always crapped themselves when they swung, as did men of course, although men had their trouser legs tied round their ankles. For some reason, the authorities thought it was more degrading in the case of women.

Hampstead Heath was a real Gobbler's Gulch in its day. All sorts of people having it off in the good weather – and the bad for that matter – but you could find some really funny things going on there. Like the time in July 1968 when the park keeper heard hammering and there was a Joseph Richard de Havilland being nailed to a twelve-foot cross. There was all sorts of stories about how it was a sex thing, but it seems de Havilland had told one of the men nailing him up that by being crucified he'd make the world a better place with no sin and no racial discrimination. When it come to it, though, they seem to have been doing it for the money with photographs going to the newspapers. One of the men got a twelve month but they never prossed de Havilland. Maybe they thought he'd suffered enough.

There was another very funny case on the Heath in the middle of December 1991. A woman walking her dog found Ghebre Luul Kassa, an Ethiopian refugee, hanging from a tree in West Heath. He had been bound with white washing-line rope and blindfolded with a red silk tie. They reckoned he had been killed close to where his body was found and he had then been hanged. His gold and black onyx ring with the letter 'K' was missing. He'd had a briefcase and that had been opened and the contents lay all around.

The police discovered that the previous day he had spent most of his time at a café his brother owned in Cricklewood Broadway. He'd told his brother he'd got a job working as a chauffeur for a wealthy Arab family. He rang up a garage on the Finchley Road where this man's Mercedes was being repaired and then after he left the café around six p.m. he was never seen again.

Of course, people thought politics, but no one could prove that he was close to any refugee or dissident groups. There was some story he'd gone to the Heath to meet someone around ten p.m. and there was another that it was a mugging gone wrong, but it was a funny sort of mugging if that was the case.

It's not the same today but when I was in the nick after Mr Smith's you could almost count the number of black people you came across on one hand. One of them was a fellow called Kayode Orishagbemi. He'd done a young girl, Grace Fayodi, who was related to him in some way in July

1966, but I've never been sure he really meant to kill her. He said she was a witch and he was trying to exorcise her, but the Pros said he was a conman who was trying to shut up a witness to his frauds.

The girl was found trussed up like a chicken in Merton Rise not far from Swiss Cottage tube station. All her hair had gone and her thumb had been crushed. Orishagbemi said he'd tried to get her to disclose her secrets as a witch because he said she'd made his wife ill. In fairness his wife was in hospital, I think she'd got TB. Anyway he'd hang Grace on the door jamb every day when he went out to work and cut her down when he come back. Eventually she just give up and died. He said she'd been pushed downstairs by a ghost.

What the Pros said was that he was running a scam, pretending to be the secretary of the 'London Girls Modern College' in Plimsoll Road, Finsbury Park. They found letters saying he would be willing to pay the fares of Nigerian students to come over but there wasn't any such college. He got life. A few years earlier and he'd have been topped.

You don't get too many killings in a hospital except by the medicos (just joking) but there was one in the Royal Free Hospital in Hampstead and it was done in May 1992 by the girl the coppers say was the first woman hitman in this country, Rangimara Ngarimu. She took out Graeme Woodhatch, who was said to have swindled his partners of over £50,000. He was in hospital having his piles operated on so he wasn't exactly mobile. I don't know that I'd employ her. First off she couldn't find the ward he was on, then next day she goes back and does the business. She then caught the plane to New Zealand. Unfortunately a bit after she gets there she got religion and when the police went and saw her she told them everything and the men who'd hired her got life. She wanted to clear her conscience, she said. I don't know of a second hitwoman but I'm sure there'll be another.

4

My Uncle Andy, who'd enlisted in the First World War at the age of fourteen, took me to see Arsenal on Boxing Day 1928 along with my elder brother. I was on my uncle's shoulders and we was on the North Bank opposite the clock. I don't know now who we played or even if we won, but it was my team from then on. If he'd taken me to Accrington Stanley or Port Vale that would have been the team I'd have supported the rest of my life. I suppose, by all rights, really we should have gone to see Millwall.

It was in the Seven Sisters Road down the Holloway Road end, not all that far from the Arsenal, that Ronnie Marwood stabbed the copper, Raymond Summers, when he tried to stop a fight outside Eugene Grey's Dance Academy in December 1958. The Nash brothers were very good. They and the Twins arranged for him to stay out of sight for a bit but, when it was clear that the net was closing, rather than cause them any more trouble he give himself up.

Sometimes Eva and some of the other Forty Thieves would go out in the sticks – that's what they considered the Holloway Road to be. There was a nice little store there, Jones Brothers, which they used to visit. It's shut now, only closed down a few years ago but stuff from there featured in one of the biggest cases of the last century. It was a first in some ways. The first time anyone had been nicked through the use of the wireless telegraph. It was the American Harvey Hawley Crippen and his girlfriend, Ethel le Neve. He was done for poisoning his wife who was some sort of music hall actress when they lived in Hilldrop Crescent. She'd gone missing and some of her friends reported it to the police. When Inspector Dew came poking round Crippen got the wind up and him and Ethel went off to America. The copper followed after them when the captain of their boat telegraphed that he thought he'd got them on board. Meanwhile they'd found the wife in the cellar.

Where Jones Brothers comes in was that Crippen had done a bit of dismembering of the body and said it couldn't be her, because no one had been in the cellar since he bought the house. The brief who was prosecuting sent the policeman to Jones Brothers and they was able to show that the pyjamas the bit of the body had been wrapped in hadn't been on sale before Crippen bought the place. That was the end for him. Ethel le Neve simply disappeared for years and years, with people saying she'd gone to Australia and so on. It was one of those things they had in the papers back then, 'What Happened to X?' And then when Ethel was an old lady it turned out she'd been living in Lewisham for years. The house where they'd lived got turned into a block of flats years ago.

There were another couple of big murders in North London around that time. In 1912 Seddon poisoned his tenant for her money in Tollington Park. That was the case where he made a Masonic sign to the judge to try to get him not to sentence him, but although the judge started to cry he wasn't having it. Then there was George Smith, topped in 1915, who murdered his wives by drowning them in the bath. He did one of them in Waterloo Road off Highgate Hill. Seddon's place is still there but that Waterloo Road is gone.

If you go out further you come to Highgate and the woods and the cemetery. The gambler Brandon Hale was shot there back in January 1997. He'd been given around £100,000 to launder by some people. Now, a relatively easy and safe way to do that is to play red and black at the same time on the roulette wheel. You clean your money nicely and that way it only goes wrong if zero comes up too often. Instead what does he do but blows the whole packet. It seems he got a beating before he was shot as well.

I was reading the other day they're not going to allow plastic flowers in the cemetery no more. Not posh enough.

5

Joey Martin, who was in the nick with me over the years, came from round Tottenham but that bit of London never brought much luck for him. He was done in 1960 over shooting a girl he knew and he was hardly out when just before Christmas he goes on the Express Dairy raid not far from the Wood Green tube station in which a milkman is shot. He got a six for the first and life for the second. I knew him well over the years in the nick. He was in Durham when he and John McVicar and Wally Probyn tried to get out and only John managed it. I'm glad to say at long last Joey's out and about again. He did well over 30 years.

One of the best of the bank robbery teams of the 1970s was the one really run by Bertie Smalls who come from Hornsey. In a way they changed life in Britain. Before then everybody had to be paid in cash, and so every Friday morning there was a load of trucks being driven up to banks with people's wages inside. On top of that banks were friendly then; just a counter, no grilles, no bars, no nothing. And, just like I'd done a few years previous, Smalls and his team did the banks on a regular basis. It was partly a result of that that the law was changed so that people could be paid by cheque, and it was certainly Smalls and the others who forced the banks into putting up grilles and bullet-proof glass.

Robberies wasn't always really organised well in advance because someone might go in Tommy McCarthy's Log Cabin in Wardour Street and say, 'Anyone want to work tomorrow?' The next day they'd go in, get on the counter, fire a shot in the ceiling, take the cash after it had been delivered and off till the next weekend. They made fortunes. And then, who'd have thought it, Smalls turns out to be a wrong 'un and grasses up all his mates. I suppose you might have suspected he was a bit odd because in his early days he'd run a few women – which wasn't usual. There wasn't half some porridge handed out.

There were some good men went down as a result –
Danny Alpress, Micky Salmon and Bruce Brown, who was
the captain of his local golf club in Wembley. Another was
Bobby King, who I see died only a bit ago and who was a
great friend of Bobby Maynard. And then there was Philip
Morris, who also got seventeen years for the shooting of a
milkman during a Securicor raid down at Ewell in Surrey.
He took all the blame for that one. There was one other
curious man on the raids with Bertie and that was Donald
Barrett. He rather puts the bubble in when Smalls and
Bobby King got out over a bank robbery in Bournemouth.
Barrett put his hands up. Then later on he became a
supergrass on his own account, did his short bit of bird and
goes out on other jobs and turns supergrass a second time.

Sometimes grasses live out their lives happily – I hope
they don't. I don't think Smalls had that much trouble
and, like I say, people worked with Barrett even when
he'd done it twice. There again, you've always got to be
looking over your shoulder. Take that Peter McNeil who
grassed up a whole lot of people. He'd been a drug dealer
himself for years and he helped set a trap for a man from
Detroit who ended up with eighteen years. Unfortunately
for McNeil, his name come out at the trial and he said
from then on he'd be a wanted man. That was back in
November 1988. It wasn't until the 1990s that he was
done down in Hampshire. Opened his front door and
whack.

Mickey Greene was one of those big robbers at the
beginning of the 1970s. He got nicked for the Ilford bank
robbery and got an eighteen for it along with Ronnie Dark
– no relation to the one who was later done by John Bindon
down in Fulham. It was the one where Jimmy Saunders got
nicked and Smalls give evidence to get him out of it. Over
the years from time to time Mickey and me were in the same
nick. I saw he'd been nicked at the beginning of February
last year. The coppers had chased him all over Europe and
America for that matter.

He'd done about half his eighteen when he come out from the Ilford robbery and he teamed up again with Ronnie Dark. They were amongst the first to realise how easy it was to make money buying gold coins, which didn't carry VAT, melting them down, selling them back and this time charging the bullion house the VAT. The coppers said they cleared six million in just a few months. A few of the team was nicked, but by then Mickey got over to Spain in the days when there was no extradition. The next thing there was a story that he had tried to get a ransom for a businessman who'd been kidnapped in Spain but, if he did, he was on his toes before they come for him. Then he started moving a bit of puff – well quite a big bit, actually – and he got caught for a couple of kilos. He got bail and was on his toes to Morocco but he had to leave behind all sorts of boats he owned.

Next he managed to get seventeen years in his absence in France – they can do that there – after the *flics* there found a whole load of bullion and cocaine, but no Mickey, in his flat in Paris. He was off to California where he rented Rod Stewart's flat under a moody name. The FBI picked him up whilst he was by the pool and put him on a plane. What does Mickey do? When it stops at Shannon he just walks off. That would be about 1994, but next year he accidentally runs over a taxi driver and he's prosecuted and banned. That's when people discovered who he was and he disappeared again. The Gardai took another load of his things, like his two houses there.

I was glad to read this summer Spain had refused to extradite him over here, but it still leaves France of course.

Islington can be a bit of a dangerous place. Billy Fisher, who was a friend of Marilyn's dad, Tommy Wisbey, was killed there in 1991. He just opened his front door and he was shot, and Brendan Carey was shot in the Prince of Wales in the Caledonian Road. A bit earlier in 1985 that moneylender, Alan Smith, who had a green Roller and looked a bit like Steptoe, was shot in the Duchess of

Devonshire. He was having a drink one Saturday night in the pub when five men turned up. He was shot across the bar with a sawn-off shotgun and as he staggered out into the street he was shot in the head. He wasn't popular. If you owed him money he could be hard on you. They said that when people heard he'd been done there'd be parties on every council estate in London.

On the whole, though, you don't get too many professional hits out in North London but there was one in Arden Road, Finchley, a couple of years ago when Saul Nahome, who was said to be a financial adviser to the Adams family, was shot outside his home. It was a job off the back of a motorbike again. There was another one out in Barnet; a fellow was shot when he come back to his home in Moxon Street, just off the High Street, near a trading estate. No one ever was done for either of the jobs and I don't think they was even connected. That's the trouble, you can rent a hitman nowadays for not much more than a few hundred quid.

EAST END

1

I used to get all over the joint as a kid out thieving. You had to be shrewd enough not to stick locally. From the time I was eleven or twelve I was all over offices and shops. The City was the cream. Eva was that bit older and she would come out with me most of the time, sort of look after me. If I was caught – and thank God that wasn't too often – she'd be there to say she'd take me home and this was the first time and my Dad would give me a whipping, and it usually worked.

The East End was different; much harder work. Full of Jewish people, of course, and they were a bit warm in looking after their shops. Opportunities were definitely limited but what there was about we took and brought it back to the Elephant to sell, mostly through Lumps and Bumps, the old woman who wore no knickers and would hoist her skirt to warm her bum in front of the pub fire.

Funnily, although the East End was meant to be where the Chinese lived, I don't remember seeing many of them about. There weren't Chinese restaurants on every street like there are today. I suppose Eva and me just never really went into Limehouse which was the Chinese bit. We concentrated more on Mile End, round there. What people don't realise is that in them days the East End was a series of villages which was really separate from one another. People say the East End but Limehouse was far more different to, say, Upton Park than the Elephant was to Brixton.

Pennyfields was where the opium dens was when I was young. That and gambling clubs. It's where the man they called the Brilliant Chang operated. He was deported over drugs when I was about three but there was still legends about him. How he'd come back to England and was going to be like Fu Manchu and take over England. They was just old wives' stories, of course. There was a fair bit of smuggling Chinese into England when I was young and, of course, there is even more now. It's not that many years ago – 1995 I think it was – that a couple of Chinese turned up dead in Glasgow Road in Plaistow. They'd been stabbed to death a bit before, but it was only when the neighbours complained about the smell that anyone took any notice. The coppers said that it was to do with illegal immigrants.

I suppose Aldgate really marked the divide between the City and the East End. It's all changed today, but there was a tailor's the chaps used to go to just by Aldgate tube station. Max Cohen it was called and it had been there years – run by Hymie and Henry Cohen. I got my first made-to-measure suit in Brick Lane when their father had his shop there. Then they moved to opposite Sir John Cass School, whose emblem was a red feather. The story was that Cass had a haemorrhage just as he was signing the deeds of the school and bled all over the quill pen he was holding. I don't know if it's true but it's a good story.

If you stood at Aldgate tube station, looked east and turned left you went down Mitre Street. That was where there was a long firm running before we all got nicked over

Mr Smith's. Long firms are nothing new, they've been around for years and years. There was about a hundred of them running at any one time in the 1920s in the City and Manchester. In an LF goods are bought on credit and sold and the vendor is given his dough. You do this a few times and build up credit and other vendors, and then you buy a whole lot of stuff on credit and knock it out cheap. Back in them days it was rare if anyone got nicked, let alone convicted. Firstly, you generally put in a front who had no convictions and you changed him around a few times, so that he could genuinely say he was only there part of the time. Then since most of the buying was done on the phone there was no question of identifying who'd bought the goods.

If the geezer was ever nicked he could put it down to inexperience and bad trading and, best of all, since both the coppers and the Board of Trade was involved they often didn't know what the other was doing and so nothing happened for months or even years. By that time the front man would be on a long cruise somewhere.

Another good thing about a long firm is that you can have a fire. You show the goods was bought and stored on the premises and it's gone up. Of course you've got the goods out before the blaze and so it's double profit. Then when the coppers or someone comes round you just say the business was ruined by the fire. Things is more difficult now but in them days they worked a treat.

This time the warehouse was to go up at a weekend but as luck would have it, after petrol had been poured all over the premises, the fellows who was doing the job saw a courting couple in the street. By the time they had gone the fumes had risen and so, when they aimed a Guy Fawkes rocket at a semi-basement window, instead of just getting a fire which would burn nicely the place blew up and demolished half the street. Charlie Richardson wasn't at all pleased.

1 Corner of Frith Street and Old Compton Street – Albert's fight with Jack 'Spot'

2 Wardour Street – Tommy McCarthy's Log Cabin, the best place in the 60s

3 Gerrard Street – the New Cabinet Club, run by Billy Hill's wife, Aggie

4 Great Windmill Street – Jack Solomon's gym, where the faces hung out

5 Seven Dials – where Billy Hill was born

❶ Cornwall Road – My birthplace (the building is now part of the station)

❷ Blackfriars/ Union Street – the Ring as it was – now it's moved to the opposite side of the road

❸ Walworth Road – my parents' flat, where we moved when I was five

❹ Walworth Road – and just about opposite their flat was the Reform Club, which is how I came to join the Richardsons

❺ Walworth Road/ Manor Place – Manor Place Baths, where we used to go to bathe

❻ Lower Marsh – where I saw my first dead bodies

Above Ron and Reggie
Kray with their mother, Vi

Right Jack 'Spot'. I told
him it was on and it was

Left Double spy, George Blake. This picture was issued by Scotland Yard after his escape from Wormwood Scrubs prison, West London, in 1966. He seemed a cut above us, I suppose he was

Below Mandy Rice-Davies leaving the Old Bailey. A tough girl – she told Ronnie to take his hands off her. And it cost Peter Rachman several grand

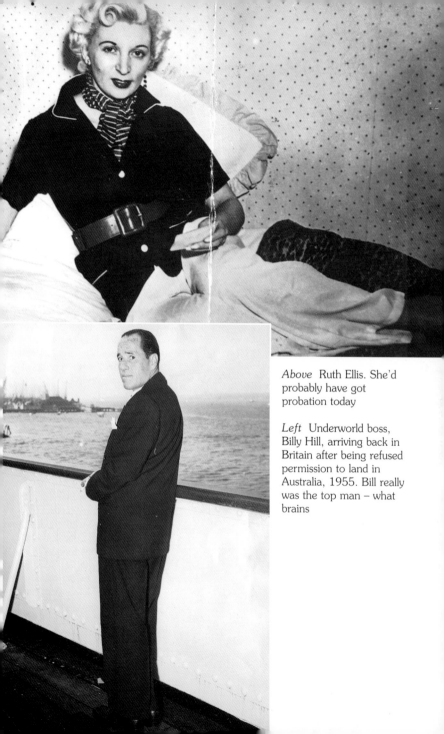

Above Ruth Ellis. She'd probably have got probation today

Left Underworld boss, Billy Hill, arriving back in Britain after being refused permission to land in Australia, 1955. Bill really was the top man – what brains

Above The Messina brothers, Eugene and Carmelo, 1956. Just about *every* West End girl on the game belonged to them and their brothers

Left Flower sellers at Piccadilly Circus, 1925. This was the London I grew up in

Left Rev. Harold Davidson, Rector of Stiffkey, with his daughter Patricia, outside court during his trial for grave immorality, 1932. He said he was saving young girls – more like, saving them for later

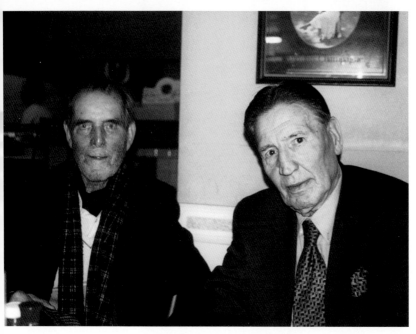

My old mate, Jimmy Robson, the gamest of the game, with me, March 2001

The Hampton Court Palace pub, where Lennie Garrett fought with Jimmy Robson

Left The Castle Hotel, formerly the Reform Club, Walworth Road

Below My wife Marilyn with me and her parents, Renee and Tommy Wisbey, at the launch of Marilyn's great book, *Gangster's Moll*, in what was Murray's Cabaret Club

2

It was round the corner from Mitre Street in Mitre Square that Jack the Ripper did one of his women. Well, around Aldgate was where he operated the whole time. There was terrible slums and tenements there; brasses were literally tuppenny uprights. There was over 200 lodging houses in Whitechapel alone, and they took in up to eight and a half thousand. A single bed cost fourpence and a double twice that.

The first of the girls was done on 31 August 1888, when Mary Ann Nichols was killed in Bucks Row, and the last was on 9 November, when Mary Jane Kelly was killed and he really took out her lights in Millers Court which was in Dorset Street. In between there was Annie Chapman on 8 September at Hanbury Street, and both Elizabeth 'Long Liz' Stride at Berner Street and Catherine Eddowes, who was the one in Mitre Square. He did the pair of them on 30 September.

There was a couple of other brasses done earlier that year. Emma Elizabeth Smith in Osborn Street on 3 April and, four days later, Martha Tabram in Grove Yard Building. Emma lived long enough to get to hospital where she copped peritonitis. There was a lot of fighting gangs and youths who went round demanding money so it may have been one of them, like the Old Nichol gang, that did for her. The other one may have been done by a soldier.

A copper called Ernest Thompson is thought to be the only person who may have seen Jack the Ripper, but that's if you count Frances Coles as being one of the girls. He'd only been on the force a bit over a month and he was out on night duty for the first time in his life in February 1891 when he walked through Chambers Street and saw a man come running out of Swallow Gardens towards the Royal Mint. He ran after him but fell over the body of Frances. It upset him quite a bit. Nowadays he'd have been able to have counselling and probably make a claim but there was no chance of that then. A James Saddler was nicked for her murder but the case got chucked early on.

In fact the copper did turn a bit odd and he reckoned he'd never die a natural death. He was right. He was stabbed to death at Alder Street and the junction with Commercial Road at the beginning of December 1900. There was a man, Barnet Abrahams, accosting women at a coffee stall and when Thompson went to talk to him, he was stabbed in the neck. He held on and, so they say, died with his hands still on the man's collar. Abrahams claimed he had been given a severe beating by the police and so remembered nothing of the incident, just like Podola in Kensington all those years later. He was lucky with the judge because he got a manslaughter verdict and twenty years' penal servitude. It didn't do him no good, though. He might just as well have been topped because he died in prison.

Who was Jack the Ripper? Well there's almost as many theories as I've had Christmas dinners in the nick and none of them really stands up. It's almost as if people don't want him named because that would spoil all the fun and ruin the industry and all. The story I like best is that it was some Masonic plot or other, or that it was that James Maybrick, who was poisoned by his wife up in Liverpool, but who knows? I suppose if they could ever get DNA samples they might find out, but those who support another man would say the samples was contaminated and they shouldn't count.

One of the most elaborate murders down the East End in Victorian times was when Henry Wainwright did his mistress, Harriet Lane. It was a bit earlier, in 1874, and this time there's no doubt he did it. That was another of those cases where the murderer kept the body. He was already married, of course – a pillar of local society – but that didn't stop him and Harriet having a couple of kids. Then his business – he was a brushmaker – started to go wrong and Harriet was on the booze the whole time so he introduced her to his brother Thomas. She thought she was just being transferred to a new owner but they had it in mind to put her away. The day she went off, as she thought to live with the brother, she was never seen again. Well, she was seen a year later because over the winter a paint room in a warehouse owned by Wainwright began to smell so bad that the tenants moved. The next summer he was made bankrupt and the warehouse was sold so he had to move Harriet. It's amazing what Wainwright's brother would do for him, because he agreed she could be put in the cellar of his shop.

They'd put the body in quicklime but it had worked the other way round from usual and the body was preserved, which was why it smelled. It was in parcels and Wainwright, instead of sending a boy for a cab, asked him to look after the parcels. Being inquisitive as kids are, the boy opened one and there was Harriet's hand. They put the parcels in a cab and Wainwright drove off to his brother's. On the way he saw another girlfriend and she got in the cab with him and Harriet. The stink must have been something rotten because he started smoking a cigar. Meanwhile the kid had found two policemen but all they did was laugh at him, and so he had to go looking for another pair. Coppers didn't go singly round the East End then, otherwise they'd have found themselves pushed down a manhole and been lucky if the cover wasn't put over them as well. Eventually they caught up with Wainwright and wanted to see what was in the parcels and that was the end of things. His brother received seven years as an accessory and the kid got £30. Wainwright got scragged.

3

I have to admit it, though I hate to do so, that Frederick Lawton, whose father tried to do me all those years ago, could defend properly. He defended in another East End murder towards the very end of the war, after Lilian Hartney was found early one morning at the beginning of August 1945 in Rich Street with her feet pointing to

Grenada Street. Whoever done it had turned her dress back to show her fanny because she hadn't pants or stockings on. She'd been strangled and someone had bitten her. Whoever it was was missing a couple of teeth.

The Pros' case was that she had been done by her husband, Patrick, who had TB – which was a killer in them days. The story was that he was tired of her being out, putting it about in Chinatown night after night. As you know when people die, particularly when they're being strangled, they often have a riddle and there was a patch of urine in the bed. It was the same when Sidney Fox strangled his mother in that hotel in Eastbourne. The Pros said that showed Lilian had been killed at home. When the coppers come there was her husband fully dressed.

Though it hurts me I have to give Lawton credit. He hadn't much to go on but he got the jury to believe that this man who had consumption couldn't have carried his wife's body two hundred yards down the East India Dock Road. Wrong, when you have to do something, you find the strength from somewhere. It wouldn't have mattered much. Although he didn't know it, Hartney was a dying man already. They might have done him a favour by topping him, but there again they probably wouldn't have hanged him for what they called mercy. Just like the man they didn't hang, down in Hampshire, for shooting his wife because he'd shot himself in the jaw and it was now so brittle the noose was likely to break his jaw, slip over his head and make a fine mess of things.[1]

A bit after, a Patrick Hartney was lucky not to swing for a murder he done down the East End. The man was a regular burglar and he did for a Mrs Goodman in Stepney. The wire was that although she lived very poor she'd got a lot of money. A neighbour called round one morning in

---

[1] This was the case of William Gray who ambushed his wife on 31 December 1948. He pleaded guilty to murder at Winchester Assizes and was sentenced to death but reprieved.

January 1946 and there she was, dead on the floor wrapped in a blanket. The only thing that gave the coppers the alert was a bit of cloth on the pantry window. It was so small that it seemed like only a child could have got through but that copper Fred Narborough, who spent so much time trying to find out who killed a girl in Sussex and never managed to prove it, knew there was a dwarf in the neighbourhood. It shows how poor people was. When he got the pull he was still wearing the same trousers, which had a tear that matched the bit of cloth. His story was that she'd surprised him when he was screwing her drum and he'd thrown a blanket over her head to keep her quiet. He'd given her a push and she'd fell and banged her head. His appeal got turned down but the Home Secretary gave him a reprieve. Maybe it was because he was only nineteen or maybe it was because he was a dwarf.

Not that being a dwarf has always saved you from the rope. There was one up in Nelson in Lancashire, went and killed a woman in a burglary before the war. I'm sure that what did for him is that he went and hanged the woman's dog from the bedstead with a bit of string when it tried to defend her. He had not a hope in hell with a jury. Lawton's father didn't die when I hanged him and his dog on Wandsworth Common. Given the option I'd have swung for the dog, not for him.

4

Just about all the small halls have given up doing boxing shows. They used to be at the baths and there was Seymour Place, Manor Place near me, Lime Grove, though I think they did more wrestling, Porchester Hall down Paddington way, West Ham, there must have been up to a dozen of them. Now there's just about only York Hall left. That's just by Bethnal Green tube station. It was outside there that the boxing promoter Frank Warren was shot and the lightweight champion Terry Marsh got prossed. Frank, who's Bobby Warren's nephew, had done very well for Terry, but they'd had a falling out and the Pros said this was the reason for Terry doing the shooting. Frank had been on the way to a show when a man in a hood comes up and blasts at him. Not surprisingly, Frank can't recognise the man who's on his toes straight away. A few people chased after him but he got clear. Then a bit later Terry's nicked. He had that top brief Richard Ferguson, the Irishman, defend him and he got a not guilty.

Cinemas were thought of as easy knock-overs, and for some reason when there was a murder in one it became famous in its time. Maybe it was because real life had taken over from the fantasy people had been looking at. There was that famous one in Liverpool just after the war when Jimmy Kelly got topped. I see from the papers they're trying to re-open that one, prove him and the man who swung with him was not guilty. But the one I remember most was at the Eastern Palace Cinema in Bow Road in September 1934. The cleaner found the manager dying when she went to take some milk up to his flat. There'd clearly been a big fight and there was blood all over the place. He'd been hit on the head with an axe. Someone had opened the safe and a century had gone missing. That was headlines. It's not like today when a murder doesn't even make the news in brief because there are so many. A murder-robbery like that was news for months. When you think about it there probably wasn't 130 murders a year throughout Britain, and many of them was husband and wife and would get written down to manslaughter. It was really the same with robberies during the war. They made the headlines simply because they were so few.

The fellow that did the Bow cinema job, John Stockwell, worked at the place. He'd grown up in Salvation Army hostels until he'd been taken in by a lady in Empson Street. Then he'd started walking out with the woman's daughter, Violet. Good-looking girl she was from the photographs. Of course, the police started combing the neighbourhood but

Stockwell had an alibi. He shared a room with Violet's brother and the boy said Stockwell had been in all night.

It's funny how when people have got money from something illegal they start tossing it around and everyone becomes suspicious. What does Stockwell do? He takes the day off work and goes to Southend. Then he takes Violet to the Tivoli cinema in the Strand. Long gone, that is. He's only just got work and suddenly he says he'll take the next day off and take Violet up to Lowestoft for the day. She tells him not to waste his money but by then the coppers know about his day off. She goes to work but he went up to Lowestoft anyway. Then it's just a matter of time. His picture is put in the papers and his landlady up on the coast recognises him. He sent a note to Violet saying he'd changed his name to Jack Barnard and another to the coppers saying he was going to drown himself.

Then he goes and leaves his clothes on the beach just like that MP John Stonehouse who was in the nick with me. It doesn't often fool people for too long. Fishermen usually know where a body will wash up and if it doesn't, well, then people start wondering. He went and booked in a third name into a place in Yarmouth and the manager blew the whistle. The police were waiting for him when he got back from buying new clothes. The jury recommended mercy because he was so young and he hadn't had any parental guidance after his father had been killed in the war, but it did him no good. His girlfriend visited him a couple of times. He had a pint of beer with his last supper and he's meant to have said 'Here's to the next world' but that can just be one of them things you hear in prison.

5

There have always been some dodgy doctors down the East End. The Twins had one straightened out and Christopher Swan was another one. He'd got a surgery in Queensbridge Road, Hackney. He took the place over from another doctor, John Peto, who'd copped it for not keeping proper records. The police claimed that Swan had been doing abortions and running a drug racket and he was charged with conspiracy. Eventually in January 1969 the abortion charges was dropped and he got fifteen years on the drugs, as well as soliciting a copper to commit murder. He'd wanted a few witnesses taken out and was trying to get a bargain price: four grand each for the first two, or ten grand for four.

It's funny how pubs change their names nowadays. In my time they never did but suddenly you look up and the Dog and Duck has got some funny name like the Fart in the Colander. There's two pubs down the East End, though, that will never change their names. Go down Mile End Road and just before you get to Whitechapel tube station there's the Grave Maurice. That was one of Ronnie's favourite hang-outs. It was at the trial that his brief, John Platts-Mills, started to explain how the place got its name. It seems he was some sort of Polish nobleman, the brother of Count Rupert, but the judge, Melford Stevenson, cut him off before he got very far so no one never learned, not that day anyway. The Grave Maurice was where I met Ronnie when he told me things was going wrong, and that the coppers were out looking into me and Charlie and Eddie.

Then if you go down the road just another hundred yards you come to the Blind Beggar, which I suppose is just about the most famous pub in all London. That's where Ronnie shot George Cornell the night after the Mr Smith's Club fight. That pub was named after a story about a blind beggar who had a beautiful daughter. Really he was a rich nobleman and he was disguising himself so people wouldn't marry her for his money. The other story is that the beggar was a soldier who got blinded in the Hundred Years War and his daughter, called Bessy, became a brass to keep him. That sounds more likely, and there's a Bessy Street off Roman Road.

George had been visiting my friend Jimmy Andrews, who worked with us at Atlantic Machines and who'd been shot himself, and he'd just gone into the Beggar's for a drink. It's funny how things come round in a circle. The record playing when Ronnie walked in that night was 'The Sun Ain't Gonna Shine Anymore' by the Walker Brothers and only this year they had me on telly explaining why that was such a big hit. Jimmy Andrews was often getting himself into bits of trouble. I shot both Checker and Teddy Berry over him. I shot them in the legs because I was only doing it to warn them. If you're going to kill you don't go for the leg. They'd given Jimmy a seeing-to and that was the comeback. Guns was easy to get hold of in them days, just as easy as it is now. The Malts in Soho always had them. Afterwards you gave them back, or if things had gone a bit wrong you chucked them.

Another very famous place in its heyday was Charlie Brown's. Really it was called the Railway Tavern and it was just in the West India Dock Road in Limehouse. Before the war people used to drive down there after a night out in the West End just to slum. It was an adventure for them, something they could tell their friends the next day. 'Oh listen, we was in the East End last night and look we survived'. The original Charlie Brown had a big collection of stuff he'd bought off sailors when they docked and he'd got some more stuff he'd show the men in the party in the back room.

There was a killing there during the war. A local man, George Gilbey from Bethnal Green, was done by a United States serving man, Gunner Matthew Smith, who was only nineteen. According to the man who'd taken over, the Americans were 'blowing their heads off' by which he meant they was having a sing-song, and he ordered them out calling 'bring me my stick'. When he had cleared the pub a door panel was smashed in and Gilbey was stabbed. The boy maintained that although he had been there it was not his knife which had killed Gilbey. The really funny thing was they held the court martial in Regent Street of all places and he was found guilty and sentenced to death, but because of his age it was commuted to life imprisonment.

The pub's still there but it's changed a lot. The other big place, the Blue Posts, was opposite the Railway. Then there was the Crown and Anchor which Queenie Watts ran in Pennyfields, Chinatown. She was a great pal of the Twins. She used to sing the old Cockney songs for them when they had the Double R and the Kentucky.

Just like Soho, the East End was full of clubs and spielers and when it come to it the Twins was getting a good nip out of a lot of them. It may not have sounded much but it added up. The owner of Dodgers in Brick Lane paid them £15 a week and there was another of the same from a betting shop there. There was a spieler in the Commercial Road that paid the same as well. The Green Dragon in Aldgate paid up £40 and there was more when a blackjack table went in the club. There was a tenner from another place in the Whitechapel Road. And that was only a part of it. When you think that about that time you could buy a house in Tottenham for £500 you can see it was good money. We had one or two machines over the East End but we wasn't really interested.

6

'Little Legs' Brian Clifford was a mover, a buyer of gear. He did Johnny Mangan down the East End in 1979. Two in the nut and somehow Johnny survived and Clifford got acquitted of attempted murder. A few years later Clifford got done himself but there was no mistake this time. I've heard it said that everyone but him on his manor knew it was on top. People come to his door one night, pushed his wife aside when she opened it, thundered up the stairs and shot him whilst he was in bed.

People talk about gangland feuds but so much of it is personal and not business. It's never really been like Chicago, where Capone was wiping out the opposition to his booze trade. It was in Cheshire Street that Ginger Marks was meant to have been shot just after New Year 1965.

He'd been out doing a bit of work when he thought someone called his name. He looked up and he was shot for his trouble. That was a mistake by all accounts. The man who was wanted was Jimmy Evans. At least that's what he said when he give evidence ten years later at the Bailey against Alfie Gerard, Freddie Foreman and Jerry Callaghan. The case was slung. That was another personal matter.

Of course so much of the East End went in the war. Places like Grenade Street where Zoe Progl was born just don't exist any more. She was a very good thief, hoister, screwer, anything really. She was a girlfriend of Tommy Smithson before he took up with Fay Richardson. She got out of Holloway, which was a pretty good feat, not too many women have managed that. Shirley Pitts, from that good family off the Lambeth Walk, did it too and she was well pregnant at the time and all.

There again you find places still standing like Batty Street near Brick Lane where the Jewish man, Israel Lipski, was hanged for the murder of one of the other tenants back at the end of the nineteenth century. He was found half-unconscious underneath her bed. The Pros said he'd been trying to rape her although she was well in the club at the time. Right at the end Lipski said he'd killed her in a robbery, but there's always been an argument that maybe he was asked to confess because there was such anti-Jewish feeling at the time and this was a compromise.

People have always said the East End is clannish and I don't suppose there's a much better example than when in July 1992 Kevin Fox, wearing a hood, was shot with his own gun after he had blasted the landlord's son, Mark 'Chalkie' Smith, three times in the stomach at the Memory Lane public house in Plaistow. The landlord had said he wasn't having drug dealing in the place. Fox had a gun and he fired shots at the crowd as it went for him. He was hit over the head with a fire extinguisher, punched, kicked and then shot. Eleven people were questioned over the killing but the coppers got nowhere. Good riddance you might say.

There was a couple of killings down Stratford Broadway which never got solved back in the summer of 1986. Peter Morris, who'd been about, was done a week or so after Micky Collins who'd owned the Moonlight pub in the Broadway went down. Micky had been a bit unlucky. Someone had decided to stripe him on the buttocks – noughts and crosses it's called – and they hit an artery. The pub he'd owned had once been in the hands of Bobby Moore the footballer, and Collins had been mouthing off about how he was going to take over the East End. That was one week and the next Morris is shot and stabbed outside the Telegraph pub only a few hundred yards from where Collins had copped it. No one was charged for either of them.

Another man who went down in a pub was my old friend Jimmy Moody, who helped carry me out of Mr Smith's when I was shot by Dickie Hart. He was killed in the Royal Hotel, Victoria Park, which was an area I'd had a wonderful touch in years before. On 1 June 1993 Jimmy was standing at the bar when a fellow comes in, puts two in him and he's off on a motor cycle. Jimmy had been another man in a good escape. He'd been in the Thursday Gang of the 1970s who'd specialised in blaggings and eventually when he'd got nicked he had gone to Brixton. Along with Stan Thompson who'd been in the Parkhurst Riot with me, and an IRA man called Gerard Tuite, they cut through the brickwork and were away in December 1980 and he'd more or less never been heard of again until right at the end. Then he'd been involved in a row with a family down Walworth way and had come over to the East End for a bit and he was living under the name Mick. I knew it was on top and that night I made sure I was on my way north, as there was nothing I could have done about it. After he was done there was all sorts of stories about the number of contracts he'd carried out. Who can tell? Maybe it's like Teddy Machin after he was done in a domestic in West Ham. Or that Gilbert Wynter who, now he's dead, is said to have done all sorts of things over in North London. As for Stan and the escape it was a bit of a waste of time. I'm glad to say the jury chucked his case out whilst he was still on his toes.

7

Just like Epping Forest, the marshes over Hackney have always been a good place to find things, and back in December 1980 the body of Colin Osborne, who was known as the Duke, turned up there. I never really knew him on the outside but he'd been a friend of the Twins over the years. He was a sort of minor villain really; a bit of a gofer for them. He wore a rug and thought people didn't notice. He got involved with Lennie Watkins who was known as Silly Eddie because, when he'd become rich from smuggling drugs, he used to light cigars with £20 notes. Nothing like drawing attention to yourself. Dukey, who was bright, was actually the one who put together this smuggling but it all came on top when a Customs officer was killed not far from Tower Bridge a couple of months earlier. I think there was a lot of people looking for the Duke and they wasn't only people from Customs and Excise. He was said to have had a heart attack but there was some story he'd been kept in a refrigerator – which I suppose might be enough to give anyone a heart attack. Watkins got life for the Customs officer and, after a breakout failed, he went and topped himself in the nick.

Rotherhithe tunnel was where I got nicked and pulled twenty months just after the war. Spindles Jackson, who got a two, and Charlie Rainsford, who got eighteen months, was with me and so was Danny Swain and Dido Frett. They got away after we had done the town hall at Rainham for some petrol coupons. We'd set off an alarm and we were chased all the way from Barking until we run out of petrol in the tunnel. I should have got away as well, but I ran straight out the end of the tunnel where the coppers were waiting, instead of going up the stairs which was an escape route if there was a fire. On the whole tunnels is good places for jobs. Charlie Knight, who was a top class thief, was probably the one who made the best use of tunnels. I remember looking at the tunnel from Waterloo Bridge into Kingsway with Jerry Callaghan just after it opened, and we was saying how if a security van went down you could just block it from the front and cut off the rest of the traffic with a Road Closed sign. We watched it for a long time but it turned out to be no good. People don't realise the planning which goes into jobs and half the time they come to nothing for one reason or another.

Nowadays the East End's changed. I was walking round there the other day in Brick Lane, Banglatown it's called, and it's wall to wall restaurants. Not like when I was on the run from Stamford House and Patsy Fleming's people hid me out down there back in the 1930s. The places just line up one beside the other and I don't understand how they make any money. There's also a lot of Yardie-like killings down there. I was reading the other day that there's more murders in the Lower Clapton Road than there is on any other street in Britain. Where we used to have a straightener and sometimes knives got used, now it's guns and more guns.

There was a real spate of killings that year, in particular all over London and the people who got the blame this time were Yardies. What you have to be wary of is the way the media hypes things up. It sells papers and it's often like it was with Billy or the Twins and others like them. They'll make out they're Yardies so as to get more attention and some kudos. Mind you if you're looking down a sawn-off shotgun I don't suppose you care whether it's a Yardie holding it or someone else.

Things have changed down in Hackney from the Twins' time and one of them is the Regency Club. That was really their flagship, a nice place where you could take your family of an evening for a night out, a Chinese meal and a spot of gambling if you wanted. They once turned Jack 'The Hat' McVitie away because he was wearing Bermuda shorts. He was also carrying a machete at the time. That's where he was collected before the party in Evering Road where Reggie stabbed him. It's become Trenz nowadays and a lot of Stoke Newington is Yardie country now. Two brothers and Leon Meshack Walsh was shot outside the club back in April 1997. The coppers said they wanted to interview a Rudi King but he was shot over in Walm Lane, Willesden that November.

I don't care what is said, since that Lawrence case the police have been treading very warily in arresting black guys. They'll only do it now if it's cast iron. What is it that Macpherson said? Racist conduct is racist conduct if that's what the guy who's on the receiving end thinks it is. Easy to put up, isn't it? If you're nicked and there's nothing found on you then all you've got to do is scream that the reason you were nicked is because you're black. You're the one who sees it's racist and therefore it is. Now black villains is poncing it for all they're worth and you can't blame them. I suspect there'll come a time when white guys will be able to scream they're being picked on and that's racist too.

WEST LONDON

1

What really was the best prison escape? I've often thought about it since the last book and whilst I've been writing this one. Sometimes I decide one and then the next day I think, no maybe that one was better. Was there one better than when the Welshman, Ray Jones, the cat burglar, broke both his legs getting out of Pentonville and still got away? I never knew whether it was him or Peter Scott who stole Sophia Loren's jewels all those years ago at the Edgwarebury Country Club out in Hertfordshire. May 1960 it was, when she was filming *The Millionairess* with Peter Sellers. Both Peter and Ray claimed the credit and it was a good job whichever done it.

I suppose Jones' escape could get the vote for the best of the single-handed escapes – no help from outside – but I think Biggs and Flowers out of Wandsworth must be one of the best team efforts. Talking of Ronnie, it's sad the condition he'd got himself into. I don't blame him coming back, doing it for his boy really, but I think if it had been me I'd have stayed out there, only because of the effort other people put in to getting me out and to Australia and then to Brazil. It would feel to me as though I'd slung it all back at them. I do understand his reasons but I couldn't have done it. I hope they'll let him out. If they want a hostage sort of thing I'd do a few years for him. It may sound daft but I would.

The time when the Twins got Frank Mitchell out of Dartmoor can't really count because he was on an outside working party. Mind you, Charlie Wilson out of Winson Green can't have been far behind the Biggs escape. People come over the wall at night, up into the security wing and out again. That was some feat and there's no way you could do that now. In fairness, when you look back it was incredible how they kept any men in during those days. What happened? The orderly officer went round early in the evening and double-locked the prison doors and then came and opened them in the morning. That was just about all, except for those walls with leg-breakers on them and a bit of wire.

But maybe the springing of George Blake out of the Scrubs was the best. After all he was doing 42 years for spying and you'd think the authorities would take extra care of someone like him. From the time he was weighed off in July 1961 there had been all sorts of stories floating around about how he'd tried to escape or how someone was going to try to get him out. You can never tell how good these kinds of stories are. There's always some con who wants to cause trouble to another or brown-nose a screw, and an easy way is to say that Frank Fraser or someone like me is going to be sprung. Then it's out of circulation for the poor devil.

There was one really good story about the Blake escape which seemed so far-fetched it couldn't be true. An ex-con who knew the prison well was going to be got over the wall into the nick wearing prison clothing and the trusty's blue armband. He was then going to get into the mail bag shop where George was working and take him out on some excuse or other. Then a helicopter was going to land in the yard, pick them both up and off it was to East Germany. The ex-prisoner was a sort of ne'er-do-well from Eton and Oxford – he'd been thrown out of both of them. The man who was to be the pilot was going to escape first and he was the one who blew the story to the screws. In fact the authorities took it seriously and interviewed everyone in sight and decided that the man who put the story up was mentally unstable. Fantastic though it might seem they couldn't rule out that something like this might not happen. If you think about it, well it could. People had got into Winson Green and got Charlie Wilson out. Years later there was a helicopter landing when John Kendall and Sidney Draper, who'd been done with my friend, Billy Murray's boy up in Scotland, got out of Leicester. There was one only the other day from a French prison.

Then they couldn't rule out an East German connection. After all there was Paddy Meehan, doing an eight, who got out of Nottingham with a load of others whilst they was watching a cricket match and came down to London where he got a bit of help from Eva before he pushed off to East Germany. You'd have thought someone would have heard bells but they still left George in the Scrubs. The place was thought to be just about escape-proof. No one had got out of 'D' Hall, which is where they had George, for six years or more. And they can't have thought George was much of an escape risk anyway, because they took him off the escape list within a few months of his sentence.

It all went wrong for the authorities twice over. Firstly, in June six men got out at slopping out time and five of them got over the wall with a rope they'd made in mattress manufacture from the prison workshops, and grappling irons they'd made from metal rails on the landings and stairs. If you think about it that must have been one of the best and all. What was even better in a way was that, although someone had grassed them and the police told the screws, they still got out. They'd even named two of the men. One of the men who got out was Martin O'Day, who'd worked for Eddie and me at Atlantic emptying the machines. They wasn't out long. Like I've said, that's the problem with escapes. It's not necessarily the getting out that's difficult. It's the staying out.

Of course, after Martin and the others' escape there was a great fuss with emergency towers being put up in Wakefield and Maidstone and an observation tower at the Scrubs with walkie-talkies for the screws.

Then came the killing of the coppers in Braybrook Street, which of course was nothing to do with security at the prison except they thought, quite wrongly as it happened, that there was a plan to spring me. What had happened was that Harry Roberts, John Duddy and John Witney had been going to do a rent collector when they were pulled by some coppers over a tax disc. Witney called out to Harry to shoot them and he killed two straight off. The third one tried to drive away but Harry shot him as well. Someone had seen their motor and it got traced back to Witney, who grassed up the others in short order.

As I say, it was in the papers they had been there to spring me, and I was taken out of the Scrubs faster than you could say Old Bailey. Duddy's father had been in the Glasgow police; done years in the force there. I knew Duddy in the nick. He was a good man but you always look twice at people who've got relatives in the police. That other one, Witney, he not only grassed them up, he grassed people up in the nick and all. Who would have visualised he was a right snide? When Charlie Richardson and the others did that great feat in Durham and barricaded themselves in the prison officers' room and were going through the papers, Witney was meant to be with them but he went and locked himself in his cell like the coward he was.

Duddy died in the nick and Witney was released some years ago. Then in 1999 there was a good piece of news in the papers for once. Someone had killed him in Bristol where he was living. I'm not sure the whole story come out in court but a much younger fellow, Nigel Evans, went and hit him with a meat tenderiser after a quarrel over the rent. He said he'd only done it when Witney attacked first but the jury was against him. Evans also went and pleaded guilty to stealing Witney's cheque book and bank card and he got life in May last year. Harry is in an open prison and with luck by the time this book comes out he may have been released. I knew him well in the nick. His mother, who used to visit him all round the country, was a lovely woman.

But, back in 1965, they still didn't move George Blake. Really, when you think of it they'd only themselves to blame when he walked out – which is what he did on 22 October that year. The cons had been watching the wrestling on ITV and he was telling a couple of screws at 5.30 p.m. how he thought it had been faked and by half six at the very latest, some people say it was by six, he was gone. He'd gone onto the landing on the second floor and kicked the bars of the window. There was then a drop of a bit over twenty feet but he could get onto a covered way which was about half the distance and then, if he lowered himself off, it was a drop of no more than four feet. It was raining at the time and the visibility was poor and he'd only got twenty yards to cover to the prison wall. He still managed to damage his ankle whilst he did it and they had to get a moody doctor to look at it.

The funny thing was, after the alarm went off, so to speak, the coppers couldn't find a picture of Blake in his file at Scotland Yard and that give him a bit more time. Almost all the Sunday papers had been printed and the only one they could eventually get a picture in was the *News of the Screws* but George was long gone by then.

What happened was he had teamed up with Mike Randle and Pat Pottle, two anti-nuclear campaigners who were doing eighteen months apiece, and they agreed to help him. He was also helped by an Irishman Sean Bourke, who got him a walkie-talkie of all things. Although the coppers thought he'd go straight to Germany he stayed in London until nearly Christmas, when Mike Randle smuggled him out in a van and drove him to Berlin. I think Blake's still in Moscow. Pottle and Randle then went and wrote a book about how they did it. The authorities did nothing and then a year later decided to pros them. It looked like it was one of those open and shut cases but the jury refused to convict. Maybe if they'd prossed them sooner they'd have got a conviction. Anyway when it came to it the pair never got all their royalties from the book. I don't suppose they minded that much.

Of course what with Blake's escape and that of Frank Mitchell and Biggs and John McVicar getting away from a prison escort down in Winchester all happening within a few months of each other, there was bound to be an inquiry and they got Lord Mountbatten, whose wife was in love with Hutch, the nightclub singer, to conduct it. Apart from things like having dog-handlers and links with police stations, one of his recommendations was that there should be better hygiene and living conditions for the cons so they wouldn't want to escape so bad. Nearly forty years on the conditions are probably worse in some nicks.

I've never escaped from anything except the remand home and that was more or less a question of walking out. In fact I only had one serious go after approved school and that was when I was still a kid at Feltham and we tried to get to the wall. All we got was a spanking and a half for our trouble.

I know, though, what it is like to be nicked when you think you are away clear so I suppose I know what it is like to be out and over the wall and then get pulled in. If a Londoner was, say, in Manchester in the old days he'd stick out like a sore thumb if he wasn't out of the town quick. You've got to have transport outside the nick and a place lined up to go to. You feel you want to go back home but that's where the coppers are going to be looking for you first. Then there's always the fear someone's going to bubble you. Look how much of their dough the Train Robbers had to give away just to stay out. And the cleverer the escape the more it must hurt. Take John Kendall for a start. He'd been a member of Billy Tobin's Hole in the Wall Gang, which used lorries to ram warehouses long before people called it ram-raiding, and he'd picked up eight years. He managed to get away when he was being taken to Parkhurst and stayed out nearly two years, but he was finally nicked and they took him to Gartree to do him on other charges for what he'd been up to whilst he was out.

That was when Sidney Draper and him got out in that helicopter on 10 December 1987 but John didn't manage to stay out long. They picked him up in a flat in the King's Road at the end of January along with the man, Andrew Russell, who'd hijacked the helicopter in the first place. He picked up an additional seven whilst Andrew drew a ten. They didn't find Sidney for a long time but, when it came to it, he'd gone back to his old stamping ground in Enfield.

It was the same with Roy Webb, whom they called Rubberbones. He was a great escaper, but although he could get out all right, he never seemed to have the contacts to stay out. He come from the North, Cheshire way, and he'd been in the Coldstream Guards in the war before he was done for damaging a gun. He always said it wasn't his fault and it really soured him. He was forever escaping, and he turned up in London at the end of the war when there was literally thousands of deserters. He did a jeweller's and in a panic hit the man over the head. He got eight years and Flash Jimmy, the man who was with him, got a ten. They both had a birching as well. He got off the Dartmoor train once but he was out only a few days before he was picked up, exhausted. But then he also got off the Moor in 1951, I think it was. He'd dug away at his cell wall with a needle of all things, every night shifting about half a pound of concrete which he washed away the next morning when he slopped out. He managed to get into a tunnel that had been there more or less since the prison had been converted back in Victorian times and which come out only a few yards from the wall. He was away but his real trouble was he didn't have any back-up and, of course, it was only a matter of time before he was caught. He got to London, but he was betrayed by a barrow boy. He'd got a few clothes with him and he tried to sell them. The barrow boy told the coppers and that was that.

He got out of Wandsworth in the 60s and said it was to show he could do it, the screws had been saying it was easy enough to get out of Dartmoor but their place wasn't so simple. Again he was only out a few days. I've no idea what happened to him. Like so many others, he just faded away.

My main thing would have been to try and stay out after an escape. If I'd got clear and I hadn't had things planned in advance than there was a number of people I could go to, friends of the family but who weren't known as such. First off I would have stayed in London and then I'd have gone up North, perhaps even abroad. Don't forget Albert had friends in Paris who'd put me up whilst I was having trouble in Brighton with Harry Rogers down there in the 1960s. I'd stayed in a place of theirs in Pigalle for about a month. It wasn't smart but it was clean and decent and they'd even send a gorgeous girl up to keep me company, as well as give me a lovely present for my boy, Francis, when I left. Of course our lot did the same when one of theirs was in trouble. Jacques Mesrine, a really high-class robber and kidnapper for that matter, who was one of the most wanted men in France back in the 1970s, was hid out in Pallister Road, Barons Court, back in 1978. He was later shot dead back in Paris.

Quite amazing. I read the other day there's been a top Italian mafia man living down the East End in Hackney. Fellow called Raffaele Cadarelli got sentenced to twenty years in his absence around the end of the 1990s. He'd been working in a shoe shop. But if what you read is right there'd been plenty of people turning up in smart cars with dark windows, wearing shades and looking like something out of *The Sopranos*. No wonder people got suspicious. Funnily, in 2005 another top Mafia guy Francesco Tonicello was nicked at Vauxhall tube station. At least he'd been selling papers.

If you could stay out, say, four months then the hue and cry would have died down and things would have been better. Remember, in those days if you could stay out for the whole of the rest of your sentence it was wiped out. You was free.

The time that did for me was when I thought it was all right to come back after the Spot slashing. I was in Ireland and I heard Dido Frett and Ray Rosa had been nicked for doing Johnny Carter. I felt responsible. They'd been helping me with my quarrel with the Carters so I arranged to come back to see what I could do to help them. Little did I know the phone was tapped and there they were waiting for me at London airport. Of course, we'd heard rumours about tapping but we didn't take no notice of them. I phoned Doreen in Brighton to say meet me off the plane and that was what did it. I thought it would be nice to have someone meet me. Right sickener it was. One minute I'm walking about as an ordinary passenger and the next someone calls out 'Frank'. I look up and I don't see light of day for seven years.

It wasn't until George Blake got out that the government really started to pay attention and if he hadn't been a spy then I don't think they'd have thought too much about it. They might have swallowed Frank Mitchell leaving the Moor and John McVicar getting away from the coach at Winchester but this was national security. I met Blake when I was in the hospital at Wormwood Scrubs, getting treatment after I was shot in the leg in Mr Smith's Club. He come over to the hospital wing a couple of times. He was rather austere, as if he was superior to the rest of us, which I suppose in a way he was.

2

Black-marketeering was the thing just at the end and a bit after the war. We really kept things to ourselves but there was a bit of trade with people like the Poles who'd come over here with the Polish Army. It was a couple of them who got nicked over the arrest of a Russian called Reuben Martirosoff, whom they called Russian Robert. He used to be a big card player in a club called the Bees which I think Italian Jock, Albert's brother, took an interest in.

Martirosoff was found dead one morning at the beginning of November 1945 with his hat over his head on the back seat of a car, an Opel it was, in Chepstow Place, North Kensington. It's smart today but it wasn't then. Someone had shot him through the back of the head. There was blood everywhere, including the steering column. Easy enough, you'd say. All the coppers had to do was match the prints and there it was.

You'd think that the people who did it would have taken his money or whatever and thrown the rest of his stuff away but no. A couple of days later a Pole called Marian Grondkowski was found down the East India Dock Road with Robert's watch and cigarette lighter and his wallet. I know some people get touches of guilt and want to be caught but this man was meant to be a pro. What he then did was grass his mate, Henryk Malinowski. And when they nicked him, in turn he said it was Grondkowski. When it come to the trial each of them said it was the other who had shot Russian Robert and forced him to go along with it. It had been a robbery and they'd got about £150 between them. You might have thought that Grondkowski, the one with the wallet and watch was the one who really did it, but which one had never really mattered. They both swung. But it shows you the dangers of dealing with people who can turn on you. Mostly I, and people like me, dealt with people from approved school or Borstal, or from the neighbourhood who we knew or who someone had vouched for. It was much safer but you couldn't do it all the time.

It was risky being in the black market in the sense of getting rid of the gear. The blag was easy enough but then you was at the mercy of other people. At the end of the war when the black market was at its best, if you got hold of any silk stockings then you was your own master. Them, snout and Scotch were winners and you could ask your own price. Tom was even better because you could carry it around in your pocket.

If I wanted to sell and I hadn't got a buyer lined up I'd go down somewhere like Bobby's Club in Rupert Court off Rupert Street and do a deal. If you was lucky you'd have the gear in a garage but cars weren't all that common and people like us didn't always have garages. You couldn't leave it in the car and so very often it would be in someone's front room. One problem was the nosey-parkers, people who'd look on from behind their curtains. The plus was that they didn't have phones, so if you was seen loading up by some curtain twitcher then chances were you'd be on your way before they could put on a hat and coat and run down the nick. If you'd got the gear in a house then you'd do the deal after dark. The man would come over or send someone with the money, and you'd have someone with you so you could count and load at the same time. What you tried to do was have between five and ten really decent buyers over all London; people whose money was solid. If you couldn't unload it on them then your troubles was just starting.

Of course the police would try and stop you. By the end of the war and just after there was night-time round-ups and I remember in January 1946 they closed all the bridges over the Thames from Hammersmith to Blackfriars in the hope of catching people. It wasn't a great success as I recall. What they was after was the professionals, but all they ended up with was a few people in unlawful possession of petrol.

There had been another raid in Soho the previous month; everyone they could find there and in Mayfair got rounded up. I remember Billy Hill telling me about it. All they got that time was a few deserters. Mind you, Billy was having identity papers and army passes printed by the dozen around then, so I suppose it was a tribute to his work that so few people got done.

You never really needed to go to, say, Leeds unless a place was stuck up for you. It was a long way, petrol was rationed and there was always the chance of a pull. Anyway, there was enough little factories around the back of New Oxford Street to keep you busy. That's where they made women's clothes. Very often there wasn't a burglar alarm at all and they didn't even take very much notice of security. You'd have your Stillsons and clip off the padlock and that was that. If you thought there was a burglar alarm then you'd have a bellman with you. Jock Robinson, who was known as Jock the Fitter, was a good man and Charlie Gibbs was another good bellman. So was Jimmy Ford. He was one who had a bit of bad luck once when he did a job with Albert Baffy in Sloane Square. Albert was nicked straight away but Jimmy, who'd done a bit of boxing as a boy, got clear. He'd been on the run about twenty months when he was recognised by an off-duty copper who'd known him from the boxing. Jim had been a good soldier, very brave. He was at Dunkirk and he picked up a medal.

3

Billy Hill lived in a flat in Moscow Road just off Paddington. Sometimes the chaps would go down the Turkish baths at the Porchester Hall which was just nearby. They've all more or less gone, nowadays, but at one time they was all over London. There was a hotel in Russell Square had one and there were big baths in Jermyn Street. If you was out on the town and missed the last train you could go and sweat the booze off in one of them. You'd have some steam and then be given a straight massage – no question of a hand job or the risk of getting your ring felt – wrapped up for the night in a sheet and next morning you'd get a cup of tea before you left. It wasn't at all expensive either, but I never really fancied them myself.

Whiteleys, the store in Queensway, was a home from home for Eva and her mates. It was considered really posh and they were always at it there. The founder got himself topped on the premises by Horace Rayner, his illegitimate son of all people; same first name as Lawton, although the judge never used it. Anyway Whiteley wouldn't recognise Horace, who was absolutely on his uppers, when in January 1907 he went and got a gun, took it to the store, and demanded his father recognise him as the son and heir and all the loot that went with it. You have to give the old man credit. He wouldn't and Rayner shot his father between the eyes and then turned the gun on himself. He shot himself in the eye and the bullet exited through the cheek and he recovered. It was rather like when I was shot at Turnmills, except that never hit my eye. They found a letter in his pocket saying it was his father who had brought it on himself. The judge thought he was bound to swing but he was wrong.

Public opinion thought Horace had been hard done by and something like 200,000 people signed petitions for his reprieve. It shows what public opinion can do sometimes. He was reprieved but he tried to top himself twice whilst he was in the nick and he wasn't out two years before he died.

People tell me the best Chinese restaurants in London are in Queensway but I don't think I've ever been in one. I was well out from being in one of them back in 1977, when the Wo Sung Wo did for their rivals the Sui Fong. They just turned up with cleavers and swords and three customers got slashed. That was the end of the Sui Fong as the stars of London. It was almost all Wo Sung Wo after that. But they keep themselves mainly to themselves.

4

I suppose the biggest villain in West London was one who was never ever done and that was Peter Rachman, the slum landlord. When he died in 1962 he must have owned near enough 500 properties, from flats to houses to brothels in St Stephens Gardens and round there. He come over after the war and a spell in a Russian labour camp and he started buying up tenanted houses, getting rid of the tenants and letting the properties out again, mainly to West Indians. He wasn't too particular how he got rid of the tenants either. He'd encourage a whole load of West Indians in the next door flat to have all night parties and once he simply had the roof taken off over some people who wouldn't move out of a place in Bayswater. Then he had a whole collection of rent collectors, like Norbert Rondel who'd put the fear of God in you simply by looking at you. Norbert got a few years after he was convicted of biting someone's ear off. He then said he hadn't been properly defended and tried to sue his barrister. He got all the way to the House of Lords but it went against him. It became a famous case in the law reports and he was still trying to get his conviction quashed the last I heard.[1]

Rachman was a friend of both Mandy Rice-Davies and Christine Keeler and he had an affair with Christine. He died when he was 42, and the story is that he'd been humping some girl so hard he collapsed the next day. He was rushed to Edgware General Hospital but he died. He'd got a gold bracelet with all his bank account numbers engraved on the inside. There's another story that he didn't die and the body was switched, so he must be sitting on some island somewhere with JFK and Elvis.

5

If you're a brief in England you're fairly safe from the chaps unless you start doing business with them. That's what made the disappearance of the solicitor Janice Weston, who lived in Holland Park, back in September 1983

---

[1] Rondel v Worsley. [1969] 1 AC 191.

so surprising. She worked for the big firm Charles Russell and when she didn't show on a Monday they raised the alarm. Her body was found up the A1 near St Neots. She'd been badly beaten and the coppers said it was probably with a car jack. Her husband was working in Paris and she'd gone home after doing a bit of overtime on the Saturday. On the table in the flat was her meal not cleared away and she'd left her bag behind. It wasn't sex, because she'd not been assaulted, and it wasn't robbery because her purse was under the driving seat. No one could work out what she was doing up there on a wet Saturday. A few years later there was a story given by a prisoner that she'd been killed by a South London face called 'Chic' Fowler, but if he exists I've never heard of him and no one I've spoken to has either.

It was down at Gloucester Road tube station that someone killed the Polish Countess Lubienska, a very different class from those black marketeers. She'd been a very rich woman and nothing really had gone right for her. Her husband had been killed in the Russian Revolution. Then her son was killed in the Second World War and then she was carted off to Auschwitz. She survived and come to England when, at the end of May 1957, she was stabbed not even late at night, just about 10.15 p.m. as she got out of the train. She died before they could get her to hospital. No one was ever sure who did it. There was one story that it was some Teddy Boys who were around at the time and another that it was political. Sometimes in the nick you heard whispers about who it was did something, but in all the years I was in I never heard a word about her death.

It was funny because a few years before, August 1953 I think it was, there was another case involving a Pole which was never solved either. It wasn't in London but in Bradford and the man was a priest called Henry Borynski. Someone telephoned him, and his housekeeper heard him say he'd go. He just walked out of his home and was never seen again. His housekeeper watched him turn the corner and he just vanished. Never took any money from his bank account either. One story says he went behind the Iron Curtain, but I don't know.

There's always crime at tube stations. There was another over in North London at Finsbury Park in December 1992 when a man, Jonathan Zito, was stabbed in the eye by a schizophrenic, Christopher Clunis. Clunis just went up to him on the platform. He got sent to Rampton and the last I heard he'd started an action against the local council who'd had him in care before the stabbing, saying they shouldn't have released him. I never heard if he got any money. Zito's wife set up a trust to help victims.

In October 1984 Johnny Maile, who was known as Johnny the Flower and who ran a flower stall at Earls Court tube station, was shot dead at his flower stall. He had witnessed Charlie Richardson's arrest after his escape and then he'd given a long account to the papers. There was talk at the time that somehow Charlie had been involved, but I'm pleased to say that at Johnny's inquest the police said there was no truth in the suggestion whatever. They never got no one for that either.

It wasn't exactly a crime, although some people wasn't sure he hadn't been done, but Charlie Taylor, who was a big fraudsman and once was a great mate of Billy Hill's, dropped dead on the tube coming home from giving evidence at the Bailey back in the 1960s. He'd turned grass which goes to show sometimes there is a God after all, like Stinie Morrison said, when he heard one of the coppers who give evidence against him in the case had been killed in an air raid.

One of the most famous cases come in July 1959 just after the police tried to arrest a man at South Kensington tube. It led to a copper being shot dead. What happened was that a German crook, Gunther Podola, broke into the flat of a model and stole some of her jewellery and furs. He also went and took some letters and he thought he could put a bit of black on her. Good for her, she wasn't having any and she called the coppers. They had a trace on her line and the next call came from South Kensington station.

Two coppers were sent to arrest him and, of course, Podola was on his toes. He was chased into a block of flats at 105 Onslow Square. One of the coppers then went in search of help and the other, a Sergeant Ray Purdy, remained on guard. They can't have searched Podola and Purdy must have turned away an instant because he was shot at point-blank range. The other copper was after him at once but they lost him and Podola made his way to the Claremont House Hotel in Queen's Gate where he had a room.

He was traced there and officers broke in. By the time they got him out he was unconscious and after a spell in the nick he was taken to hospital. It's funny. The police was going through a good spell after the killing of PC Summers, but now things turned against them and there was stories that Podola had been beaten up. There'd been a fund set up for Purdy's widow but now the contributions started to dry up.

On anyone's showing Podola was in a mess. There was questions in the House of Commons, because when he come to court he was walking supported by a couple of coppers. There was all sorts of questions being asked, but the Pros said that he'd been behind a door and when that had been knocked down it and a big copper fell on him. Podola had been knocked over a chair and he landed in the fireplace.

Anyway the first thing was that he began saying he couldn't remember a thing about what had happened, and if he genuinely couldn't then he wasn't what they called 'fit to plead'. And if that was right then he couldn't be topped. So they had a jury in to decide if he was faking it. The doctors who saw him was split two each for the Defence and the Pros. In fact it went against him because he went and recognised someone who'd brought him cigarettes in the nick when he was on remand. The jury said he was fit to plead and the second jury had no doubt he'd done it. Topped.

6

It's amazing how things can get out of hand sometimes. When there was a gun battle in Fulham back in February 1968, just a couple of years after the Torture Trial, people was saying how it was a war between scrap metal merchants, but it was nothing of the kind. It had all blown up over Tony Lawrence, who had a site in Waterford Road, not being served after hours in the Queen Elizabeth in Bagley Lane something like two years earlier. He'd got the hump and there'd been a big fight and it all came on top from there on in. Some people were prossed over the fight. Others said they was grasses and should have kept their mouths shut. And then a bomb got thrown into the scrapyard of one of the witnesses. It was after that Tony started buying in weapons and a bit after he got a pull from the police over the bombing. He got the hump even more and it all ended with Tony Lawrence's foreman, Baba Elgar, being shot dead and Tony ending up getting fourteen years at the Bailey for conspiracy to cause a dangerous explosion.

7

Just as legends lived on in prison, so they did in Broadmoor where I ended up. This one was well before my time in 1922. He was Ronald True and there had been a lot of trouble about him not hanging when a young kid swung at the same time. It was always said that he'd been reprieved and sent to Broadmoor because somehow he'd got connections and this kid Henry Jacoby hadn't.

True had been well educated but apparently he'd always been one of those who'd tortured small animals when he was a child. Then he was sent abroad by his family and he learned to fly. He was a conman, really. Took a fellow for a lot of money and was forever passing dud cheques and walking out of hotels leaving the bill. Then he robbed a brass, Olive Young, and took up with a Mrs Wilson, threatening to shoot her if she went out dancing with other men.

One night he just turned up at Olive Young's flat at 13a Finborough Road in Fulham, spent the night with her and clubbed her to death with a rolling pin after he brought her a cup of tea the next morning. The landlady saw him and he give her half a crown as a tip to let the girl sleep on. He can't have been all that mad because he started pawning her jewels. Of course he was nicked in a matter of hours, in a box at the Hammersmith Palace of Varieties where he'd gone for the show. He got convicted but he was reprieved. The doctors said he'd got some mental condition brought on by drug taking and there was also some suggestion he'd got the pox.

He lived on in Broadmoor until he died in 1951 just a few years before I arrived. Even then he was talked about as being the life and soul of the parties they had there. They'd had a concert party, like the end of the pier shows, called the Loonatics or something like that, and he was one of the stars.

You expect streets in Soho or the Gorbals or the East End to have more than one murder take place in them but you don't really expect it in the same street in Fulham. However, in May 1948 in Finborough Road they found the body of another brass, Winifred Mulholland. She'd come down from Durham and had been living in Brixton. There was some story she was going to go to Canada to get married. When they found the body they weren't sure if she'd just fallen off a balcony, or if someone had tried to make it look that way, and then they decided on the second. After that it wasn't too difficult to work out it was a man called George Epton who lived in a flat just near where she was found. At first he said he'd never seen the woman but what he'd done was beaten her with a hammer and a flat-iron for good measure. Later he said he'd picked her up in Piccadilly and taken her home for dinner. Then he'd missed £9 from his pocket and beaten her up when first she said she hadn't taken it and then he'd seen it by her shoes. He said he only used his fist and after he'd given her a couple of blows he then went to sleep and when he woke up found out she was dead. He was another who kept the body for a bit and then tipped it over the balcony. He was lucky and all. They were still talking about stopping the death penalty at the time and he got reprieved.

8

If there's a killing or a failed attempt it's never really squared up. Maybe if something goes on top in a pub or a club, spur of the moment sort of thing, well that's one thing but otherwise it's not forgotten. There's always going to be repercussions even if it takes years. It's no different from them Corsican vendettas in Paris just after the war. Things can run twenty years. If you've got a very strong man such as Billy Hill, well sometimes if he was dealing with minor villains he could call things to order. But not with the big boys.

When I think of it Peter Hennessey's a good example. In fact, he caused so much trouble over the years – even though he didn't know it and he didn't mean to. It went on all over South East London, Kensington and ended up back in South East London again. He was the one who was having that straightener with Eddie Richardson in Mr Smith's Club when Dickie Hart started shooting and I ended up on the murder charge. That started a chain of events which brought down poor Charlie Richardson and ended with me having a twenty.

Then when Peter was at the Royal Garden Hotel in High Street, Kensington, for a boxing evening, he gets a bit drunk and he begins causing all sorts of trouble. He was trying to start a whip for some charity of his own which wasn't the charity of the evening and he ends up dead on the floor, stabbed 60 times. Paddy O'Nione, who was known as Paddy Onions, was meant to have been the one who stabbed him, him and Jimmy Coleman who was related to the Arifs were put on trial. I'm pleased to say they was chucked. But things didn't end there.

Paddy Onions had done a good bit of work with me over the years. He was with us in Manchester when we did a tie-up job on Mrs Post and also in that job with the Gibbs brothers in Bedford when I was done. Paddy's mother was with Jock Robinson, Jock the Fitter. Anyway Paddy gets shot in November 1982 outside a wine bar his son owned in the Tower Bridge Road. Someone had had a go at him a few months earlier and shot him in the face but he'd survived.

Then the man who was said to have done him for five grand died in a police cell. He'd been in Parkhurst with Peter's brother Mickey and he was a wild man. He was going under the name Jimmy Davey but his real name was Bowman. He'd had a brother who was killed and that was when he'd changed it. Earlier Jimmy had done a six for cutting a copper. Anyway he was arrested in Coventry and when the coppers come to take him back for questioning over Paddy they say he lunged at one of them. He was put in a choke-hold and he lost consciousness and the doctors switched the machine off a couple of weeks later.

It was in the Ranelagh Yacht Club in Fulham that Johnny Bindon stabbed Johnny Darke to death in November 1978. This Darke wasn't related to the good fellow who was a friend of Mickey Green but a man who'd been a grass for years. I'm glad to say the jury ruled it was self-defence. A solicitor come to see me in the nick about giving evidence of what Darke was like but they never called me, which was just as well. In none of the cases where I've given evidence for anybody has it worked out well. John did better than having me give evidence, he had the actor Bob Hoskins tell the court what a good guy he was.

John was a good actor. He was in that film *Poor Cow* which was such a success and in lots of TV series but he went on the river and become unreliable. Women thought the world of him, though, and he lived with the model Vicky Hodge for years. They say he could hang a few beer glasses – half pint ones, mind – on his thin and thick. I never saw him do the trick myself. In the end though he got AIDS.

It seems so long since he died; October 1993 it was. I went to the funeral, of course.

9

It was down in King Street in Hammersmith that the Welsh girl, Elizabeth Jones, got picked up for the killing of a taxi-driver, George Heath, who'd been found shot at the beginning of October 1944 on the Great West Road, near Staines. Someone first found a wallet and took it to the local nick, and then about an hour later another geezer found the body. The man had been shot in the back. He was a driver for a car hire firm and his Ford saloon was missing. It wasn't Brain of Britain work to reckon that if you found the car you'd be close to finding who killed him and the car turned up in Lurgan Avenue which is just off the Fulham Palace Road, funnily enough not far from where Virgin Publishing's got their offices. Three days later a copper on his beat found it and then it was a question of waiting to see who came near it. The man who did was a US army deserter called Karl Hulten. When they nicked him he'd got an automatic pistol with him, and at first he said he was an officer in one of their parachute regiments. It shows how bright he was. He gave his correct regiment – not that it would have taken long to find out – just promoted himself. Then he give varying stories about how he'd got the car and finally he said he'd been with a girl called Georgina Grayson, so he went and took the coppers to where he said she lived in King Street.

Georgina turned out to be Elizabeth Jones. She said she was a cabaret artiste but really what she did was a bit of strip-tease, funnily enough in the Blue Lagoon in Carnaby Street where that Margaret Cook (see Chapter 2) worked. They had her in and released her but then she met up with a man who was a War Reserve copper, and she said if he'd seen what she'd seen he wouldn't be able to sleep at night. Then it all fell out.

Hulten had told her he was a Chicago gangster when she met him at a coffee stall in Hammersmith and they went on a four-day spree of nicking cars and doing a bit of blagging. He went and knocked a girl cyclist off her bike and stole her money and then he told Jones he wanted to rob a taxi-driver, because I suppose he thought the man would have more money than the girl he'd done. In the meantime they done another girl – hit her over the head with an iron bar and got five shillings. Big time.

It was after that they flagged down Heath and got him to take them down the Great West Road to where the Chiswick flyover is now. The driver was boosting his price, because he'd wanted ten bob for a short ride when he'd seen a man in American uniform. He must have thought he was a soft touch. It was down the road that Hulten shot Heath and the girl took over the driving.

When it came to the trial they went against each other. She'd written him a letter from Holloway, blaming him and saying he'd forced her to go through Heath's pockets, which the authorities intercepted, and that really did for him. It didn't help her much because he tried to put the blame equally on her. She got a recommendation for mercy but of course they was both sentenced to hang. Eva was in Holloway at the same time as her, doing six months for hoisting.

It was a big thing. For a start it was about the biggest trial at the Old Bailey since the war had begun and a lot of women didn't have much time for the girl. There was even one factory in Scotland which threatened to strike if she didn't swing, which wasn't going to do much for the war effort. She got reprieved eventually but he swung. I read somewhere once that Winston Churchill, who was the prime minister then, thought it was wrong and she should have been topped as well. A few years ago they made a film about the case.

George Sewell, the father of the actor, always fancied himself as having sort of stood back to back with Darby

Sabini. He liked to be known as the Cobblestone Kid and he was a receiver and a grass as well. He give evidence against Jimmy O'Connor, who was known as Ginger, when Ginger was done for the murder of a coal merchant in Hampton Road, Kilburn, in 1941 in a robbery which went wrong. He said Ginger had sold him some tom which came from the robbery. Ginger swore he hadn't, but he still come within an ace of being topped. The authorities must have had some doubt because he was reprieved the night before he was due to go. Later, Ginger went and married the brief, Nemone Lethbridge, and for a time he did well writing plays. He come out of North Wharf Road, Paddington, which itself wasn't the best bit of a very bad area.

10

The Towpath murders in 1974 were the ones which created the biggest stir in West London and it was one of them cases that, because the authorities never released the name of who they suspected, there's been so much speculation that it was a very famous boxer. Personally I've never believed it was, but that's the trouble. If people don't say what's what then rumours are bound to fly and they hurt innocent people.

Whoever done them became known as Jack the Stripper; after Jack the Ripper, of course. This was a bit clever because most of the girls were found naked and, if they did have the right man, because he worked in a paint-stripping business. The first girl was a thirty-year-old brass called Hannah Tailford, who went under a number of names. She turned up on 2 February 1974 in the Thames near Hammersmith Bridge. Most of her clothes were missing but her stockings were still around her ankles. She'd got bruising on her face and her knickers were stuffed in her mouth.

Hannah seems to have been mixed up in the porn business. Although she lived in South Norwood, she worked out of a flat in Victoria and when the police looked there it had studio lighting equipment and a camera. Most brasses who aren't actually on the street keep a book with the names and telephone numbers of their punters – the black book they call it, maybe after black for blackmail – and that was gone. So the police thought it might have been a client who'd done her to stop her leaning on him. Funnily enough, though, when it came to an inquest there was an open verdict and since there was no evidence to show that she was murdered the police didn't go on treating it as a crime. That was despite there having been another brass done in the area in the meantime.

This time it was at Duke's Meadow. You hear it on the television when they're having the Boat Race 'Oxford is leading as they come to . . .' The new girl was Irene Lockwood and she had been strangled. Again the police thought she might have been blackmailing her former punters. She'd provided the alibi for a man accused, a year earlier, of murdering another brass, Vicki Pender.[2]

Then the body of a third brass turned up when Helen Barthelemy was found a couple of weeks later, a little way from the river in a driveway near Swincombe Avenue in Brentford. She used to hang around the Jazz Club, in Westbourne Grove, which had a big black clientele. Four of her teeth were missing and she had traces of paint spray on her body – which made the police think it might have been kept in a paint-strip shop before being dumped. There was traces of sperm in her mouth and they worked out she had either been orally raped or that she had plated the man before she died. Now they reckon that if one man was responsible for the murders the blackmail theory was wrong.

The next day the coppers must have thought their Sundays had all come at once when Kenneth Archibald, a caretaker, walked into Notting Hill police station and

---

[2] On 2 July 1963 Colin Welt Fisher received life imprisonment for the murder of Vicki Pender at her flat in Adolphus Road, Finsbury Park, on 19 March 1963. The prosecution alleged both had been taking drugs.

confessed to killing Irene Lockwood. He worked in a club for Joey Cannon of the big Notting Hill family. There were some good men amongst them but Joey was a toe rag and a grass. After the fight in Frith Street he'd been hired by Spot to shoot Albert and Hilly, but I'd taken the gun off him and explained the facts of life. Then he was meant to be the bodyguard to Spot, but he wasn't there the night I did Jack outside Hyde Park Mansions. Just as well, it was probably the best day's work he didn't do in his life. He was the one whose eye I tried to put out in Pentonville.

Anyway Archibald fitted the bill. He told the coppers he must have lost his temper and strangled her. Then he'd taken her clothes off and rolled her into the river. He'd taken the clothes home and burned them. Unfortunately there was no way they could tie him to the murders of either Tailford or Barthelemy so that theory went out the window.

They put Archibald on trial at the Bailey for just Lockwood's murder. Of course, at the trial he took his confession back and luckily for him the jury believed him. They was only out 40 minutes. Just as well for him since he didn't do it. What seems to have happened was that there'd been a break-in at the club and he thought he had been in the frame. He'd gone and drunk six pints of beer before he walked into the police station and made this moody confession.

It was funny, though, that whilst Archibald was in custody the murders stopped. It was as if the killer knew what he was doing and wanted the blame to fall on someone else. Maybe the brasses were just being a bit more careful in their choice of clients, but I can't believe that's right. Most of this lot weren't what you might call quality and they'd need to take what was going. The next murder come on 14 July when Mary Fleming, a mother of two, was found in a sitting position near a garage in Berrymead Road, Chiswick. She too was naked and her denture was missing. Again, someone had come in her mouth and traces of paint spray were on her body.

The next one turned up in the November, when Margaret McGowan was discovered on a pile of rubble in a car park in Hornton Street near Kensington High Street. Again spots of paint covered her body and she had a tooth missing. She'd been missing a month. The last of the killings was discovered in the middle of February the next year, when the body of Bridie O'Hara was found behind a store-shed off Westfield Road, Acton.

There was links between all the killings and the police went back to the theory that it had to be one man. The girls was all small and they all worked the Bayswater-Kensington beat. The scientists could tell from marks on their bodies that they'd all been suffocated before their clothes was taken, and they was convinced the girls were kept in a store before their bodies were left out to be found. Finally all were found in or near the Thames.

The coppers managed to trace the paint on the bodies to a covered transformer near to a paint-spray shop on the Heron Factory Estate in Acton. Whilst they were still working on the 7,000 odd people who were employed on the estate in June 1965 a married man from South London topped himself, leaving a note saying that he was unable to stand the strain any longer.

What is certain is that the killings stopped and the police put it about that this man was in fact Jack the Stripper. Then the rumours started, because it was about this time that the boxer Freddie Mills topped himself or got took out in Goslett Yard, a little turning off the Charing Cross Road near where the Astoria is, and just round the corner from where Freddie had a sort of Chinese restaurant club. There was all sorts of stories about that. Some people said he did himself because the place wasn't doing well; that he was half gay and couldn't cope; that he was upset because he wasn't being used as a commentator for boxing on the radio no more; that he was being leaned on for protection and wouldn't pay, or that the Twins did him or that the Chinese Triads did him. Pick any theory you want.

Then there was the story that he was the Stripper. The tale went that some coppers knew it and told him he had to top himself because they didn't want to have anyone arrest him. That's the story that's grown up, and despite the fact that it all happened near enough 40 years ago it has never really gone away.

There was another view that the Stripper was an ex-copper who was a heavy drinker. The story went that he was married but had always fancied brasses. He'd taken up drinking when he wanted to go to the plain-clothes division and they wouldn't let him, so he'd resigned. But who knows?

There was a funny killing just nearby in Ealing. You don't get too many done with crossbows but Diana Maw had a six-inch crossbow bolt in her head when they found her body on the landing outside her flat at Stanley Court in Woodfield Road in July 1988. At first the coppers thought she had been shot by a mugger, but then it emerged that she'd been stalked by her killer for the previous six weeks. There was a photofit issued of a man but then the coppers changed tack and a woman interior designer, who'd been a former girlfriend of Diana's bloke, was charged. There really wasn't any evidence – something like a single witness and you know how chancy that can be. The Pros said the woman was obsessed but when it come to it they offered no evidence against her.

The only other crossbow murder that I can think of offhand was that girl, Debbie Lee Parsons, who got done over in North London back in June 1990. She'd been working in a sauna and, that evening, had meant to go over to help out her boyfriend who had a restaurant. She never turned up and when they found her in Epping Forest she'd been done with a crossbow. They never nicked anyone. One suggestion was she'd been trying to put the black on some serious people, but once again, who knows?

Paddington had some big families and some good clubs and it was here that Jack Spot thought he might pitch up and open a club or two after him and his wife Rita put me and the others away for slashing him. He got it wrong. Firstly, Billy Hill had taken up with Gypsy Reilly and she was done in March 1957 for trying to put a man's eye out in the Miramar Club, in the basement of the Miramar Hotel in Paddington, which was really Spot territory. What was she doing over there in the first place? It was Hilly just letting Spot know he was around. She got acquitted. It was one of Patrick Marrinan's last defences before he got thrown out from being a barrister because of his association with Billy.

Then Rita goes into the Market Club in Shepherd's Bush and some people take objection to her being let in. The club gets busted up. After that in June 1958 Spot opens up the Highball in Lancaster Gate on the money Rita's made from selling her life story, but that got done over badly the next month. And a month after that it was burned down. And that was it for Spot – he was off to Ireland.

There was some seriously tough clubs up in Notting Dale. There was one run by Ernest Bell. Him and his sons fell out with another local family, the Smiths. The feud was another which ran for years and in May 1960 James Smith got shot. The end result was that Ernest Bell's son, Ernest junior, and a neighbour picked up seven and five respectively for manslaughter.

The most curious of all those clubs in West London was the Celebrity at 10 Ruston Close. It was run by Charlie Brown – no connection with the man who had the Railway down the East End to my knowledge. Charlie was the doorman of a club in Kingley Street in Soho and when it shut down for the night he'd send the punters to the Celebrity. What the punters didn't know was that 10 Ruston Close was really 10 Rillington Place, where John Reginald Halliday Christie had murdered all those women back in the 1940s. The club got raided and there they all were in the room where Christie had done the girls. It got closed and I think the whole place was torn down and rebuilt without No 10. The other story about Christie is that apparently the pathologist who did the post mortem of someone who had been topped was allowed to keep bits and pieces of him for medical research, and the one who did Christie kept his orchestras for his students to work on. Not that much different from keeping the kids' parts, like these hospitals have done, when you think about it. Even murderers usually have families.

Before the place got torn down, though, people had been paying half a crown to see the rooms where the bodies were, and someone was done for nicking the door handle of the place.

Keeping the bits reminds me of that dog, the prison governor Lawton, after Harryboy Jenkins had been hanged for de Antiquis (see Chapter 4). He woudn't return Harryboy's clothes, saying he'd been topped in them but here were the buttons, braces and shoelaces which they'd taken away in case he'd harmed himself and cheated everyone out of their fun. It was rather like that case long ago when a man hanged himself in a cell in Sunderland. The widow wanted his clothes but the Poor Law Guardians said they were entitled to them. Eventually the Home Secretary was brought in and he told the magistrates they had to give the widow back the clothes, less the cost of the application and postage.

12

I see that Bert Wickstead died in March this year. He'd been a Commander at the Yard. I never come across him myself, but I knew scores who did and they included some very good men such as the Tibbs family and Alan and George Dixon, Reggie Dudley and Bobby Maynard. He was reckoned to be just about the King of the Verbal. When Reggie and Bobby got done for that Epping Torso Murder, when Billy Mosley got cut up and Mickey Cornwall got killed as well, Wickstead was asked by a defence brief if he had a tape recorder when he was interviewing the men. He said he did. Then when he was asked why he didn't have it on, he replied he was a police officer and police officers didn't use tape recorders.

I was never verballed too bad but it was what your barrister was terrified of, and nine times out of ten there wasn't anything you could do about it. What you'd have was a trial within a trial, with the jury out of the room to see if you could get the evidence ruled inadmissible. The judge would listen to what the coppers had to say about how you'd come to make these remarks which did for you. The coppers would say how they'd written down the answers not at the time but at the earliest opportunity, and that could be up to nine hours later in the canteen. Then they'd be asked if their colleague had helped them recollect and they'd say it was completely independent. After that they'd be asked how the reports were word for word the same and the judge would interrupt and say 'That's because they've remembered accurately'. They could have been interviewing you for hours and the questions and answers, when they was read out, took about five minutes at most. Why was that then? That was because they'd only written things down which was relevant. Later on, when they got a bit more savvy and sussed no one was believing them, the coppers would agree they'd compiled their notes together in the canteen, but said they'd only been refreshing each other's memories.

Of course nine hundred and ninety-nine times out of a thousand the judge would let the evidence in. You got a second bite at the cherry because the jury would come back in and you'd go through it all again and sometimes, thank the Lord, they'd think the coppers had made it up. I could never understand how people believed that serious and experienced men like me and others would start to confess the moment we got to the nick. Or we'd make some damaging remark on the way in the car and then say nothing at the station. That dog Lawton said once in a judgement that it was not surprising that men like us would want to unburden themselves. Something like that.

One of the most famous cases over verbals was that case of Whiteway who murdered a couple of girls – he'd been a family friend of one of them – on the towpath down at Teddington. He was done by that copper Herbert Hannam and it was always thought he'd verballed him up rotten. Two teenage girls were found raped and murdered at the end of May 1955. I think some of the old-time coppers got a kick out of being in the witness box and fencing off the briefs' questions. It's like, if they'd come from different circumstances, they'd have been briefs themselves and Hannam was one of them.

What happened was that Whiteway signed a confession and then denied it. What else was he to do, and old Peter Rawlinson, who was later Lord Rawlinson, put Hannam through the paces about how he'd got the confession out of the man. It was the first time any brief had ever done it to a copper, with that much success anyway, and he did open up gaps in Hannam. Even some other coppers thought Hannam had been pushing it too far, but the jury wouldn't have it that it was totally manufactured and they weren't out 50 minutes. After that there was a bit of an outcry, with the public writing in and saying it was wrong to make these attacks on coppers.

It took years before the public realised that coppers made things up. What was so wrong was that people who'd defended you and knew what was going on just turned a blind eye when they got on the bench a couple of years later. They were the ones who could have put a stop to things if they'd wanted.

13

I suppose the murder which had so much to do with West London, even though it didn't take place there, and which has lived on in people's memories is the Hanratty case. It's funny how so few cases are known by the victim's names. You think of Heath, Cream, Craig and Bentley, Hanratty or even the place where it happened, but you don't often know of the other way around, certainly not if the fellow was caught. I suppose the Hulton and Jones case was known as the Cleft Chin Murder because the taxi-driver had a cleft chin, but who knows his name?

The reason it's so tied in to West London is that it was at the Vienna Hotel in Sutherland Avenue, Maida Vale, that Peter Alphon was staying on the night of the killing. He was the first person picked up for the murder of Michael Gregsten and the rape of Valerie Storie, his girlfriend, back in August 1961. It's also the area where the characters who put Hanratty away come from. Whoever done the killing picked the pair up when they was in a car parked up at Dorney Reach near Slough. He made them drive around and eventually shot Gregsten at a place called Deadman's Hill on the A6 and then he raped the girl and shot her, paralysing her.

The car was found abandoned in Ilford and they had an Identikit out in no time. A landlord in Finsbury Park said it looked like a man staying there. It turned out to be Alphon, who'd booked in there the night after the murder. When the coppers questioned him he said he'd been in the Vienna. The police took a statement from him and let him go. There was no things like police bail then.

Then the gun turns up down the seat of a No 36A bus and the next thing that happens is that the manageress of the Vienna finds a couple of cartridge cases in a chair in Room 24 which link up. Then the manager on the night of the killing, a man called Nudds – well that was one of his names – who'd been given the hoof by now, said that Alphon had been out late on the night of the killing and was looking nervous when he saw him the next morning. The trouble was that Alphon had been in Room 6. The fellow who'd been in 24 had signed in as J. Ryan, which was a name that Hanratty used. Then what does Hanratty do but ring up the copper in charge and say he was in Liverpool, but he's not coming in because he's wanted for housebreaking.

He got nicked in Blackpool and Valerie Storie picks him out on an ID parade. She'd already got it wrong when Alphon had stood on one earlier. There was also a prison grass who said Hanratty had confessed. I know the Pros used to use them more in those days, when juries didn't know any better, but even so they must have realised they had a weak case. However, Hanratty's alibi went belly up, and even though well into the trial he said he was in Rhyl – and in fact it looked as though he could have been – it didn't do him no good.

Over the years people have been on to Alphon to say he done it, and from time to time he half says he's done it and then he goes and says he hasn't.[3] One of his stories was that he and Charles France, who was meant to be a friend of Hanratty's, had framed him. Charles was the one who told the police about Hanratty saying that shoving things down the back of a bus seat was the way to hide stolen tom. The Pros made a lot of it but you'd think every jewel thief would know about that. France had been the manager of the Rehearsal Club in Archer Street, but he'd got the sack and was making a few bob marking at the snooker club under Jack Solomon's offices. He topped himself between the verdict and Hanratty being hanged. He left a number of letters but the authorities have never released them.

Hanratty's friends and family have always fought and fought to get his name cleared and just about every piece of evidence for the Pros has been discredited in one way or another. But the DNA test put paid to that – it looks as though it may have been Hanratty after all.

---

[3] See for example the *Sunday Times*, 14 May 1967.

MAD FRANK'S BRITAIN

INTRODUCTION

W hen I get an offer of work nowadays it's usually
television or radio, but if a friend or friend of a friend
wants some real help I'm always happy to try and give a hand.

I had a call a bit ago from a man I've known for years.
His son was on his toes. Could I help? Of course I said yes,
I could. Get the boy to ring me. I'd only seen him once to
my knowledge. It's like if you're in a coffee shop and
someone comes in and the man you're sitting with knows
him. You get introduced and that's it. Next I hear the boy's
in London and he's lost. That's the thing with mobile
phones. The thing is it's a Saturday and this kid is red hot.
It's a case of the most dangerous man in Britain, until the
next one comes along that is. I give him directions how to
get to South London and a bit later he's on the blower
saying he's lost again. He's been asking people directions
but you know how it is. Everyone you ask's a stranger
himself and if he isn't he's got a cleft palate. The kid says
he's in a motor outside the Post Office in King's Cross just
opposite the station and I tell him to stay where he is – get
the motor round a corner, of course, and I'll come and get
him. What else could I say? I didn't want to frighten him

saying he was even hotter there with the police cleaning out the druggies and brasses and their pimps.

I hop a lift and we was there inside ten minutes. There's a little turning just up the Euston Road and we double-parked there. I go round to the Post Office and there's the kid. We walk back to the car I'm in and suddenly I see two coppers. It was just one of them things but all they did is walk on by. I rushed him back to his car and got in it with him, but he said it would be better if he followed on behind and we got home safe.

In a way things turned out well. When Marilyn had gone she'd taken the kitchen cupboards and things with her and though I'd been down to IKEA and got some new stuff, I hadn't put it up. Funny thing is, now she's living in the same block where the Twins was nicked. So, the good thing was I wasn't having people round because I didn't want them to see the state of the place. There was no danger of my family or friends coming round. I'd been fobbing them off for months. The other good thing was the kid was good with his hands and he had stuff on the walls in no time.

We parked his car – it was a ringer, of course – in a side street and every morning we'd be up at half seven, quarter to eight to move it into the car park. Fiver a day it is. We'd load up with silver and shove it in the machine. If you'd left it in the side street you'd have been ticketed for sure. 'Greedy bastard,' the wardens would think. 'Too mean to pay for the park round the corner', and they'd have blistered it straight away. The car was safe enough during the day in the park but if you'd left it there at night it would have been stripped. Nice car it was. Not too flashy and not too beaten up. No one would raise an eyebrow at it. Like that advertisement all those years ago, 'Not too little, not too much.' So once it was dark we moved it back to the side street where kids wouldn't be so likely to break in. Moving the car was the dangerous part. There's a great big modern police station in Manor Place near where the Baths used to be, took over from the old nick Carter Street in Walworth.

There's squad cars going up and down Browning Street the whole time; that and coppers on the beat. I said to the kid he should walk on ahead and I'd follow a few yards behind. I'm often seen on my own in the road but there's never anyone with me regular, so if they had see another person they might have wondered. With me behind, if they had come looking I could have gone steaming in like a terrier and tried to cause enough trouble for him to get away. I'd never have succeeded and I'd have been nicked for certain, but it might have given him that bit of time if there hadn't been too many of them. I'd have had to try.

You couldn't invent what happened next. All my life and all the people I've known and they've known and the kid and his friends have known it's never happened to them. One morning we go to drive the motor round to the park and the boy said, 'Oh, Christ'. I thought what had happened was someone had banged into it or scratched it but what's happened is someone's nicked the front plate. Why not both? Well, I suppose whoever done it had the first one off and then there's a twitch on the curtain and they don't fancy hanging around for the second. I reckon someone must have wanted the plates for a short time job.

Along the Walworth Road you can buy anything. Anything that is except plates. We walked up and down it until we come across one shop which said they could make some up but not until the next day. Then the fellow tells us there's another shop in a little cul-de-sac where they might be able to help, so round we go. Blow me, on the pavement there's a man talking to two coppers. I was all for walking on by but the kid says, 'No they've seen we look like we're going in the shop, if we spin off they might get suspicious.' First thing the woman wants to know is have we got the insurance certificate? I pat me pockets. 'Blind me, I've left it behind.' 'Have you reported it?' Then she says she can't do it 'til the next day anyway. And so out we come. We got a cab back to the shop that sent us to her and there's another man there. He'll fix us up by four in the afternoon.

So I get a lift to go back that afternoon but now there's the worry the woman may have done her duty and given the station a bell. 'Officer, these two men . . .' Maybe there's some law that shops who make up plates have to report things. I thought the best thing was to go back on my own and if there's trouble then the driver can at least get back to the flat and get the kid out. But no, it goes sweet as anything. 'Do you want me to wrap it?' the man says. 'Yes, it's better with it on the bus.' I don't let on I've someone waiting across the street. As soon as I got back the kid went straight down and put it on. The driver was terrific, she'll know who I mean.

You might think with my connections it would be easy to ring up someone, even one of my boys, for plates but I didn't want to know. It wasn't the money, though someone would have charged three or four hundred. Speed was of the essence. One of my boys could have rung someone up but he might not be there and then he would have to ring someone else and before you get it right there's half a dozen people know I want some plates. There was always the worry that the law might have nicked the plate and it was a get up.

I liked having the kid around. I don't smoke and he didn't and I don't drink in the house and nor did he. A couple of times he went away to do a job here and there but I didn't ask, though he told me one had been a right touch. Then he says he'd better be getting on. I didn't ask him where he was going. It's better you don't know then it can't slip out somehow. The last night we sent out to the local Italian, *La Luna*, and had a decent meal brought round with a good bottle of wine; a sort of celebration, and we had a good laugh about the plates. And he was gone the next morning. He wanted to pay me but I never took a penny. Putting the cupboards up was good enough. I had a nice card saying thanks and I had a Christmas card as well.

BRIGHTON AND THE SOUTH

I was never in Lewes Crown Court myself. Not in the dock, anyway. I've watched a few trials from the gallery and when I did a bit of work for Harry Rogers from Brighton all those years ago, like torching a rival bingo place in Eastbourne, I also had a look at a juror at the court. You only had to get hold of one in them days although you always tried for two as a sort of insurance.

The building itself is really pretty if you like that sort of thing. It's in the High Street and just about opposite the hotel, The White Hart, and people reckoned that after the Old Bailey it had had some of the best cases in the country. One of them was Tony Mancini. No relation of the Tony Mancini who got done for topping Hubby Distleman in the Palm Beach during the War. This one was a bit before the War, in the '30s. It all came on top because of someone leaving a body in a trunk at Brighton station. I've said before how I can't understand how people think they're going to get away with that sort of caper. It's a bit like those mafia killings where they leave the body in the boot of a car at Miami airport. Two days later and it's going to smell like anything. Of course you can't do it at stations now with security. They don't have lockers or a left luggage now for a start. But even when you could, and though it's not as hot in Brighton as it is in Miami, it was going to get the stationmaster in soon enough.

What happened was a bit of bad luck for Tony. At the beginning of June 1934 someone went and left a trunk made out of plywood in the cloakroom at Brighton and by the middle of the month it had started to stink. They opened it, of course, and there was a woman's body without a head and legs. Maybe that's why they called it a trunk murder, just joking. They had that pathologist, Bernard Spilsbury, down to have a look and he decided it was a girl about 25 years old. A bit later they found her legs at King's Cross station. There was about 700 women reported as missing at the time but they never managed to identify the girl. She'd been in the club so it could have been a boyfriend or a botched abortion, but why leave the body at the railway station?

Over the years there's been quite a few heads rolling around. After Billy Moseley was killed in what they called the Torso case, his head turned up in a lavatory in Islington, during the trial I think it was. Then, a bit after Jimmy Waddington was killed in Romford over some trouble or other, someone chucked his head at the local nick one night. In New York, when the Westies killed someone in the bit they called Hell's Kitchen, they took his head for a farewell tour of the bars giving it a drink and putting a cigarette in its mouth.

Anyway, as for Tony he'd kept the body of his brass, Violette Kaye, in a trunk at Kemp Street near the station. His story was that he'd come home and found her dead on the bed and since he'd got form he didn't think anyone would believe him and he'd panicked and hid the body. He was defended by that brilliant brief Norman Birkett who told the jury to 'Stand Firm'. When they give a not guilty, Birkett says to Tony 'Go home and be a good boy to your mother', which shows how soft some briefs can be even if they're brilliant.

Years later, I met Tony in a club, in Brighton. His real name was Cecil Louis England and he had almost more aliases than I had Christmasses at home – Antoni Pirelli, Luigi Mancini, Hyman Gold and Jack Notyre were some of them. He was born in Newcastle back in 1908. He'd been on the fringes so to speak for years. I half remember he was mixed up with Darby Sabini and his mob at one time. He worked as a counterman and bouncer in pubs all over the place. I'm not sure he wasn't a dancehall gigolo at some time either. A bit before he died he went and told some reporters he had actually killed the girl. He got a few quid for his story but I don't hold with doing that. Keep your trap shut in cases like that is my motto. Up in the North there was a fellow a few years back got acquitted of killing a brass but he gets put away for something else. He's another who can't keep his trap shut; he tells a screw all about how he did it. They can't do him for the murder again, but they did him for perverting the course of justice and he got a six.

The club where I met Tony was owned by Bud Flanagan of The Crazy Gang, on the front it was, near the derelict pier rather than the big one near the Aquarium. For the life of me I can't think of its name at the present. Lovely place it was; lovely baby grand piano. Bud opened it just before the War – 1938 or 1939. It ran for years.

Over time you get a few women who stuff their leavings in trunks. They've usually had a bit of help though. One was the brass in Paris called Gabrielle Bompard. At the end of the nineteenth century she and her boyfriend killed one of her clients. He got topped and when she was released she became a bit of a celebrity, being invited to people's boxes at the races and things, so idolising the likes of us is nothing new. Then a few years later there was a woman, Maria Goold, who did a woman in Monaco. This time her husband was helping her. They were about as incompetent as I was the time I did a smash and grab in Oxford Street just after the War and the car wouldn't start. They thought

241

they'd take the body to Marseilles and ship it to London. When they got there the body wasn't just ripe, it was leaking blood. They both got a guilty but, when it come to it, she died of typhoid and he topped himself.

I suppose the most famous was that Winnie Judd who got known as The Tiger Woman in the 1930s. She did a couple of her girlfriends and went with their bodies from somewhere in Arizona to Phoenix. Made sure they arrived at their destination so to speak. Same as the Goolds in the South of France, someone noticed the trunks were leaking. She was going to be topped but they reckoned she was insane. I read she was released a few years ago.

I've written about Brighton before and how it was an open town with that Chief Constable Ridge who rode on a white horse up and down the promenade. He was a good drinker and he'd be in the clubs with the best of them. I remember there was a Chief Constables' meeting in Brighton one year and Ridge had a whole lot of them in a club where I was, all of us having a drink together. Didn't do me no harm.

But Brighton wasn't too good for a number of people I've known. Alf Gerard was one. He died down there when he was on the run. He'd been a good man in his time; a good crook and a good cook and if you was in a spot he was one to have at your back. Funnily, like so many of us he wasn't a tall man, just a big one. For a time he had a restaurant, The Blue Plaice, south of the river. There's so many stories about how he died – cirrhosis is one of them and that he choked on a lobster is another. I like the second one better.

Then there was Alan Brown. He didn't die down there but he just about signed his warrant. He didn't turn up from release and when he was found down in Brighton at Britannia Court it was with what they said was the biggest haul of amphetamines they'd found so far.

People who say the death penalty stopped killing is mostly wrong, I reckon. I suppose there's an argument, and as a rule we didn't go out with guns on a job, so I suppose to that extent they're right, but take the case of Victor Terry. The day his friends get topped he goes out and does a bank job and shoots the guard.

The people who were topped were also my friends – Flossie Forsyth and Norman Harris. They'd gone down for killing a bloke down Hounslow way; kicked him to death with those shoes they called winkle pickers. There was all sorts of petitions but it didn't do them no good. Flossie got topped at Wandsworth and Norman at Pentonville in November 1960. That was the way it was. Normally if you was one side of river you would be hung in Wandsworth and the other Pentonville, but by then the authorities didn't like topping two people in the same case in the same prison on the same day anymore. Not like in Canada where they literally used to tie them together and hang them back to back.

Anyway Vic hears about them on the radio and sets off for Worthing with a couple of mates, and when the bank guard tries to take the shotgun away from him it goes off and he's killed. Vic and his girlfriend then went on to Portsmouth where he bought himself another shotgun and from there it's off to Scotland. There's rewards out all over the place. I don't know what he was thinking because he gets in a taxi there and tells the driver to keep the change from a ten-bob note when the fare's only a tosheroon. With his cockney accent he must have stood out like a camel in a back garden.

After that it's only a matter of time before him and his girlfriend gets picked up in a hotel in Glasgow and he's brought back down to Sussex. Vic runs a diminished responsibility defence. Says he's possessed by the spirit of that New York gangster, Legs Diamond, and so he's not responsible. There's two doctors say he's genuine and the one for the pros who says he isn't, of course. What the judge does is, instead of reviewing the medical evidence out loud, he gives the jury a copy of the transcript of what the three doctors have said which he's marked in red ink where he thinks something's important. When Vic gets a guilty there's an appeal and he's unlucky. The Court of Appeal says the judge was wrong but what it was all about was whether Vic was pulling the wool over the trick cyclists. It depended not on them but on what the jury thought of Vic. That was the end. Poor old Vic was topped at Wandsworth just like his mate Flossie. Twenty-sixth of April 1961 it was. They did things much quicker then than they do now.

I'm too lazy to go on holiday really. I think the last time I went abroad was with Marilyn to Mexico and I can't say I did enjoy that. I go down to Brighton a lot. The neighbours were good to Doreen and my boy Francis when I went away for what turned out to be twenty years. There was no ostracising them even though there was a lot of publicity. But, there again, I'd been a good neighbour. There was never any trouble with any of them and I kept the house looking nice, of course. It was the first place I had which had a bath of its own. Doreen lived there all the twenty years and that's where I first come out to when I was released. It was sold when she died but Francis still lives in the area with his family. I go down quite often. There's a little jazz band plays of a Sunday at the back of Montefiore Road. Good they are too. I listen to it and put a few bob in the hat. One man come across when they was having a break and said, 'Do you remember me, Frank?' Blow me, it was the man who had the corner shop all those years ago.

I used to be a good swimmer, after all I saved Billy Murray when he got into trouble near what's now the Oxo building when we was kids, but I've given it up now. I swam a bit after I come out from the twenty but I've always been a bit worried about showing my back with the scars on it from the floggings. I don't want people upset or staring for that matter. One thing the school did was take us to the Lambeth Baths every couple of weeks or so. If you didn't have a costume they rented one for you from the attendant.

I don't recall getting lessons from any master. It was more or less left up to the older boys to show the younger ones how. We used to walk past my Gran's in Cornwall Road, and when she knew I was coming she'd throw me a ha'penny or perhaps even a penny – mouldies they was called. On the way back I'd treat myself and friends to the bread pudding you got home made from the corner shop in Oakley Street – it's Bayliss Street now. It was gorgeous. Her house is gone now but it was there until ten years ago, when it was one of the ones which had to come down for the Jubilee Line extension.

For the life of me I still can't understand why Freddie Foreman went and admitted the killing of Frank Mitchell and tipping the body out into the Channel. There wasn't any need. I don't think he got much dough for it and it didn't help his reputation any for it. It didn't help when it looked as though him and the grass, Albert Donaghue, stood and looked at each other on the escalator. I know that can be done by filming them separately and then cutting the film but it didn't do no good.

Mitchell's body's never been found but the one that turned up near Newhaven was that of Scotch Jack Buggy. He'd been done in the Mount Street Bridge Club in Mayfair where he'd been causing a bit of grief trying to get the money back for my friend Roy James from the Train. Roy had left it to be looked after whilst he was away and the money seemed to go for a walk. Jack, who'd been in the nick with Roy, was just trying to help. For his pains he was shot, wrapped in a carpet to get him out of the club and then bound with baling wire and tipped overboard. He floated up just about Derby Day 1967. Years later a couple of people was charged but their case was chucked out at the Bailey.

Of course that's where Lord Lucan is said to have disappeared, over the side of the Newhaven–Dieppe ferry after he was meant to have killed the nanny, Sandra Rivett, by mistake for his wife. It seems amazing it's back in 1974 his Lordship went AWOL. Mind you, I'm not sure he's not still alive somewhere like South Africa. He could easily have been hidden away. There's still a lot of people who don't believe he's dead. There's also a lot of people who don't believe that JFK and Elvis are gone either, or that singer Jim Reeves, so maybe they're all together somewhere.

If you went the other way out of Brighton you'd get to Shoreham on the way to Worthing. That's where the body of a biker turned up in the harbour. Just down the road was Shoreham and in April 1973 a body come out of the harbour there with its legs tied to a block of concrete. Clive Olly, the fellow's name was, and he'd been reported missing at the beginning of March. It turned out he was a member of the Mad Dogs Chapter of the Hell's Angel's (Brighton). The Mad Dogs seem to have been a bit of a poor relation because they didn't have bikes of their own.

It seems Olly'd had it off with the girlfriend of Brian Moore, another Mad Dog. Moore had put Olly in a van and hit him with a truncheon and then thrown him in the harbour. Him and another fellow was convicted of the murder. They had a girl with them and she was convicted of manslaughter, but that got slung out on appeal.

One man got a re-trial over what went on in a hotel in Brighton. Not the usual sort of hanky-panky the town's been famous for, but when the jury got sent to a hotel overnight some of them put together a ouija board to get a bit of advice. The fellow was Stephen Young and he was meant to have shot Nichola and Harry Fuller at their cottage in Wadhurst in 1993. Harry used to boast about how much money he had on him and the pros said that was why Young went and shot him. He was in debt but the day after the topping he went and paid six grand into his bank account. They never found the gun but it seems the bullets were like some the coppers found at Young's place.

The jury goes off to the Albion Hotel for the night and around eleven o'clock four of them go to one of their rooms and since they don't have a ouija board they put together the letters on bits of paper. They get a wine glass and the glass moves to the letters spelling words out. It says it's Harry Fuller and so they ask it, 'Who killed you?' and it says, 'Stephen Young'. After that they ask it how and where the money is and things like that, and then it tells them to vote guilty. Anyway although they agree to say nothing about it one of them blows it all out at breakfast. They still find Young guilty but one of the other jurors gets in touch with a brief. Now one of the problems is that the Court of Appeal can't ask jurors what's gone on in the jury room once they've retired to consider the verdict but it's a bit crafty. The court says the jurors weren't in the jury room at the time and so it can hear what went on. They quashed the conviction and give Young a re-trial, but it doesn't do him any good. It's another guilty.

It's funny how you think if people are part of a firm then the only harm that's going to come to them is in the way of business. It's not right of course. Take Charlie Clarke who was with the Twins. He wasn't generally liked. He kept a room for Ronnie as a hideaway for him in Walthamstow. He'd been a grass for years but Ronnie Kray never found out, which was just as well for Charlie. He also set up Lennie McLean, 'The Guv'nor', to get a beating. They was going to strangle Lennie with chicken wire but he escaped and as a result Charlie had to pay good money in compensation.

He was another who moved to the seaside and later he had one of his legs off. In March 1989 he's stabbed to death at his home in Dover. Apparently he surprised a kid, Shane Keeler, when he was screwing the place. Funny, because Charlie had been a good cat burglar himself in his day. Keeler pleaded guilty to manslaughter on the grounds of diminished responsibility but he still got lifed off. Charlie was 71 at the time.

* * *

I suppose one man who did more harm than any three judges put together was that pathologist Bernard Spilsbury. When I was young he was the great God in the courts. All he had to do was turn up and say some man had done it and the jury was knocking their heads on the box saying, 'Yes, Sir Bernard, of course Sir Bernard'. But now it seems that he wasn't necessarily all that great. One of the men he did for was Sidney Fox and there's been an argument about whether he was right in that case ever since.

Sidney and his mother were a pair of confidence tricksters but by October 1929 they was well down on their luck and they'd got rooms in the Metropole in Margate. I think things was so bad for them that she was wearing all the clothes she had on top of each other. She'd been ill and they put it about they'd been visiting the graves of his brothers in France. Her story was that she was the widow of William Fox, founder of Fox's Flour Mills. What she was really was the widow of a railway signalman. It's true her boys had been killed in the War, but they'd never been near the graves. Sidney liked to be called Captain Owen Smythe.

Just before midnight one day he runs down the stairs saying there's a fire in his mother's room and a fellow comes and pulls her out. It seems like the armchair and the carpet was on fire. Poor Sidney was so upset they had to give him a shot of something to quieten him down. What he was worried about was a pony that was in his mother's bag. They found the bag but there was no dough in it. His story was that he woke up, smelled burning and tried to get in his mother's room but got beaten back.

He was nearly home and clear because the doctors at the inquest reckoned she'd fallen asleep and part of a newspaper had caught fire and set the place alight. What did for Sidney was that he'd taken out insurance on her for £3,000, which was good dough then, and the policy was due to expire about twenty minutes after she snuffed it.

It all came on top for him when he tried to get the money from the insurers. They got in Spilsbury who reckoned there was no soot in her lungs and she must have died before the fire started. By this time Fox was inside for getting credit by fraud and he never come out. What Spilsbury reckoned was that he'd given his mother a few doses of port and then he'd strangled her. He'd then gone and shut the doors before he raised the alarm. He said he'd done it to stop the fire spreading, which isn't a bad answer. But the really funny thing was that if you strangle someone you can't help not breaking what's called the hyoid bone and this hadn't been broken. Spilsbury said he had seen bruising but the other pathologists, Sydney Smith and Keith Simpson, said it wasn't there when they saw the body and it could have just been putrefaction. They reckoned the jury convicted just because Spilsbury was Spilsbury.

Fox never appealed and he got topped in April 1930. I suppose it come out right because a bit before Mrs Fox died Sidney had been having it off with a widow and she'd woken up and found the gas tap on. He'd persuaded her to make a will in his favour and then insured her as well. She give him the chuck after that and he's walked off with her jewels. He got a year-and-a-half for that. Some people think he did his mother because the old girl had Parkinson's and he was practising euthanasia, or 'old dear topping' as we call it. But even years later Smith wouldn't have it as murder.

I think people in insurance companies have got smarter over frauds these days. You used to be able to have a fire and there was no questions asked. Provided you didn't do it too often everything was all right. Mind you when Joe Wilkins and me set fire to the place off Wardour Street we was lucky to have that hooky assessor help us out. Of course, some people don't go about it the right way. I saw one in the papers where the husband got a good payment from the insurance, going about like he was crippled for life, and then he goes and leaves his wife. She's so cross she shops him. There's a story, I don't know if it's true, of an assessor who hounds an Irish builder who's slipped off a ladder and can't work anymore. The man's convinced the builder's a fraud but he can never catch him going ten-pin bowling or anything. Anyway the fellow gets a big pay out in the High Court and he's being wheeled away when the insurance assessor runs up beside him and says he'll never stop chasing him and he'll get him one day. The man just smiles and says, 'It won't do any good. I'm booked to go to Lourdes next Monday.'

Being in a wheelchair doesn't stop you working though. In fact it can be a good cover. There's just been a woman in America, Ernestine Williams, 65 she was, run a gang of pickpockets from a wheelchair. She'd got high blood pressure, she was arthritic and she'd had kidney failure, but you have to admit she was game. The team worked from Miami up to Atlanta and they was clearing $1,000 a day each. She'd started off as a family business using three of her kids and one of her grandsons and she'd expanded. She taught her fifteen dips the tricks of the trade, like who you should nick from. She reckoned elderly whites in supermarkets was the easiest touch. She used to trade the credit cards her team nicked with crack cocaine for the kids she was using. By the time she was nicked herself it was reckoned she'd cleared hundreds of thousands of dollars.

Going back to Spilsbury, he started out his career as the pathologist in Crippen's case and he went on from there. Eventually he topped himself. He'd had a stroke as long back as 1940 but it still didn't stop him working. Then he had another couple, and then at the end of 1947 he went and gassed himself in his workroom. I reckon it's impossible to say just how much harm he did to people over the years.

In my time there wasn't that many policemen killed. I think until the early 1950s there'd only been four in the previous ten years. I know people will say one is more than enough but it shows how violence had grown in recent years. There was a copper, Evan Davies, shot whilst questioning a couple of youths in a Cardiff air raid shelter at the beginning of the

War. They was never nicked. Then there was a William Avis only a couple of months later in February 1942, while he was searching a house in Bognor Regis. Then come Nathanial Edgar who killed Donald Thomas in Southgate in February 1948. There'd been a lot of burglaries about that time in the area, which had some big houses, and the copper was patrolling Wades Hill. Edgar was found in Clapham with a Luger under his pillow. It was funny how he went wrong. He'd been captain of his school's cricket team but once he'd been called up at the end of the War he become a deserter. He'd done six months in detention and he was on his toes again. He was lucky they was discussing abolishing hanging at the time because he'd have swung for sure otherwise.

But the one which created a big stir was a kid who'd escaped out of Feltham Borstal in June 1951. I think it was because he was so young. He'd been bullied there and he did it to show that he was as tough as anyone else. Derek Poole he was. He come from Chatham and he got himself back there and barricaded himself up. He killed a copper, Alan Baxter, before he shot himself. There was something like 200 coppers at the siege.

Portsmouth was the place we'd be taken to go over to the Island. We'd go down on the train and then let out at Portsmouth Harbour and have to walk in our handcuffs across to the boat with everyone watching. Sometimes there'd be a chain looping through the cuffs. Then it was in a big cabin to ourselves and at the other end a coach to take us to the nick.

Portsmouth was also where Alfie Hinds' father did a big raid in the 1930s. He got the cat for it and it ruined his health. It was also the place where the fellow Harold Loughans, who was missing a few fingers on one hand, was meant to have strangled a woman who ran a small hotel. Mrs Rose Robinson she was and she ran the John Barleycorn in Commercial Road. At the end of November 1944 she'd been found strangled and there was scratches across her throat. Whoever done it got away with a bit under £500. It was one of the few mistakes Spilsbury made that ever got showed up. He was appearing for the defence that time.

Loughans got nicked because he was heard saying he'd done the woman but although Keith Simpson give evidence that even without his fingers he could have strangled her, the jury at Winchester disagreed and when the case was reheard in London Spilsbury gave evidence. What he said was that it was impossible for Loughans to have killed the woman because when he had caught his hand in the machine that took off his fingers, in trying to pull away he'd also done in the muscles in his arm and he wouldn't have had the necessary strength. Loughans got a not guilty but within a couple of months he got a five for screwing. Then he got a fifteen years PD. When he come out in 1963 the *People* had done a series on the barrister J. D. Casswell who'd prossed him back in 1944 and in it they said Loughans had been lucky to get away with the murder.

It's as I've said so many times. The likes of us shouldn't go near the libel courts – Darby Sabini, Jack Spot and me are just some who've all come croppers. Anyway Loughans had a run at the paper though I don't know where he got the money; in those days you didn't get legal aid for libel and it was illegal for a brief to take it on and share the winnings.

Joseph Moloney was the brief for the paper and he was the one who later prossed us at Parkhurst. It was a jury trial and he was able to put Loughans' form to him and he called Simpson to repeat what he'd said nearly twenty years earlier. He'd kept his notes all those years. Anyway the jury said they reckoned Loughans had done it, and they was right. He'd got stomach cancer and a bit before he died he walked into the paper's offices and made a confession saying he hadn't long to live and he wanted to put things straight. They took a photo of him writing out that he'd killed Mrs Robinson.

There was another man who had a deformed hand who said he couldn't have done a murder. He was Ronald Lewis and he went down for killing a nurse in 1969. He pleaded guilty and now he says his brief persuaded him to and he was shielding someone else. The last I heard he was still inside. He'd had a bit of trouble with his home leaves. First he tried to top himself in a hotel in October 1989 and then he'd gone to Grendon and it turns out a woman who'd been seeing him when he was in Leyhill complained he'd been round to her home and made threats. He says he never did but it's been enough to have him kept inside. He may be out now and I hope he is but, if so, it's only recent.

It was down the road in Southampton that Lady Docker lost her jewels; back in 1958 when I was doing time for Spot it was. She'd left about 150 grands-worth of stuff in the boot of Sir Bernard's Roller. They'd left about £20,000 of stuff behind. The assessors put up the usual ten per cent. It was a well-planned job. The boot wasn't forced so someone had a key. Bernard said he thought there was only two keys in existence, one with him and the other with his man-servant, but there must have been three. Billy Hill went to see Her Ladyship and said he'd do what he could to get the stuff back. This time he didn't manage it like he'd managed for Gordon Richards when that good climber Billy Benstead nicked his racing trophies.

Hilly had met her at a party at Gennaro's in Soho when his book come out. Albert Dimes had given her a slap when he went into the upstairs room and found Billy giving her one. Albert could be a bit straightlaced and he thought it showed disrespect since her husband was downstairs.

I suppose the biggest murder case there's been in South-ampton come in the 1920s when a fellow, William Pod-more, did a man who worked in the same company, Vivian Messiter. What had happened was Podmore, who was a sort of an all-rounder, had applied for a job as a salesman at the Wolf's Head Oil Company. Sensibly he didn't give his own name and he was calling himself William Thomas.

Once he'd got his feet well in, he starts writing up fictitious invoices and collecting the commission on them. When the company sends Messiter round to see what's going on Podmore kills him with a hammer and hides the body behind boxes in a garage.

There's no way you can just leave a body like that and, of course, someone sniffs it out. There wasn't a lot of evidence against Podmore – a few letters which tied him in – and he had a brief who was really big at that time, Edmund O'Connor, who appeared at the inquest. He wasn't a barrister, just a solicitor but people said he would have been as good as Marshall Hall if he'd gone to the Bar. He defended my friend, Freddy Ford, over some gambling clubs and drinkers he was running.

In those days – in fact up to the Lucan case – an inquest jury could name the killer and that worked as a sort of committal proceedings. O'Connor was brilliant; he managed to get a verdict of murder by persons unknown and Podmore walked. Like getting chucked at the magistrates' court it didn't count always as an outright acquittal and they could charge you if there was new evidence. Podmore didn't last long on the outside because he picked up a six months for an earlier fraud in Manchester and then on his release he collected another six months for robbery. Then he was nicked again for the murder, and this time they'd got those so-called cell confessions made to other prisoners.

From what I read of the committal proceedings O'Connor produced a trick really worthy of Marshall Hall at his best. Podmore was quite a small man, not much taller than me, and O'Connor challenged one of the doctors to try to move the 'body' of Messiter, a much bigger man. He'd got one of Podmore's friends to play the part. All the doctor succeeded in doing was to rip the buttons off the man's shirt. It must have been a bench of lay justices. A stipendiary wouldn't have allowed that sort of thing. O'Connor also did a lot with the jail evidence, but the beaks committed Podmore and when the trial come the pros had its house back on the bricks. There was an application for a reprieve but the Home Secretary said the there wasn't any doubt. By the time Podmore was topped, O'Connor was reported to be in Paris looking for a so-called mystery enemy of Messiter who might have done it. More likely he was off drinking and gambling because that was the downfall of him. He ended up penniless and doing a seven for fraud.

MIDDLESEX AND HERTFORDSHIRE

When I read how the police complain they can't get convictions and juries throw cases out I think they've only got themselves to blame. Over the years when I was young there wasn't really any point in challenging police evidence. Juries who come from the middle classes had no experience with policemen except that they saluted and told them the way to Piccadilly Circus when they was lost. Then over the years, little-by-little, it come to them that the coppers lie same as anyone else. What's worse the magistrates and judges are as much to blame. The defence briefs knew coppers were lying but when they got up on the bench themselves it was the same old story, 'Brave old PC Jones, why would he lie, members of the jury? Have twelve good policemen risked their pensions and prison conspiring against Fraser?' If they'd put a stop to it back in the 1950s and 1960s then things would have been a lot better.

Take that thing with notebooks. Coppers used to say notes had been made up independently with no help from their mates and yet they was word for word and full stop for full stop the same. How could they be independent? So they got over this by saying they'd refreshed each other's memory in the canteen some five or six hours after the interview. There's a story about that top brief who's got a junior brief behind him who's meant to be taking notes. The judge misses something and asks what a witness has just said. The man behind the leader didn't get it down and the senior brief gets up and says, 'I'm afraid he hasn't written down what the witness says but he and I will be compiling it in six hours time in the wine bar.'

I think the first person really to go on the attack in a murder case over verbals and statements was the man who became Attorney General, Peter Rawlinson, when he was defending Alfred Whiteway in what they called the Towpath Murders in Teddington back in 1953. Here was the man on trial for his life and people said that Rawlinson had gone in a bit strong against the copper Bert Hannam. He was cross examining him over Whiteway's confession and he didn't half lay into him, saying he'd more or less composed it himself. It didn't do Whiteway any good. He was on trial for the murder of a young girl and there was another one who'd been killed as well so he wasn't going to get any change out of the jury. But Rawlinson was one of few who dared give it a real go. It was a bit of a funny case altogether. The copper who found an axe which Whiteway was supposed to have used took it home for himself. When he was asked why he'd done it he said it was the rule that if a driver found anything in the car he could claim it.

Hannam may have got away with it that time but he come a cropper with the case over that doctor, Bodkin Adams, who was meant to have done his patients in at Eastbourne. Mind you, more or less the whole of the pros' witnesses come a cropper in that.

What's come out over the years is that it wasn't just verballing but they had a thing called scriptwriting. If there was a bank job or a hi-jack, something like that, then there'd be one officer who's job it was to write up a script giving all the coppers their parts to play. The result was when it come to court they couldn't make a rick by one of them saying he could see DS Smith the whole time when DS Smith was saying he was round the corner. Then when it was all worked out, the copper would give the script to each of the others and they'd write up their parts in their notebooks.

You don't associate Potters Bar, at the start of what used to be called the Great North Road, with murder but there's been a couple of what you could call good murders there and in Wheathampstead, which isn't that much further up the road. That wasn't solved and nor was one of the ones from Potters Bar.

The first was back in 1947 when a fellow Albert Welch, who was known as Snakey to his workmates, left a note for his wife Phyllis on the kitchen table saying he'd gone for a walk and wouldn't be back for tea. They lived on an estate which is near where the rubbish tip is nowadays on the way to the M25. He wouldn't be back at all. Next day she told her neighbour, who was a retired copper, and she reported him missing. He'd taken his ration book and identity card with him but he didn't turn up for six months until a kid was looking for golf balls in Potters Bar Golf Club, where Tony Jacklin used to be the assistant or the pro, and turned up a hand with manicured nails. Bit by bit as they dredged the pond up come Albert, or what's left of him. Someone had cut off the head and burned it. They managed to get a fingerprint which identified the bits as Albert but Mrs Welch wouldn't have it that it was her husband. She never went to the funeral saying it wasn't him they was burying. She said he'd got rough workman's hands but his mates said he always wore gloves to protect them. I suppose it's possible the fingerprint was wrong but if it was no one can say where Albert finished up. No one ever found out a reason or who killed him.

Funnily there was another murder at Potters Bar Golf Club about eight years later, when a boy called Michael Queripel hit a woman, Elizabeth Currell, with a tee-marker.

He was only seventeen and he got detained. You'd think that Queripel was such an unusual name you'd never hear of two of them in your life but in 1993 a little girl called Stacey Queripel was found in the woods near where she lived in Bracknell. At first they thought she'd caught her necklace on some branches and strangled herself but then they realised someone else had done it. At one time they arrested her mother but she was released. She told the coroner that she'd gone to check on Stacey and found her missing so she'd got her lodger to go searching for the little kid with her. No one was ever prossed over it.

The case in Wheathampstead was one of those real mysteries which ran for years. A girl called Ann Noblett was a seventeen-year-old who disappeared at the end of December 1957 on her way home from a dancing class. Some men with their dog found the body a month later in some woods about seven miles from where she'd last been seen. She'd been raped but what was really odd was that she'd been kept in a deep freeze. The family got a detective agency to look into things and three years later they lit on a man who was wanted on a fraud charge and had left the country. He said it was nothing to do with him. Him and another man had a refrigeration company. I think the family tried to bring a private prosecution but it never got off the ground.

Private prosecutions for murder are rare but not as rare as it used to be. What's more common now is that families, where they don't like a not guilty verdict, bring a civil action where they don't have to prove so much. O. J. Simpson's a classic example and there was one in Scotland not long ago, as well as the one brought by the family of that doctor in St John's Wood. But there was a proper private prosecution over the death of a girl in Sussex back in August 1948. There's always a danger with them. Either the Director of Public Prosecutions can step in and offer no evidence and there's nothing you can do even if you don't agree or, worse probably, if the fellow gets acquitted you can be liable for a lot of dough.

Anyway Joan Woodhouse's body was found by a fellow in the grounds of Arundel Park. There was a neat pile of clothes by the body. She'd been dead about a week. They thought she'd been raped and strangled. She'd been living in the YWCA in Blackheath but originally she come from Barnsley. She'd arranged to go and see her father over the Bank Holiday and that's where she told her roommate she was going but instead she goes down to Sussex. The copper Fred Narborough was in charge and he could never get enough together to make an arrest. Of course they fancies the man who found her. The family instructed a private detective and the Yard then got that Reginald Spooner to have another look. He says there's no evidence but the family isn't satisfied, and that's when they took out a private pros. The DPP steps in and this time he does go on with the case. Two hours later to great cheers the magistrates say the man hasn't got a case to answer and that was the end of things, although the family did try and get what's called a Voluntary Bill of Indictment, which means a case goes straight to a jury. That's what the pros did in the case of the prison officers they said had attacked the Birmingham Six. This time though the judge wouldn't grant one to the Woodhouse family. It seems that Spooner thought since a big relationship had broken up she'd committed suicide and that accounted for the neat pile of clothes, but Narborough never agreed with this. He always reckoned a man would speak up out of turn in a pub somewhere and then he would have him. But if there was such a man he never did.

It's not often you get two killings in exactly the same place. Well, I suppose you can if you're thinking about Chicago or some club or other, maybe a beach or some moor, but off hand I can't think of many like that here. One place was an exception and that was Rooks Farm at a place called Stocking Pelham out in Hertfordshire. That's first of all where Muriel McKay ended up, poor woman, and then a kid called John Scott gets done there as well.

The McKay case was famous. It was one of the first kidnappings for ransom there'd been in Britain and the coppers didn't have much experience in dealing with it. That and the fact the Hosseins didn't have lifts going up to the top floor, certainly not as far as crime went. For a start they kidnapped the wrong woman. Two brothers, Arthur and Nizamodeen, from Trinidad they were. Arthur was quite a good tailor down the East End. They'd been watching television and seen Rupert Murdoch who had bought the *News of the World* talking to David Frost about what a beautiful wife he had and what he was worth, and they decided they'd kidnap her and get a million quid for her. They went to Fleet Street and by chance saw Murdoch's right-hand man, Alick McKay, get in a blue Rolls and they mistook him for Murdoch. They follow the car out to Wimbledon and went back and kidnapped his wife.

They took her out to the farm and no one quite knows what happened to her. She needed medicine and she may just have died because she didn't get it. They sent off the demand for a million and there was drops of money arranged. I think they even had a million printed up in fake notes. Anyway it didn't do no good but the Hosseins was using their own car to go on the run for the money and a copper took the number. After that it was just a question of time and the next morning they picked them up. Both of them got life. I knew them in prison a bit. They kept themselves to themselves. They weren't that popular for having done that to a woman but I never heard of anyone giving them a seeing to. They're still in I think. No one ever found out what happened to Mrs McKay. The best bet is they fed her body to the pigs but they never would say.

After the brothers had been put away, a publican down the East End, Tony Wyatt, bought the place. Seventeen-and-a-half grand it cost him back in the early 1970s. Anyway, in September 1972 there's a wedding reception for his sister-in-law, Avril Hurst, and during the festivities John Scott gets himself done with a sickle. It was a bit of a funny case. The holes in the kid's body is plugged up and he's dressed in fresh clothes and taken to Ranelagh Road, out Leytonstone way, and left in a van. Schoolkids found him a day or so later which must have put them off their lunch.

Tony Wyatt was done for the murder. He said he'd only killed Scott because he was being offensive to the women at the party and Scott'd attacked him when he'd tried to get him to go. He pleaded guilty to manslaughter at the Bailey and was defended by that good brief, Michael Corkery. He got three years and was out just after one. He never even lost his licence. What made the whole thing so funny was that he couldn't have moved the body all on his own and yet no one was done with him, although that copper Bert Wickstead was involved and he used to pride himself on how he solved cases. At the time Wyatt was a big witness for the pros in the case Wickstead was running against the Tibbs family and there was a number of other witnesses at the wedding. The farm was sold again and this time it was worth around £46,000.

BROADMOOR

Back in 1953 I got taken from Durham straight down to Broadmoor in a taxi. It was a long drive in the days before the motorways and there was an overnight for the screws which meant overtime. That pleased them and paid for a part of their holiday. No one told me where I was going. I just found out when I got there. They didn't actually talk to me on the journey. I went straight into Block 6, the refractory block, and I stayed there the whole time. At one time you did every day of your sentence if you was in Broadmoor; there was no remission. The benefit was the regime was easy there. But as years went by prisoners tried to get in and out of Broadmoor and back to prison just before the end of your sentence. If you was doing say a seven then you did a couple, went to Broadmoor for a couple of years and back to the nick. You'd be out in four years and eight months if you'd lost no remission and it had been an easy run.

Generally you worked your way up through the blocks and apart from Block 1, which was a sort of assessment block at the time I was there, the lower the number the more the privileges. There was some wealthy people in

Broadmoor over the years and in Block 2 some of the men had others being sort of batmen or valets for them, giving them a few bob a week. Even if I'd got out of refractory I'd never have done that.

I was in Broadmoor just after John Allen, the so-called Mad Parson, had escaped. He got the name because he'd been part of the Broadmoor concert party, a sort of end-of-pier show, and had dressed up as a vicar for one of his parts. He'd managed to hang on to the collar and the stock front and he climbed out one night, jumped into some telephone wires which broke his fall and he was off. November 1947 it was. There was a big hue and cry but he was clever. He wore slippers and carried his shoes and the bloodhounds followed the scent to a pond where he'd thrown them in and the dogs got confused. I don't think bloodhounds are that bright myself. Some got used in the hunt for Jack the Ripper and that lot got lost. Anyway, Allen gets a lift into London from a fellow. That happened then. If you saw someone walking by the road it was courtesy to offer them a lift. It can't happen now. Women are generally too frightened. Men ought to be as well. I read of a case the other day where some girl made a speciality of getting herself lifts and then telling the men that if they didn't give money she'd go to the police and say they'd tried to rape her. Back then vicars in particular were respected, and if you saw one then of course you'd stop. Allen was dropped off at South Kensington tube and he made his way to Paddington and got a train to Devon.

He was out two years before he got nicked up St John's Wood way. He'd been working in a baker's. Back in 1937 he'd been some sort of chef when he killed the little girl of one of the women he'd been working with. Nothing sexual or anything like that. He just got in a temper because the mother had been chosen to bake some cakes in preference to him. Up till then he'd been devoted to the kid. He got the death penalty and was reprieved and sent to Broadmoor. He'd been in the hatch twice already before he killed the girl.

There'd been a few murders in St John's Wood about the time he escaped. One was a brass and another was a woman beaten to death in her shop one lunchtime and, of course, Allen was in the frame. He was put on an ID but he was never picked out. He got sent back to Broadmoor but they only kept him another couple of years. By then he certainly wasn't mad. When he was back inside he applied for a rebate of tax he'd paid whilst he was working on the run.

I remember one of the times when Alfie Hinds escaped, the papers got hold of Allen for his comments about what he would be doing if he was in Alfie's position. He wrote a book and all. He'll be well in his eighties if he's still alive. Several people got out of Broadmoor and stayed out, but there was one who come back. He'd been sent there in the 1880s, James Kelly his name was. He always talked about escaping and that's just what he did. He joined the merchant navy and went to America. Then at the end of his life he came back and demanded to be let in, said it was his home. He'd been out 39 years. It dwarfs Ronnie Biggs really. And he was meant to be mad and all.

I suppose the really big man who was in Broadmoor just before me was Ronald True. He'd been the one who'd killed a brass down Fulham way and got reprieved. People said it was because he was well connected, as when a poor kid called Jacoby, who's never had any sort of a life, kills an old girl in her hotel, he swings. I've written about both the cases before.[1]

True had been the sort of King of Broadmoor of his day. He'd been another leading light in the concert party. People were always speaking about him. He died in 1951. He'd been there 28 years, happy as a sandboy. There was talk that he knew some of the Royal Family, and that counted a lot even if it wasn't correct. People was very snobbish in them days. If you was Sir Charles Brown or Sir William Smith then people looked up to you no matter what you'd

---

[1] See *Mad Frank's London*.

done. There wasn't any of these knighthoods for sport or acting you have now. I think Stanley Matthews must have been the first. You wouldn't have got one for rowing up and down a river in them days. Maybe it was Gordon Richards, the jockey. There used to be a joke on the music halls, 'If they made Gordon Richards a knight why can't they make Wigan a pier?'

Another toff who was in Broadmoor a bit before me was Thomas Ley. You don't get too many times when a former cabinet minister, even if it's an Australian one, gets done for murder. But that's what happened a bit after the end of the War. November 1946 it was when the body of a bloke named John Mudie was found in a chalk pit down in Surrey.

Really Ley's story was a good one. He'd gone from here with his parents to New South Wales when he was eight, back in the 1880s, and had been a paper boy. He'd left school at ten and become a junior clerk in a solicitor's and he'd managed to work his way up and qualify. He even had his own firm, and by the time he was 25 started to go into politics. He got into the State Parliament and then wanted to go for the big time. There was a whiff about him even then. His opponent claimed there was bribery involved and he disappeared when he was on the way to a meeting with Ley.

Then there was another bit of trouble. Ley was a director of a company and when that got investigated the man who was causing trouble disappeared over a cliff top. Then there was another man died, with Ley a bit too close. I suppose he was really a serial killer, not for kicks but he just cleared people who was a nuisance out of his way. Anyway this time enough was enough and they kicked him off his Parliament seat and he came back to England. He'd got a middle-aged mistress by then; Maggie Brook was her name. He tried to get a sweepstake off the ground and did a good bit of profiteering in the War.

By the end of the War his girlfriend was getting on a bit. She was 66 and you'd have thought getting on for retirement from it all, not looking at other men. But Ley got the idea in his head she was having it away with his son-in-law and then later with a barman called Jack Mudie. I don't suppose for a minute she'd had it away with the son-in-law, and all poor old Mudie had done was just speak to her. But it was enough to do for him. Ley recruits a man, Lawrence Smith, and together they find out Mudie's address, lure him to Beaufort Gardens where Ley is living and strangle him. Then they take the body to a chalk pit near Woldingham.

It's not that long before the body's discovered. The trial was a big one. Lord Goddard, the man who it was said had two pairs of trousers with him when he give someone the death sentence, was the judge. The story used to be that he had to change because he'd come as he was saying the words. His family denied it but, like Mandy Rice Davies said, 'They would, wouldn't they'. My friend Alfie Hinds, who was up in front of him more than once, used to say you knew he'd lost interest in your case when he started picking his nose.

Ley ran a number of defences and that top pathologist Keith Simpson really got on Goddard's wick by saying that it was possible Mudie had topped himself. I don't know how he come to work that one out. Then there was another Aussie who come along to say he'd tried to do a screwing at Beaufort Gardens, had found a man tied up and he'd pulled on the ropes. God knows where they found him and how much he must have been paid to say that. It didn't do Ley and Smith no good whatsoever. They both was sentenced to death – I don't know if Goddard had three pairs of trousers that day. Ley was going completely round the bend by then and a bit later he was found insane and sent to Broadmoor. That was what saved Smith. They couldn't really top him if the man who'd started it all was reprieved and so he was lifed off. Ley didn't last long. He had a brain haemorrhage within a few months. That was the case where a neighbour of ours in Howley Place, the all-in wrestler Chopper Sims, give a bit of evidence. You could see him at the Ring, Blackfriars and the other shows before the War. It wasn't his real name of course.

Ronald True wasn't the longest inmate in Broadmoor by a long chalk. A lot of people lived a long time there, if they kept out of the refractory block that is. One of the reasons people did is that they didn't have any worries. Everything was done for them. The other reason was the air was so clean. The place is just on the edge of Windsor Forest. When Allen was in there was more than 50 inmates over the age of 75. There was a fellow, Peter Murphy, who'd been in Broadmoor 55 years when he died at the age of ninety. He played the drums in the band they had. That was in the 1930s. Then again just before me was Frank Smith who was there from 1893 to 1947.

Bill Giles was the oldest man in Broadmoor. I'd gone by the time he died in March 1962. He was 87 and he'd been there over 75 years. He'd been sent there in 1886. The place hadn't been open 24 years then. He'd set fire to a hayrick and that was the last he saw of the outside world. He was so small he was kept in the women's wing for the first five years until they decided he was big enough to stand up to the violent men in the main block. That's where he stayed. He was the best floor scrubber they ever had. People did come and see him for the first few years but gradually he outlived them all. I don't suppose he was dangerous for years but there again he wouldn't have been able to cope outside. Just think, he was in during the Boer War let alone two world wars. He was there before there was proper electricity and the motor car. He must have been taken there in a horse-drawn van. When he died, there was spokesmen saying how people used to play tricks on him, nailing his bucket to the floor, and how he enjoyed it saying he'd have them expelled. Just like he was a schoolmaster. They give him a new suit each year and a birthday present. There was stories about how he corrected new nurses if they got the routine wrong. Made him out to be a proper little character. But what a life for the poor devil. Now he'd have had probation.

Another big thing happened when I was there and that was the death of a kid, John Berridge, from cyanide poisoning. He'd been in a few years after shooting his parents in Pembroke Dock back in 1959. Now how did he get the poison? Or who give it him? There was all sorts of rumours flying around. Of course, we all fancied the screws, but when it come to it the coppers reckoned it was either one of the inmates or that he topped himself. A whole load of inmates give evidence and there was a lot of talk about how easy it was to get poisons at the time. There was also talk that he'd been blackmailed over tobacco debts. It seems like someone had shoved the cyanide into chocolates, just like in an Agatha Christie book, and John had picked them out.

There was another even more fantastic story. Young Berridge had been in the RAF and the reason he gave for topping his father is that whilst he'd been in Germany some fellow speaking perfect English had asked him to be a spy for the Russians. There was a bit of boodle in it and he'd agreed and told the man about some practice bomb or other. When he come home he told his father and the old man said he was going to report him to the authorities. That's why he blew him and his mother away. No wonder they put him in Broadmoor. Anyway one story which come out at the inquest was that he'd had a parcel which he said had come from the Russians and that it contained cyanide.

My friend Timmy Noonan, who was with us on the Parkhurst Riot, was one of the witnesses. The jury went and decided it was suicide. Seventeen of them there were. For once no one could say I'd had anything to do with it. I was on Block 6 like I've said and this took place on Block 4.

I've said before how I was advised there was two sorts of medicine they give out, one which put you to sleep and one which just about put you to sleep permanently, and most of the people in the refractory were on one of them. We'd be woken at seven and slopped out and then it was down to breakfast. There was a series of tables and benches cemented into the floor so the inmates couldn't use them as weapons, and you had the equivalent of plastic spoons to eat with; some of the men just used their hands, shovelling it in with both of them. The screws sat at one end of the room so they could watch us. You'd have three or four men on each table. The screws would supervise breakfast and once that was cleared away we sat at these tables until it was time for what they called airing court, which was our half-hour's exercise. When you went on exercise you walked in a sort of courtyard where the walls was smooth so you couldn't injure yourself by rubbing your face against them.

A lot of the men were just slumped over the table with their heads on their arms and they only moved when it was medicine time. They'd come to life and then they'd slump over again. Then there was lunch and the same thing happens until it's tea and then we went back to our cells at seven in the evening. And then it was the same the next day and the one after. If you wanted to go to the toilet you had to put your hand up and go under the supervision of the screws. If you weren't mental when you come in, there was a fair chance you soon would be.

In fairness the screws weren't bad. They never tried to provoke me. They knew there was nothing wrong with me and I behaved myself. There wasn't a minute's trouble from me. I was there for a rest from the prison screws and the prison screws was having a rest from me. So, I got some privileges. The screws would have the morning papers and they'd hand the linens out for those who wanted to read them. The trouble was if someone who was really daft got hold of it first then when it was your turn it might be in shreds already. So they was good. They'd let me have the paper first so's I could read the sports. The other good thing was they put the radio on. Now that was unheard of in prison at the time.

As for treatment I never got none but then, as I say, I wasn't ill. Some of them were getting electric shock treatment which was popular in them days. The men was in fear of the next dose. There had been talk earlier of me having it but fortunately, what with the fractured skull I'd had when I was a boy, that went away.

All in all though it was better than prison. The food wasn't bad by prison standards, not good but not that bad either. There was none of that cell work sewing mailbags we all hated so much. There couldn't be – you couldn't leave the inmates with needles. They couldn't give you bread and water, just a bit more of the liquid cosh. Visiting was better too, about every fortnight and it was at a table, not through glass. It wasn't far for Eva to come, and you could get more letters. She was terrific, she was always writing in, keeping up the pressure, making sure they remembered there was nothing wrong with me.

People today would be appalled, but that was how it was on that block fifty years ago. Jack Rosa was in there when I went in and he pulled a bit of trouble and got sent back to refractory so I had a bit of company. He was still there when I left.

Things got a lot better over the years and there was people who set up Broadmoor's League of Friends so that relatives and friends of the prisoners could get a lift to and from the station. They'd also go and see people who didn't have no visitors. It went belly up for one woman visitor, Rita Fry. She and her husband were both volunteers but what does she do? She goes and falls in love with one man and ends up under the patio. The man she fancied was Paul Beecham who'd put four bullets into his father, another nine in his mother and then shot his grandparents as well. That was back in February 1969. He kept the bodies in the bungalow and spread a load of fanny about how his father had had an operation and had died in hospital. It all come to an end when a window cleaner looked into the bungalow. He pleaded to manslaughter and got popped in Broadmoor. The doctors said he'd had a brainstorm, which sounds about right. Rita started holding hands with Paul on visits and kissing him. It wasn't surprising her marriage come to an end. They let Paul out after about ten years and he took up with Rita. Everyone liked him and it went well for years and years. Her kids liked him but she never told them what he'd done. Then she started to believe he was killing people and she went into hospital for depression. That's when she told the kids about Paul's conviction. When she come out in October 1997 he invited one of the kids, who'd grown up and left home by now, around for dinner and when they got there he'd blown himself away and there was no sign of Rita. Police dogs found her under the concrete about a month later. He'd hit her on the back of the head with a hammer. He'd been all right for eighteen years and then it all went wrong again.

I went back to see people a few times. Jack Rosa, of course, and later Ronnie Kray. That was after I'd done the twenty. I was going down with Stephen Berkoff when Charlie Richardson rang me up and said one of his old mates, an Eddie Jones who'd been an LF man years earlier, wanted to go. Could he come with us?

Anyway, things had changed a lot in visiting since I was there. No question of having to put your hand up to go to the toilet and when Eddie goes Ronnie follows him. They're gone quite a time and I get a bit worried because Ronnie could sometimes be a bit careless where he put his thin and thick so I go along too. When I come in there's Ronnie with his hand on Eddie's shoulder saying, 'Frank, I was telling him what a lovely day it was.' When we was leaving I asked Eddie was everything all right. 'No,' he says, 'When he come in, it went all down my leg.'

Eddie was on the box a few months ago in a programme which was slagging Reggie and Ronnie off. I couldn't bring myself to watch it really and I couldn't hardly recognise Eddie. He was described as a former gangster. He's put on a lot of weight.

EAST ANGLIA

It's always interesting to see who was topped or killed on your birthday. Mine was the 13 December 1922 and there was a couple hanged side by side at Lincoln Prison. There was Frank Fowler who went and killed Ivy Prentice in the White House pub in Market Deeping. She'd only been married three days and she went down to look at her wedding presents when Fowler turned up and shot her. He must have been an old boyfriend and he held a grudge. The second was another boy and girl romance which had gone wrong. George Robinson cut the throat of his girlfriend, Frances Pavey, when she broke off the engagement. He cut his own throat as well but they nursed him back to health so's they could top him.

Over the years there has been a lot of people who've been acquitted of doing someone by saying they was sleepwalking at the time. Round the world I suppose it's getting on for a hundred. It's often the case though that people say they've got away with it. It was like that in the Essex case in the 1960s when that American airforceman, Wills Boshears, wakes up on the floor and there next to him is a girl, Jean Constable, he picked up at a New Year's Eve dance. The trouble is she's dead. Not a good way to start the New Year.

Boshears' old woman was up in Scotland visiting her parents and what had happened apparently was that him and another man had gone home with the girl. They'd all had a skinful and they all fell asleep in front of the fire. The other man woke up and went home, and then a bit later Boshears wakes up and finds he's strangling the girl, and she's a goner. He then starts to cut off her hair, gets a touch of seconds and puts her body in the spare room and goes off back to sleep. He kept the body in the flat all day and then put it in a ditch a couple of days later. He burned her clothes but he kept her watch.

It wasn't what you'd call a good defence but some people have all the luck. The jury chucked it out inside two hours. There was no question of manslaughter. It was murder or nothing, and there was a joke going around that it should have been 'guilty but asleep'. It's not a defence for the likes of me though. If I tried to run it I'd be laughed out of court.

I suppose in a way it all worked out for the best. Boshears went back to America and got chucked out of the Force for something or other. It wasn't long before he was killed in a car smash.

Wartime was a good time for women getting killed. Soldiers was always on the move and you could be out of the country and maybe killed yourself, doing your duty for your country, before they ever found the girl's body. I suppose the most famous was the Wigwam case, like I've said, and there was that Canadian soldier who got topped after taking a machine gun to a woman who wouldn't go out with him. He was the longest there's ever been in the death cell. I was on punishment in Wandsworth at the time and he was opposite me.

There was a killing up near Beccles, which doesn't get too much in the way of crime usually. It was Winifred Mary Evans who was strangled in November 1944 at Ellough by

Arthur Heys. She was only eighteen and worked as a wireless operator in the WRAF. It seems she'd left her barracks a bit after midnight. She'd been to a charity dance at an American base and she was already late for duty. The coppers reckoned that was when she ran into Heys. They was sure he'd been drinking and he wanted to have it off. They reckoned she fell in a ditch and whilst she was laying there Heys jumped on her back causing her liver to burst and begin to haemorrhage. Then he pulled her shirt up tearing the buttons, ripped off her slacks, got rid of the rags and had her from behind.

Her body was found the next morning by a special copper cycling along the Ellough Road. There was a girl who'd seen Heys in the area and when the coppers got to him he said he'd been to a dance in Caxton Hall, Beccles. He'd gone back to his barracks and fell asleep. There was a bit of scientific evidence that he'd washed his trousers around the crotch, and they matched some cat's hair from them with some on the body.

He tried his best. Whilst he was in the nick waiting for the Assizes he wrote an anonymous letter purporting to come from the murderer, saying Heys was innocent. In the supposed confession the man said how he had had an appointment to meet Winnie Evans shortly after midnight, that he had seen a drunken aircraftman [Heys] and that Winnie had arrived after that. The letter said the girl was 'unclean', which was the polite way of saying she was on, and the coppers reckoned only the killer could know that so, if the letter was genuine, it let Heys out.

They found out that he'd had access to paper and crayon and that he'd got someone who was being discharged to take the letter out. It wouldn't have been difficult. When I needed to get an authority out for my libel action to start against the *Empire News* that's what I did. Not that it did me any good.

As for the murder, they called up that fingerprint and handwriting expert, Fred Cherrill from Scotland Yard, to give evidence that the letter had been written by Heys, and that was just about that.

What was really interesting is he was working his way up to be a serial killer. On the file was the unsolved murder of a female in Colne, which is where he come from, before the War. Someone stabbed her in the back and it was reckoned to be down to him. He'd also been suspected of an attack on a LACW at the RAF station in Leuchars. This time he couldn't be identified and he said he'd been vomiting up booze. Heys had also been on site when another woman had been assaulted, this time it was at Thornaby.

There was a fellow put his wife under the floorboards in Newmarket and she didn't show up for ten years until a purchaser was looking the place over. In Field Terrace Road it was and the woman was Margaret Bennett. She disappeared back in the middle '80s. Her husband Frank reported her missing in January 1985. He told the coppers they'd an argument three days earlier and when he come back from work she was gone with a suitcase and a pony in cash. She'd gone missing before and it seems no one thought too much about it. Then three years later it looks like he topped himself. His body was found by the tracks at Welwyn Garden City and it seemed he must have walked in front of a train. There's a belief that people always leave suicide notes but a lot of them don't and Frank was one of them. The coroner returned an open verdict. There was all sorts of stories about how dogs wouldn't go in the house but it was another five years before the police got a tip and they dug up the patio. She wasn't there of course and the place stood empty until 1995 when this fellow buys it for thirty grand and starts to check for rising damp.

I didn't know Tony Maffia who was called The Magpie that well. I knew his mate Alfie Hinds much better. We come from the same bit of London and we did a lot of our bird together. I've written about him and his escapes a lot before.

Tony did a good job getting him away from the Law Courts when Alfie had gone there for an appeal. They locked a screw up in the carsi and it was off and away.

Tony's body was found at the beginning of June 1968 in the front passenger seat of his Jaguar in the car park of the Midway Restaurant – it was midway between South-end and London. The staff noticed a smell and went to have a look. It's funny; if the car had been parked there nowadays it would have been clamped and towed away inside a couple of hours. He'd been shot behind the right ear and in the right eye, a proper professional killing you could say. There'd been a bit of a heatwave and the body was so swollen they could only recognise him from a ring he wore.

Tony had a car business, Justice Motors, as well as being one of the big receivers in England. There was nothing he wouldn't touch in the way of jewellery, antiques, a bit of porcelain, coins, currency, you name it, and there's no doubt he'd made a few enemies. He'd got a nasty tongue on him. I don't mean that unkindly but he could take the mickey out of people and they didn't like it. When the police searched his house they found it was just like a magpie's nest, full of stuff that shouldn't have been there including a bit of gold from a big robbery in Clerkenwell which had gone off the year before. He didn't get rid of stuff, he just seemed to hoard it, which is how he got his name.

Then a funny thing happens. A fellow called Stephen Jewell from Manchester walks into a nick to speak with that bent copper Kenneth Drury, who picked up an eight and got it down to a five when a load of officers from the porn squad went down. Like father, like son. Drury's old man was a copper I used to give money to when I was on the run at the beginning of the War. I've never understood quite why Jewell went in. There was plenty of other candidates and you'd think any sensible person would stay out of harm's way until at least the first heat had gone out of the fire. Maybe he wanted to get his oar in first. He said he'd been trying to sell Maffia a few forged notes and at the same time buy his place in Buckhurst Hill which he fancied. It wasn't all one way. Maffia was trying to unload a boat he'd got in a marina at Wallasey Island.

Jewell's story was that just after him and Tony left the marina after looking at the boat three men in a Zodiac stopped them and told him to go away as they wanted to talk to Tony about a deal. They was Essex heavies he said. When he come back both Tony and the Zodiac was gone and so was a pistol there's been in the Jaguar. Jewell had left his coat in the car and there was blood on it. So, what does he do? He takes the car and drives off to London and whilst he's on his way he throws the coat into a field. Then he parks the car at the Midway Restaurant.

You can see why the coppers might fancy him for it. Can you believe the killers saw the car and thought let's put Tony's body back in it? Anyway he went down on a ten to two majority. Of course, Alfie Hinds' name's been mentioned all through the trial – not too favourably either, and at the end Alfie's allowed to have a brief make a statement that it was nothing to do with him. The man he had was that Roger Frisby, who was wonderful until the drink got to him. I saw he'd died last year.

Whilst he was in the nick Jewell wrote to Tony's brother, Arthur, saying he wasn't responsible but I heard Arthur had a few friends ask about and it come back they was satisfied it was Jewell. Still when he come out there was a programme on the telly showing how it was a miscarriage of justice. He's dead now as well.

I never really knew what it was about. Maybe Tony legged him over and Jewell got upset and shot him. There was a lot of cash and coins on Tony when the body was found so it wasn't robbery. If it was a contract, well it wasn't the best done that I've heard of. The story which floated around most was that Tony had worked a little trick over Jewell with some forged notes and when he fell for it,

Tony kept on baiting him till the man lost his temper. Like I've said Tony did have a spiteful tongue.

There was some funny hangings at Norwich Prison over the years. Well before my time, of course, but it was still part of legend when they hanged a man called Robert Goodale for doing his wife in. Back in 1885 it was, but the way people talked you'd think it happened yesterday. They'd just changed over to Marwood's method of breaking the neck in a hanging instead of strangling the man to death. It was all done on a table of weights. The heavier the man the longer the drop had to be. Anyway the screwsman decides he isn't going to go on the table of weights and shortens the drop. What happened was the drop pulled the man's head off. I think that people always had that sort of fear, not necessarily about being topped but having their head pulled off even though they probably wouldn't have known, nor would the family because it would be straight down to the prison graveyard and a report that everything had passed off all right.

There was another funny topping at Norwich much nearer my time. It was the case of Harold Bennett. He come from South London and there was real doubt about whether he did his wife, Mary, or if it was someone else who did for her. They made their living selling faked violins. It was just the old con game. She was the young widow forced to part with her late husband's most cherished possession. They were also at the badger game and a bit of insurance fraud thrown in. Good all-rounders they were. Somewhere down the line they fell out, and when it come to the trial there was the landlady saying she'd heard Bennett saying he wished his wife was dead and that if she wasn't careful she would be. Good stuff for a jury. She pushes off to Bexleyheath and now he's going out with a parlourmaid. He gives the maid a ring, but he doesn't seem to want to add bigamy to the other things he's been up to. Just like me. That's one of the few things I've never been done for. Then he goes and sees his wife and suggests she takes a holiday up in Yarmouth.

I've never been able to work out what they were up to but it was certainly something. Maybe they was putting the partnership back together because she's using the name of Hood. Then she tells the woman she rents a room from that she had been escorted by her dead husband's brother-in-law who was both madly in love with her and madly jealous. There's certainly some man she was seeing whilst she was up there. I think maybe they were going to work the badger game again with Bennett playing the brother-in-law.

Anyway the week after, Bennett tells the parlourmaid, Miss Meadows, that he has to go to Gravesend to see his grandfather who's ill, and off he goes to Norwich. Well, that's what the pros said. That night there's a courting couple on the sands at Yarmouth who sees another couple on the beach and hears the woman call, 'Mercy, mercy'. Then there's a moan but they don't do anything about it; simply get up and walk away. Later that evening, a man gets a room in the Crown and Anchor hotel, saying he had missed the last tram to Gorleston. The pros says that's Bennett.

They find his wife's body the next day. She'd been sexually assaulted and strangled with a mohair bootlace tied around her throat, but she wasn't identified for some six weeks when she got traced through a laundry mark on her clothing. Bennett was nicked and, when his room was searched, the police found a long old-fashioned gold chain together with men and women's wigs and a false moustache. There was also a bit of evidence that he had given a number of his wife's possessions to Miss Meadows. Just like Crippen gave away his wife's stuff to Ethel Le Neve.

Because local feeling was so strong against him the case came down to the Old Bailey. The evidence wasn't strong against Bennett. No one could agree whether the chain was the one she'd been wearing and Marshall Hall, who was defending Bennett, called an alibi. The real problem was that Bennett wouldn't give evidence himself. Some people say that you shouldn't give evidence unless you have to, and

I don't think I've ever been acquitted after giving evidence. If I have it's only the once. But people I've been in the nick with have told me you really had to do it in a murder case when there was topping around. Anyway, he should have done, because the jury was out about 35 minutes.

They sent him back to Norwich Prison to be topped on 21 March 1901. They used to run up a black flag to announce the death in them days and as it was being raised the flagstaff snapped. People said it was a sign of Bennett's innocence.

Executions was regarded as one of the few entertainments the working classes could have. People took time off from work and women put on their best dresses to go and watch. After they stopped public executions people still crowded outside the prison gates waiting for the notices to be put up. Men would be called in off the street to be witnesses to the topping – a bit like how they used to put a coroner's jury together – and they'd get five bob for watching. It seems that people who worked in the neighbourhood would hang around the prison and hope to get picked so they could pick up the extra dosh.

The funny thing was that a few years after the Bennett case a girl, Dora Gray, was found strangled with a bootlace on the beach at Yarmouth in July 1912. Dora told a girlfriend she'd met what was called a gentleman friend in them days, and she was going to see him again. Her body was found just near where Mrs Bennett's was and the bootlace had been taken from her boot. The story went around of course that Bennett was innocent but I don't suppose too many cared. Her killer was never found and it got put down as a copycat but whoever it was it can't have been Bennett.

Of course overall, being a screwsman didn't bring out the best in people. Some of them couldn't take it after a time. One of them was Jimmy Ellis who went and topped himself. He'd tried to do it before in the days when attempted suicide was a crime. He was up in front of the bench and they just told him not to do it again. Many a person had been sent down for a few months for trying. He'd also appeared in a play when he was Marwood, the man who actually topped Charlie Peace. The climax was right at the end when he hangs Peace on stage. People loved it but there was an outcry and it got took off after a few days. I was about ten when Ellis started chasing his wife round the kitchen one day, threatening to kill her, before he did himself finally.

Talking of hanging people on the stage, I remember seeing Tod Slaughter at the Canterbury. It was amazing what value you got for your money then. Two films and a stage show often enough. He was always the villain in those Victorian melodramas. He'd be the Squire who got the local unmarried mother turned out of the tied cottage when he was the baby's father all along. Wonderful he was. People loved him. Great big man who was just as big a ham. Like Donald Wolfitt but he never got a knighthood. He was hanged on stage night after night. One night, in Derby I think it was, he's hanged same as usual and just goes back to his lodgings and dies. What a wonderful way to go. You can still see him in those old black-and-white films on the telly in the middle of the night.

I could see what a ham he was because St Patrick's, where I went to school, was more or less across the street from the Old Vic. When we was old enough groups of ten or twenty would be taken to see the matinées. Even if I never really understood what the plays was all about they got to you. I don't know that I saw anyone famous but I must have done because Gielgud and Olivier and the others were at the theatre then and whoever they were they was different from Tod.

Talking of hangmen, there was that Syd Dernley. He should have got the sack. He was an assistant when he goes to hang a man, Norman Goldthorpe, at Norwich for killing a brass; 1950 it was. He'd got a book with him and he starts reading that poem *The Farting Contest* whilst him and the hangman, Harry Kirk, are in the room over the condemned cell. They'd had a few drinks and soon they and the screw they're with are laughing so loud that the people in the condemned cell have to knock on the ceiling to get them to shut up. What made it worse was the next morning the poor sod gave Dernley the Woodbines he hadn't managed to smoke before they come for him.

Of course the biggest case come out of East Anglia in recent years is that Tony Martin who shot the burglar and got lifed off for it. People had been turning his place over regular and one night when some blokes come round he opens fire. A lot of people thought he'd get a not guilty. I think if he'd gone straight to the coppers and said, 'Look, this is what's happened', he'd probably have been all right but when it come to it he didn't. Then it come down to manslaughter in the Court of Appeal but he still got a five.

Mind you, there's always been a bit of vigilantism about. Take that case up in Darlington back at the end of the 1970s. A man screws a neighbour's house and they nail his hand to a railway carriage. Just like that film *Boxcar Bertha*. The nailer got three years and his stepbrother who'd given him a bit of help gets a three. It was a bit like pot calling kettle black. Both the geezers had a bit of form for screwing.

PORTLAND BORSTAL

I don't think I'd like to live in a village called Borstal but that's where it got it's name from – a bit like Dum Dum in India where they made the bullets. Borstal's in Kent, on the Medway near Rochester. They'd been talking about having an institution for young offenders for years before the first one opened. Around 1908 it was.

The early ones had a matron, a figurehead really but something to show how caring they was. If you was sick you reported to her, and if you had trouble at home she was meant to be an ear to wig. They looked good when the Commissioners come to do an inspection. They was wheeled out then but otherwise they was kept very much in the background. I've heard people say they was called Maggies but I never called them that. In fact, I was in punishment so much I don't think I ever spoke to one. They wasn't allowed near the punishment wings when I was in. They was mostly what you would call comfortable-looking women, female screws coming to the end of their service, that sort of person. The idea was that none of the boys – and remember they could be up to 26 by the time they left Borstal – would fancy them. One or two had a go at them and they was phased out. Nowadays, it's the other way around and you get some of the women who work in prison fancying the men all the time. They take up with them after their sentences but it doesn't work out all that often. There wasn't anything like that in my day.

The Borstal idea was to make it a bit like a public school and promote teamwork and self-sufficiency. The blocks were to be called houses and there was to be inter-house rivalry with football matches and things so you could feel proud. The staff wore civilian clothes and the inmates was called 'lads', but that soon became trainees. We all wore shorts. In Billy Hill's book there's a picture of him and some others in their kit. I was looking through a book on prisons the other day and there was a photo of a gymnastic display, everyone balanced properly like a display team at that Service of Remembrance. People said it just made young criminals fitter.

They might have a point. The grandson of one of my friends got a report from the probation office saying how well he'd done in the karate class. His brief said he couldn't use it. The magistrate would have had a fit. I've never gone for probation reports myself. I don't mean they don't mean well, but when you have someone who's bashed old ladies and threatened them with knives after getting in their houses pretending to be from the gas and it says, 'Henry has begun to show a real insight into his offences and I feel he will benefit from probation', that sort of baloney, it only annoys the beak. Does more harm than good.

The staff at Borstals in the early days was really being trained as well, before they moved on to proper prisons. Of course, not everyone thought Borstals was a good idea. There was plenty who still fancied the short sharp shock. There was good results at first but as the years went by that fell off. People realised that just like prison or probation, Borstal would do the trick for some people and not others. By the time I was there they wasn't doing as well as they had at the start when there was much fewer people in the country. Judges who sent people there were putting married men with families along with seventeen-year-olds in them. You heard it a lot. The judge would say 'I'm going to give you a chance.' You thought that here was a spot of probation until he added, 'You'll go to Borstal for three years. Take him down.' Eventually it was Maggie Thatcher had the courage to do what should have been done years earlier and that was to shut them down. It's amazing, it's over twenty years since they were closed.

One of the things we did at Borstal was breaking those stones. It was one of the useless tasks they set prisoners in them days. It was a sort of carry on from the treadwheel, which was before me I'm glad to say but the old men who was in the nick with me and had been on it said you could break a man. You had to do just under 8,700 feet a day. Like climbing up the Post Office tower a few times. If you didn't do your distance there was either a whipping or a cut back on your rations. Men use to cry when they was put on it.

One of the other useless things they did was to have you move stones. Not just pebbles but like the boulders they use in the Strongman competition on the telly. They'd keep prisoners at it all day. Moving a series of stones to one end of the yard and then back again, all day and all week and all year long. In fact once the stones come in useful because in the First World War a whole lot of prisoners was sent from Parkhurst up to Peterhead to build foundations for aircraft hangers. The idea was that they threw boulders into the sea to make a sort of platform. One of them was that fellow Charles Smith who shot Eddie Guerin, the man who escaped from Devil's Island, back in 1906. He was still inside and he'd only wounded him. When the men got there they found that there wasn't no tea served like at Parkhurst and they had a protest saying they wouldn't work without it. That did them a lot of good. Two months' remission lost all round and nine months for the Irish fellow who led them.

The treadmill and stones didn't stop crime, any more than Borstal did. The thing is that if you're a proper criminal you don't think you're going to get caught, and if you are you're not going to get a guilty, and if you do you're not going into the nick. That's the only way you look at it. And better than half the time you're going to be right. If you're going to do a job which will pull in twice what you'll earn in a year doing nine to five in an office, for one night's work and a bit of planning, you can see how people might fancy it.

When I went to Borstal the system was you were sent to Feltham for assessment to see whether you should go to an open one, but I tried to escape. I was never a great escaper. The time a few of us had a go at Feltham we never even made the wall so it doesn't count really in my mind but it meant I was sent to Rochester. That was where the other two escapes was from. At least we stayed out overnight then, not that it did us any good long term. They was within a month of each other. The first was on 8 October 1941. I sawed through the bars in one of the recreation rooms. You was mostly in there unsupervised to play cards or chess, things like that. If you were good the screws would put the radio on sometimes during evening association. There was a big window and one of the other fellows in with us had a job in a workshop. He took a hacksaw and smuggled it back in. It wasn't that difficult – no metal detectors then; the screws would give a man a pat down and if he was trusted they wouldn't even bother half the time. It wasn't properly planned. Eva never knew anything about it to try and get a car down but there was a chance you could make it in the blackout. A fellow named Cutler come with me. I can't think of his first name after all these years but he was a smashing fellow. I met him again in Wandsworth in 1948 but I never saw him after that.

We never got far that time and it was down the block for me. That's when I got out the second time. A good bit of the Borstal had been taken over by the Navy then and part of it was fenced off. When you was doing the pounding two screws would sit and watch. The Borstal had a back gate with big double doors, but not a second set like you get in most prisons. At quiet times it would be open for parties who'd been out bringing in vegetables and six of us just steamed at the screws and made a run for it. Three was nicked straight away but three of us got away. We were chased, of course, but we stayed out all night. Charlie Jennings was one with us. A big fellow he was, and then there was Tony Byrnes. I think he come from Lancashire. We was all in shorts and they looked pretty silly but because I was small and young looking I could pass a bit more easy. We screwed a small shop for some food but the coppers got us the next day on the banks of the Medway. Like I say it's easy enough to get out. It's staying out that's the trouble. It was down the block again and that's when I half drowned Holy Joe, the screw who was looking at me when I was having my bath. I wasn't having that. I tried to drown him but a couple of the other prisoners yelled for help and they pulled me off. So it was down to Portland. I went in a car with a special escort all the way across from Kent; 1942 it would be.

To get to Portland Borstal you had to go to Dorchester and then down to Chiswell Beach on a long road with waste land on either side. You'd come to Portland which was at the end of a peninsula and then it was uphill to the prison. In my day it was one of the four closed Borstals – Rochester, Sherwood and Feltham were the others. Before the War you were sent to Wormwood Scrubs for assessment but they shut it down at the beginning and MI5 used it. They still pretended it was open by having Black Marias going in and out but the prisoners had been transferred. It may have fooled the Germans but it didn't fool the likes of us.

I went back to Portland the other day to see my grandson, who was doing half a stretch for driving disqualified. He's the third of my five grandsons to have been away. Keeping the family flag flying. This time we took a taxi from the station. The building's just as forbidding. The prison visiting room's smarter but apart from that it's not much different from when I was there. The sea air doesn't half get into the fabric. That was when it all come back to me.

I remember when I was in there I was in E Wing, which was the punishment block, most of the time. All the wings had names after British admirals, Drake, Rodney and Benbow and so on to make us proud, but the block didn't have no name. If it did I suppose it should have been Claggart because it was really rough. He was the villain in that book, *Billy Budd*, I read. I've said before that was the one good thing about prison. The books I got to read, they was mainly classics. Nothing like *No Orchids for Miss Blandish*.

A lot of kids tried to escape but there wasn't really anywhere to go. The beach was mined and there was both Army and Navy in the area. Where was you going to go? I don't remember anyone even having a visit let alone escaping successfully. Of course, it wasn't long before I was in the punishment: chinned a screw same as usual.

In punishment we did stone pounding, out in the open and too bad if it was raining. The screws sat under a canopy and watched us. Two-and-a-half hours in the morning and another three in the afternoon. When you finished the screws would give you a little shovel and they'd watch while you put all the stuff you'd pounded into a sieve and shook it into a box. If you hadn't filled it up, then you was reckoned to be slacking and you did a bit more time on punishment to teach you.

In the punishment block there was a name scratched in the wall, John Lee. Babbacombe Lee he was called and I suppose he was one of the most famous people ever was in Portland. Everyone learned and remembered his name because he was the man who they couldn't hang.

He was meant to have killed the old woman who he worked for back in the 1880s. Even though he was only nineteen he was an ex-con then and she employed him as a footman. There was a bull about the way he did his work and she docked his wages down to ten pence a week. The pros said he did her with an axe and then cut her throat right through to her back. After that he set fire to the house. It was all circumstantial evidence and, in them days, Lee wasn't allowed to give evidence to tell his side of the story. That didn't come in for another ten years or more.

The thing was they couldn't hang him. He must have been the only person who stood on the trapdoor three times and it wouldn't open. In Exeter Gaol it was. Berry, the hangman who later got religion, was the one who mucked it up. They take Lee out of the cell and put the hood over his head, pull the lever and nothing happens. They take him off, stand him on one side and have a practice. It works perfectly. Put him back on and nothing happens. They take him off again and the door works. Then its back on and it still won't open. The reports all say how calm he was. Not so the prison chaplain. He can't take any more and walks off. They took Lee back to his cell and a reprieve come through in a matter of hours. He served 22 years and then when he was let out he went off to America. He married and died there in 1933. After he come out he wrote a book, *The Man They Could Not Hang*. He'd got a bit religious and well he might. He said things like it was the Lord whose hand stopped him being topped. He kept on saying he was innocent, and I suppose he might have been.

There was many stories about what had happened including one that there was a convict underneath who shoved a wedge in every time Lee stood on the trapdoor. Berry thought that the iron catches of the trap doors weren't heavy enough and they bent with Lee's weight. Most likely the doors had become warped. Apparently there'd been a lot of rain over the weekend before he was to be hanged on the Monday.

There was another got religion in the punishment block at Portland. A fellow called Fred Lemon so the story goes. One day he sees Jesus. I suppose it's as good a place to see

Him as any but there's not many who do. Anyway Fred gives up crime and becomes a vicar. He wrote a book as well. It didn't go down too well. The phrase 'a right lemon' is meant to refer to him but I don't know if it's true.

As for me, one day I just put down the pounder and said, 'Bollocks to this' and chinned a screw. Even though I was officially too young the Home Secretary, Herbert Morrison, had me sent to Wandsworth and then on to Chelmsford, which is where I first met Billy Hill.

It was whilst I was at Wandsworth that I was taken in front of the medical board and that's where I made a mistake. They asked me if I was fit and instead of saying I'd had a fractured skull and suffered from memory loss, I said 'Of course I am.' I was really a bit angry because they could see I was keeping myself fit. I got a Grade 1 instead of Grade 4 which I was entitled to. It was true I'd had a fractured skull. I'd been knocked down outside on our street when I was about six, running into the road to blag cigarette cards off of the lorry drivers. I was in hospital weeks.

So more or less the minute I come out I'm meant to be in the Army. I wasn't having that.

WEST

What happened to us all after Parkhurst? Well, we was dispersed all over the country and I never saw some of the fellows again. That same afternoon I was taken off the island and transferred to Wakefield into the hospital there. Billy Blythe, no relation to the good man who was with me over Spot, was eventually released and took up with my niece, Shirley, but he turned out to be a wrong 'un. Martin Frape did a couple of years in Leicester. I heard of him a bit back when I was doing a signing. He was out and about. Had been for years. Andy Anderson mixed with the Scots mob in King's Cross for a time but I haven't heard of him in years. You've got to remember that what with the couple I got for receiving, I did over twenty after that before I finally come out. You lose touch.

One of us who had it hard was Timmy Noonan. He went to Liverpool and he was put straight into solitary. He'd been in solitary since well before the trial even. In fact one of the reasons for the protest on the island was the treatment that Timmy and others had had in the punishment cells. There'd been a round robin signed by 120 prisoners complaining about what was happening to him.

As I say he'd been in Broadmoor with me but there wasn't much talk of sending him back, even though he did a dirty protest and found a moth in his cell to talk to. By January 1973 he'd been in solitary for 1,041 consecutive days, which people said was a record. I thought I'd had the record myself but I'm happy Timmy should have it. The authorities said that when he come back into the prison proper he got into fights with the other cons, but if he did it was with the screws. And can you blame him? Three and a bit years banged up on your own 23 hours a day. He'd made himself some playing cards out of lavatory paper but they'd taken those away from him as well. They could keep you on Rule 43, which meant you could be kept out of prison proper for 28 days at a time, and then the magistrates had to reconsider things. That meant they'd considered it forty times and still wasn't prepared to allow him up.

That MP Ernle Money, who was meant to defend in the riot trial before the election came and ruined it, took up his case but it didn't do no good. By then there was a special wing at Parkhurst for cons who was violent. The idea was to give them a bit of controlled association but they never took Timmy there. Whilst he was in Liverpool in 1971 he had a heart attack and he was only 35. He lived in fear he'd have another and no one would notice. Of course, poor Timmy did have another attack and this time it was fatal.

It's funny how some words last in slang and others come and go. People make it up, particularly rhyming slang, as they go along. Very often it's done on people who are famous at the time. Some of it lasts, and we still say Oscar for cash, but who remembers that Oscar Ashe was the star of *Chu Chin Chow*? Nowadays people is saying Britneys for beers but I don't suppose that'll be around in a hundred years. Some of it's quite clever. Bill Wyman for hymen, but I don't suppose that'll last any longer than they do. But take Sweet Fanny Adams. How many people know where that comes from although it's been around for getting on for 150 years and it's still as popular as it ever was?

She was a little girl who was done by a solicitor's clerk, Baker, down near Alton sometime around 1860. It was about the time that tinned beef was introduced in the Navy and there was a joke that what they was getting was Sweet Fanny Adams, and it went on from there.

You hear all about it when our sort of people kill others so it's quite good when a copper goes and does it. I was thinking about it the other day after that copper who went and killed his whole family and then topped himself. Absolutely wicked it was. There was all that rubbish about his suffering from depression but I reckon that's a load of fanny. You go and top yourself, not everyone else, kids and all.

Still, I suppose it wasn't as bad as that copper down in Worcester a few years after I was born. November 1925 it was. Herbert Burrows was his name. He'd been a probationary copper and he wanted some dough to go on leave, so what does he do? He stays drinking after hours in The Garibaldi, the pub opposite where he's got his lodgings, and then goes and shoots his friend Ernie Light, who was the landlord, in the back. Then, when the man's missus goes to find out what's happened he does her too. He's ransacking the house and the baby starts crying so he kills him as well, strikes him over the head and fractures his skull. He lets the six-year-old daughter alone but then, when he's got about seventy quid, he tries to set fire to the place. Throws paper all around the cellar and sets light to it. Then he goes back across the road to his digs and goes to sleep. Next morning he's back on the beat as though nothing's happened. It was only when he dropped into the nick for his breakfast and starts opening his gob that people get suspicious. He makes a fanny of a statement saying how he's brought disgrace on the force and apologises to them.

After that he pleads not guilty, saying he's got the pox and that was what made him do it. He doesn't seem to have cared much whilst he was waiting to be topped either, sang to himself and played cards until his day come on 17 February. They didn't hang about then so to speak. Good riddance.

Funny how sometimes things runs in families. Ignatius Lincoln was the son of Trebitsch Lincoln, who'd been an MP and was a spy. The boy, whose mother was German, enlists in the British Army and then with one of his mates decides to do a drum in Shepton Mallet on Christmas Eve 1925. Him and the other fellow, Ian Stewart, can't find any money in the house, so instead of hopping it they start drinking the man's booze and piling it up by the front door. Of course what happens but the man comes in and tells them the game's up. Lincoln just shoots him stone dead. Fifteen minutes was all it took to find him guilty, and about a third of that to top him.

I know my niece Shirley got found with a head in her fridge, a bit like John the Baptist, but she'd been forced to keep it there. Anyway it wasn't on the shelf more than a few hours, but I don't understand how people can have bodies on the premises for years. Not that I'd be afraid of having one there but surely it's got to be the first place for the coppers to look if the person's a relative. Yet people do it time and again. And sometimes if they've got enough front they can get away with it. In the past if they did it long enough there was no evidence how the relative had died and they ended up getting convicted only of things like drawing their social security for ten years. Look at Christie, the Notting Hill murderer. He had half the brasses in the neighbourhood walled up in his kitchen. When the next tenant took over and started re-papering he near enough died of fright.

Then take that family down in Weston-super-Mare, that small town in Somerset. They lived on The Boulevard and Joy Mayes was a mother who did everything she could for her boys. One of them went to university and the other to a good school. She took a job waitressing to put the money together. Then one of them, Roderick, gets himself hooked on LSD and she thinks he's in for a long drawn-out death, so she tops him in his sleep. She puts a handful of sleeping pills in a mug of cocoa as he lay in bed and when he's become unconscious she fractures his skull with an iron bootscraper and cuts his throat. The other boy, Sean, is with a rock band off touring abroad when she done it. April 1972 it was.

Understandably when he comes home, the boy says he wants his brother to have a decent burial and so him and his grandfather, who's been a Commander in the Navy, helps take the body which she's hidden under the bed, wraps it in a candlewick bedspread and plastic sheeting and they dig a shallow grave in the back garden. Friends were told that Roderick had gone to live with hippies. No one took that much notice.

The old boy dies a few years later and then Mrs Mayes pops off in 1992. That leaves Sean and by 1995 he's got HIV and he's on his way out too. It's then he tells the coppers what's happened to Roderick and there he is in the garden. This time, because of the plastic sheet they wrapped him in, the body was well preserved and they could prove who it was from the teeth. No charges were brought against Sean. Quite rightly, no one thought it was in the public interest to prosecute him.

The Commander had left a diary with entries which looked like he was referring to the killing. That got read at the inquest. Within a couple of days of Rod being topped he'd written 'Terrific operation'. They thought that meant the burial. He doesn't seem to have minded too much about the loss of his grandson. He'd also gone and written, 'Such a relief with R and friends not popping in and out.' So I suppose when it come to it things was a bit quieter and everyone was reasonably happy. Though if I'd been Sean I'd have been a bit worried when me mum asked if I wanted a drink before bedtime.

You could get away without being topped if you did yourself badly enough. That was why they made you keep your hands above the bed clothes at night when you was in the condemned cell. Stop you spoiling their fun by doing yourself first. In the last 24 hours they increased the number of warders in your cell. Still some people managed it. There was a fellow Ernest Wood, up in Durham nick, cut his throat very badly. It wasn't that he was going to die from it but the thought was that the rope would pull his head off and it would make so much mess that he got a reprieve.

A long time ago that was, but then there was the fellow William Gray, who made a good end to the year by shooting his wife Una on New Year's Eve 1948. He's quarrelled with her and she's round at her mother's in Andover. He'd had it in mind for a bit because he'd talked to a friend who'd told him not to do it, but he'd gone ahead and put a down payment on a gun, gone and paid the balance and bought some cartridges.

He went round to his mother-in-law's and as Una leaves the house with three friends and mum he comes up, calls out, 'Is that you, Una?' and then 'Stand clear' to the others and blasts away. I suppose he's in a third category of my murderers. The ones who plan, the ones who do it on the spur of the moment, and then those who try and top themselves straight away. You can never tell with those who fail if they was just making it look good, giving themselves some sort of an excuse – in which case they go straight back into the planners' category, or when it comes to doing themselves in they think life's going to get better and they bottle out. Whichever it was Gray's found later that day laying on a bank beside the road. He had blown part of his face away with the gun. He put his hands up to it at Winchester Assizes but now his jaw was so brittle the noose would have been likely to break it and so slip over his head when they tried to top him. So his sentence was commuted to one of life imprisonment.

That wasn't the only time when a fellow had been saved from the gallows because he couldn't be hanged properly. Back before the long drop one fellow who was done for killing a gamekeeper had a bent neck, and so to strangle him, which is what happened in those days, would have caused him too much suffering. He got reprieved, which was just as well because whilst he was in the nick another bloke came along and admitted he'd done it.

Another deserter from down West in the First World War was Percy Toplis and he went on to do a string of blaggings. He'd started off life with a conviction for fraud at the age of seventeen and then he did a couple of years for attempted rape. There were stories that he had been in the RAMC but he'd deserted during the Somme campaign. He was found in a little village outside Le Touquet, Rang des Fliers, and was arrested, but when him and another was taken to a guard camp, they dug out in the sand and got away. The other fellow was nicked but Toplis made it to Paris and there he hung out until he was able to get back to England.

I don't know if that's true but certainly it was after the War when he was at his peak. He was a master fraudsman. He'd got an Oxford accent by now and he could persuade people he was a half colonel. He'd even got the nerve to dress a couple of subbies down for not saluting him properly when one of them had been an officer in Toplis's regiment.

He worked the West Country mostly and that's where he shot a taxi driver near Andover in April 1920. He'd already thrown another cabbie onto the pavement in Bristol. He made his way to Wales and then came up to London. By this time there's a full hue and cry and in the six weeks he was out there was more people reporting they've seen him than saw Lord Lucan. There was 1,097 different sightings and he was meant to have gone to the Derby as well. He even went back to the camp he'd deserted from.

He tried to get back to Paris and he was a bit unlucky. He'd been staying at the Union Jack Club in the Waterloo Road near where we lived and no one had sussed him then. But when he was waiting for the boat train at Victoria station he sees some coppers. He thinks they're after him but in fact they was there for another reason; instead of holding his bottle he panics and goes off to Skegness and works his way up to Scotland, where the coppers find him in Upper Banffshire. He holes up in a gamekeeper's hut and when the man and a copper come to see why there's a fire burning he shoots the pair of them.

Then a couple of days later he's on his way back down south when near Penrith he runs into a copper who recognises him and sends for help. There's a gun battle in which he's shot. Best thing for him really.

It's amazing how often it happens. You see coppers and think the worst and they probably haven't even heard about you. It was the same with that brilliant housebreaker right at the beginning of the last century. A foreigner he was. He's done countless big houses in London, got the nerve of the devil, and he's sitting on the promenade in Ramsgate when a copper sits down next to him. He thinks it's all on top and instead of just saying 'Good Morning' or something and walking off, he starts to run. The copper follows him and the man turns and shoots. He misses and then turns the gun on himself. He was a better burglar than he was with a gun because he didn't top himself, he just took his own eye out. It didn't stop him getting a fifteen at the Assizes. Later he got out of Portland, I think it was, and for a few days he's on the run before the gentry turns out on their horses and they get a pack of hounds and run him down.

There was another soldier who swung for a killing in 1952. He'd been a bit lucky he hadn't swung before. John James Alcott his name was. He hadn't learned from a previous time when he was done for the murder of a caretaker in Germany in 1949 when he'd been in the Grenadier Guards. The conviction was quashed, because no one it seems had told his mother he was on trial. This time there's no mistake. He killed a railway booking clerk, Geoffrey Dean, who was known as Dixie of course. It was at a station called Ash Vale near Aldershot where the barracks are. He was topped on 2 January 1953 so I don't suppose he had that good a Christmas. Still, there can't be that many people in this country who've offed two people by the time they was 22.

You wouldn't think Bournemouth was the place for crime, but you'd be wrong. The Twins had interests down there, sort of supervised by Bill Ackerman on their behalf. There were stalls at markets which had a bit of protection and a couple of clubs here and there. You've got to remember, where there's people making money on the side there's always someone stronger or who's got a bit more clout who's going to take a nip out of them. Bill came a tumble once or twice in the '70s. There was one case when he was asking for bail and the copper told the court that Bill was the No. 1 Criminal in Bournemouth, which must have caused a bit of a laugh to those who didn't know better. Bill tried to turn the Twins over once. I don't rightly know what it was about but I do know they didn't half have the facts of life explained to him.

Bournemouth was a useful town. There was a good bit of protection going on and there was a lot of jewellers to blag. The trouble was if a job went bad in the town you had to have a stow, someone who had a place where you could bake-up for three or four days until someone sent a motor to collect you. Bournemouth wasn't the only place like that. If you were doing a small town, say Scarborough or Blackpool even, then it was essential.

I wasn't the only person who walked out of barracks during the War but some people who did caused a lot more damage than me. There was that fellow Leslie Goodall down in Bournemouth, who ended in Broadmoor in my time. He didn't want to be a soldier anymore than I did and he wasn't any smarter with the fitness board than me. He went and told them that he was a Communist, and when that didn't work he said he was a conscientious objector. All that did was get him a sentence for refusing to be medically examined and the moment he was released they had him in again. He got sent to the Royal Fusiliers and he didn't last long there. He got away as far as Scotland where he was picked up, and he got another spell inside before they took him down to Bournemouth where the regiment was. It's funny, no one ever thought he was completely bats because the next thing he does is go absent again. I suppose they thought he was just trying to work his ticket. He lasted two days on the outside this time. At least I did a bit better.

He's found in the centre of the town and handed over to the military, and he's put in barracks at Wimborne Road where he's left to scrub some floors. Only a few hours later he's off again but now he's got himself his rifle and some ammo's missing from the barrack room. He just shoots two soldiers dead. A couple of NCOs go after him, and one of them gets through the ceiling and into the room where he's hiding and persuades him to give up the gun. There's no question of anything but guilty but insane, and he had that really good brief, J. D. Casswell, for him.

Casswell was really big in his day. He defended in a lot of murder cases and didn't lose many. The pros said that Goodall just didn't like authority, but Casswell ran it that Goodall was suffering from a split personality and the jury agreed. They took less than half an hour when it come to it and off Goodall goes to Broadmoor. He's there for years and eventually they let him out on the proviso that he'll go back up to where his father was at Morpeth and become a patient at a hospital up there; 1964 that was. He did all right. Then his father died and he started causing trouble, having fights with other inmates. Goodall had a sister in Hampshire and he wanted to get back to Broadmoor so she could get to see him. He even went to see his MP about it but nothing come of it quick enough for him.

It seems that the patients at St George's hospital got a good bit of freedom. There was one nutter who thought himself the store detective at Woolworths in the town. He just walked up and down the aisles all day. He never arrested anyone and he didn't cause trouble, so they left him alone. There's shops like that. They're good that way. They let people alone if they don't do any harm. I was signing one day in London and a fellow dressed up as a Highlander kept coming in, walking round the shop, shouting at a couple of people and then leaving. He must have been in half-a-dozen times in the couple of hours I was there. Seems he thought he was security as well.

Anyway Goodall gets a knife and back at the hospital does the man who thinks he's a store detective; stabs him in the neck. When he's made sure the poor fellow's dead he goes down to the police and tells them what he's done. He pleaded guilty up at Newcastle Crown Court in 1977. They couldn't have him back at Rampton or Broadmoor at first because there wasn't any room, but I think he got moved out of the nick fairly quickly. The judge said he hoped he'd never be in a position to go and buy a knife again.

I suppose the most famous case which Casswell defended was Neville Heath, although there was a lot of others. There was the porthole murder where that man James Camb pushes the girl he's had it off with through the porthole when she dies when they're having sex. That was one of the cases where there was a question about not convicting him because they couldn't find a body. They did though. Then there was Mrs Rattenbury. I was in the nick with the man who did her husband. She got a not guilty but she went and topped herself all the same. The man got a reprieve. There was those Russians at the end of the War who killed a blackmarketeer, and there was also that girl, Elizabeth Jones, who took up with an American deserter and did a taxi-driver down Hammersmith way. I've mentioned both of those cases in *Mad Frank's London*.

Anyway Heath, after he's done a half brass in London – flogged her to death and bit her nipples off – comes down to Bournemouth to hide out. This time he's pretending to be an officer and a gentleman again. When he did Margery

Gardner in South Kensington he'd been Lt Colonel Heath, but now he'd demoted himself and was Group Captain Rupert Brooke. There was a big search going on for him at the time. Anyway he stays at a hotel near the sea and that's where he meets a young girl, Doreen Marshall, in July 1946. They go out for a walk in the chines, those zig-zag paths down to the sea, and that's the last anyone sees of her alive. Something like five days later she's found with her throat cut and a whole lot of injuries in Branksome Chine. In the end he was done for the murder of Margery Gardner rather than her.

There was a whole lot of talk that Doreen needn't have died. Some of the top coppers wanted a photo of Heath circulated as wanted, but because there was a question of an ID it was decided not to do it. If they had he might have been nicked before he got the young girl.

One fellow from down there was in the condemned cell a bit longer than his marriage lasted. That was Reginald Woolmington. He was another who was defended by Casswell. Poor devil, he was a 21-year-old farm labourer. His wife Violet, well she was only seventeen and she was well in the club when they got married in August 1934. The kid was born a month after the marriage. It wasn't like it is today when it's a sort of competition for young girls to have a kid as soon as they can and get a council flat of their own. This pair lived for the first few weeks with his parents in Milborne Port where, of course, everyone knew just what everyone else was up to.

Then they moved into a farm cottage at a rent of three shillings a week. A week later their son was born and from then on it was the usual story. The cottage was tiny; the baby cried; Reginald was out working long hours; he was only earning 33 shillings and they didn't have enough money. Thank God, I've never been in that position. When I was out I was always able to earn good money, even if we never had a bath of our own.

Violet had worked with her mother making up gloves at piece rate for local manufacturers and so mum come round bringing work for her to do. He started to think she was trying to get Violet to go back home and of course that's what she did. They hadn't been married three months when he comes home and there's a note saying Violet had asked her mother to have her back and she was going into service. If that had been all, I suppose he might have worn it, but it was a bit worse than that.

A fortnight later he meets her brother who tells him there's a new Mr Woolmington on the horizon. The next day he get a double-barrelled shotgun from his governor, saws the barrels and cycles over to his mother-in-law's. He pleads with Violet to come back and when she blanks him off he shoots her. Of course even the local coppers could work out who to look for and there's a note in his pocket, 'Goodbye all. It is agonies to carry on any longer. I have kept hoping she would return. This is the only way out . . . Have no more cartridges, only two, one for her and one for me.' Of course, he didn't use the one for himself. He's also written a note for his employer, 'I shall not be coming to work today. I have shot my wife.'

When it come to it I don't know if he was lucky. The first jury at Taunton couldn't agree and the second was told it was for him to show he hadn't acted maliciously. That's where the pros come unstuck. It got all the way to the House of Lords with him in the death cell and they say the judge was wrong. He shouldn't have had to prove anything. First rule of British law and all that; it's up to the pros. Out he went. Not even a manslaughter over him. But he'd been 81 days in the condemned cell.

The further west you get the less real crime there is. For a start it's a long way and there's always the trouble of getting out. There's not much in the way of motorways in Cornwall and there's always the danger of a road block. Even so there's been one or two good little cases – more domestic than professional really. One was that boy Miles

Giffard in 1952. His father was a solicitor and the Under Sheriff of Cornwall, and when it came to it he had a bishop come and plead for him so he'd got good connections. He'd been to Rugby. He topped his parents because they didn't approve of his playing around in London. By the time he was in his mid-twenties he was a remittance man. Those were the days when things like all-night jazz parties were happening at places like Cy Laurie's club in Windmill Street and people was fearful what their kids might be doing. I remember reading in the linens about a girl who was suing the man she claimed was the father of the baby, and when she was asked where she'd fallen pregnant, she said in a box at the Chelsea Arts Ball at the Albert Hall.

Giffard come down to his parents' place on a cliff top at Porthpean near St Austell, and there was a big row. He was in love with a girl in London but his parents wanted him to come back to Cornwall and make something of himself. So he did them, just battered them to death with an iron pipe and then tipped them in the ocean. His mother was still alive when he did it. Then he took his father's car and drove to London to see his girlfriend in Tite Street and popped his mother's jewels. He took his girl to see that Charlie Chaplin film *Limelight*, and as they come out of the cinema there was the coppers waiting.

His brief, who was John Maude, ran a defence that he'd been unstable since he was a kid and that a cruel nurse had locked him in the cupboard, but that was never going to work, even though a doctor had said he was bats at about the time he was fourteen. He got topped in the November. He might have thought that a bit of class prejudice would work in his favour like it had for Ronald True all those years earlier but it didn't.

THE MOOR

It was interesting reading at the beginning of the year the coating Dartmoor got over conditions there in a report. Screws calling the cons 'vermin', wire cages for exercise, things like that. It's funny because it isn't the end of the prison road where all the villains are sent as it was in my day. It's been down graded to something like a C class prison since I've been there. Even so, whatever it's like it can't be as bad as it was when I was there. I know every old con is going to say things like 'You youngsters haven't half got it cushy', but it was really tough back in the 1950s and worse before that as well. There were people who inspected prisoners but they didn't get notice taken of them.

If you was in the punishment wing, which I was mostly, you were meant to get an hour's exercise every day but it could be cut to half an hour for what they called special circumstances. And that could mean anything – staff shortages, sickness, you were the type of prisoner who'd cause difficulties, anything they could drum up. You were never told what it was. When it come to it you got about twenty minutes.

When you did get your exercise it was in a small cage about ten foot by ten foot. You couldn't see who was in the next one to you. You'd be let out of your cell and the first would be taken to his little pen before the next was let out and so on. One side was open so a screw could walk up and down and see you weren't doing anything wrong.

You had ranks in those days. When you'd done four years you got a blue circle sewed to the sleeve of your coat and that meant you went in D wing on the Moor. This was what they called special stage and there was two landings. There was about twenty or more prisoners at any one time. Now you could have a radio, but of course you had to have it sent in. I was lucky, I'd got family and people like Billy who was looking after me, but of the twenty or so men I shouldn't think ten had family. Remember, they'd already done four years and by now they'd be half forgotten. They'd have had a Dear John letter that their wife's going to have a baby by some geezer, if they had a wife that is. And those whose wives were still faithful, well the girls probably didn't have the money to spare anyway. You got released straight out of Dartmoor in those days. Just before their release one or two lucky guys got sent to Wakefield where there was a sort of camp but the only open prison was Leyhill and it wasn't for the likes of me or anyone else who'd been sent to the Moor.

The trouble with prisons in the old days was that it wasn't the Governor who ran it, it was the screws. From the reports it looks as though in some nicks it's still the same.

There was always someone who could make alcohol in prison and when I was in Dartmoor, Wino Richards was the man. He worked out on the Moor itself and he distilled the stuff when he was on a work party. Remember how lax things could be with Frank Mitchell just drifting off to the pub when he wanted to. There was also another lag whose wife wanted to get in the club, and she'd drive down in a van with a mattress in the back and he'd get in and have it away. I never knew if she fell. I reckon Wino used to make some of the drink for the screws and that's why they turned a blind eye.

I suppose the reason they let us see the film *The Blue Lamp* in the nick at Dartmoor was because it was meant to be a warning to us. Shows there is life after death for coppers. Dirk Bogarde, who's the little tearaway, goes and shoots honest old Jack Warner who's PC Dixon. Bogarde gets topped but Jack comes back for a television series. That bit was filmed just near the old theatre, the Metropolitan in the Edgware Road where Max Miller used to appear so regular. I remember in the film 'Two Ton' Tessie O'Shea was meant to be topping the bill there. Big Welsh girl she was, looked a bit like Diana Dors, played the ukelele and sang smutty songs. Well, smutty for those days you know. Some line would end with 'witch' and you know what the end of the next one would be, except she'd smile and give a clunk on the uke. Bit like a female George Formby.

Anyway, the film wasn't that much of a warning as Harold Thirkettle found out. He was stabbed to death during a showing of *The Blue Lamp* in the prison chapel at Dartmoor, the middle of June 1961. He'd got a number of convictions and was doing twelve years for the manslaughter of the woman he'd been living with. When she said she was leaving him for another man he'd attacked her with an axe. A black guy, Matthew Nwachukwa, was charged with his manslaughter. There must have been more knives in the audience than on the screen that night. Nwachukwa was reckoned to be a grass and someone had stabbed him during the film already. He got the knife out of his back and went and stabbed the two men nearest him. Neither had been involved in the attack. It all got chucked. Who cared what cons did to each other back then?

BIRMINGHAM AND THE MIDLANDS

The first bit of work I ever did outside London was in Birmingham. It was during the War. People all over the country was on the run, deserters, and a couple we met in London had stuck up this firm. I was on the run myself. I looked young and I was small. People wouldn't really give me a second look. The job was the usual story. The bosses would send a couple of men to the bank on a Friday morning for the wages and the workers would get their dough by four that afternoon. There was no question of cheques. Nor did they ever think it was a good idea to vary the time the men went or the route they took. Dead on nine or ten whichever it was. It was a piece of cake. As far as I can remember we took two grand, which was serious money.

How did we get there? Well, petrol wasn't that difficult to obtain. Billy Hill had the market in forged coupons and we had a hooky man who ran a garage just off the Waterloo Road. We'd give him a drink and he'd fill us up. Sometimes he'd take Billy's coupons, others he wouldn't bother. Birmingham was good because you could be back in the day. We used to take two motors. One was hooky and we'd use that for the job; we'd probably dump it and come back in the straight one. But if the job was sweet we'd bring it back and keep it for another day.

During the War I was hardly out but, when I was, I was an enthusiastic thief. I was living at home and of course my mother would be given something. By now she must have realised what I was up to but we still went on pretending. Eva was dividing her time between my mother and our Gran, and she was the one who looked after my dough for me.

One of the big rivals to Darby Sabini, who I worked for on the racecourses when I was a kid, was the Brummagem Boys who was led by Billy Kimber. What it was all about was a struggle for control of bookmaking on the racecourses. You could make real money if you had the bookmakers in your pocket. You could make them buy chalk for writing the odds on their boards, the paper with the runners and riders, you could have them employ a kid like me going round with a bucket to sponge down the chalk between races. Of course, they could have done all these things themselves, but if they didn't want cutting or rows in front of their boxes and people calling out welsher at them then they paid up and looked pleasant about it.

All through the 1920s there was trouble over who ran the racecourses. There'd been fights in London and Bath and Doncaster as well as Yarmouth and at some of the trotting tracks which were popular then. But the biggest set-back for the Birmingham boys come on Derby Day 1921 when nearly forty of them got nicked after they'd attacked the wrong people.

They'd been put up to it by that crooked financier, Horatio Bottomley, who'd got the magazine *John Bull*. He was sounding off about how it was all wrong that Italians and other foreigners should be running the courses when good Englishmen back from the War wasn't getting a look in. A meeting was arranged in a hotel off the Bull Ring and instructions were given to attack London bookmakers taking taxis back home from the races. It didn't matter if the Sabinis wasn't among them, it was going to be a lesson who could protect them. The idea was to ambush them in the Ewell Road. After the big race the Birmingham men left and blocked the road with their charabanc and attacked the first cab in sight. One of the men inside lost three fingers to a meat cleaver. The cabs were overturned and the occupants routed. Unfortunately it wasn't the Sabini bookmakers who was in the taxi; it was people from Leeds who wasn't at all pleased.

Of course, the coppers heard of it pretty quick and they seem to have thought it was a Sinn Fein riot, but when a Sergeant Dawson arrived on the spot he did for the lot of them single handed. First, he took the sparking plugs from the charabanc and then he threatened to shoot the first of the men who moved. That way he kept 28 of them under control until other coppers turned up. In all 17 out of the 28 was found guilty and there was some good bird handed out. After it was over people wrote suggesting that Dawson should get a subscription set up for him but the police didn't seem to think that he deserved anything. A vote of thanks was about all his reward. One of the blokes who went down was Edward Banks who'd been involved in the shooting of Darby Sabini at Alexandra Park the previous year, and there was talk he had been going to get some Mills bombs, so you can see it was getting to be heavy stuff.

But a bit after that there was a big alliance between the Midlands and London. It came about through 'Brummy' Sparkes, who was Maggie Hill, Billy's sister's first husband. He might have been her only husband for all I know. She was much older than Billy and so was very much older than me. That sort of cemented things because Maggie was a big shoplifter going all over the country. Maggie Hill really took over the Forty Thieves as they was known, from another Maggie who was married to Ted Hughes, the one Billy called Odd Legs in his book because he was gimpy.

Maggie was only 25 when she picked up a three at the Bailey for lifting back in 1923. It was reckoned that she and her team had cleared over £100,000 in the previous twelve months. She used to go down to Brighton a lot where the coppers reckoned she had a receiver, but if she did he was never picked up. She was good with a knife as well. The previous year she'd done a girl real bad but she was never prossed. Brummy Sparkes was a big burglar in his day, good for country houses.

Lord Woolf never did me any harm. In fact he did me good. When I went down for three years over receiving coins a bit after I'd come out from the twenty, he wouldn't quash the conviction, but him and two others knocked the sentence down to two years. Good man, known to be liberal, so I did wonder what he was saying earlier this year about people who mug mobile telephones getting a minimum of four. Still, I suppose that what they're doing is knocking women and kids about to get the phones so they deserve what they get. There was that Judge Michael Argyle at the Bailey. He'd been the Recorder of Birmingham and there was a rash of stealing from telephone boxes so it got that you couldn't find one which was working. He started potting people for long stretches and the word soon got around. It was the same back in the 1860s when there was what was called garroting going on. You put a chokehold on the neck of the man and nicked his kettle. Apparently if you didn't know what you were doing you could kill the bloke. People got the bash for that. Twelve strokes as you went in the nick and another twelve just before you came out, so you had something to look forward to. That stopped it pretty quick. So maybe Lord Woolf's right.

I suppose that what Argyle'd done in Birmingham earned him promotion and that was when he went to the Bailey. I read a couple of years ago that Argyle had died. I was never in front of him but enough of my friends was. He was a funny man; dead keen on racing. He'd go out to the betting shop in the lunch adjournment. His wife's racing colours were nigger brown and black cap and he couldn't for the life of him see what was wrong with that. He was the one who remanded that Richard Neville and his mates over the magazine *Oz* and said the prison authorities should make sure they had a short-back-and-sides before they came back to court. He chucked a kid's bicycle in the river as well. No question of charging him with criminal damage though. He got his come-uppance in the end. The people who'd run *Oz* did very well in business later on and Argyle libelled one of them in an article he wrote. The man sued and got a lot of money for charity.

People don't remember how the cinema was before there was television. You'd get what they call a B picture, something like a Randolph Scott Western, then you might get a travelogue, you know the sort of thing, 'Now as the sun goes down over the island, sadly, we leave the land of bare-breasted women.' Of course you never saw the bare-breasted women except at the other end of the island. It was like those nudist films they had in the 1950s, you never got a shot of anything at all. They were always playing beach ball with the ball covering up everything. Anyway, then there'd be the news with a good bit of sport; one of the boxing matches or cricket or a big race like the Grand National. They used to rush it out for the Monday and there'd be queues round the block even though we all knew the result. Then there'd be the main film. But what they also had was advertisements for people who'd gone missing and the police wanted help finding them. Sort of an early version of *Crimewatch*. The War was about the best time to get rid of a wife or girlfriend. You could say they'd gone away to the country or gone off with some other bloke. People would accept it and the police was too busy to go searching for every wife who'd gone off.

Even when they found a body they couldn't always link it up to anyone. That's what happened in November 1943 when one turned up at the water level at Osborne Bridge Road in Luton. They had the pathologist Keith Simpson and he reckoned she'd been done within the past couple of days. He reckoned she was in her early thirties and she was well in the club. She was missing a few teeth and all. She'd been put in sacks and they came from a local potato merchant.

This was when they used the cinema and, like usual, a whole lot of people come forward to try and identify the body but it didn't do no good. It was sheer luck that they found out who she was. It was some months later when a dog nosed out a shoulder-pad from a woman's dress off a rubbish tip. The copper in the case was nearby and it was given to him. There was a dyer's tag on it and it was traced to the Sketchley dye works in Luton. Once they'd made that step it was only another to Caroline Manton who lived in Regent Street. In fact there'd already been a house-to-house enquiry and the two kids there had been shown the photograph but had failed to recognise their mother.

When the coppers asked her husband, Bertie, about Caroline he said there'd been trouble over her going with soldiers; she'd left him to go and live with her brother in Grantham and had then moved on to London. He was another like that man down in Hampshire who got caught because he couldn't spell. He'd been writing letters to his wife's mother saying they come from Hampstead, but when the coppers got him to write the word he left out the 'p' just the same as on the letters. Then they started to turn over the place in earnest and there was some blood splashes and a fingerprint. That was more or less it for Bertie.

It was the usual wartime story. She complained he did nothing but work and had thrown a cup of tea over him. He'd hit her with a stool and it went on from there. The trouble was he was a boxer and even if he has to hit her, there was no need for the stool. Then there was the usual fanny about how he had a blackout and wakes up to find she's dead. He put the body in the cellar and that evening, when the kids are out, he put it on his bike and pedals off to the river. He'd gone and smashed up her false teeth because the kids knew their mother always wore them.

There was a big petition to save him being topped. I think it was something like 30,000 signatures, and they reprieved him. But he didn't last all that long. He died in Parkhurst in 1947. Funnily, if he hadn't tried to get rid of the shoulder pad he'd probably never have been caught. What made it worse for him was there wasn't even any blood on it.

Over the years I got to know a lot of murderers who'd been reprieved. They'd all had the pressure in the condemned cell to make them think they were going to be topped. Condition them so that when it came to their being swagged that last morning it would be easy. Once they got the verdict and was back to prison they'd be taken straight in to the cell and there was a wall with a screen just like you'd have your photo taken against. They never realised that on the other side was a door and that's where the handle was.

If they was reprieved then the sheer joy could last a few years. I know it sounds silly but that's what happened. By the time they got their act together maybe they'd done three or four years, sometimes longer, and they'd become a proper prisoner. Then they could start to sail through their bird because they'd got that number of years behind them.

These were straight guys. In their wildest dreams or maybe nightmares they never thought they'd be going to prison. They was the kind who wouldn't steal an apple in the market. Then they'd found their old woman was having it off with the bloke two doors down the street and they'd lost it. You had to be wary of them. They were straight mugs and the screws could lay a cherry in front of them because they didn't know any better. They thought if they brown-nosed they'd be let out earlier. 'Anything you hear you've got to tell us. That's the rules.' And they'd go on, 'That Fraser, anything you hear about him . . .' Poor sods, there was a perpetual carrot. Their probation officers would

be the same, 'Anything you hear let the screws know . . .'
At that stage they'd shop their own mother.

Of course some turned out to be terrific guys. They'd tell
you how the screws had approached them, but unfortunately they was rare. Little did they realise that if they kept out
of trouble and had someone on the outside to look out for
them and give them a home they'd no need to be grasses to
get out after a few years.

You tend to forget that the IRA has been active for years.
When I was in the nick in the 1940s there was still a lot of
the IRA in prisons here left over from before the War.
There'd been a lot of IRA activity in the '30s. When people
of my generation talk about the Birmingham Bombing they
could as easily be talking about the one in August 1939.
What happened was a bomb was planted on a bicycle left
in Broadgate. Five people was killed. The coppers was able
to trace the owner from its serial number and five people
were charged. Three of them got off but two of them, James
Richards and James Barnes, were found guilty. There was
no question of a reprieve for them and they got topped in
February 1940.

One thing that's changed crime is DNA. Not so much in
what was my line of work, because there was always
fingerprints and palm prints, but in rapes and what you call
domestic murders. It's changed things so much.

The first time it was used in England was in a case in the
Midlands. There was a very nasty rape and murder in a
village, Littlethorpe near Leicester; back in 1984 it was. It's
amazing to think it's nearly twenty years ago. Then there
was a second one two years later. The chances are in
something like that it's someone who knows the area well
enough. One, maybe it's a stranger, but two – that's pushing
coincidence.

They had one kid in who confessed, saying he'd probably
gone mad when he done it. Here's the good thing about

DNA; the samples they took from him and the girls proved he couldn't have done it. He still did three months in custody though whilst they was sorting things out.

The next thing they did was to try and get samples from all the young men in the neighbourhood, well up to the age of 35. Of course you couldn't make people give samples but if they didn't you could go round and have a look at them. It had been done with fingerprints before then. They got a good turn out of people. You had to take some ID to the local hall and give a sample there and then. Of course, these things can go wrong and it did in this case. One fellow goes and gives sample for another. The man who should have turned up was called Colin Pitchfork and he persuaded his mate that he should give the sample for him. Of course what happens is that the fellow talks about it in the pub and one of the women in the group knows a copper and reports it to him. Not surprising that Pitchfork didn't want to give a sample. He'd got a couple of convictions for indecency already.

It was only a matter of hours before the coppers went to see him and straightaway he says he's done it. But really it was the girls' fault. He intended just to expose himself but they'd seen who he was and could identify him so they had to go. That's what his sort always say. It was just like that man in Bradford caught having it off with a bull terrier. The dog made the first approach he said.

Apparently in one case Pitchfork's taken his wife to evening class, killed the girl and then gone and collected her. The baby had been on the back seat of the car in a carry cot when he'd done it. He said he'd exposed himself to over 1,000 women, which shows people don't report this sort of thing as they should. I can see why they don't but if someone had then maybe he'd have been locked up before he got to the girls. He got life, of course, and the bloke who'd taken the test for him got a bender.

I was looking at the linens the other day about the chef, also from Leicester, who's been done twenty years later for killing a young girl. It seems the pros' evidence is all DNA. The fellow says there must be some mistake. I wonder if this DNA thing is all that it's cracked up to be. In a way it's just like fingerprinting was a century ago. The scientists said your little finger print matched something found on a cup and you put your hands up. Now, a hundred years later, there's doubts creeping in. Briefs didn't know how to deal with it. If the scientists said it was a match, well then, a match it was. Juries simply lapped up that sort of evidence. I remember that case when the brief John Platts Mills said that a copper had lifted a fingerprint and planted it. The judge, who was that Melford Stevenson, was so cross he tried to have his fees taken away from him. I reckon in ten or twenty years' time it's going to be the same with DNA, and there'll be a whole lot more people queuing up for the Criminal Review Commission. Platts Mills acted for me in my libel trial against the *Empire News*.

There was a really funny case in Peterborough a few years ago and the bloke was lucky he didn't swing. A few years earlier and it would have been a posthumous reprieve, which doesn't do too many people much good. One day in October 1973, around lunchtime, Albert Taylor calls on his girlfriend, Gillian Seaton, in Mountsteven Avenue to tell her how he's got on at a job interview, and he finds her fifteen-year-old sister, Jackie, stabbed to death and with a dog-lead around her throat. She had seventeen stab wounds and someone had interfered with her.

Instead of calling the police he panicked and ran, caught a bus and went back to his room at the Great Northern Hotel in Peterborough. He noticed he had blood on his trousers, from the time he had knelt by the body to see if Jackie was alive, and took them to the cleaners. Not the most sensible thing to have done. He then met Gillian as she left the local technical college but he didn't tell her of the murder. She went to another class and Taylor went to her home, but by then the coppers had already arrived.

He had an alibi. What he said was that he'd been on Peterborough railway station buying a newspaper at 1.15 p.m. Then he went for his interview which lasted half an hour and then he went to his girlfriend's home. He said he knew it was 1.15 p.m. when he was at the station because of the peculiar ticking noise of the station clock. The pros wasn't having that and they called evidence to show that the clock was electric and didn't tick. Guilty, My Lord.

Taylor wasn't having it though and he managed to get the case re-opened and coppers from another force to investigate the thing. The man in charge managed to trace the clock which had been removed when they'd done up the station. He found that it did tick, but only in cold weather and then at certain times of the day. It would have ticked at 1.15 p.m. on the day of the murder.

Taylor explained the reasons why he had not told his girlfriend of the death of her sister by saying that he thought he had imagined it. As to the cleaning, he said if he had killed Jackie he would have burned his clothes, and anyway, there was blood on his coat which he had not had cleaned. So far as running away from the scene of the crime was concerned, he said both that he had had trouble with the police before and that he had seen a cyclist killed under a bus as a child. After that he couldn't stand the sight of blood.

Very often, the Court of Appeal is grudging when they allow an appeal against conviction. It's never a straight, 'We think he's not guilty'. It's more usual that they say 'The conviction's not safe', which means we still think he might have done it. They did that a lot in the Irish terrorist convictions. They wouldn't come right out. It was the same here. 'Not clear where the truth is.' That sort of thing.

Taylor'd served five years and five months of his sentence and he got £12,000 compensation for the wrongful conviction. It doesn't seem much nowadays, what with people getting hundreds of thousands, but then the pay-out rate was about two grand a year and there was no guarantee you would get it. He was always hoping he'd get back with his girlfriend after he was freed but it didn't work out. She'd married someone else by that time and said she'd told the local papers she didn't want to see him again. So he changed his appearance and put an ad in the local linen for a new girlfriend.

Things seem to have gone better for him after that, until May 1980 when the house he was living in with his new girlfriend and their four-year-old daughter, Donna, caught fire. He didn't panic this time. He caught their three-month-old baby when it was thrown to safety, and then he went back in to try and get Donna. He got very badly burned. Brave thing to do. You like to think you would do it yourself but until it happens you never know. There's many a person would stay outside waiting for the fire brigade.

Birmingham was the place where Ray Rosa and Dido Frett got caught when they was off to Ireland after they did the Carters with me back in 1955. I was off there as well but I was travelling separate which was good for me. It wasn't their fault neither. What had happened they was travelling with Patsy Lyons, who'd been such a good man in his day. He was the one who did a jewellers in Victoria with me at the end of the War. Later he mixed with the wrong people. He was with Charlie Mitchell who turned against the twins when Mitchell has a bull down Fulham way and ends up prossing the pair who did him. Patsy shouldn't never, ever have been in the same car as Mitchell.

Anyway, Patsy's driving Ray and Dido up north. In fact they're on their way to Leeds when they get a pull. What's happened is that Patsy had done a jewellers in Birmingham the previous year. What people didn't know is that in them days jewellers used to buy wholesale and a lot of them belonged to a chain. The suppliers would drive round delivering fresh stuff and taking away the stuff which hadn't sold, moving it around. It was a routine just like sending a couple of men to the bank at the same time on a Friday. Anyway Patsy was in his own car and he got nicked. He was in Winson Green a few months before he got a not guilty.

In them days you had to wait for Quarter Sessions, which in the beginning was just that, every three months, and if you missed it you generally had to wait for the next one. Sometimes there was a bit of compassion. There was one case in the north, Durham I think it was, that a woman got arrested for killing her old man on the Friday and appeared at the Assizes the next week. It was the quickest there's ever been. If she'd missed it she'd have had to wait for months. I seem to remember it was some sort of mercy killing and although she got sentenced to death everyone knew she was going to be reprieved.

Patsy's in his own car again and the coppers see it and bang. This time it's the jackpot for them because there's warrants out for Dido and Ray over Carter. Patsy gives them a story, says he didn't know they were on the run and they have to let him go. Jack and Dido weren't so lucky. They was brought down to London.

Like I say I'd been in another car and I got to Liverpool and over to Dublin. I was met off the boat and stowed away safely in the suburbs. Bill had arranged it all. I stayed very quiet but when it come to it I wasn't there long. If I'd stayed there longer I'd have made myself useful, done a bit of work, but when I heard they'd been nicked, I was gutted. I felt responsible and I come back to London to see if I could help straighten things out. That was me gone as well. I wasn't out of the baggage hall at Heathrow when I was nicked.

Birmingham was a lucky place for my friend Ruby Sparks, the great smash and grab man and escaper, though. He knocked down a woman after a smash and grab raid in New Street in November 1924 and she died. For a time there was a chance he'd be done for murder but he stayed away and by the time he was nicked there was no chance the witnesses would pick him out on an ID. The coppers never managed to trace him or the other two who was with him. They'd left behind a load of stuff in the Buick when they abandoned it, including a Van Heusen collar with laundry marks on it. It was the first smash and grab raid there'd been in Brum and they nicked over a grand's worth of jewels.

Funnily, two days later there was a second smash and grab. This time a couple of fellows did a pawnbrokers. They was chased by a man on a bicycle but they got on a tram and he couldn't pedal fast enough.

It's amazing what ordinary straight people kill over and how you never know your neighbour's a schizophrenic until it's too late. Look at that case in Birmingham a few years ago. Jeffrey Gould couldn't stand his neighbour James Bourke, playing classical music and so he battered him to death. He thought Bourke had been sent by what he called the Divine Lord to spy on him. Then there was two people on different occasions when neighbours killed each other over the gardening. One of them happened quite recently in Leicester. A fellow called Sandor Bata goes and kills his neighbour Mick Willson because he was dumping his clematis cuttings on his allotment. He says Willson was abusive so he goes and gets a shotgun. He was lifed off in September 1999. The most amazing bit of the story is that Bata was 73 when he done it.

What with modern science I don't suppose now there'll be too many more cases where girls have been cut up and put in parcels all over the railway and no one can find out who they are. But I expect people will still have a go. There was a girl a few years back found in a suitcase on the Wolverhampton train from London. Well, a bit of her was. Her head and legs was missing, but they soon worked out she was Asian. Then a bit more of her turned up and then, finally, her head was found in a duffel bag over Wanstead Flats. It turned out her father had done it. She'd been going out with a married man and got herself in the club. She wouldn't give the man up and her dad hit her over the head with a coal hammer.

Whenever I watch those news bits on TV with grieving boyfriends and husbands saying they can't think who'd have killed their girls and someone must be able to help, it's then I start to wonder. Of course a lot of them are genuine but sometimes I think the police have people on so they can see how they behave. It's not that rare to see them weeping on the telly one week and the next being hustled into the magistrates' court with a blanket over their heads.

Look at that Gordon Wardell back in 1994. His wife Carol's body was found in a lay-by near Nuneaton. The building society where she worked had its branch robbed after her code had been used to get in. There he was in a wheelchair weeping on the box. Then there was him throwing a personal note into the grave at her funeral. What had happened, he said, was that a gang had broken into the house, and had been waiting for him to come home. They'd tied him up and taken Carol off to the building society and killed her after they'd got the money. What the pros said was that he'd suffocated her and gone and done the building society himself. After that he'd tied himself up and he'd been in the house for fourteen hours before the police broke in and found him, but he hadn't even wet himself. The jury agreed. The last I heard he was still saying he was innocent and the coppers had made a lot of mistakes in the enquiries.

NOTTINGHAM

S herwood Borstal near Nottingham was for older boys. You could still be sent to Borstal at the age of 23 and so some of the so-called boys was grown men with families. Kenny Strickson got topped for doing the matron there. Mrs Phillips was her name, and she was only 46. In 1949 it was.

She must have been quite good looking for a matron and it seems like he'd made a remark about her figure and she hadn't put him down hard enough. She'd said something about it was a good job she was broadminded. He told another inmate that he fancied his chances with her. He was told he'd get three years, but he went to see her back up near the chapel, locked the door and did her. He didn't touch her sexually but he didn't half bash her about. The doctors reckoned most of the blows had come when she was on the floor and he'd broken up a couple of chairs to use. He goes and confesses straight away. He'd have been better off sticking to Widow Palm like the rest of us.

The trial was over in a day. The pros called the boy he'd talked with to prove he'd done it deliberately. The fellow had done eighteen months for rape, which shows what lenient sentences there were then. Kenny's brief tried to show that the fellow had made it all up and was trying to get an early release but, of course, the bloke denied it. The brief didn't call Kenny and relied on a medical report that his father had been in a home and had epilepsy, but it didn't do no good. The jury can only have gone out for a smoke. They were back in 25 minutes. But by then the big story in the papers was of John Haigh, the acid bath murderer, who'd done that Mrs Deacon down in Crawley and a whole lot of others it turned out. I was the hospital in Brixton with him before his trial. All murderers went in the hospital in those days so they could get a nut and gut report on them. I'd just been nicked over a torch but because I'd been in the hospital at Cane Hill they had to have me under observation. Haigh seemed perfectly normal to me.

It was a fellow from Nottingham that went and confessed to a newspaper reporter. Newspapers were really big on crime a bit after the War. Each of them had their own special reporter, often more than one, and they had good contacts. There was people like Tom Tullett and Peter Earle. Like I've said before, Edgar Wallace knew an uncle of mine and he was always down the Elephant picking up bits of gossip. Anyway this bloke, Herbert Mills, telephones Norman Rae, the reporter on the *News of the World*, in August 1951 to say he'd discovered the body of a woman and it looked like murder. He said he'd read a poem when he found the body while he thought about what he should do. It's funny how often the killer reckons he's discovered the body. That way, in the past at any rate, he's got some sort of explanation for how blood got all over him.

What had happened was Mills had strangled the woman after trying to steal her necklace. He seems to have been one of those committing the perfect crime, or so he thought. He fancied himself as an artist and poet and took this middle-aged woman out to the cinema and arranged to meet her the next day, which was when he did her. He went and made a long confession, which he wrote out himself, and the paper gave it to the police. He was on the blower trying to get the *News of the World* to buy an exclusive of his story when the coppers traced the call to a coin box and they give him a tap on the shoulder whilst he was still talking with Rae. That was the last time he saw daylight. He'd wanted £250 for the story.

He tried to run the defence he'd discovered the body. If there'd been only blood he might have done better, but there was fibres from his suit under her nails. That was a bit too much to swallow. They topped him at Lincoln even though he was only nineteen. There was a report that his heart beat on for another twenty minutes. It must have been a bit iffy whether he was all there.

Paddy Meehan got out of Nottingham prison with three others in August 1963. It was the same month I was bombing the screws' houses in Pentonville and Wandsworth and when it come to it the Nottingham local paper give that more coverage than the escape. But Paddy's was a story and a half. In 1961 he'd come down to London to do the Co-op Store in Edmonton along with Billy Gentry, and it looked a million to one that someone grassed them. I think Paddy was trying to put money together so's him and his family could go to Australia.

Paddy was just the explosives expert and when he looked at what they was doing he reckoned there was enough jelly bobbling about to send them and half the neighbourhood to kingdom come. That was why the English boys had to get in expert help. If you didn't know what you was doing you could blow yourself up. That's what happened in Liverpool one time. Some fellows were trying to blow the safe at the Bootle Dock Board which had got the dockers' pay in it. They must have used too much. I don't think they killed themselves but there was blood all over the place. It's at times like that you've got to have a tame doctor. You don't want to be booking into the local casualty department. Anyway Paddy's taking the jelly out of the lock with a knitting needle when Old Bill arrives. He got an eight at the

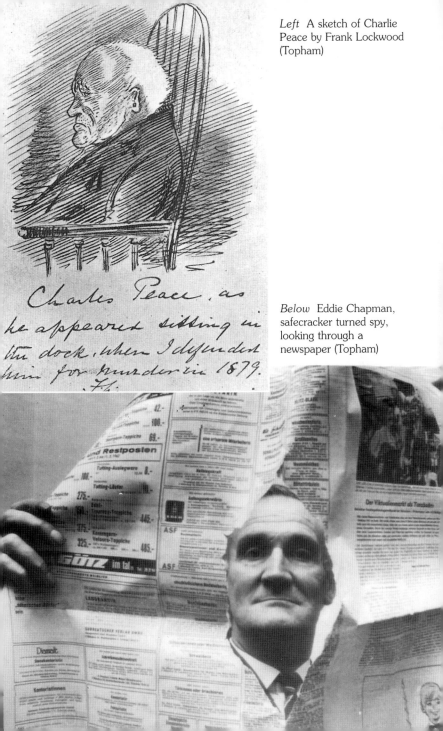

Left A sketch of Charlie
Peace by Frank Lockwood
(Topham)

Charles Peace, as
he appeared sitting in
the dock, when I defended
him for murder in 1879.
F.L.

Below Eddie Chapman,
safecracker turned spy,
looking through a
newspaper (Topham)

Left Archibald Hall: the butler killer (Topham)

Right Peter Manuel on the closing day of his trial for 8 murders (Hulton Archive)

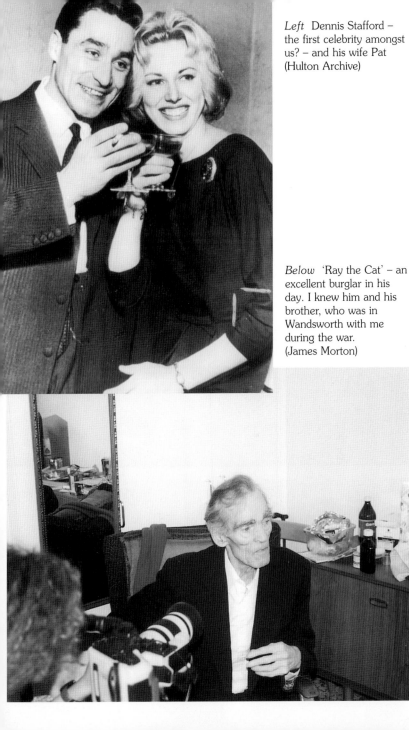

Left Dennis Stafford – the first celebrity amongst us? – and his wife Pat (Hulton Archive)

Below 'Ray the Cat' – an excellent burglar in his day. I knew him and his brother, who was in Wandsworth with me during the war. (James Morton)

Top left Arthur Thompson's Glasgow – his 'ranch' . . .

Middle left . . . the Barrowlands dance hall . . .

Bottom left . . . and the Provenmill Inn, where his funeral was held. (all James Morton)

Right Me, a little more comfortable now.

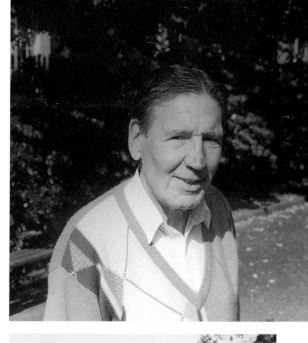

Right Me outside Lincoln Prison with a couple of well-wishers.

Left The forbidding entrance to Dartmoor Prison as I remember it (Topham)

Right A prisoner on the security wing at Durham (Topham)

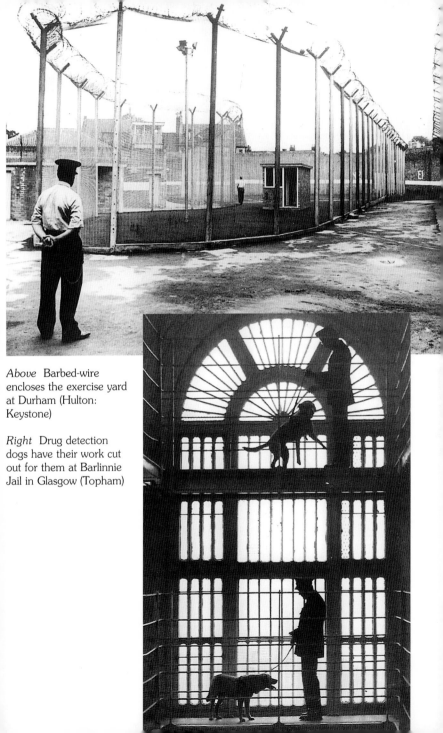

Above Barbed-wire encloses the exercise yard at Durham (Hulton: Keystone)

Right Drug detection dogs have their work cut out for them at Barlinnie Jail in Glasgow (Topham)

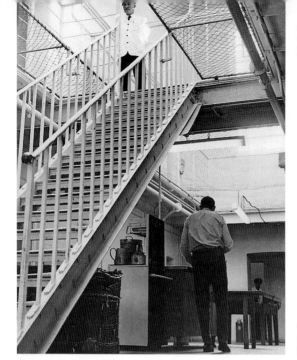

Left Inside the security wing at Parkhurst on the Isle of Wight (Topham)

Below Outside the security block at Parkhurst (Hulton Archive)

Bailey under the name Patrick Carson. Judge Maude was the one put him away; a very aristocratic man he was. Good sense of humour if you wasn't on the end of it. He once told two top of the roofs who'd been caught plating each other not to do it again, but if they felt they couldn't control themselves then not to do it under his favourite bridge.

Paddy tried to get out in December 1962 and all he got for his troubles was six months' loss of remission and some bread and water. Then in August 1963 he tried again. There was a diversion set up when they was meant to be watching a cricket match in the nick and they was away through the fence. There was a car waiting for them. That's what I mean when I say it's no use just getting out. You've got to stay out, and for that you need help. They all come down to London and go round to Eva who's only too glad to help them out and give them some clothes and food. Paddy and a man called Hogan go back up to Scotland and then, if you believe what he said, and wrote for that matter, Meehan had the most amazing time.

He went over to Dublin and then went on to Frankfurt. After that he took a train to a place called Badhersfeld and then he got a bike and cycled over into East Germany. It was there he got nicked. It seems like he'd been to some Communist meetings in the past and he'd run into one of the men there a few months before he'd been nicked over the Co-op. According to Paddy his name had been put up as someone who might help spring a spy – there was a few of them in the nick at the time – and when he'd got to East Germany he was pulled. Once people started interrogating him, he told them that he could spring a spy and gave them details of the lay-outs of some of the nicks and so forth. It didn't work out too well for him because by the time he'd given all this info, the East Germans simply took him to Berlin and at Checkpoint Charlie handed him over. After that it was back to Wandsworth to finish off the sentence. MI5 interviewed him and what he used to say was that he told them the Communists wanted to spring the Krogers and George Blake. According to the Mountbatten Report into how Blake got sprung, Paddy had said there wasn't much interest in him. By that time Paddy had got sent to Parkhurst, which was where he met Jimmy Griffiths.

What I wonder now is why more people didn't try and escape in the old days. There was the great prize. If you stayed away until the end of your sentence the authorities sort of called it a draw and you didn't have to go back. It didn't do you no good if you failed to go the distance. You didn't get any time wiped off for the days you was out. Got a bit more, more like, but if you kept away from them then the sentence was scrubbed. I suppose the reason there wasn't more escapes was that you was watched so much. There were so few prisoners at the time. No question of two or three in a cell. Half the time there weren't enough cons to fill them. There wasn't much work and so you was locked up most of the time except for exercise. You could expect a cell search every ten days and, since when you was out, all the cell doors were open the screws would be able to look in. There was no question of other cons stealing because there wasn't anything in them to nick. Anyone who was even suspected was branded a cell thief and could expect a very bad time. There was no Rule 43 then so people couldn't ask to go into isolation. Rule 45 it is now, but I don't suppose it'll be known as anything but Rule 43 for years. Even though a man who was thought to be a cell thief might have been innocent, it stuck and it would follow him around.

If you got caught trying to escape you'd be put on special watch even though that wasn't much. You had to put your clothes outside the cell door at night. Not that that stopped Charlie Wilson getting out of Winson Green and that was years later. People also had to wear patches. They refused at first and there was a tear up in Wandsworth but, of course, it was like trying to stop the tide coming in.

I don't know about women who marry men who are doing life or a long sentence. If I was a psychiatrist or a miracle man maybe I could give you the right answer. To some of them the man represents something different. It sounds silly but it's a bit of glamour. Dead straight women are never going to meet men like that in their lives. There's also a theory that for some of them, they do it knowing the man's not going to be out for years so there's no pressure on them. Some of them do it just for the publicity. The more famous you are the more interest you get from the outside. A guy gets the headlines and women write in. Years back Ruby Sparks used to tell me women wrote in after his escape from Dartmoor and the news of him being in the riot there. As I've said you usually weren't given letters from people you hadn't written to in the first place but sometimes they'd let them through. By the end of my twenty even I at my age was getting a few bits of love mail. Of course by then it was easier to get letters.

Then there's the women who think that, despite all the evidence, they're going to reform them. Love of a good woman and that sort of thing. They're the ones who are going to make the men change. Sometimes it works out really well but as often as not there's problems. Stands to reason there's going to be. It's difficult enough when someone comes out after a long stretch to readjust to life on the outside with people he knows, let alone with someone he doesn't. All these years he's been under pressure to keep his cell tidy and clean and now he finds his new wife, however tidy and smart she is when she comes to see him, doesn't make the bed or leaves the toothpaste all over the bathroom.

Of course a lot of men who've had long stretches will come out with nothing. The Discharged Prisoners Association would give them something in my day but it was a real problem. You haven't got any dough. This woman you've married, and who you've only seen outside the warehouse for a couple of days, is on at you to get work and so there's a real temptation to do a job. If you get away with it that's good but you don't really care if you get nicked and it's back in the warehouse. It's an option. If a Chap comes out that's different. He's going to get help and cash from his friends.

As I've said before it was never any hardship for me readjusting. The moment I was out I'd forgotten what it was all about. If someone said after I'd been out 24 hours, 'What were you doing this time two days ago, Frank?' I'd have to think, and then I'd go, 'What's the time? 2.30 p.m. Well, I'd have been banged up.'

It's difficult enough for the woman who's already married and then discovers her husband's a murderer. Is she going to stay with him? Does she send a Dear John straight off or let him down as the years go by? A lot of women start working for the man's release. There was one who got her bloke's release almost by accident. The fellow was a vet and he'd gone down for life. She was Catherine Crooks who'd married Ryan James from Burton on Trent whilst he was in Gartree. She'd known him before and in fact they'd been having an affair before he was put away. What the pros had said was that Ryan James had given his wife, Sandra, an injection of Immobilion, which they drug horses with, to clear off his debts with the insurance money. The jury gives him a guilty and the judge says what an evil man he is. How wrong can you get? Catherine's going through James's old papers and she comes across a note from the wife stuck in between the pages of one of his books, saying that she wasn't leaving him anything except the note, and she'd added, 'If you find it in time'. It really confirmed she'd done herself. You wonder how many other cases like it there are.

Mind you, marrying a man you know's committed a murder and done his time for it must be better than marrying a bloke who's done a girl 24 hours before your wedding and you not knowing it. That's what a fellow David Blake did in Leeds back in 1934. Strangled a waitress, Emily Yeomans, and tried to rape her as well. He was done because he kept her powder compact and the girls she worked with recognised it because it had a torn lid.

He'd already done time for attacking a girl and stealing her necklace, which he gave to the girl he was going out with then. There was a big effort to get him a reprieve but he was topped.

Taking little girls off the streets and killing them isn't really anything new. Frederick Nodder was one of those nonces who do that. His was a bit of a legal case, like the one in London I've mentioned.[1] It was straightforward in a way; a little girl, Mona Tinsley, disappeared in January 1937 and Nodder'd been seen with her at a bus stop near Retford. When she never turned up he was done for abduction and got a seven. It was really one of those no body cases where they reckoned they couldn't pros for murder without one. The judge was convinced the kid was dead, saying things like '. . . may be that time will reveal the dreadful secret which you carry in your breast'. It's amazing to think that they actually spoke like that in them days.

Anyway, three months after Nodder's been potted, Mona's body is found in the River Idle and so they try him for murder. In fact the only reason she was found was that a medium predicted where the body was. There was no doubt she'd been strangled. His brief tried the defence that he'd been tried once and so couldn't be tried again. When that did no good they reckoned she must have met a stranger. That didn't wash either, and he was topped at Lincoln just before the year's end.

Nottingham was where the judge, Mr Justice Watkin Williams, dropped dead in a brothel. He'd been touring on Assize in 1884 and he was having a bit of relaxation in the evening when the dinner and the port and then the effort was a bit much for him and his heart give out. The place he copped it in was on Low Pavement. They got him back to his lodgings and tried to cover it up but these things never

---

[1] See p. 17.

work. Then they tried to hide the inquest away as well. Coroners could hold inquests any hour and wherever they wanted, even in their own front rooms, so as to keep people out. But again it did no good. The linens got hold of it. 'Corinthian pleasure' they called it. The girl he had been with, who was called Nellie Banks, said the old gentleman had given a sort of grunt and she thought he'd come, but he'd gone. He wasn't even that old, only 56.

NORTHAMPTONSHIRE

S ometimes I think the killing's the easy part. It's what to do with the body that's the trouble. Billy Hill was all right when he had the man at the crematorium squared. Drop the body in, give it the military salute and that's that. They don't come back from the ashes. But over the years a lot of good people – and bad ones for that matter – have come unstuck trying to be too tricky about what to do with bodies. Epping Forest's always been a favourite place. That was where they found Jerry Hawley, the so-called tattooed man who starred in his own porn films, as I've said in *Mad Frank's London*.

Then there was that copper who liked to take pictures of girls tied up. The man had been on duty outside Downing Street once upon a time, guarding Mrs Thatcher. He started off with them prettily enough, little pink ribbons on their wrists, things like that. Then it was a bit more serious, and eventually he got done over an eighteen-stone lesbian brass in leather and chains, who was blind drunk and went and suffocated in the mask he'd got her to wear.

This was down in his place in King's Cross and now he's got problems. He can't hardly go to his superiors and say

'I've got this eighteen-stone les in an armchair in the flat and I can't move her', because, for a start, coppers aren't meant to be going out with brasses. So what does he do? He gets her in the bath and starts sawing. It's summer and the neighbours think there's a smell, but he gets her in moveable bits and it's off to Epping Forest where there's every chance she won't be found until the foxes have had a good go. Bad luck on him. Some kid sees her bum and starts using it for target practice. The kid goes to see if he's hit anything and now it's all on top. He got done for murder and went down for it, but the Court of Appeal said all he should have had was a sentence for hindering an inquest and he could have five years.

Other people have tried to burn the victims. It certainly won't work now when even the smallest bit of bone is going to be identifiable, but Alfred Rouse, who was a commercial traveller, tried it in the 1930s.

It was a really big case, not just the murder itself but the trial. He just got himself in a terrible mess. He had women all over the place and I think what he really wanted was to disappear. He'd been in the First World War and he'd been injured, so you have to give him credit for something; they'd operated on his head. I don't know whether it was what made him a bit funny but he couldn't keep his hands off women. He's got to have been a charmer because they reckoned he had eighty illegitimate children, and there was always some bum bailiff knocking on the door with another court order. He also went and had a bigamous marriage which, I suppose, is about the only thing I've never done. He was a right Hans Christian Andersen as well; said he'd been to Eton and Cambridge when he'd been to the local council school. When he decided he had to disappear he was meant to be getting married to yet another girl, Ivy, who was in the club and thought he was going to move her to a big place down in Kingston. More fool her.

What he does is set fire to his car in the middle of the night in a place called Hardingstone in Northamptonshire.

November 1930 it was, and it was big stuff in the linens. Remember, there wasn't all that much murder in those days. No Yardies opening fire in a club every second night in some drugs battle. A murder was headlines. It was bad luck for him that two men was walking by and saw him climb out of a ditch. What was more there was a body in the car and the coppers traced the plates back to Rouse's home in Finchley. They had his wife go to Northampton, and she had a look at what was left and said it looked like her old man's stuff.

So far so good, but this is where Rouse went and made another mistake really, and I've never been able to work out why he did it except that Ivy was in a bad way with the baby. Instead of getting out of the country, which was the only thing for him, he goes to Glamorganshire to see her. Her father went and showed him a picture of the burned out car and all. There was also a description of him by the two men who'd seen him in the ditch. He must know his number's up and he gets on a bus back to London. He's nicked at Hammersmith bus station. By this time he's thought he's got up a half-way decent story. What he tells the coppers is that he'd given a lift to a man who was hitch-hiking and he'd stopped to refill the petrol with a can he had. After that he'd gone over to the ditch to have a jimmy and suddenly when he looks back the car's in flames. He thought the man must have struck a match and that was when the car went up. It wasn't the best story but it wasn't a bad one in the circumstances. Remember scientific evidence wasn't like it is today. What the pros said was that he'd set fire to the car with the man still conscious.

What really did him was his own expert. He called a man who said he was an engineer and tried to explain that there'd been a spark and it was all an accident. Norman Birkett, who was doing the pros, asked him, 'What is the co-efficient of the expansion of brass?' When the man said he didn't know Birkett just ripped him to pieces after that, making out he wasn't an expert at all. People said it was an unfair question, but the brief said he'd got it out of a pocket diary for engineers and if it was in there then the man should have known. It didn't matter much because Rouse went and made a confession to the *Daily Sketch* who'd put up the money for his defence. That was the rules. They'd pay your brief but if you was topped you was expected to have left them the story of how you'd done it so they could get their money back through selling more papers afterwards.

They had a waxwork of him in Madam Tussauds in the Chamber of Horrors there. There used to be a sort of jury box where all the great murderers like him and Seddon and Charlie Peace were sitting like they were doing the deciding. There was also an exhibit of torture through the ages and a man hanging on a butcher's hook. I used to think that was much the best.

The copper who did the Rouse investigation got called in a few years later to have a look at a murder in Dunstable even though it wasn't in his county. The reason was it was a girl who'd been the fiancée of a Bedfordshire copper who was done. Ruby Keen was engaged but she was still quite happy to go out with other blokes when the man was on duty. She was done back in 1932, strangled with her scarf, said Spilsbury. The reason they was being a bit discreet was because she'd been seeing another copper, as well as a fellow called Leslie Stone. He'd been out with her and then done her. Although there was no sexual assault he got topped at Pentonville and the other copper was booted out the force. The girl's fiancé was asked to resign, which seems a bit hard. Losing your girl and your job at the same time don't seem really fair.

Funnily, the day they topped Stone was the same day of the year they'd had the first private hanging in the country. Back in 1868 it was. A young fellow, Thomas Wells, got the sack from his job with the London, Chatham and Dover Railway and he went and shot the stationmaster. It was the first time a hanging hadn't been done in public, although there was plenty of reporters there. It seems it was a botched job and the boy just strangled slowly.

MANCHESTER

Manchester was a good place to be just after the War and one of the best of the men there was Bobby Critchley, who had a bulletproof car. I've no idea where he got it. He was a large man, distinguished looking. There was a big Jewish population in Manchester and Jack Spot came to the city in search of a nightclub to mind. The club Spot fancied was Critchley's Jacaranda in the Stretford Road, but Bobby saw him off. Over the years Bobby had been involved in racecourse protection and he'd done a bit of bird in his youth, but when I knew him he'd got some property and he was more of a putter-up. The Mrs Post job I've written about was one he gave us.[1]

There was plenty of others though. A good man who wasn't a villain but who mixed with us was known as the Aga because he looked like the Aga Khan. He was a brilliant card player, straight as well as hooky. Very often there was no need for him to cheat. If he went down a spiel you could see the punters lining up to play cards with him or have their man play with him. It was like that Paul Newman film,

---

[1] See Mad Frank.

a card player would have backers who'd stake him out and take a percentage of his winnings. Sometimes the Aga'd string them along, let them win a bit and so the next night they'd be back for more, thinking he wasn't as good as he was cracked up to be – then Bosh. There was big money floating around both Manchester and London. No disrespect but the better players were in London. Up there they wasn't quite up to the mark and it was like having a baby over for him. As I say he wasn't a villain but he admired villains. To him anyone could play cards – of course they couldn't, not like him – but it was a different thing going out and risking your liberty. A couple of times when I come out he slipped me a few hundred. He faded away. He needed to be smart and he got ill and was never the same. For a time he played in a spiel Billy Howard had in Brixton but he went right down the pan.

Then there was Bobby MacDermott, a really good man – King of the Barrowmen, and a good thief and receiver in his time. He was probably the king of them all, linked up with Billy Hill and Arthur Thompson. I don't think people realised quite what a network there was even back in them days. He'd come and see me in the nick when I was doing the rounds and when I was up his way. He didn't drink. He'd done a bit of bird in his youth after a fight when he'd been drinking and he just give it up.

I'm not sure Manchester was a good city for me or for many of us. I was never nicked there but all the jobs I did didn't exactly pay for the trouble. There was that job we did with Jock the Fitter, a tie-up on Mrs Post which come to nothing. Jerry Callaghan and Jimmy Robson lost a load of jewellery in Manchester, along with Danny Swain. He was the wheelman, of course, in a smash and grab but what Jerry and Jimmy do in their hurry is not shut the door properly as they're getting in and the stuff goes all over the pavement. They couldn't stop and pick it up but at least they got away all right. It was the same with the Aussie, the one they called Joe the Bash, when he did a job in St James's before the War. It shows there's more to a blagging than breaking a window.

In fact the more I think back, in my earlier days Manchester wasn't a good city to me. The info where Jack Spot was the night I did him and got a seven came from a contact in Manchester, though I don't suppose it was Manchester's fault for that. Then in a way it was down to a fellow from Manchester that I got the five which led to the twenty. Not his fault, of course, but he came from Manchester.

There was some good clubs up in the place. Not as good as say Churchills or Winstons, but good clubs and Owen Ratcliffe had one. Cromfords it was, a lovely place. If I remember rightly Jack London, the old heavyweight boxer, was on the door. There was also a lot of what they called Sporting Clubs. Nice places they was in the main. You could take your wife and there'd be a couple of bouts of all-in wrestling, not people on the big circuits, but those who was billed as The Fighting Irishman versus Red Mask, that sort of thing. Then there'd be a cabaret, someone like Wee Willie Harris, and a bit of Bingo. All for just a few quid. The ex-wrestler 'Big' Bill Benny, who was massive, owned clubs including the Cabaret Club; he used to advertise it as 'The South of France comes to Manchester', and Chez Joey with roulette and blackjack tables at the back. When the police come the doorman would try and delay them a bit to give the punters time to clear up. The story was always that Big Bill died in bed and had to be sort of winched off the girl.

It was Owen who set me on my way to the twenty. Not that it was his fault, but Owen and his partner Paddy McGrath had opened Mr Smith's in Catford and were having a bit of trouble there. That was when me and Eddie was asked to look after the place and put a few of our machines in. The very night we signed up there was the fight with the Haywards and Dickie Hart was shot.

* * *

It was funny how reprieves went. Sometimes you couldn't see neither rhyme nor reason. Look at that fellow Patrick Monaghan who killed a woman in Swords, near Dublin just before the War. Beat her, raped her and then suffocated her. The jury recommended mercy on the grounds that he hadn't intended to kill her and he got a reprieve. He only served eleven as well. When you think poor Charlie Richardson got 25 for a spot of GBH in a case they wouldn't even bring to court today. I suppose that Monaghan case was in Eire so they may have done things differently there.

Contrast that with the case of James Makin who does a brass, Sarah Clutton, in Manchester in 1925. She was only 24 and she'd been poxed up before; now she thinks she's got it again so to cheer herself up she goes and buys herself a new green hat. The pox isn't going to stop her working though, and she picks up this Makin fellow in the city centre. They start having a few drinks and she insists he takes her to his home. He's married and living with his wife's uncle out at Cross Street in Newton Heath which is four miles away. He must have been mad to agree but off they go on the bus. His wife and the uncle are out working but there's plenty of neighbours twitching the curtains, so to speak. They see the pair go in and notice her hat in particular. Usual thing, they thought they'd been drinking but wasn't drunk. Then an hour later he comes out alone. When the uncle and his wife come back from work, under the bed is what's left of Sarah, who's had her throat cut and whose legs is sticking out. Makin meets a pal and tells him what he's done before he goes and gives himself up. What seems to have happened is that after they've had it off the brass starts crying and asks for a bowl of water. He realises he may have caught something and does her.

It turns out that his eldest brother had died in the asylum and that Makin begun to get depressed after the War. He'd thrown himself in the Rochdale canal three times. His sister said she'd had to turn him out because of his moods and the threats he made against her and her husband whilst he'd been living there. His wife said he'd threatened to kill her and she'd hidden his razor but it didn't do no good. The jury was only out twenty minutes, and he didn't bother to appeal. It was all a bit of a waste really because it comes out there was nothing wrong with the brass after all.

It was in Strangeways when I saw a Flying Saucer. I was in my cell one night and it just came past the window. Fortunately Stan Cahill saw it from his cell too, otherwise people would have thought I really was mad. I hadn't liked to say anything until Stan mentioned it first. I think there was word of it on the radio the next day. Stan was a good boxer in his day. He trained well in the nick and was allowed out to take part in the ABAs as a light-heavyweight – under escort of course. I don't think he won but he did quite well. His trouble was he couldn't get the real training you can outside. He turned pro when he come out but he wasn't really up to it. I think he opened a couple of clubs in the North. He was big in Liverpool.

I think the last time I saw him was when he came to my seventieth birthday at Jack Trickett's place in Stockport. He brought a half dozen of champagne over to our table and we had a good chat. That was a good evening. I remember seeing a whole party of dwarves at one of the other tables and I couldn't think what they was doing. I don't think I'd ever seen as many at the same time. The comedian had a good joke with them and they loved it. Then I realised they must have been up for the pantomine, *Snow White*. Poor old Stan, he's doing a long stretch up in Scotland now; something like a twenty.

Mrs Van Der Elst reckoned she spent more time protesting about executions in Manchester than anywhere else. When she first went up there in 1935 it was over the killing of a girl called Amelia Nuttall who was known as Milly. It was her boyfriend John Bridge who was in the frame. He was only 22. He'd known her most of his life but then he'd met a girl, Eileen Earl, at work and he got himself in a right mess. More or less engaged to both of them. Eileen breaks it off and starts going out with another fellow; then she breaks that off because she realises she's in love with John, and he reckons he's in love with her. So he makes an appointment to break it off with Milly, but he's late and she starts a bull with him and comes at him with a poker. He takes the poker from her and bashes her with it and then he takes a bread knife and cuts her throat and pushes off. He's nicked when he comes back later. The coppers say it was to see what he'd done because there's plenty of people like to come back to the scene of the crime. That's why coppers turn out at funerals, just to clock the faces of who's there.

The jury recommended mercy and that's where things went wrong. The lawyers decided there shouldn't be an appeal and they'd go straight to the Home Secretary, but he wouldn't wear it. Mrs Elst was on the blower day and night it seems and sending telegrams but it did no good neither. She held a rally at the Free Trade Hall the night before the topping and 2,000 turned up. She was urging them to protest outside Strangeways the next morning and a lot of them did go there as well. In fact they say it was the biggest crowd ever to go to a non-public hanging. I don't suppose it would have made Bridge feel any better even if he'd got to hear of it. Mrs Elst had a row with the people there, shouted they was like the French Revolution, and they said they was mothers and what about poor Milly. She went to the inquest on Bridge and the coroner got quite sniffy. He said 'this matron' would be better off if she devoted herself to saving souls, which, I suppose, in a way is what she was trying to do all along. Then one juror pipes up that he agrees and there'd be a lot more killings if there wasn't hanging.

Brasses have a hard time. It's said you're most likely to get done by someone you know but in their case it must be the reverse. I saw a bit in the papers a few months ago saying there was a survey amongst brasses in Glasgow and at some time or another 80 per cent had been attacked or raped or knocked about in some way. I should think if you did a survey they're killed more than anyone else. That's one reason some girls don't mind working for pimps. There's a bit of protection from the punters knowing there's a bloke round the corner who's there to look after you. That and they always think the ponce is going to marry them and they can give up the game just as soon as he's become a lawyer, or written a bestseller, or gets a try-out with Man United. There's always some excuse.

The danger is you can just meet a psycho. Look at that girl Annie Riley who meets a Jewish boy, Solly Stein, just before he's 21. Back in October 1931 it was. He'd never been with a girl and he thinks he ought to give himself a treat for his birthday. He's been out celebrating with his mates and he meets her in New Bridge Street just by Deansgate. They go to the Station Temperance Hotel and he puts down ten shillings for a room. He asked for a knock on the door so he wouldn't be late for work. Next morning, when he wakes up he looks and sees she's a right old scrubber, and I suppose he's a bit ashamed at what he's done so, instead of just walking out and writing it off to experience, he strangles her with his tie. He put in granny knots so the poor girl can't undo them. Stands and watches her apparently. Then he wanders around Manchester and stays out a second night just when his family is preparing to have his 21st for him; he gives himself up the next day.

When he comes up at court he pleads guilty. His brief can't understand it and tries to get the judge to disallow the plea because he knows it's a topping matter, but the judge won't have it. After the case the boy won't see anyone but his father and then only once, and he won't appeal. He just kept on saying he was guilty. I think he was only the third Jewish man ever to be hung at Strangeways.

There was a story that the hangman James Billington was in the Fox Tavern in Wigan at the end of the nineteenth century and he's introduced all round and shakes hands with people. One fellow, Elijah Winstanley, says he wouldn't like to meet him in his official capacity and there's a good old laugh. Anyway Elijah and his mate go out to do a screwing at the local railway depot which goes wrong and a copper's stabbed. The man who gets topped by Billington is this Winstanley. It a bit like that story of Albert Pierrepont, who was called Tish by his mate in the pub he had, and he calls him Tosh. One day he's called to do the job and he finds it's Tosh he's going to hang. Pierrepont was the man I did at Wandsworth when he came to hang Derek Bentley.

If you were in punishment and reported sick, the doctors came to see you, but on the morning of an execution you were taken over to the hospital. E wing was just a few yards from the hospital. They tried to discourage prisoners from going sick on the day of an execution. On E1 you had to have two screws unlock you if you were in the single cells; this day, a mug screw did it on his own and told me to wait at the end of E2 landing. I said, 'Which end? The hospital end or the centre end?' He said the centre end. I went down the corridor as he'd said, there were two other prisoners already there. Patsy Lyons was one, and a fellow called Spiro. Now it's a bit after eight and out of F2 wing come Pierrepont with two burly prison officers on each side. One was Jack Manning. I'd already lost my remission after doing Carter. I did Pierrepoint – *bosh* – and kicked the door of the cell, shouting out, 'God bless you son, I know you're innocent.' It was only a few seconds before they was on me. Next day I was charged with assaulting a servant of the prison.

Like I've said before, it's not too often a man goes on to do a second murder. My friend Jimmy Essex was one and another was a fellow, Walter Rowland. Just after the War it was, in Manchester. He'd been in the death cell before for killing his two-year-old daughter. That was well before the War, back in March 1934.

The second time was in October 1946 and it was a funny sort of case altogether. This time he stood trial for doing a Manchester prostitute, Olive Balchin. There was no doubt as to his guilt in the killing of his daughter, but there were considerable doubts over the verdict in the Balchin case.

In October 1946 she was found battered to death on a bombsite. A blood-stained hammer had been left by her body and the evidence against Rowland was a witness, MacDonald, who said he had sold the hammer to him on the day of the murder. There were also traces of hair which could have been that of Olive. There was human blood on his shoe but it was impossible to type it with the tests they had then. What was in his favour was there was no blood on his shirt, nor were his prints on the hammer. On his arrest he'd asked, 'You don't want me for the murder of that woman do you?' Nowadays you'd reckon that was a typical verbal.

He pleaded not guilty, but he went down. Whilst awaiting his own trial a prisoner in Liverpool, David Ware, confessed to the murder of Olive Balchin and the confession was the big ground of the appeal.

The Court of Appeal wasn't going to call Ware like Rowland's brief wanted. Goddard was saying how often people made confessions when they'd nothing to do with a case. If anyone was to re-examine the case then it was for the Home Secretary who had infinitely more resources. As he was taken down Rowlands really went beserk, shouting out how innocent he was. There was a KC appointed to head an inquiry and he acted fast. There was another ID and MacDonald failed to pick out Ware. Ware went and withdrew his confession and it was reckoned he'd learned most of what he wrote from the newspapers. Rowland was topped at the end of February. He'd been in the same cell after he'd done his daughter before his reprieve.

It didn't end there because in November 1951 Ware turned up at Bristol Assizes, charged with attempted murder. He'd told the coppers, 'I have killed a woman. I keep having an urge to hit women on the head.' It was off to the bin for him. If you're the one the police fancy then the confession must be right.

There'd been another case like that before the War when George Armstrong, who was manager of a Manchester clothing store, was beaten to death at the beginning of May 1929. The man they had up for it, George Fratson, was nicked a bit afterwards in a brothel in Preston. He made over a dozen statements to the coppers but at last he come up with the one the police said was right and that was when he confessed. At his trial he tried to take it back, saying he made it only because he was despondent and wanted to die. He was convicted at Manchester Assizes in the July and he got a reprieve in the August.

After his trial it turned out that a cardboard collar-box in the shop was stained with blood and it had a finger or palm print on it which matched neither Fratson nor Armstrong. So his case came before the full five-member Court of Criminal Appeal. A senior copper gave evidence that he leaned towards the view that the impression had been made by the hand of a police sergeant who had visited the premises in the course of the investigation. I don't know why the sergeant was never printed so it could show things one way or the other. A second ground of appeal was that the pros knew that a raincoat belonging to Fratson and sold by him shortly after the murder showed no traces of blood. The Court wasn't having it and knocked out the case, saying there was nothing in the prints and he might not have been wearing the coat. Whilst he was in the nick Fratson became insane and was hauled off to Broadmoor.

Even then it wasn't over. In July 1934 Walter Prince, who'd been found guilty of murdering a young woman and had been sentenced to death, confessed to the murder of Armstrong. He got a reprieve and slung in Broadmoor. If he was insane his confession couldn't be right, now could it? I don't know if they ever met. Fratson's conviction was never overturned but if that new Criminal Cases Review Commission ever runs out of work they might like to have a look at both it and Rowlands' as well. But they never will, run out of work that is, and there's no one to keep pestering on Rowlands' behalf, or for Fratson for that matter.

It was like that case in Wales when Stephen Miller was convicted in 1989 of the murder of a brass, Lynette White, in Cardiff. He was questioned for hours and hours before he said he'd done it, but the Court of Appeal's had a bit of a change recently and they said it was oppressive and threw the conviction out. They've come to realise if you question someone long enough they'll say what you want just to get you to stop.

People generally had a lot more respect for the police years ago and so that's why when the Mayor says the coppers wanted to take everyone's fingerprints in Blackburn back in 1948 and they'd be destroyed when they'd been checked, people believed him and they come forward in their droves. Mind you it was the killing of a little girl who was in hospital so in a way it's not surprising. If someone had killed me and they wanted to check fingerprints I don't suppose there'd have been the same response.

What had happened was the kid, June, had been nicked out of her bed in the children's ward at Queens Park Hospital. Poor kid had been in there with pneumonia and she was due out the next morning. A nurse had checked the ward at 11 p.m., seeing to a child in the next bed to June's; half an hour later she had been working in the kitchen when she thought she heard a child's voice in the corridor.

She went outside and saw a door to the garden open. There'd been a wind that night and she thought it had just blown open so she shut it and went back to work. A quarter of an hour later she makes another round and this time she sees what looks like adult footprints, either barefoot or with thin socks, on the polished floor. I don't suppose nowadays anyone would notice in most hospitals but back then things was always highly polished. You could literally eat your

347

dinner off the floor of a ward. She started checking and she could see June's bed was empty and under it was a bottle of distilled drinking water. She went to see if the little girl had gone to the toilet and when she wasn't there she raised the alarm. They found the body up against the hospital wall in some long grass about three hours later.

They had that copper John Capstick, who liked to be known as Artful Johnny and who'd tangled with Eva and the rest of the Forty Thieves, down from Scotland Yard. They fingerprinted everybody in sight and the only print they couldn't match was the one on the water bottle. It was the same with the files at Scotland Yard. There wasn't a match and the print got sent abroad in case it was a sailor or foreigner, but that didn't do no good either.

That was when they decided to see if they could fingerprint every male in Blackburn. They reckoned they'd need to take about 50,000 prints. In the May the Mayor made a public announcement saying that the prints would be just used against the bottle only. They'd not be checked against a list of wanted men nor would they be used to solve any other crime. Now people wouldn't have believed it. The work would be done on a house-to-house basis. There would be no need for anyone to attend a police station. By the September they'd got around 45,000 and there still wasn't a match. Then they decided to have a check on who'd been sent ration cards, and there was still another 800 people to be printed.

In the middle of August a copper calls a place in Birtley Street and asks if a Peter Griffiths, who's nineteen, will give his prints. If he hadn't I suppose they could have made some excuse to nick him but he gave them willingly and this time they check out. Once they've got him things fall into place and they matched up fibres from a suit he'd popped with some found on the body and there was bloodstains as well. He didn't even try to say it wasn't him The briefs said that he killed June whilst suffering from schizophrenia. His old man had been in the bin, but the jury wasn't having it. Less than 25 minutes they was out. A couple of weeks before Griffiths got topped all the fingerprints were shredded in public at a local paper mill.

Blackburn wasn't the only place where there was mass fingerprinting. There was more claims for nationwide fingerprinting when 'Aunt Polly' Mary Ornesher and her sister Margaret got battered to death in Ormskirk, Lancashire in May 1956. Fifteen thousand fingerprints were taken over a period of six months of every male over sixteen years of age, but none matched with the prints left behind. It happened again in Reading and also in Beeston over the murder of an elderly shopkeeper, Lily Blenkarn. There was fingerprints on a toffee tin and also on the backdoor latch. Something like 24,000 prints were taken in 1974 but they still couldn't get the man. Then a seventeen-year-old fellow, Anthony Hunter, threw a brick through a window and he was fingerprinted. It turned up a match. He'd managed to get round the big fingerprinting by getting a mate to practise his signature and do it for him. Just like Pitchfork did all those years later.

Not everyone reckoned everyone should be fingerprinted after 73 year-old Florence Gooding was found battered to death in Oxted. There was a bit of a straw poll and there was just as much objection from older people as from younger ones. It wouldn't matter to me since my dabs have been on file since the 1930s.

Back ten years ago contract killings weren't as popular as they've come to be nowadays. Of course, like I say, there was always work to be had if you were in that line but husbands and wives didn't go out looking for people in pubs who'd do their loved ones in for them. Looking back I don't think there was that much killing of straight people in business. Just like solicitors, provided they didn't meddle accountants were safe as well. It's only when people like them run up debts or start to get into business with the likes of us that there's generally trouble. That's what happened to David Wilson from Chorley in March 1992. He got involved in a cigarette smuggling scam. He was big in debt and he wanted to clear the books but it all went on top.

The people who done it must have been watching for their opportunity because when it came there was only Wilson and one daughter left in the house one evening. The others had gone off visiting. It's always easier to control just a couple of people at a time. If there's too many in a place there's always the chance someone will manage to slip off and bell the coppers. This time the Wilsons hadn't been gone for five minutes before a couple of men in balaclavas burst in and did a tie up. Then when the others came back they was tied up as well and made to lie on the floor. David Wilson was taken outside and they thought he was being kept hostage because that was about the time when kidnapping and hostages was making a bit of a show in this country.

Eventually they managed to get loose and then they find that the telephone wires had been cut and they drove to get help from a neighbour. When they came back they found David Wilson's body face down. He had been shot point blank. When they'd heard it earlier the family had thought it was a car backfiring, but it wasn't.

At first the coppers said things like nothing known to his detriment but it began to leak out in the press. It always does. There were suggestions it was the IRA and that Wilson was a bit too close to some drug gangs. He'd also been a bit close to a shipping fraud for his own good.

Then a year and a half later most of the story come out when Stephen Schepke, who'd been an art restorer, was charged with conspiracy to murder him. The shipping fraud over a non-existent cargo of fags had involved £26.5 million and the original plan had been to pass off cheap Mexican cigarettes as Marlboros, but Hector Portillo, who the pros said was really Michael Austin, and who'd been Wilson's partner, pulled a double cross. There were no cigarettes nor was there any gold which Wilson was buying for an Isle of

Man company from Portillo. Instead of keeping stumm or trying to get someone to make a deal for him, what does Wilson do? He goes to the CPS. He was also sending off faxes to Portillo complaining and saying he'd never forgive nor forget. Portillo decided he was too dangerous and talks to Schepke.

In October there was a bit of a funny verdict. Schepke was found guilty of aiding and abetting Wilson's murder but the jury was unable to agree a verdict that he had conspired to have Wilson killed. It didn't make no difference – he was lifed off.

The rest come out at Carlisle Crown Court in early 1995 when Hector Portillo, who was a top-class fraudsman in the States and was reckoned to be worth around £60 million, and who'd paid £1.5 million in cash for a suite in the Trump Tower in New York, got convicted of conspiracy to murder Wilson. He got life as well. All it had taken to organise the murder was a series of telephone and fax messages. It was a bit like that film *The Thomas Crown Affair* with cut-outs so that no one knew who anyone else was and all you did was leave messages on an answering machine. Once the number was changed, something which frequently happened, the contact was broken for ever. I'm not sure that the actual killers was ever caught.

The trouble with drug wars is that innocent bystanders cop it, far more than in our day. For a start we didn't spray whole areas with bullets. Really guns was not that common and there was no such things as drive-bys. When you think, when Babe Mancini got topped in 1941 he was the first so-called Soho gangster to be done for over twenty years. Now, if the death penalty was in force they'd have to have a dozen hangmen working several days a week to cope with the deaths from shoot-outs. Take the case of that girl in Old Trafford. By 1993 the drug wars had moved out of Moss Side, and Old Trafford, where the cricket ground is, was suffering. In April that year five houses got sprayed in one go and in one of them was a young student, Andrea Mairs. All she did was pull back the curtains in her bedroom window and she gets a stray bullet in the stomach. She lived, which is one thing, but there's many who haven't.

I know I keep on saying it but we did what we could to keep our bits and pieces well away from innocent people who could get hurt. I know the Carters turned up to do me when my wife and kids was in the flat that Christmas after the War, but there's no way they would have kidnapped her and set fire to her. That's what happened to that girl in Blackpool. She was just another in the wrong place.

The really bad case I've always thought is that little kid, Dillon Hull, killed when people opened fire on his stepfather John Batts, when they was walking in Bankfield Street, Bolton in August 1997. He was only five but he saw what was happening and tried to jump in front of his dad. He got wiped out and Batts was hit in the side. There'd been an attack on Batts earlier in the afternoon and someone was laying in wait. Batts had run drugs in Blackburn and had moved out to Bolton when things had got a bit warm. He'd upset someone there as well, wouldn't co-operate and so a contract was put out on him. They got the fellow who took it up. The man was Paul Seddon and £5,000 was the price. They got around £4,000 of the money back but they never got the man who took the contract out. They don't too often. Seddon got lifed off, of course.

Some women do have all the bad luck. Look at the woman whose son was taken off by Brady and Hindley. She adopts a little boy, Benjy Stanley, and he gets wiped out when he goes to the local takeaway to get a goat pie or something like that. He was wearing a scarf showing he was a Manchester United fan and the first story was he ran into a turf war. Like in America the Crips and the Bloods have blue and red colours – I forget which is which – so did the Gooch Gang and the Pepperdines over Moss Side in Manchester. Afterwards people said he wasn't all that innocent and he'd got over twenty grand in his building society account which hadn't come from baby sitting, and what was he doing with a £900 mountain bike?

Just before my seventieth birthday party at Jack Trickett's good hotel in Stockport there'd been a double killing just down the road. A couple of MoT inspectors was shot in a garage, Chestergate Auto Centre. Whilst they was talking to the manager a fellow in a mask come through the door and just blew them away. There was all sorts of talk that they was investigating a big ring of stolen certificates and it was a gangland contract which had got the wrong people, but it turned out nothing like that. It was the owner of the garage Tommy Burke. They called him the Milky Bar Kid. He'd had his brief to do MoTs taken away and he'd just lost an application to get it back. He took the men out as revenge.

LANCASTER

There's a saying that if a wife gets topped, look for the husband and if the husband's a doctor don't bother to look any further. Of course it's not always a hundred per cent. Look at that Dr Sam Shepherd in America, accused of doing his wife years ago and now it looks odds on his story he was attacked himself is true. Not much help to him though, he's been dead years as well.

But one which shows the rule's often right is the fellow Buck Ruxton from Lancaster who did his wife in the 1940s. Did the maid and all because she walked in at the wrong moment, and then chopped them both up and distributed them in Scotland at Gardenholme Linn between Moffatt and Edinburgh. Sometimes I wonder how people think they're going to get away with things but, in a way, it's as I say. Murderers do it on the spur of the moment or they think they're so clever they'll never be caught. But it's not enough to tell the coppers that the wife's gone off to see friends or run away with another bloke but he doesn't know his name or where he's gone. The Bill must be thinking, 'Pull the other one' as they nod and say 'Sad for you, sir', whilst they wait for him to cock it up like Crippen, who had

Ethel Le Neve wearing his wife Belle's jewellery whilst she was still just about warm in the cellar. Wrapped in his pyjamas, she was. They'd got a label on them. He said it wasn't his wife and the body must have been there before they bought the house. The coppers showed the local shop didn't sell those sort of pyjamas until well after he'd moved in.

Ruxton was a Parsee and he'd met his wife, Isabella, when she was working in a restaurant in Edinburgh. She'd been married to a Dutchman but she set up housekeeping with Ruxton in Dalton Square, Lancaster. They were quite well off; they'd a live-in maid, Mary Rogerson. He always reckoned that when his wife was out of his sight she was having it off somewhere and he'd give her a good tongue-lashing or, if he felt like it, a beating. He'd got some French phrase which would appeal to Women's Rights nowadays, 'Who loves most, chastises most.' It all came on top in 1935 when he's convinced himself that she's having an affair with someone from the Town Clerk's office. She wasn't, but there was no persuading him otherwise.

She goes over to see the Blackpool Illuminations in the middle of September that year and there's no doubt she came back because the car's there, but there's no sign of her. As far as anyone can tell, since Ruxton said it wasn't him, what happened was there was a big quarrel when she went up to bed and he started strangling her. Mary hears what's going on and comes out of her room and he does her too. It was a Sunday so there's no patients and no one around and he spends the day cutting them up. Then he goes to one of his patients and says the decorators are coming in the next day, would she mind helping out scrubbing the stairs. There's a lot of blood about as you might expect and he says she can have the stair carpets. He tells her he's cut his hand opening a tin of peaches.

Then of course he's got to explain where his wife and the girl is and he makes up a lot of stories. Her and his wife have gone to Scotland for a holiday; the girl's in the club and Mrs Ruxton's taken her to see someone; his wife was on holiday; she'd gone off with another man. But once the bodies turned up, even though at first they was said to be a man and a woman, the tongues were wagging. His real mistake was that he used part of the *Sunday Graphic* as wrapping and there was an insert with details of the Morecambe carnival which was only distributed in the Morecambe and Lancaster area. Then Mrs Rogerson identified one of her daughter's blouses, and he'd used his kid's rompers and they were recognised as well. The trial lasted eleven days, which was a long time in those days. Norman Birkett defended him and Ruxton was in the box for two days. He wasn't a good witness, shouting and weeping, but it didn't do no good. He got topped at Strangeways. Apparently he left Birkett a set of fish knives in his will, which Birkett sent back, but the brief made sure that Ruxton's kids were educated.

Some people get away with it for years though and it's just bad luck when it comes on top. Look at that airline pilot Peter Hogg, who reported his wife Margaret missing back in 1976. He'd been a bit of a hero when the airline he worked for in Halifax, Nova Scotia went out of business. It looked like the aeroplane was going to be impounded and all the passengers trapped so he made a daring escape with them. He said he thought his wife had gone off with another bloke, which seemed quite likely because one of the neighbours said that she ate men for breakfast, but I don't think they meant it the way it sounds today. Anyway it's nearly ten years later before her body's found, and then it's by accident. A French girl, who had been walking near Wast Water in Cumbria, had gone missing and they was dragging the lake to find her. It's the deepest lake in the whole of England. They don't find the girl but wrapped in a carpet and weighted down is Mrs Hogg. They can work that out from the wedding ring which has got the date of the marriage on. What had happened, he said, was that there'd been a quarrel and he'd strangled her. He'd driven north and dumped her body from a dinghy. If he'd rowed just a few yards further it would have been the deepest bit. He was defended by that wonderful brief Patrick Back who did so much for us at Parkhurst, and he got a four for manslaughter. It was a couple of months after he was weighed off they found the body of the French girl. She'd just fallen about 300 feet.

There was another body turned up. This time it was in Coniston Water not that long ago. It had been there 21 years and was found by some amateur divers in some plastic sacking and weighted down. The woman had vanished after she'd said she wasn't feeling too good and wanted to stay at home, not go away with her husband and their three kids. When the family comes back she's not there. Once the body turned up the coppers arrested the husband, but there was no evidence against him and although he was charged, the CPS soon chucked their hand in.

One fellow who come a long way to end up in a lake in Lancashire was that Marty Johnstone. He was found by divers in Ecclestone Depth back in October 1979. Someone had taken his hands off but what they should have done is taken the Chinese long life pendant from off his neck. Not that it worked. Johnstone had been a founder member of what was called the Mr Asia drug syndicate which ran out of Australia and the Far East; huge it was. Eventually it was run by a fellow called Alexander Sinclair who was also known as Terence Clark, and when Johnstone'd been caught skimming money to set up his own syndicate he had been killed on Clark's orders.

Clark persuaded Johnstone to go to London to set up a Scottish deal and another bloke, Andy Maher, was to drive him. Once they got near Carnforth Maher had asked him to take over the driving and as he got out of the car he was killed with two bullets to the head. His body was then mutilated but Maher and another man with him, James Smith, forgot to remove the pendant. The body was taken to Ecclestone Depth and rolled down the bank into the water but it caught on a ledge under the surface. When the aqua club members found it they thought it was a tailor's dummy, until they learned better that is.

Clark went down in July 1981, after a 121-day trial and the judge, who was that Rose Heilbron, was told he was worth £25 million, give or take a million or two. During the trial one of the fellows in the dock at Lancaster Castle complained it was cold. 'Not as cold as Mr Johnstone is,' says the pros. Roars of laughter.

Clark was another of those who died in prison. He had a heart attack in Parkhurst. He'd been ducking and diving and there was a story that he'd been taking drugs to try and get himself into the hospital wing so he could get out from there. He might even have been the second man off the island. With his money there'd have been no problem in having a helicopter come for him. The dough was said to be invested in restaurants in Sydney, a silver mine in Indonesia, and Swiss bank accounts. But he won't be using them now. Funnily one of the others in the case got nicked again and was put away last year after a big drugs case.

There was some more people who was cold in Lancaster Castle. Most of a family got wiped out inside a year. It seemed that the first was old man William Bingham, who'd been a sort of caretaker and guide to the castle. He suddenly started having diarrhoea and sickness and he died within the day at the end of January 1911. But when it come to it his daughter Annie had gone the previous November. Then his son James took over being the caretaker and he invited his half-sister Margaret to come and do the housekeeping. She lasted only a few days and died in July. The doctor said it was a brain tumour. James next got hold of his sister, Edith, to do the housekeeping but she was not a success. She's missing a few sandwiches in the picnic basket and she's mucky and stays out all hours, so he gets a Mrs Cox Walker to came and replace her. But before she can do so, down goes James. This time the doctor says it's arsenic. They dig up all the rest and only Annie doesn't have arsenic in her.

In them days a coroner's jury could say who the actual killer was and they nominated Edith. There wasn't much against her though. She didn't actually get any benefit from the deaths of her family and she wasn't exactly being put on the street when Mrs Cox Walker come. In those days the pros had to nominate which murder they was going with and they picked the one of James. They could bring evidence of the others in to show method but there was also a bit of trouble showing how she'd actually done Margaret in. Everyone had had some of the same tin of beefsteak for breakfast that day and it hadn't harmed the others. The judge, Avory, was on her side, which must have been about the one time he ever helped anyone out, and she got a not guilty. Most people think she was very lucky at that.

BLACKPOOL

Blackpool was a town and a half, going back. There was a man there, Henry Starr, who got a not guilty first time he was charged with murder, but he never learned his lesson. He did his wife in when she wanted a separation after finding out he'd been seeing other women. Back in 1903 that was; topped in Liverpool. Then that fellow George Joseph Smith, who drowned all his brides in the bath. Did one of them in Regents Road back in 1913 and got £600 insurance for her. His landlady chucked him out but all he did was come down south and swindled a girl in Bournemouth. She was lucky; a century and her clothes and jewellery was all she lost; then it was on to Bath, which was quite appropriate, where he did another.

There was a bit of a sad case a few years after that. A fellow called Frederick Holt killed his sweetheart, Kitty Breaks; shot her on the sand hills at St Annes on Christmas Eve 1919. He'd left his gloves and a revolver near the body and it was easy even in them days to trace his footprints. Next day he called at the hotel where he'd been staying and asked for her. The pros said he'd done it for £5,000 insurance and going to see if she was at the hotel was all part of the plan, but Marshall Hall who defended him reckoned he was off his trolley. He tried to get a verdict that he was unfit to plead but that didn't work. The pros said he was faking it. It didn't help that his family tried to give him an alibi. He got a guilty but then a doctor wrote in and said he'd treated Holt for the syph in Malaya and that he'd thought he was shell-shocked from the War even then. They brought that up in the Court of Appeal but it didn't do any good; the Home Secretary wouldn't give a reprieve. You didn't get reprieved where you'd done someone for money. The story is that after the verdict he just folded the evening paper and put it in his pocket. When he got back to the nick he said, 'Well, that's over now. I hope my tea won't be late.'

Another fellow who passed through the town years later was James Hanratty, the one there's all that fuss over whether he killed Michael Gregsten and shot the girl on the A6. He'd dyed his hair so he wouldn't be recognised but a couple of coppers grabbed him. Last space he walked as a free man. Peter Manuel, who killed all those people up in Scotland, was another. He came to Blackpool to try and make a name for himself just after the War but he didn't last. He got chucked on a burglary but he wasn't trusted there anymore than he was in London. He couldn't keep his yap shut.

It was for a job in Blackpool that James Griffiths got his four following a tie up. He was working with three men from Rochdale and one of them falls over when they get in the house and the gun he's carrying goes off. Griffiths' got a bayonet and he stabs a couple of men but after that he gets a bandage for the man's hand. They cleared £700 but a couple of guns was found in Griffiths' flat. When you think of it four years wasn't bad even though conditions in the nick were so much worse. A ten would be more likely nowadays. As I've said he went on to get off the Isle of Wight.

Just as Brighton was to London, so Blackpool was to both Manchester and Liverpool, although the Liverpool boys really preferred Southport. Blackpool was a short drive away and at one time, just like Brighton, there was a dodgy Chief Constable which meant it was an open town. Stanley Parr, that was his name. There'd been trouble about him being appointed and then he wound up on something like thirty disciplinary charges in the 1950s and got the hoof. I knew him, not well, but he'd drink with the Chaps, just like Ridge did in Brighton, which isn't a good idea when you're the top copper. Good for us mind. He'd straighten things out. Back then top coppers could go hooky without much risk. There wasn't that investigative journalism in them days. The top crime reporters was interested in murderers and there was no TV investigations. Coppers had reporters in their pockets. Look at Percy Hoskins from the *Daily Express*. He used to travel with Fabian so there wasn't much in the way of what you might call critical reporting going on was there?

Blackpool was a town you could work. There was always a lot of punters on the look out for a bargain. I remember in the early 1960s when watches were a bit more scarce than they are today there was a whole lot of Swiss watches on offer. They was smuggled into England, sealed into car bodies or people wearing special waistcoats like they used for gold smuggling a few years later. Then they was dumped in Blackpool and unloaded on the punters. The watches was sold at a fiver each and was worth thirty bob top whack.

There was a hotel there, the Norbreck Hydro. It's very fashionable today. In the '50s, when I'm talking about it, it was reckoned to be the place to go with someone else's wife. You had to sign in and strictly it was an offence if you did it in a false name. There was no sharing rooms then. If you wanted to go case it was a walk along the corridor in your slippers and dressing gown. It wasn't all that odd because in a lot of hotels there wasn't private bathrooms so there was always plenty of people wandering up and down with their spongebags. The story was a bell was rung at 5 a.m.

for you to go back to your own room. If it was I never heard it but then I've always been a good sleeper.

One of the best pubs in London for the Chaps was run by Ruby Mancini, one of that big family. They all seemed to be cousins or half-cousins, straight people and all, and they was all over the place. Ruby'd got a pub off the Tottenham Court Road. I can't remember its name. No one ever called it the Queen of Hearts or The Admiral's Head, to the Chaps it was always Ruby's. He used to play the piano marvellously. I think he'd got another place over Paddington way. Then he suddenly sort of retired and went to Blackpool. Bought himself a small hotel there and he was gone.

I met him again after I'd had a bit of an escape. It was after I come out from the receiving of the coins and I was still working. Some of us had a van in our sights over Waterloo way but somehow the coppers got wind of it and nicked two of us. Brian Perry was one of those with me and we were just over there having a look. If it had been right we'd have done it and we'd have slung caution to the winds but it was still really in the planning stages. I wasn't sure the law hadn't seen me and all so I was off. I rang Wally Downes, he's dead now – God rest his soul. He got hold of Louis and Vinnie up in Manchester and I was on my way. When something comes on top like that speed is of the essence. Speed for us and speed for the coppers whilst it's still warm. It's all right if two are nicked but if two more get nicked then someone's bottle may go.

I didn't even go home for a change of clothing. Fortunately I'd got some dough on me. I didn't let anyone drive me. I just got the train and got off the station before Manchester and Vinnie and Louis sent someone to meet me. I was away about three and a half months but by the end I'd started coming down, trying to gee things up for the two who was nicked. If you don't do things yourself and rely on other people they get slack. They think they'll do something the next day when they should be doing it right now. I'm pleased to say the boys got chucked. Billy always used to say that a thief's best partner was himself and he was right. Anyway Vinnie mentioned that Ruby had this hotel and when things was all over Marilyn and I went over there for a break and he remembered me. We had a really good time.

I liked Abie Tobias. Abie come from Manchester and then he went to Blackpool. He was a top man in the town. One of Abie's daughters had been walking out with a copper and the man got called in to say he shouldn't have no more to do with her; not because Abie was a villain, which he was, but because he was Jewish. Think of that for prejudice.

It was Abe who had good connections with London and he put up a lot of screwings. He had the Continental Café in the town at the time. He come undone with one at the end of November 1953 though, when he had Alfred Curtis from Waterloo and Siddy Golder from King's Cross come up to Blackpool with Danny Swain and another bloke, to do the wrestler Jack Pye's drum in Cornwall Avenue on the North Shore. Danny was the driver, of course.

Jack used to wrestle most Friday nights at the Empire Stadium in Liverpool and they knew he'd be out of the way. After that he'd look in on his club, the Horseshoe, in Dickson Road. What they had to do is make sure his boy Dominic, who lived in the same house, was out of the way as well. They knew he'd go to Leslie's Bar at the Metropole and they found out he was wrestling over in Rochdale so he was gone as well. He was a big man, bigger than his father, and he was strong. He was dangerous when he'd been drinking as well. He turned a man's car over on the promenade once because he was annoyed with him. It was Dominic that Owen Ratcliffe was chasing when he fired a shot in the ceiling of the Horseshoe. Poor Dominic, he topped himself a few years later.

Abe and the others piled tyres in the place and coats to muffle the sound and they got the safe with Pye's money and savings certificates out. They also took a mink stole with them. What they didn't know was there was a bottle of haircream in the safe. The trouble was Abe's car had been seen by a copper who wrote the number down. Abe's brief come a tumble over that at the trial. He asked the copper why he'd noted Abe's number down in particular and the copper replied that all of them was under instructions to make a note of where they saw Abe or his car. Danny did the 19 miles to a farm near Preston, where they was to unlock the safe, in 36 minutes, but once they go there they couldn't get any keys to work. They had to rip the front off and the fellow whose place it was noticed the bottle of haircream. Pye always had long black hair and he'd put the haircream on in the ring to annoy people, and make sure it never got pulled too strong as well.

Anyway Pye gets the word that Abe's had something to do with the screwing and he takes Dominic and a couple of brothers and the old boxer, Paddy McGrath, round to the Continental for a chat. You can imagine what that was like. Abe gets humpy and says Pye isn't going about it the right way and that if he'd approached him properly he might have been able to help. At the court Pye was asked why he'd gone mob handed and that's another mistake. He says it's because Abe runs with the London mob and they've always got guns. After that it's all on top. Abe's in custody and he and Siddy get sent up the Assizes for the screwing, and Alf goes up as well on a conspiracy charge.

Danny was never nicked and he did what he could whilst he was out. One of the pros' witnesses was in the nick and Danny posed as his brother and got to see him at Lewes. Said there was a cow's calf down and another £50 after the trial if he changed his evidence. It didn't do no good. Once the trial was running you could see where was it was going. There was just too much for Abie to get over. He said the copper couldn't have seen his car because it was parked at the café. That was about the strength of his alibi. The judge asks him how many witnesses have been wrong about him during the trial and Abe says 'About six'. He got a seven and Siddy a six. Alf got a three. I was in the nick at the time but it wasn't long after I saw both Abie and Siddy in Dartmoor, where I heard all about it.

Another of Abe's daughters, Sheila, married Georgie Porritt and she got herself in all sorts of trouble. Georgie had a great escape when in May 1961 he killed his stepfather and was nearly topped for it. He'd got involved with Florence 'Fluffy' Copeland, who was the former girlfriend of Edwin Copley who we called Cadillac Johnny. Poor old Johnny had killed himself when he crashed at 75 mph in a chase over Tower Bridge. She'd taken up with what the Copleys saw as one of their rivals. There was a quarrel between her and one of the Copleys in the Manor House Club near Wrotham down in Kent and later that night, so the pros said, six armed men came to the Porritt home. George had always been keen on guns and he's got quite a few. He reckoned they was attacking his stepfather and so he shot at them, missed and topped his dad. And, of course, they did him for capital murder.

He got convicted at the Bailey but the jury recommended mercy. George was sentenced to be hanged at Wandsworth Prison in the July. Thankfully, when it come to it, the scragsman didn't get his fee. Fluffy did a lot of good work collecting signatures for the reprieve and the Copleys, give them their credit, joined in. They said they hadn't nothing against George and it was his stepfather who was the trouble.

In fact his appeal was allowed on the day before he was due to hang. Neither the pros nor the defence had raised the question of manslaughter and the court said that was no reason why the judge shouldn't have done it himself. So George got a manslaughter and ten years to go with it.

Fluffy went back to her own people and whilst he was on the Moor in March 1963 George married Abie's Sheila. That didn't turn out too well when it come to it. She was later convicted as the driver in a wages snatch back in Manchester. What she'd done was taken her kid from a former relationship along with her because she could not find a childminder. Later she did find a minder for an evening and paid her £2 out of some of the stolen money. It was traced and she picked up five years whilst others in the team drew up to fifteen. One of them, Albert Reddans, one of the brothers from Canning Town, collected ten years and this got made consecutive to another ten he'd collected the previous month. Albert put it about on that television programme *Hard Bastards*, which Kate Kray ran, that he'd chinned me in the nick. His memory must be going. Albert wasn't really a great credit to himself. He got stabbed. I thought it was in Reading, which made it appropriate but Charlie Richardson said it was Gartree. Anyway he went and gave evidence against the people who done him. He chinned Charlie in Durham in the security wing but it was in front of three screws so Charlie never got the chance to retaliate. As for chinning me it never happened. If he had done it would have been the talk of the nick.

It was George Porritt's brother, Roy, who worked with us in Atlantic Machines, the one-arm bandits Eddie Richardson and I ran. I still think that fight in Mr Smith's Club in March 1965 was because one of the Haywards had been having it off with Roy's wife. Seeing me and Eddie and Roy in the club together with him meant we was going to have some words over it. I'll never know now. What I do know is that I wasn't the one who killed Dickie Hart. I know who did but I've never said and I still won't; though I was charged I was found not guilty. Good luck to the man.

I haven't heard of Abe Tobias in years. There was a story he'd gone to Israel and it might be right. All I know is he'd be nearly ninety if he's still alive.

I knew Freddie Sewell quite well. A few years earlier and he'd have swung, no questions asked. He came from South London and he got life for killing a copper in the town. It was meant to be a routine job. He and four others go up North to do a jewellers in The Strand, what they call the Golden Mile; 23 August 1971 it was. They reckoned they'd get around £100,000 but one of the staff in the joint manages to set the alarm off and from then it's all on top. They hadn't noticed the sales manager get into the back office. They was still just about putting the jewels in bags when the coppers arrived. There was a chase and one copper was shot in the leg and another in the chest. Then a Superintendent Gerald Richardson goes after Freddie and pulls him down. That's when the gun goes off and the copper is hit in the stomach. Freddie managed to reach the getaway car and was driven off in the boot.

Fred gets away down South but, of course, half the country's looking for him and there's rewards all over the place, including one from one of the newspapers putting up ten grand so its only a matter of time before he's given up. People didn't get out of the country then as they do now so someone was always going to lolly him if he stayed here. Lolly him they did. The coppers found him in Birnham Road, Holloway at the beginning of October and it was back to Blackpool. He got a recommendation that he do thirty years. The story was that a club owner put him away hoping to get a bit of rest from the coppers but you never know. There's another story that it was the well-known grass, Philly Herbert, who put a handful of people away including his parents over the years. That's the sort of son you want to have.

Of course, Fred wasn't going to get any sympathy from anyone and there was reports in the papers about how he was looking bruised when he comes to court the first time but no one said anything about it. Just a few days before he was nicked Arthur Skingle had picked up life, and the judge said that should mean life, after he went down for shooting a copper in Reading. Peter Sparrow who was with him got a recommendation of 25 years. After his conviction Fred ends up as a waxwork in the Chamber of Horrors at Louis Tussaud's on the Central Beach.

Years ago if you was a good murderer and you was convicted you went straight into Madame Tussaud's in

Baker Street in the Chamber of Horrors. There was a sort of jury box with all the old villains like Charlie Peace and others who'd been topped in it; all looking out and serious, as well they might. Many of them was in their own clothes because the firm used to try and buy them to make it more realistic. There was one fellow who sued for libel when they made a waxwork of him. He was a con man, William Monson, and he was well connected. Back in 1893 he'd done in a fellow called Cecil Hambrough whose investments he was meant to be looking after. Hambrough was suspicious Monson was helping himself, and first Monson tipped him out of a boat but the man swum to shore. The next day the pair and another fellow went out shooting; the target was Hambrough. Monson got that funny not proven verdict you can get in Scotland and when his figure was put in the Chamber of Horrors he sued. He won but he got a farthing damages and had to pay the costs. I've said before that when the likes of us sue it generally doesn't do any good. Anyway, it was a couple of years later Monson turns up at the Old Bailey and gets a five over a share fraud.

It's amazing how many people do for themselves by opening their traps. I suppose it's human nature to boast but if you're thinking of killing someone it doesn't help you if you go around spouting away before you've done it. I can't think how many times the pros has brought in evidence remarks about how husbands was saying they'd do their wives and wouldn't mind swinging for it. Which as a rule is just what they did. That Louisa Merrifield was one. If she hadn't opened her big mouth she might be alive today. Well, hardly since she'd be just about a hundred, but you know what I mean.

In March 1953 she'd only just got married – the third time it was – to a man much older than herself. She'd been married before the War to a Joseph Ellison and they lived quite comfortably – an eight-room house near Wigan. She was something of a party girl because she had four kids and they all got took into care. She'd done a bit of bird just after the War, something to do with ration books. The authorities liked a few convictions for that sort of thing. It kept everyone toeing the line. Then her first husband died in 1949 and she starts talking to old Alfred Merrifield who's 79. He was a patient in the same hospital as Joseph, but he's not husband No. 2 though, because she marries a fellow called Richard Weston who's a year younger than him. It seems she wasn't after him for his money, only his pension, but he didn't last long. Ten weeks later he's had a heart attack and now it's Alfred's turn. They got jobs as housekeepers and caretakers and it was about job number twenty in Blackpool when she latched on to a Sarah Ricketts in Devonshire Road in the town.

The old girl must have liked her because within a fortnight she made her will in favour of Mrs Merrifield and Alfred. Next thing is Mrs M. opens her trap and tells a friend she and her husband have come into the bungalow worth £4,000 and the old girl has died leaving it to them. The trouble was she wasn't dead for another three days. Mrs Merrifield kept on though. She told a friend she has to lay the old girl out and when the friend asked how long she'd been dead Mrs M. replies she isn't but it won't be long. Mrs Merrifield was all for trying to get her cremated but the doctors called for a postmortem. You've got to give her credit for a bit of style. She had the Sally Ann band come and play 'Abide With Me' outside the bungalow. Rat poison was what the doctors said, and not only does she open her mouth but she kept the spoon in her bag. It's like I say, people are so confident they think no one will find out.

The funny thing was that poor old Alfred gets nicked. He's allowed to see her in the cells when she's waiting to be committed and next thing he's in the dock with her. From what I heard and read she made a bad witness, arguing and boasting. There was the question of why they hadn't called a doctor and Mrs Merrifield said she didn't like going out on the streets late at night and Alfred said he was crippled which he wasn't. She never fancied she was going to get a guilty but she did and she was topped in the September. The jury failed to agree about Alfred and he was let go. He stuck it out, claiming a share in the house and eventually he got a sixth of its value, provided he left the place straight off. The story is he told a reporter, 'The old bugger was going to do me next.'

NORTH

The more I think back to the people who was reprieved and who wasn't, the less I understand how the decisions were reached. There was a couple of cases up in Lancashire just about the same time which could have gone either way. It was in 1964 and first there was Joe Masters who got done for the murder of an old age pensioner in Clitheroe, a bit outside Preston. Straightforward robbery it was. He'd got a bit of form for violence as well. Knocked the old boy down and he hit his head. At the trial he said he was only there to borrow money, not to steal anything, but since he was wearing gloves that didn't do him any good. Then suddenly he gets a reprieve. It was just about the time that topping was coming to an end and people thought if Masters wasn't going to swing then you wouldn't put money on anyone swinging ever again. Maybe what saved him was he was only 22. Not that over the years many people younger than that haven't gone down.

But there was a couple more. Peter Allen and Gwynne Owen Evans swung on the same day – 13 August 1964; unlucky for them. They'd done a man John West in Kings Avenue, Workington, not far from Carlisle where the pubs used to be owned and run by the Government. Again it was a robbery. They were behind with the rent and they'd got to pay fines of a tenner each in Preston. Evans, I think it was, knew the old boy and thought he'd got a bit of money. They went to see him in the middle of the night. Evans got the man to let them in and then they did him with an iron bar and stabbed him. Completely botched job it was. Just as if they'd said come and find us. Evans left behind his mac, together with a Royal Life Saving Society medallion with his name on it. They didn't get any money even, although there was a fair bit hidden. It was only a question of time before the coppers picked them up. Each blamed the other for hitting him with the iron bar but the jury convicted them both.

You'd have thought they might be reprieved because they weren't much older than Joe Masters, and Allen had young kids. You were never told you hadn't been reprieved until right near the end. There was some baloney about it being kinder to let people go on hoping until the last possible moment. Allen was topped at Walton and Evans at Strangeways.

From what I heard, at the last meeting Allen had with his wife he really went berserk and smashed the bullet-proof glass, just like my friend Nicky Carley did when his girlfriend came and told him she'd met another man. Mind you, I don't like giving that Governor Lawton credit but he did good then. Carley was doing something like a ten and Lawton could have sent him outside for punishment which could have added another five, but he didn't. He kept it to the Visiting Magistrates. Just about the only bit of compassion he must have ever showed.

Everyone had closed visits in them days. Screws would pace up and down outside the booths. You were meant to get half an hour but they'd shave it down to twenty minutes or even less if they could. You might get an open visit if someone had died. Dartmoor and Parkhurst was the only places you got open visits. You might be allowed a kiss and a cuddle at the end. After all, when Doreen come to see me she'd had a three-day journey, there and back. It was expensive and all. Princetown Station had closed down and when you got off the stop after Exeter you had to get a cab. It was a thing for a man to get a visit. Outside working parties would wave and cheer it was so rare.

Evans and Allen went in the record books as the last men to be hanged in England but, of course, they didn't live to know it. Funny, the hangman in Evans' case was also called Allen.

I read the other day there's a proposal to sell off the old prisons to raise money for modern ones. The idea is people will buy them for lofts and things. I wonder what they're going to do about the bodies. There's got to be around a hundred each in most of the prisons where there was topping. I suppose they'll have to notify the relatives. It's only, what? a bit under forty years since Allen and Evans, and there were a good few just before them. It's likely the wives of some of these men will have moved away from the area and maybe re-married. Some of them may have changed their names. They'll have kids by new partners and there'll be grandchildren. It's going to be a bit embarrassing if they get asked what they want done with the bodies. The grandkids may have been told Grandpa was lost at sea. Now they'll find out he was lost at Swansea, or wherever.

LIVERPOOL

The only time I put my flame thrower to use was over some people from Liverpool who was troubling the James's and their Kingsway Club in Southport. Not that the James's knew I was going to use it, nor anyone else for that matter. They'd have said 'Lay off Frank'.

We'd had a bit of trouble before with local people throwing their weight about at the James's. That was when there was a fight with Peter Ioannides in a club up there. He got a bit lippy and Eddie had to sort him out. As we was driving off some heavies chased after us and set a dog on us, but we sort of kidnapped it, put it in the car and only let it out when we'd gone a few hundred yards. As I've said before Eddie was nicked over it and John James was nicked for a thing a bit earlier when I'd done a few people. Fortunately it all blew over at the magistrates' court.[1]

I'd got the flame thrower from a friend, a real craftsman he was. If you couldn't get a silencer for a gun he could make something which would cut the sound, make keys, that sort of thing. He never charged me; he just wanted to

---

[1] See *Mad Frank*.

know it would be used well. So when there was people causing trouble at the club I said I'd come up and meet them on the seafront late one night. They turned up and there was just me and my flame thrower. I didn't talk to them, it was just bosh. It stopped them in their tracks. Monty would have been proud of me. A couple of them was quite badly singed but they was straight up people, good men really. It was between us. They didn't go to the bogeys and after that they left the club alone. I think they spread the word because we never had any trouble again anywhere in the North.

The James's looked after us when we was in the nick over the Torture Trial and the Parkhurst Riot. Every month there was my money on the table and that's how Doreen was able to pay for the house in Hove and keep herself and Francis all those years. They was good. They could easily have said, 'On your bike', and I couldn't have done nothing. In fact it wouldn't have been fair for me even to think about it; I wasn't doing anything for them in return. When Eddie got out before me they suggested they give us a lump sum and I agreed, but what good people.

It was even funnier because years earlier Bert Marsh, who was Darby Sabini's right-hand man for years and who organised the bullion raid at Croydon Airport, had stuck up a caravan for us at Porthcawl, but when me and Billy Blythe – God rest his soul – got there we found the place deserted. Just as well because we didn't know it belonged to one of the James's. In fact it was Bert Marsh's mate Bert Wilkins who put them in touch with us later when they was having their trouble.

There's been some good men from Liverpool over the years, including the Grimwood family. It was Billy Grimwood who did for Amies in the Crow's Nest in the city. Amies was a right dog. He wasn't called The Snake for nothing. He was that copper Tony Lundy's man and he was one of the first supergrasses. Amies was a half iron and he was a really nasty robber. He was into what you'd call home invasions and he'd threaten to cut the victim's balls off or to rape the guy's daughter. He got nicked up in Liverpool with a hardman from there, John Tremarco, and back in October 1977 he pleads guilty. Then he comes to London and starts grassing everyone in sight. After that it's back to Liverpool to be weighed off with thanks from the judge for all his help. He's with some coppers and the night before he's due in court he wants to go and have a drink. It was quite usual with grasses. Keep them sweet was the motto. He and the copper who was actually with him went to the Crow's Nest and got a right beating. When it come to it Tremarco drew a fifteen. They brought Amies back to London and he only served something like a two. The last I heard he'd disappeared and was dead of natural causes, whatever that may mean.

There's been lots of dodgy cases in Liverpool over the years going right back to that Mrs Maybrick who was meant to have done her husband in 1889. A few years ago someone found a diary which was meant to have been written by him and they reckon it shows he was Jack the Ripper. But then there's people who says it was done with the wrong ink and anyway it doesn't really give no details which someone couldn't have got from the papers. Poor old Mrs Maybrick was one of them women in Victorian times who's meant to have killed her old man by giving him arsenic. One of her problems was they found out she'd been having it off with a bloke and that was put up as a motive. It didn't matter that Maybrick spent a good lot of his time with brasses; Victorian women didn't do that sort of thing, and if they did and was caught, well it was too bad for them. It was a funny case because most people thought she was going to get a not guilty and crowds turned up to cheer her, but at the end the judge, who was called Stephens, went against her and swayed the jury. She got a reprieve but Queen Victoria wouldn't have her released. It seems she was still in love with Prince Albert and thought that women who topped their husbands should suffer like she did. Once Victoria was dead they let Mrs Maybrick out in 1904 and she went to America. Funnily the judge went into an asylum within a couple of years of the case, and there's some people who say it was his son who was Jack the Ripper. It goes round in circles don't it?

It's funny how you could get topped because someone's hat got knocked off but that's what happened just before the First World War. December 1913 it was. A seaman, Walter Eaves, was standing waiting for his girl outside a shop in Old Hall Street and the wind caused a blind to come down and put a dent in his new hat. The next thing an assistant, George Ball, comes out to put the blind back up and Eaves demands compensation for his hat. Ball goes back and comes out with two shillings. Later Eaves sees Ball and another man pushing a cart with something in a tarpaulin and they look like they're making heavy weather of it. Next morning the owner of the shop, Catherine Bradfield, is found in the Liverpool–Leeds canal and Eaves puts two and two together. The coppers got onto the other assistant, Samuel Eltof, and he coughed straight away. Said it was because the woman had been always on at them. Ball disappeared and there was all sorts of advertisements on cinema screens asking where he was.

He was found as he left a football match a week later. He put up a wonderful fanny. Him and Sam had been threatened by a man who'd killed the owner and who was going to kill them if they didn't get rid of the body. The only trouble with that was that Eaves, who was a big man, was right outside the shop and they could have asked for help. In fact Ball had come out and paid him the money for his hat whilst the gunman was supposed to be in the shop. It didn't help that when Ball was nicked he was wearing the woman's watch. They topped him of course. The other kid, who was reckoned to be simple minded, got a few years as an accessory.

* * *

The Court of Appeal's never done me any good in the way of quashing my convictions and the only time I ever got any time off was when they knocked a year off my receiving the coins after I come out from the twenty. Sometimes I think, and I'm not alone, that they're there to try and uphold as many convictions as they can. They had that rule called the proviso which allowed them to do just about anything they wanted. They could say that the judge shouldn't have allowed the confession to come in or should have warned the jury about taking the word of a grass more strongly than he did; but when it come to it they applied the proviso – said it wouldn't have made any difference and you'd have been convicted just the same. Look at some of the things the judges have said. Take Lord Denning, who was meant to be the most humane judge ever. What does he say in the Birmingham Six case? It's better that a few Irishmen stay in gaol rather than it turns out the police have been corrupt. And that Lord Lane, who said that the longer they went on hearing the Birmingham Six appeal the more convinced they was that the men had done it. Then, of course, it comes down like a pack of cards on their heads.

Still it must be better than nothing. It all started out with that Adolf Beck at the beginning of the last century. He got convicted a couple of times of getting money out of women by false pretences. Someone was picking up these high class brasses and swindling them out of their money. He couldn't persuade anyone he wasn't the man even though the fellow was Jewish and Beck had never had his thin and thick snipped. He did over five years in the days when sentences really was sentences. We've all got to be grateful to him because after what happened they set up the Court of Criminal Appeal. That's what it was called then.

There's one man must have been really grateful and it's funny how the Court went his way. That was William Wallace who got convicted of killing his wife, Julia. I suppose it's just about the classic case in Britain; people are still writing books about it. In the early 1930s it was. It was really big; all over the papers. He was an insurance agent, a sort of the man from the Pru. who lived in Woolverton Street, Anfield. He was a member of the local chess club which played at a café in the city centre. Anyway, one night there's a phone message left for him at the club. Would he go the next night to Menelove Gardens East for a bit of business? The man said he wanted to arrange some insurance for his daughter. He gave the name Qualtrough. Sure enough, Wallace goes off the next evening but he can't find Menelove Gardens East. He asks around, including a policeman, and he makes a remark about the time. Later the pros said that he was setting up the alibi. There were a West and a North but no East, so he gives up and goes home, where he finds someone's bashed Julia to death and stolen £4 from the house.

Like it usually is, it was a question of look at the husband. The coppers, who were known as Jacks in Liverpool in them days, sets out to prove that he'd made the phone call himself to set up an alibi. One of the things they was able to prove was that the call to the club come from a box near where Wallace lived. The coppers said that as a local man who went round the city on business Wallace should have known there was no Gardens East and he'd set the whole thing up. The coppers were given the name Springheeled Jacks after *That Springheeled Jack*, a well-known Victorian melodrama that Tod Slaughter used to put on and tour with, about a man who could leap over walls and attacked people, because of the way they ran round Liverpool trying to show he could get to Menelove Gardens and back and do his wife in the time.

Anyway, he come up at the Assizes and the great thing was the pros couldn't really show a motive. There wasn't a bit on the side, and no one was saying she was having it off either so there was no story of revenge. There wasn't any blood all over the place, only a tiny bit in the lavatory pan. There's no question that forensics was as good then as they are now but you'd have expected to find some traces. There was theories that he'd done it naked and then had a bath or he'd wore a mac but no one ever found any wet towels and they never found the murder weapon. There was a kid who said he'd seen Mrs Wallace half an hour later than the pathologist said she died, but people said that was Wallace dressed up in her clothes. There's no doubt a lot of the town was against him.

He goes down but the Court of Appeal did something they've never done before, and that's say they wasn't happy with the verdict. Nothing wrong with the summing-up or anything but they just wasn't happy and they let him go. People in the neighbourhood didn't like it though and he moved down the road to Fleetwood; he died a couple of years later. He always said he knew who'd done it. There was a fellow called Parry who'd worked with him and who Wallace had got the sack after the fellow was caught nicking some of the money. He always said it was revenge. Parry denied it when people asked him and he'd got an alibi, but a few years later that fell a bit apart. He died a bit ago and so I suppose we'll never know, but it's not often you get a murder with two good suspects like that. There's been plenty of books and stuff been written trying to prove it was Wallace or that he was innocent and it was Parry really.

The most famous copper in Liverpool a bit before and after the War was probably Herbert Balmer. He'd been in the Navy before he becomes a bogey. He had three big cases and there's still trouble going on about one if not two of them. The third was much more straightforward.

There was still some racecourse trouble going on. The Sabinis wasn't as interested as they had been but there was always money to be made and, of course, the Grand National was the big thing at Aintree. There used to be flat racing there but that was stopped after that jockey, Doug Smith, nearly got killed in a fall. There was also motor racing but that was stopped after a couple of years. That was after the War of course. Just before it there was protection going on up there, according to Balmer.

He reckoned there was a gang of Australians, which was a bit funny, and another gang led by a Colonel from down South – Colonel in the criminal sense like Ronnie that is. Balmer reckoned that any trouble would occur after the National was run at a time when the crowds would begin to leave the course without waiting to see the remaining races. He was right. Him and his men found a couple of bookies been slashed. One had eighteen stitches and the other fifteen. Apparently at first they was staunch, saying it was their own fault and they should have paid, but he leaned on them a bit. Then nicked the Colonel and there was a big fight with Balmer's coat getting slashed. After that the Colonel asked him if he couldn't make it a case for the local beaks, which would have made six months max, but Balmer got him four years.

I don't know if that story was true but I do know that Charlie Wooder, who was from Little Cross Street in Islington, Jimmy's older brother I think, got six months in 1937 for being at the bottle. That was more or less the standard sentence. A carpet or half a stretch and you could reckon on the second if you was caught working on Derby Day or the Grand National. There used to be special magistrates' courts set up behind the stands to deal with the dips.

In fact there don't seem to be as many at the bottle today. It's become more a black crime. Them and foreigners. You'd think people would still fancy it what with the stuff the mugs carry on them. In the old days the bottle mobs like the Titanics from Hoxton would go out twenty handed and work trains or football crowds. If they're caught it's only three or six months and it's worth it. What ripped the arse out of the bottlers was the Criminal Justice Act 1948 when if you was over thirty and had three previous you could get eight years PD at the snap of fingers. The law come in April 1949 and it slowed people down, but a lot of the bottlers worked until middle age and later. Old Dodger Mullins was working until he was well in his sixties.

It was never my game although I went out once or twice. It was during the War and the bottle mob would come into the 21 Club in Clapham High Street or The Bungalow of an evening and when I'd had a drink I went with them, more or less for a laugh. I was the stall. The person who'd bump into them or stand behind them, but it wasn't for me. You needed long fingers and the best were the ones whose first and middle fingers was just about the same length. Bottling was at its peak then. Every big city had at least one good bottle mob. There was no unemployed so wallets was full, and there was the blackout to help you, but it wasn't for me.

Of course just like London and the other cities with docks which got blitzed Liverpool was fair game for the likes of us. There was food shortages and it was easy to get rid of stolen goods. Then because of the poor street lighting it wasn't too difficult for the dippers and the rollers to work. There was a lot of gang fighting around Park Lane, Paradise Street and Back George Street. Sailors was being lured out of the safe haven of milk bars and the YMCA with the offers of visits to illegal drinking clubs and, as a result, being rolled on the way to a girl's flat.

There was a lot of gangs after the War as well. If you've got docks you've got brasses for the seamen, and there was one lot used to work near the Adelphi hotel – that place they had a series about on television a few years back. Big Victorian pile it was but it's been done up now. And of course Lime Street was famous worldwide amongst sailors I should think. There was that song 'Maggie May' about a brass who worked Lime Street. Just like Piccadilly down South. If you wanted a cup of tea at a stall outside Lime Street station at the end of the War you had to pay 5d deposit on the cup. There weren't any saucers. Even so the geezer that run it reckoned he lost about sixty a week.

There was thought to be 200 gangs in the city just after the War but of course they might just have had two or three people in them. It was the conviction of George Kelly which broke a lot of them up, but even so there was still a good few about. One was called the Peanut Gang, which started off nicking peanuts from bags on the docks and went on from there. They became big in muggings. There was also a good network which smuggled a wanted man from family to family keeping him on the move the whole time. Then there was the Throstles, into mugging sailors having it away with the brasses. What's got to be remembered also is that people in Liverpool didn't like the police. They remembered when they was charged by police with batons in motorcycle sidecars. There'd also been a lot of religious trouble up there as well. I never really worked with the Liverpool boys. It was much more Manchester for me, but since I was in the nick in Walton with them for so long over the years I heard a lot of what had gone on.

One crime in Liverpool which never really caught on down in London was taking grids off the Nat Gonellas and getting in through them so as to screw the houses. It must have run for forty or fifty years from the 1920s. It seems the householders either did not have them mended when the grids rusted or that coalmen failed to put them properly back in place. You have to think some of the coalmen was in on it. Of course it wasn't very different from the time when 'Tom Thumb' Brindle and the others got done when they bashed the coppers after they found them getting into the cellar of the Duke of Clarence in Walworth. There was Whippo Brindle and Jimmy, Eva's husband, and there was Billy Holmes and Jimmy Robson. They took their chance when the road was being done up. The nick was only just up the road and someone must have had a dog and belled them. Jimmy Robson got a two and Jimmy Brindle, Borstal. 'Whippo' Brindle got eighteen months; he should have had the biggest because he had form but he wasn't fool enough to call out 'I think you've made a mistake'. The Clarence has been closed a few years now but it was big in its day. We never screwed houses like that though.

In those days if you got two years you had to accept that you was going to lose a month's remission and it was no use getting the hump. Petty things, talking in the workshop, not doing your sewing in your cell. Five days here, three days there, it all added up. If you got a three years' PS then you had to reckon on at least three months' loss. It was par for the course.

The first of Balmer's big cases was the Cameo Cinema murder which broke the so-called Kelly gang; there's still an argument about it today. George Kelly was a local face who'd deserted from the Navy. He'd been the barker for an escapologist before he took up running a string of girls. There was the usual game of getting a girl to go with a fellow and whilst the man was having an upright or thinking he was going to get one in an alley, doing him. Usually the girl was in on it but later in the 1980s there was people who'd just frightened the girl and make her go along. Cocky Warren was one of them. Funny, he sent me a card a bit before he got nicked in Holland over a load of drugs. By then he was stone rich, one of the richest faces in England the papers said.

But going back to Kelly, he'd done a three for desertion and also a bit for assault and receiving as well. He was a bit like me. His first conviction came when he was ten. He was always good with his fists as well. He had another line with his girls; he was one of the first to get them into cars. He took about three-quarters of their earnings and the brasses was also expected to steer punters into clip joints where they would be overcharged for their drinks. Unlike the near beer joints in Soho the men could get what they was paying for because there was often a couple of rooms at the back of the joint. He was in the nick with me when I was in Walton just after the War.

Kelly was always putting up jobs, a bit of a blagging here, what they'd now call a steaming at a funfair over in New Brighton there, that sort of thing – doing over a cab driver they thought was a grass. But what he and a fellow Charles Connolly finally settled on was a snatch at the Cameo Cinema, Wavertree.

It seems like it was Connolly who originally suggested nicking the takings from the picture place. They wanted a gun to put the frighteners on the manager and Kelly went out and got one. There was a raft of them floating around at that time what with the end of the War. The next evening Kelly and Connolly went to the cinema. Connolly remained outside and Kelly goes up the stairs to the office and tries to blag the takings from the manager. He's having nothing of it and Kelly shoots him, and the assistant manager and all. Now he in a panic and he drops the bag of money he's snatched. On his way out he was seen by Patrick Griffith, the cinema fireman.

Connolly was long gone by the time Kelly got down the stairs. He's gone at the sound of the first shot. So Kelly's now got to start to put an alibi together and he goes into the Leigh Arms and buys a drink for a fellow he hardly knows. If you're going to do that sort of thing you've got to pick a fellow you know's going to stand up and is one of the Chaps. Of course this man isn't. He's straight and he tells the court Kelly was so out of breath and nervous he asks him if he's been in a fight. Kelly says he had. By now Connolly's pushed off to meet up with his wife and sisters in a local dance hall.

The next day the papers were full of the news. Connolly's bottle has more or less gone because it's a topping matter for him as well and he says he wants to get out of the country. The real trouble, so far as they are concerned, is there's a few hangers-on who really don't have any bottle either. One of the girls who was around Kelly was a Jackie Dickson who was with a fellow, Jimmy Northam, known as Stuttie. He'd got a speech impediment; he'd been hit on the head when he'd been rolling servicemen. Another fellow I knew who had an impediment after being hit on the head was Bobby Maynard who went down for the Torso case in the 1970s with Reggie Dudley. He really could hardly speak for years but I'm pleased to say he's better now, and best of all the court threw out their convictions this July.

Then there was a girl Marjorie Dawson, called Norwegian Marjorie. Kelly'd been flashing the gun around in a pub and she'd told him to put it away but he'd loaded it there and then. She'd given over a green apron for him to wear as a mask and Stuttie had put up his raincoat. You can see where it all went wrong. Far too many people involved who don't have to be and who may not stand up.

Now Kelly's got to put the frighteners on Stuttie Northam and Jackie Dickson and he says they'll get a seeing to from his brothers if they should open their traps. Shortly after this is when Norwegian Marjorie tops herself. It's then Northam and Dickson decide to write to the police and although they don't put up names that gives Balmer something to go on. They wanted immunity and that's what they got – if they agreed the police was to put an ad in the local paper saying 'Promise' or something like that, and they did.

Even before the letter Balmer's been rounding up the usual suspects and he'd had Kelly in but he's put up an alibi from his girlfriend and for the moment it's stuck. One thing the fireman was sure was that the man had very dark eyebrows and that's what Kelly's got. Meanwhile Dickson and Stuttie have pushed off to Manchester. Not all that far but far enough for the moment, and it wasn't for six months that the coppers found them and Stuttie put up the names Balmer wanted.

If ever a brief fought hard it was that Rose Heilbron, who later became a High Court Judge. It was the first time a woman had led in a murder case but there was a prejudice against women briefs in them days. There really still is now. Kelly's meant to have said 'I want no Judy defending me' but when it come to it he couldn't have done better. If anyone ever tried, she did.

There really wasn't much evidence against Kelly and even less against Connolly. There was a bit of ID and of course Jackie Dickson and Stuttie. But out of the woodwork comes a prisoner who says both Kelly and Connolly had talked about the murder and how Connolly said he'd run away and Kelly had put up a moody alibi. All three witnesses,

Northam, Dickson and this fellow Graham, told the court how frightened they were of reprisals from Kelly's family and friends, and Stuttie and his girlfriend wouldn't even write down their addresses for the judge. It makes it look good for the pros when something like that happens.

Then it all comes on top for Connolly and his alibi was broken. He said he had been at a dance hall from about 8.20 in the evening and that his wife had joined him twenty minutes later. He also said he had entered a rumba competition and his wife, two of his sisters and their friends all put him in the dance hall before the murder was committed. What happens is the MC is sure that Connolly hadn't arrived until after the pubs closed. He remembered Connolly because he'd been wearing his hat on the dance floor and had been told to take it off.

For the time it was the longest trial they'd had in Britain. It lasted thirteen days and after four hours the jury said they couldn't agree. Now, of course, they could have thirteen nights in a hotel. It was then the prosecution had the bright idea of trying the men separately and the re-trial was fixed for a week later. One of the reasons was it was said that Jackie Dickson was dying.

This time the jury was only a bit under an hour before they put Kelly away. It often happens in a re-trial. It looks so good the first time round but the pros has learned by its mistakes for the second go and there's nothing to surprise them with. You're stuck with what you've got. Kelly was found guilty of murder – a decision in which the judge said he heartily concurred. Northam and Dickson each received £20 reward from the court.

Miss Heilbron did what she could. She went to the Court of Criminal Appeal saying that because there was a juryman who had a felony conviction the trial was a nullity and the conviction should be quashed. It come before Goddard and it certainly wasn't going to work with him. Kelly was topped in March 1950 at Walton Prison. Connolly pleaded to the robbery and got a ten. They dropped the murder.

There's been a lot of trouble over that case with allegations that Balmer leaned on and then coached his witnesses. There's plenty of briefs and a few old time coppers up there who would say Balmer wasn't straight, and I reckon they'd be right.

In a way the fact that Kelly wasn't too pleased to get a woman brief wasn't surprising. There just wasn't any around. I think Miss Heilbron was about the only one doing big crime. There was a few that did civil work – divorce and things like that – but otherwise the chances were that the solicitor you had might have a girl receptionist but even that wasn't always the case. I think if I'd had a woman brief turn up I'd have had the wind knocked out of my sails. I'd have said politely, 'No thanks, I'll wait until Mr Smith can get here.' It seems ridiculous when you think now how many of the top briefs are women but that was how it was in my day. You'd imagine the beak and the pros would have been treading all over her. It was bad enough having a really experienced man for you, let alone a young woman who didn't have the experience. The coppers would have been sneering at her. The brain trembles at the thought of it. Now, if you said no, they'd do you for discrimination. That's where the world's changed.

There was one woman magistrate appointed about that time and that was Sybil Campbell, who used to sit at Tower Bridge; she was a terror. She'd really hand it out to shoplifters but she must have liked the Chaps because she gave me and the others bail after we'd done the Town Hall in Dagenham and there'd been a chase through the Rotherhithe Tunnel. I turned up, of course. It was a matter of honour but, if I'm honest, there was also a question of finding the dough to give the fellow who was standing surety and who'd have to pay up if you went on your toes. If he couldn't pay then it was often him who went away for a few weeks.

Getting back to Balmer, his second famous case was the killing of Beatrice Rimmer, a middle-aged widow who, the SP was, had a load of dough put away in her house. The

389

fellows involved were Edward Devlin and Alfred Burns and they'd known each other for some years. In August 1951, when Burns was on the run staying with Devlin, they put up the job to a couple of girls. The idea was a straightforward con trick to get in. One of the girls was to make sure the woman was in and then she was to keep watch, knock and keep her talking whilst the others broke in at the back. A fellow they was going to use got himself nicked a couple of days before it was due off.

Eventually they decided not to use the girl and just break in and that's where it all went wrong. The woman showed up and they knocked her about with a piece of wood. The fellow they'd left out then sees a bit of an opportunity to help himself and grassed them up whilst he was in Walton. When it come to the Assizes they said they was out screwing a warehouse in Manchester and they was staying with a woman there, but she wouldn't wear it. Rose Heilbron was defending Devlin and when she went to the Court of Appeal she said she'd got evidence that another man was the real killer. Goddard wouldn't listen but there was an inquiry which come to nothing before they were topped. They was still maintaining their innocence.

Balmer's third big murder was the killing of an old junk dealer, 82-year-old George Hugh Walker, known as Daddy, in the middle of January 1953. He lived on the Warbreck Road out near Aintree. One time he'd been quite smart, well turned out and well thought of but when his wife, a dancing teacher called Madame Pepper – all dancing teachers had to be French or Italian even if they come from the next street to you – died he sort of let himself go. The place had twelve rooms and each of them was piled high with junk. The neighbours didn't have much to do with him but when his dog wouldn't stop howling one of them went over to see what was happening. They found his body, which had been hacked about.

This time it wasn't a gang or anything like that, just an unemployed labourer John Lawrence Todd, who went and hit Walker 32 times with an axe. The axe had been clumsily hidden in a chimney. Todd went to the police to explain why he might have been seen in the area but he was identified through a watch he'd nicked from the old man and then sold. He was topped in May that year at Walton. There wasn't any doubt about it this time.

Some people could just be in the wrong place at the wrong time. Take that girl Jean Larkin. She ran a company selling window blinds, and her boyfriend Gary Pettitt made his money out of selling drugs. They left their flat in Aigburth in April 1993. It seems Pettitt had had a call to a meeting in a McDonald's in Markey Street, Chorley, some 25 miles away and Jean Larkin went with him. They couldn't have expected to be away long because they'd left the television on and her dog, Bruff, was in the flat with no food left out for it. Her company was called Calypso Blinds and someone saw her van with the name on the side in Markey Street, Chorley and later it was found at Manchester airport. But they never saw either of them again.

In June the coppers started digging in woods at Coppull, which is a bit outside Chorley. There was some jewellery and burned clothing. She was just unlucky to have been around when it all came on top for her boyfriend.

YORKSHIRE

LEEDS

In my day the Chaps didn't use guns, not when we went out on blaggings that is. We might have done when we was facing up to each other, but kill someone on a robbery and that was a topping offence. You couldn't tell some people though. Take Walter Sharpe and Gordon Lannen; they was just twenty and seventeen. In they go to a jewellers, the Albion Watch Depot in Leeds, just after the place has opened and hold up the owner. November 1949 it was. The old boy who owned the place, Abraham Levine, wouldn't give them anything and he got hold of Lannen by the collar. What he got for his troubles was a stream of blows with the butt of one of the guns and then he was shot. After that the kids just ran out into the street firing. It must have been like something out of a western. No one could tell if they was just letting the guns off in panic or if they was actually firing at the people who was running after them. The old man died that night but he'd been able to tell the coppers what the boys looked like, and they were picked up a few days later in Southport.

Lannen wanted to put his hands up but the judge wouldn't let him and made him plead not guilty. What had happened is they'd broken into a gunsmith's and stolen the revolvers and gone and robbed Levine. It turned out it was Sharpe's gun which went off.

It was one of them cases when the judge has a go at films, which was what they did in them days. 'Wretched gangster films', was what the judge called them. Now it's supposed to be television which makes people go wrong. Sharpe was topped at Armley, the Leeds prison at the end of March 1950, but because Lannen was only seventeen he got detained at His Majesty's Pleasure.

For myself I can't say the films ever influenced me. I know I didn't get to see them three times a week like Sharpe said he did, but if I was going to do something, it wasn't because I'd see Bogey or Edward G. do it on the screen. It's one of those good excuses judges like and so do those people who like to work out why people commit crime. It's either because they was twins, or their dad was away or they didn't have a dad or they come from a deprived background. Look at my family. You can't make it work at all. We come from a settled family. We was poor but we never lacked food and clothes. It was a bad environment – people like to say it's environment as well – but that can't have counted. The other thing is genes. Do we have bad genes? Well, my parents didn't have criminal records. So what happens? The first three of us kids turn out fine; not a day's trouble between them. Then there's Eva. A bit of shoplifting when she was young and then only in trouble trying to help me out. Finally there's me. Never out of trouble from about ten to seventy. How can you explain it?

I never liked those local prisons, Armley, Winson Green, Strangeways. They were the ones for medium-term prisoners. There was only the Moor and the Island and, up North, Wakefield for long-term men. There was also a wing at the Scrubs for long-term star prisoners but that started in the late forties or early fifties. If there was any reforms which benefited prisoners it always seemed that they were the last ones to give the privileges. When I think back to my time in the nick, if a screw retired in 1960 that meant he'd been trained by people who'd started in 1930 and in their turn they'd been trained by people who'd begun in 1900. It was no wonder things hadn't changed much. There was the same mentality. When I started in the nick you got a letter a month. Now you get a telephone card and can ring your people every day.

Armley was the last place they hanged a man and woman together. At least they didn't do it back-to-back like they did in Canada. John Gallagher and Emily Swann it was in 1903. They'd done in her husband. She'd been having it off with Gallagher and her husband gave her a beating. Gallagher took a poker to him and there's not much doubt she was egging him on. She must have been one of the smallest women ever topped in modern times. She was only four foot two. Apparently he was on the scaffold with the blinds on when she's brought out. 'Good morning, Johnny,' she says. 'Good morning, love,' he replies and that's it.

As I've said Armley was where my mate Jimmy Essex got done for murder the second time during the War. He had a fight with a bloke in the tailor's shop. The man was coming at him and Jimmy had the knife you used to cut cloth and he done him with it. He was lucky it got knocked down to manslaughter but he still got a ten. I slipped in and see him just before the murder when I was on the run from the Army. There was always the risk you'd be caught but it wasn't that much of one. Things were a bit lax and the worst that was likely was you'd get a knockback. Otherwise you moodied you were someone's cousin back on home leave and they was generally willing to let you in. I think I'm right in saying Jimmy was the first man done for murder in prison, certainly in modern times.

Our attention was more directed at the screws and there wasn't all the association and visiting other people's cells there is today. That kept us apart. Of course, we could make knives and things but there wasn't the opportunity there is today even if we'd wanted to. There was people off their trolleys but not to the same extent and it was like on the outside if we had a quarrel it was usually a straightener. If we did use weapons the idea was to give a stripe or two but not to kill people.

Now, there's been a big increase in killings in prison over the years; not least in people who've topped themselves. There was something over fifty of them in 1999 and I think it's gone up since then. Then there's the prisoners who get killed by others. There was that big case in March 2000 when Zahid Mubarek, a black kid in Feltham, was put in the same cell as a white racist, Robert Stewart, who hit him over the head with a table leg. He just beat Mubarek to death. He'd got a poster for the Ku Klux Klan on the wall and a month before one of the staff had warned how dangerous he was. Poor kid was only doing a few months and was due out pretty soon.

That Mubarek killing was bad enough but the next week a fellow Colin Bloomfield got done in Cardiff; just about disembowelled. He was doing six months for child neglect and he was put in a cell with a fellow called Jason Ricketts who'd done a seven for robbery. Ricketts had told people he was wanting to get back to a mental hospital. He said he was going to kill and eat someone and then ring the bell for the screws, and that's just about what he did. He took the fellow's eye out and his liver and had his spleen as well. It seems like he thought that was Bloomfield's heart. He'd managed to make a sort of scalpel out of a toothbrush handle and a razor blade. He said it all come about by taking LSD and solvents when he was young. I think he was one of the ones who got his wish and went back to the bin.

There was a right man in Broadmoor after I was there, Robert Mawdsley. He'd been sent there for stabbing an iron in June 1974 in Liverpool and he'd carried on the good work ever since. He went to Broadmoor for that and whilst he was there, in 1976 he tried to kill an inmate called Monk, and later he managed it with a fellow called Francis in February 1977. That was enough for them and he was sent to the nick. He got moved to Wakefield in March 1978. When he was there he and another fellow they regarded as dangerous, Douglas Wakefield, had a spare cell in between them with a telly in it and they sort of shared it to keep them away from the others. One day Mawdsley tells a fellow in the tailor's shop that a couple would have to go and he'll be back in Broadmoor within the week. He did what he said he would and put away a couple, William Roberts and Stanley Darwood. Then he goes and tries to stab a screw. He got lifed off and the judge said he was sorry for the screws in the nick having to cope with him. So far as I know he never got back to Broadmoor but he did get a telly programme made about him. He went in a control unit.

My view is that the people who went in control units could be described as control fodder. They weren't Chaps so to speak. I mean, if they had been serious surely then I'd have been one of the first through the doors. I don't think either Timmy Noonan or Martin Frape was ever in one either.

The scheme started in Wakefield back in the '70s and if you went in the control unit you was there for two periods before you come out. The first was ninety days, when you didn't get any association with other cons. You didn't have to work but your ninety days didn't start until you did. Then you got another ninety days with limited association. At the start there was just the concrete slab on the floor and they chucked a mattress in at night. There was very heavy fine mesh on the cell windows so the con couldn't see out properly. If you didn't work or got into trouble it was back to the beginning. There was one fellow tried to get the courts say it was cruel and unusual but they wasn't having any of it. They said far worse took place in America. It was packed in a few years ago but things have gone full circle and I'm told there's a very similar system just been started again in Wakefield, although people say now it's much better.

Headingly was where they dug the pitch up when England was playing Australia as a protest to try and get George Davis released. George was very intelligent over the Ilford robbery back in 1965 when some people did the London Electricity Board in Ley Street. When he was inside he kept himself to himself and there was never the chance for the authorities to slip a prisoner into him. That was really a case and a half.

He always maintained he'd been wrongly ID'd and there was a big campaign to have him released; eventually the Home Secretary let him out in May 1976, about the time there was a lot of trouble about the danger of convicting on ID evidence only. Unfortunately George let the side down a bit because the next year he's found in a ready-eye trying to do the Bank of Cyprus in the Seven Sisters Road, Holloway. The copper who nicked him asked what he was doing and he said the shopping, and the copper says 'Why are you doing it in a balaclava George?' He got an eleven but now I'm pleased to say he's been out of trouble for years. I had a drink with him the other day. I met him down Sheila Kelly's place, the W9 Wine Bar. It's a lovely drinker, a smashing place.

There used to be a way so's women who were pregnant didn't swing. Once they'd been found guilty they could tell the court they was in the club and what was called a Jury of Matrons was put together from women sitting in the court or even in the building who then had to listen to the woman's story and decide if she was telling the tale. Sometimes of course it was obvious she was going to have a kid, but other times it was more difficult. At first they did it all by themselves but later they had a doctor give them advice. It was centuries old and I think the last time there was one was in the 1930s, but a bit before that they had a case at Leeds Assizes. It was a girl called Louie Calvert and she was a right bag of tricks. She must have been the only brass to go around in a Sally Ann bonnet.

She'd been the housekeeper of a fellow called Arthur Calvert from Railway Place in Hunslet and she convinced him she was in the club and he'd have to marry her. That's what the poor fellow did and as the time went by there's no little Calvert in the cot. You'd think she might say she'd had a miss but no, what she does is decide to go out and find a baby. There wasn't the difficulty there is now. There was always plenty of girls who'd gone and soiled the family honour and wanted to get rid of little Willie one way or another. She shows Arthur a letter which she's written herself saying her sister's invited her over to stay with her in Dewsbury for the confinement. Off she goes and sends hubby a telegram saying she's arrived safe, and then it's back to Leeds to stay with a woman called Lily Waterhouse. Then she goes and adopts the baby of a young girl and three weeks later comes back with it to Arthur.

That was on a Sunday. Next day Arthur sees a suitcase he doesn't recognise and she tells him it's from her sister and it's full of baby clothes. It turns out it's full of Mrs Waterhouse's stuff. The police are only half a step behind and she's nicked a few days later. It turns out Mrs W. has been found with her head bashed in with a poker. Louie's filled the suitcase full of crockery and anything else which might have come in handy. She claimed she was in the club but the Jury of Matrons reckoned it was another come on and she got put away in June 1926 at Strangeways. There's a story that whilst she was in the condemned cell she confessed to doing in another husband, John Frobisher, who'd been found dead in a Leeds canal in the early 1920s.

Another girl who ended up in a parcel was the twenty-year-old Ethel Wraithmell. Her head was found by a man out walking the dog in a village called Scholes near Leeds in May 1939. There was another couple of parcels with bits of her nearby. I say she was called Ethel but she'd got a whole host of names she went by. She came from the Chapeltown area and she was mixed up in a fair amount of stuff – passing coins for a gang of counterfeiters was one. Then there was a story she was a grass but the coppers denied it. People who knew her said she'd been frightened for the past six months. Eventually, nearly a year later, a fellow's charged with her murder and he goes down for manslaughter.

That bit was a strange story. In the following April he just walked into the police station and gave himself up. The pros's version of the thing was that Ethel was a brass and he'd picked her up whilst his wife was away. She'd tried a bit of black on him and he'd strangled her. There was a bit of evidence that some man had been seen with her on a tram the night she died and they reckoned he was the man.

What he said was that he'd had her pointed out to him on the street and she'd just turned up on his doorstep uninvited one night and when he tried to get her out of the place he accidentally kills her. She was in a pretty poor way by all accounts. She was homeless and she'd got a brain tumour and TB as well. The doctor didn't think she was going to live long anyway. Once she'd snuffed it he didn't know what to do. He thought if he went to the coppers they'd say it was murder and he was right. So he kept the body in the front room all night and after he come home from work the next day he cut it up. He got twelve months, which you can't say was bad.

SHEFFIELD

I've spoken to many men who've done in their wives and girlfriends. As I say they just don't think they're going to get caught, but their brains must have dropped off whilst they was doing it. They seem to me to be saying 'Look what I done?' Very often they give their wife or girlfriend's clothes or jewellery to a new girl the next day. It goes back as far as Crippen and probably a lot further. Within a few weeks

Ethel Le Neve was wearing Belle's jewellery which he said she'd left behind when she'd run off from him. Run off as far as the cellar most likely.

Then look at that bloke from Sheffield, Kenneth Peatfield his name is. They call him Concrete Ken in the nick. He's meant to be moping around the house because his girlfriend, Susan Craven has gone and left him and in fact he's out over in Oldham having dinner with his new girlfriend, a third the age of the old one as well. If that isn't enough they go and buy two wedding bands. He must have been out of his mind because he brings her back to the house and shows her the old girlfriend's body under a tarpaulin. If that isn't enough to put a girl off I don't know what is. Still you have to wonder what Susan saw in him. He'd done a ten in the 1980s for trying to hire a hitman to do his wife and daughter. From what I hear Ken still says it wasn't him.

They never found the body but they did find her head in a concrete block in his garage about six weeks later. He said he couldn't explain what it was doing there but he'd never seen it. He must have heard of the case of that lawyer Warren Lincoln in Chicago, back in the '20s. He was able to explain things when they found the heads of his wife and brother-in-law in flowerpots on his porch. He said he didn't know who the heads belonged to. He'd found them in his greenhouse and put them in concrete to preserve the evidence. Didn't do him much good either. It seems he just couldn't stand them rabbiting on together when he retired and he wanted a bit of peace and quiet.

Concrete Ken got a good beating when he went to Doncaster prison. That's not that usual. Generally people don't mind about wives getting topped. It's people who do kids in that have the worst time, and quite right too.

They seem to have had a thing about heads in Sheffield. A few years before Concrete Ken, Tony Antoniou, the boyfriend of that singer who wears an eye-patch, Gabrielle, did in his stepfather, Walter McCarthy. He took off the head as well and left the body in a lay-by at a place called

Cutthroat Bridge on the Snake Pass. You've got to give him credit for something like that. He'd certainly got a sense of humour because he called his fish and chippy The Lazy Codling. Just before Christmas 1995 it was. He said it wasn't murder because McCarthy had abused him as a child but the jury wasn't wearing it.

Back in the nineteenth century the biggest of all the criminals countrywide came from Sheffield. He was just about a one-man crime wave. Charlie Peace come from Angel Court on the corner of Nursery Street and Lady's Bridge. His father had been a collier before becoming an animal trainer and Peace himself later trained parrots and pigeons. He did his leg in when he was in the mills at the age of fourteen and when he was released they said he was incurable. A bit of red hot steel had gone through the back of his left leg, a sort of reverse knee-capping. It didn't stop him being about the best screwer in the country. That wasn't his only trade. He was a top-class pickpocket. His trick was to faint in the street and when people who'd picked him up got home they found they'd lost a tie-pin or a wallet. I know a number of faces who played the piano well enough, but he was the only villain I've heard of who played the violin. I'm not sure he wasn't good enough to play in the pit at music halls.

He was good enough to stay out of trouble until he was nineteen and then he got a month for screwing. After that it was onwards and upwards. He did the house of a local beak and his sister was caught trying to pawn the stuff. That was the standard way of getting rid of gear. It's more or less safe for the pawnbroker who's got a name and address even if it's a moody to show the police, and he's giving a price on the stuff which he knows he can resell. She was trying to pawn some boots and when the coppers searched Peace's mother's house there was a whole raft of stuff. This time he got four years.

He was like me – no remission. He'd tried to escape and he'd also tried to top himself, which was a criminal offence back then. Once he come out in about 1858 he was all over the country screwing, never staying longer than a few weeks in one place. He took up with a Hannah Ward and they was more or less together until the end. Then he was picked up in Manchester. Him and another man hid some jewellery in a sewer but when they come back for the gear it was a ready eye and he got a six with penal servitude.

Then he was in Chatham, where he organised a mutiny. For that they literally shipped him off to Gibraltar and it wasn't until 1864 he was out and back screwing. Manchester wasn't a lucky place for him either because he and the other fellow was drinking whisky instead of getting out with the gear and the servants come and did them. This time it was a seven.

If you see pictures of him he looks really ugly. This may be because he was twisting his face up so the police couldn't identify him in future but I don't think he pretended he was handsome. Not like Ruby Sparks who used to screw his face up on police pictures. Now he was handsome. Ugly or not it didn't stop Peace pulling the women. He was back in Sheffield living in Britannia Road, a couple of doors from Arthur and Katherine Dyson. He certainly took her out but whether they had it off I don't think anyone will know now. Anyway Dyson didn't like it, and they moved to Ecclesall Road and found to their horror Peace had followed them.

At the end of November he went and shot Dyson. The coroner's jury said it was wilful murder but by that time Peace was over in Hull. It was then he really start to work his way round England – Birmingham, Bath, Bristol, you name it. The railways was putting their act together and so travel was getting much easier. It was probably faster than it is today.

Nottingham was where he met Susan Bailey, and they began living together as Mr and Mrs John Thompson. He went back to Hull and of all things he rented rooms from a police sergeant who thought he was a commercial traveller. Poor old Hannah was left behind. She thought he was on the run. Finally he come down to Blackheath and sets up house with Susan and sends for Hannah who brought the kids with her. He starts going to church and plays the violin at concerts. For the rest of the time he's out screwing with his tools in a violin case; just the sort of thing the Mob in Chicago did with their tommy guns in the 1920s. He'd dyed his face walnut coloured and shaved off the front of his hair and he looks like a perfectly respectable old man by now.

It all come on top when he's tackled by the coppers in Blackheath in October 1878 as he's coming out of a screwing. He shot one of them but the man still held onto him. When he was nicked he said he was John Ward and that he was 60. No fingerprints to check in them days. A month later he got penal servitude for life. Unfortunately he asked a neighbour to come and see him and when the man does so and finds out that Ward is Thompson he goes to the coppers and then it really is on top. By the time the coppers get to Peace's house everyone's long gone, but Susan puts him and Hannah away for the £100 reward.

Then Mrs Dyson, who's now in America, says she will come back and give evidence about the shooting of her husband and when Peace is being taken up for the committal in Sheffield he throws himself out of the train. It doesn't do any good and he's picked up pretty quick.

He was never going to get out of it and it seems that in the condemned cell he turned to religion. He may have been halfway genuine because one thing he did do was admit that it was him and not a young Irishman, Aaron Habron, who'd shot and killed a copper in Manchester back in 1876. The kid, who had been heard making threats against the officer, had been sentenced to death but had been reprieved. He picked up £800 compensation for his two-and-a-half year stay in the warehouse. It seems like Peace had watched the case from the public gallery. It was Marwood who pulled the string on Peace.

He was still talked about to my day. Edgar Wallace wrote a novel about him and there was a melodrama when I was a kid where the retired executioner James Ellis, playing William Marwood, hanged the actor playing Peace on stage.

The first brothers to swing for the same offence were the Strattons back at the beginning of the last century. They're in the books for two records really. They were the first people to swing on fingerprint evidence.

Fingerprinting's been around hundreds of years in China and in India but it wasn't really until the end of the nineteenth century that it took off in Europe, and America was a bit later than that. The first person ever to be nicked on fingerprints here was a fellow who got done for a burglary in Dulwich. Jackson his name was. He got weighed off at the Old Bailey and got a seven back in 1902. That was one thing and the pros was triumphant. But the real thing was whether a jury would actually let someone swing just because a copper said that he'd made a test on a cup and it matched the man's dabs.

Then comes the big one. A husband and wife who run a small shop in Dulwich are done during a robbery in March 1905. The husband had been done on the ground floor and his wife in the bedroom. There was a cash box under the bed and it had got some dabs on it. By this time there was a sort of filing system at the Yard with convict's prints on them. There was about 80,000 of them and the prints didn't match any of those and they didn't match those of the old woman.

Really, when it comes to it, the fingerprints didn't catch the killers but they put them down. It was the usual sort of thing. People in the neighbourhood said the Stratton brothers were capable of it and one of them, Alfred, had a girl who come forward to say he'd dyed his shoes after the robbery and got rid of his coat. He'd been poncing off her and then given her a beating. There wasn't much else in the way of evidence – a bit of an ID by an old woman who saw two men running away – but it was fingerprints with that bit of support from the girlfriend.

It was a good case to test the fingerprints though because there wasn't going to be much sympathy for the pair doing in an elderly couple. The defence was unlucky. They had a man give evidence saying the fingerprints were unreliable and they didn't know he'd already written to the coppers to say he'd give evidence for them saying they were reliable. And so Alfred and Albert were the first brothers to swing. By the end each of them was saying the other done it. A bit later it was the Reubens brothers who went down together. No fingerprinting evidence here. They did a couple of sailors in the East End. Then there weren't any brothers for twenty years or so.

There was a series of gang wars in Sheffield in the 1920s and they got sorted out by the copper Sillitoe, who went on to sort out Glasgow and to be big in intelligence during the Second World War. The Fowlers, who were involved, were the last brothers to be hanged in England as far as I know.

One of the big men in the Sheffield gang wars was Sam Garvin, who was a great mate of Darby Sabini who I carried the bucket for when I was a kid. People think the Sabinis was just racecourse villains but there was a lot more to them than that. Before Sam, during the First World War in Sheffield there's been the Red Silk and White Silk gangs, who were really muggers and they wore scarves round their necks just like the Crips and Bloods today. It isn't anything new. In New York years earlier the Plug Ugly gang got its name for the sort of hat they wore, and the Dead Rabbits always had one on a pole when they went into action. There was plenty of small gangs around the country. Just two of them was the Silver Hammer gang in Hull, which ran for years working the docks, and the Nuts in Sunderland.

It was the early '20s, when there was so much trouble at racecourses round the country, that Sam Garvin and his brother, Bob, fought it out with George Mooney and his mob. Really it wasn't racecourses then, it was over the pitch and toss schools. They've never been really popular in London, not like they have been over the rest of the country, but there was big money to be made running a school and quite a good bit mugging the winning punters on their way home. The idea is you have to bet on which way a number of coins is going to fall, heads or tails. It's the same as that Australian game Two Up. They were usually held outside the town where there wasn't much danger of coppers breaking the game up and people turned up from places like Rotherham and Barnsley to play.[1]

Mooney got his men mainly from the West Bar and the Park gangs and things worked well for him for years until there was a cut in allowances for families if the men were found gaming. Mooney's men began to drift away and a lot of them went over to Sam who ran a ring at Sky Edge. The Park Brigade was also formed and soon got rid of Mooney, but he wasn't laying down. After that there was beatings and cuttings and more beatings and then there was shootings, with the coppers turning up one day to find Mooney sort of holed up in his place at West Bar under siege from the Park Brigade.

It seems that now he had a look at an alliance with Billy Kimber and those of his boys who were left from Birmingham, whilst Sam Garvin and the Park Brigade were looking for help from Darby. Then what does Mooney go and do? He gives an interview in the papers. You'd have thought he'd have had more sense but there's always villains who like the publicity. They think it makes them big. I can't think of more than a couple it's done good to. There was that Squizzy Taylor in Australia who got a lot of good publicity, and Billy Hill didn't do badly, but the sensible villain keeps his name way away from people. Mooney says there's no such thing as the Mooney Gang and it's the Park

---

[1] Pitch and toss had as many variations as venues. It was also known as Nearest the Mottie and Nudgers, Hoying and Burling. Playing had been banned on Sundays in Victorian England. It was played on any waste ground with rings, on pit banks in Lanarkshire and on the beaches near Swansea. It survived in places as a regular sport until the 1950s. See C. Chinn *Better Betting with a Decent Feller*, pp. 95–103.

Brigade who are the villains breaking up his hold on Sky Edge. Worse, he goes and names names and, not surprisingly, the men don't like it. So they start fighting with him.

By Christmas 1923 Sam Garvin's Park Brigade was well on top. One by one Mooney's remaining men was pushing off. One went down to Birmingham and in fact for a time Mooney cleared off as well. Sam was a brighter spark altogether. Once, when he was on bail for attacking Mooney, he had a boxing tournament for the families of men killed in the Nunnery colliery disaster. He also started taking an interest in politics, breaking up Labour Party political meetings. He was doing well because his family was one of the first to move into the new Walkley estate, with a bathroom. Just think, it was nearly thirty years before I could ever get a place with one.

The fighting went on for a couple of years with all sorts of people springing up. Then, at the New Year of 1925, it looked like there might be a bit of a compromise with Garvin and Mooney sharing Sky Edge. Everyone seemed to be pleased; summonses had been withdrawn and there was going to be a 50–50 split. But they didn't call Sam 'Slippery' for nothing. When Mooney's men turned up with a fellow, Tom Armstrong from Birmingham who'd moved into Sheffield, they was told to push off.

Then a fellow George Newbould took over against Garvin. And shortly after it all come on top for the Fowler brothers. In April 1925 William Plommer, who'd been a sergeant in the First World War and was now on the dole and father of two kids, one only three weeks' old, was stabbed to death. What had happened was that there's been a fight near Plommer's home in which a Garvin gang member, Wilfred Fowler, had got a beating. It seems Plommer had only been looking on but that was enough. I suppose there's a moral. If you see a fight that's nothing to do with you get on your bike. Anyway, the next night Fowler and his friends had toured the area threatening to do for Plommer.

Plommer come out of his house to meet them and was attacked by a crowd. It seems there was about eight of them and he got hit over the head with a child's scooter and then stabbed with a bayonet. Fowler and his brother, Lawrence, don't seem to have made much of an effort to run away. A copper found them with a fellow, George Wills, sitting on the steps of a shop not far from Plommer's body.

In the end eleven men, including both the Fowlers, were charged with Plommer's murder. They said that Plommer had run a tossing ring under the railway arches at Norfolk Bridge and he'd been the one who'd gone for the Fowlers with a poker and razor. They couldn't make it stand though.

Both the Fowler brothers were convicted of murder. Sam Garvin, who'd been charged with aiding and abetting, got a not guilty and Wills got a ten for manslaughter. In those days if you was found guilty you could say something to the judge about how sorry you was after your brief had spoken for you, before he passed sentence. Remember, a lot of people didn't have briefs even in serious cases. It didn't do no good usually and it didn't for Lawrence who said he'd only hit Plommer one clip with a poker. Wilfred remained stumm.

An appeal was lodged but like so many that didn't do no good either. The Court of Appeal took the view that it wasn't the Fowlers' bad luck they'd gone down for murder, it was the rest of them had good luck. If everyone had swung it would have been better. Then there was a story flew round that Wilfred had confessed and got his brother out. The trouble was there'd been so much trouble that summer round the racetracks that there was going to be an example made of someone. The brothers got topped on consecutive days – Wilfred first – at Armley. Lawrence had asked to be executed with his brother but no one listened. It was another man, Alfred Bostock, who had battered his mistress to death and thrown her in the river at Rotherham, went on the scaffold with Wilfred.

Garvin and Mooney went on and racked up a few more convictions, but they was never long ones. A bitten ear and three broken ribs was only worth nine months. When you think what we got for the so-called Torture Trial. But what the authorities did was bring in Percy Sillitoe who was given a licence to stamp out the gangs, no questions asked, and that's what he did. He had the biggest and fittest men out on the streets – one of the coppers was said to be able to hold seven tennis balls in one hand – handing out their own sort of punishment. If anyone complained and took out a cross-summons for assault the beaks weren't listening.

By 1927 the coppers had won. There was a bit of violence from people like the Junior Park but both George Mooney and Sam Garvin became bookmakers. Sam called himself Captain Mee and worked the Northern courses and Mooney, who was calling himself George Barratt by then, did some betting on the dogs at Owlerton. George, who'd had a personal talking to by Sillitoe, never got no more convictions, but Sam, who hadn't, ran up a string before he died in the 1960s.

When I was young there was a lot about the Great Yellow Peril. Fu Manchu and the Chinese was going to take over this country and only Sexton Blake could save us. In real life there was that man the Brilliant Chang, from Limehouse, who was meant to have given drugs to a couple of actresses who died as a result. Chang got deported and there was a lot of stuff in the papers warning girls from going with Chinese blokes. They was full of girls being found drugged in Chinese restaurants and so on and ending up on the game. In a way it was just like it was with the Jamaicans and the Maltese in the 1950s and 1960s. Of course, just like today the Chinese villains didn't mix with the rest of us. They have their own wars and don't like getting involved with outsiders.

In 1922, the year before I was born, there was a murder in Sheffield which, in a way, a girl Lily Siddal solved. She used to work in a Chinese laundry owned by a fellow called Sing Lee in Crookes, doing the books and marking the tabs on the washing. One day he asked her to come in special and then when she got there he didn't turn up. There was another Chinese, Lee Doon, who worked there and he said the boss had gone back to China and now he was taking over. Lily become suspicious because Lee Sing hadn't taken his hat and suitcase when he left, and also because Lee Doon was wearing the man's trousers. Lily checked out to see if Sing Lee had gone over to Liverpool to see his relatives and got a blank, so she went to the police. The coppers turned up and in a trunk in the cellar was the body of Sing Lee. At first Lee Doon said he'd killed his boss in an accident but it turned out he'd bashed him on the head and then strangled him with a rope. They topped Lee Doon. Over the years in fact there was quite a number of Chinese executed.

HUDDERSFIELD

If you've got a gun in the place there's always a danger you'll use it, even though the trouble you're in is hopeless. It's what I say about murders being done on the spur of the moment. Take that Alfred Moore who was a screwer in Huddersfield in the early '50s. The coppers come round and want to question him and what does he do? Even though he's surrounded, he opens fire and kills a couple, Inspector Duncan Frazer and Constable Arthur Jagger. He got topped at the beginning of 1953. No question of a reprieve for him.

I often had a gun about. It's what saved me from a bad beating that Christmas Day a few years before when the Carters come round to give me a seeing to. I put it to the head of one of them and pulled the trigger. I was lucky. My mate, Jimmy Ford, had taken out the firing pin or something because my young boys was at an inquisitive stage and they might have done some harm to themselves if they'd found it and started playing around. As a rule though I didn't take one with me when I went out thieving. There's no doubt when the coppers chased me back down when we did a factory in Luton, that if I'd had the gun in the van I'd have shot at the coppers. Not to kill them but I might have done. As it turned out the gun was in the other car and I got nicked. But then the reason I had that day it was in case I ran into the Carters.

I never kept crooked gear at home. Well, maybe a suit which my sister or one of her friends had lifted for me, but there was never 26 radios stacked up in the back room. Once it's found in your house the chances of a not guilty have gone out the window. What's the good of going out and getting it and then putting it where you live especially if you're a known rascal? In my day if you was found with stolen gear in your home even if you was found not guilty the pros could bring it up at a second trial if you was done for receiving again within the year, so it was kept down the slaughter. Would I have used a gun if the police come searching my home? You can never tell. If they'd been a bit flash and come on strong then my temper might have snapped.

HULL

Hull was the home of the man who killed three women over the years and got away with murder every time. William Birkett did the first of his girlfriends back in 1915. That was when he killed his married girlfriend and did nine years for manslaughter. He wasn't out a year before he did another married girlfriend, and this time he did a ten. He was out a bit longer this time. It was 1939 that he killed another married woman. He strangled this one. He'd cut the throat of the first two. He said he was jealous because they was looking at other men. You'd think they'd have locked him up for ever but he was out in 1954 and when it come to it I don't think he did another so perhaps they was right. He died a couple of years later. He'd have been nearly seventy by then.

BRADFORD

I never spent much time in Bradford but when I was there it was a lucky place for me. The first time was when I got taken up under escort to join up in the War after I'd done my 15 months for a screwing. What was so odd was that they just left me standing about and, since I was in civvies, I just walked off. There I was in Bradford with more or less nothing in my pockets and a place I didn't know. I couldn't phone anyone. No one I knew had a phone. Eva was at my parents and they certainly didn't. Even if I had got through how was they going to come up and get me? I bumped into a couple of people I knew from Camden Town who'd come up with their wives to get away from the bombing and to see if there was a couple of touches. What luck. I'd have had to take my chance and do a screwing on my own, but they pointed me in the right direction and we did both the jobs they fancied. Then we all went down to Newmarket and I made my way back to London.

The second time was when I got taken back up there again and this time I chinned the medical officer and got sent to the North Riding Hospital. They kept me there a bit and then sent me home to my mother saying I was unfit for service. I got a disability allowance and all.

There was a funny case in Bradford a bit after the War. A priest just disappeared. July 1953 it was. He was Father Henrik Borynski, an exiled Pole who lodged in Little Horton Lane. Apparently he took a call, said, 'All right I go', collected his hat and coat and walked out. His landlady watched him go walking up the road and turning right past a hospital. After that he just vanished. He took only ten shillings with him and left a few hundred quid in his bank account.

The landlady, Irena Beck, called the local police of course and the CID and MI5 was called in. The locals thought he'd been kidnapped and murdered by Communist agents. There was supposed to have been a lot of them in Bradford at the time and it was a real anti-Communist time. The Father had been denouncing them from the pulpit and people thought this might have got him into trouble.

There was another attack on a priest a bit after the Father disappeared. Someone left a message, 'Be silent, Priest' on the man who looked after the Lithuanians in town, in matchsticks on his table one night. But people reckoned that he was in a right nervous state and might have laid them out himself.

DEWSBURY

There've been some good escapes from prisons and there's been enough out of vans taking people to court or hospital, but there's not been too many out of police stations that I can recall. Mind you there was one fellow up in Sunderland when I was a teenager who did his best. He was up for disorderly conduct but when he was in his cell he managed to smash up two beds and then get out of handcuffs and a straitjacket before he set fire to the place. The coppers come and threw water on him. All he got was a month. I remember a few years ago there was a kid wanted for robbery walked out of Old Street in his stocking feet, got on the tube and went home, but he's almost got to be a one-off.

Generally people don't get out too easy. There's a lot of reasons. Firstly, people are a bit wary in the nick. It's not that they're frightened exactly but they're concentrating on their cases. There's always the chance they're not going to be charged so what's the point of escaping? Then when they are charged, it's too late. The second thing is the coppers haven't got too many people to look after at any one time so they can give people their attention. After all, in a police nick at any one time there's only likely to be two or three serious people. All right, half a dozen in the old days if everyone got rounded up after a blag, but they might not even know the others was in. The most important thing though is they aren't there long enough to do much about it. There's no chance to get organised. Anything has to be spur of the moment. The chances are the cells are underground, and if you managed to get out of the cell when you was being given food, the chances are that you couldn't get out of the cell block itself. In later years there'd be alarm bars on the walls of the cells which didn't help. Even if you did get out of the cell block you'd still got to get past the front desk. It wasn't worth giving it a spin really.

The best of the escapes from cells though was that Nikolaus Chrastny. In a way though he was different. He wasn't in the cells for just a day or so. He was in the same place for long enough to give him a chance.

What happened was that after that Bertie Smalls become a supergrass things changed. Supergrasses were kept in police nicks and they got all sorts of privileges. There was booze; they could have visits from their wives and girlfriends, and very often the coppers would take them out for a drink in the local boozer. Lots of opportunities to escape but there was none of them tried as far as I can recall. The reason for that is there was nowhere for them to go. They were safer in the nick. If they got out and went back to their manor then the chances are someone would have topped them before the day was out. They weren't all safe even in the nick. One of them, David Smith, topped himself and good riddance.

So Nikolaus Chrastny really was another one-off. Brilliant, he was; a very wealthy man and a great charmer – could get birds off of trees. He was nicked as a leading man in an international drugs syndicate back in June 1987 before these things was as popular as they are today. The customs found a whole lot of cocaine in Harley Street which isn't where you always find it. It was said to have been worth £14 million then, so you can work out what it was worth today. What he was also was a friend of Roy Garner, who'd been a top villain and a top grass at the same time.

At the time Chrastny was nicked, there was a whole lot of trouble going on at Scotland Yard with stories that some officers were involved in dealing drugs. Chrastny tells them he can help put one or two down and so, rather then let him stay down in London where there's always a possibility someone might get to him and explain the error of his ways in being a grass, he's shipped off to Yorkshire. It wasn't the last time this happened. A few years later it was thought that Garner was going to spill the beans and he got sent up to Attercliffe in Sheffield from the Long Sutton nick in great secrecy so there could be private interviews. That didn't do much good because the local paper had hold of it in no time.

First off Chrastny was sent to Rotherham, but they thought he was getting too friendly with some officers and it's over to Dewsbury. Anyway there he is in the nick in the area usually used for women prisoners. Soon, he'd got himself a television and stereo and his wife Charlotte's allowed in for dinner sometimes. Funnily enough she'd been a copper in Germany before she met him, and it's only natural they'd want to talk in German isn't it? Not too many of the local coppers was fluent but that didn't matter since they wasn't joining in. People liked Mrs C. There wasn't always a search and, it turned out later, even when she was found with £500 on her she was allowed to give it to her husband. It must have been reasonably comfortable. Apart from the telly and the stereo he was allowed to have beer and cigars, and jars of chutney, and 41 books including *The Hound of the Baskervilles*. And two files, which it was said his wife brought in hidden in the spine.

Poor devil, he's there on his own and its only right he should have something to do when they're not asking him questions and his wife's not around, so he's given stuff to make models, stuff like plasticine, Blu-tak, paint and glue.

That's one of the problems with grasses, you've got to keep them sweet. In a way you need them more than they need you. There's always that bit of gold at the end of the rainbow that's going to make you the most famous copper in the world. If they clam up it's gone. So when Chrastny gets the stuff he puts it to good use. As well as the models he's spending his time sawing through the bars. No one heard the sawing because he'd got the TV and the stereo on. That's the trouble with leaving someone in one place for too long. If they're shifted around regular enough they can saw as much as they like. It all goes to waste.

Anyway the day before he's being taken back to court in London he's managed to get through the bars. His cell didn't have a plug in it of course, and the cable for his telly ran from the medical room opposite, so that couldn't be locked. And that didn't have any bars on the windows, so he's up and running, across the prison yard, and he's never seen again; not here anyway. Of course there was an inquiry and what come out was there was a car waiting for him. It wasn't until the next morning that anyone looked for him. He was always given a lie-in, because it was 11.30 by that time. He left a note saying goodbye and they did hear from him again because he rang and said he was sorry for the inconvenience he'd caused. What was so amazing was that he was already on the run from the coppers in West Germany over an armed robbery. He'd had his face changed by plastic surgery several times. You'd have thought they might have taken more care of him.

Someone's got to suffer for things like that and they did his wife for helping him escape. She got a not guilty but she got a seven over the cocaine. After that there was all sorts of guidelines about how to keep hold of informers. No booze, no sex, officers in uniform on guard, that sort of thing. Anyway it didn't matter to Chrastny. There was some story he was in Costa Rica.

EDDIE CHAPMAN

I never tried my hand as a safebreaker. I didn't even want to try. That was a specialist's job. As a thief you had to know your limitations. In my day it was a question of stuffing jelly into the lock and standing back. It wasn't that difficult and what with the War the manufacturers took a long time to bring out new models. Even so, you always knew one or two who had died as well. It was no good unless you had training in some type of explosives. It was more or less handed down. That's where I was at a disadvantage with no one in the family interested in things like safes. I suppose I could have gone to that top man Jock Robinson, Jock the Fitter, who was with the mother of Paddy O'Nione – Paddy Onions – for years, and asked him to show me but I never did. Most of the really good safeblowers were Scots. It came from handling explosives in the mines.

Eddie Chapman was an exception but there again he came from the North East. I liked Eddie. He was class. I met him through Hilly and Albert. What a feat he'd done. All through the War he was game. He was a true working-class patriot. He come from somewhere near Sunderland, and it wasn't until he was well in his twenties that he started safecracking. He'd already got a life saving medal and he'd been in the Guards, the Coldstream I think he used to say. I think he did a bit of time in the Glasshouse as well. He'd fallen in love with a brass and when he left her she rang up the coppers to say he was a deserter. After that it was a spell in Lewes, where he teamed up with a really good blower and that's where he learned the trade. Some people say it was Jimmy Hunt but I'm not so sure it wasn't Freddie Ford, who went on to own a lot of spielers and had the scheme where brasses took suitcases into the hotels Fred had so it couldn't be said he was knowingly running a brothel.

Whichever it was they split up and in 1939 Eddie's found screwing a safe in Edinburgh with some other blokes. He got himself out on bail, and the others out when he did a screwer to raise their bail, and it's over to Jersey where he's arrested again. One of the blokes who'd been nicked with him in Edinburgh sends a postcard to his girlfriend and it's traced. The girl had a brother who was a cozzer. That copper Greeno come over from England along with Fabian to nick him, but Eddie says he's blown a safe and so the Jersey court give him two years for openers before he's to go back to the mainland. By now the War's coming and the Germans occupied the Channel Islands.

The Huns made him an offer to go over to Britain and carry out sabotage and Eddie thought if he could get back home then he could join up again. They give him the codename Fritzchen and in December 1942 they dropped him by parachute near Ely. What he was meant to be doing was blowing up the De Havilland place near Hatfield where we was building the Mosquito fighting bomber. He was told he was going to get £15,000 if it went off all right and then he'd be sent off to America to do some work there. I think he said they'd give him a grand expenses up front, which was big money in them days.

The moment he lands he gets on the blower to the local nick but he can't get the coppers there to understand what he's going on about. Eventually he does manage to get to see someone who knows what the SP is, and he's retrained by us and given the name Zig Zag. What he does next is go back with an MI5 officer and pretends to blow up De Havillands. The whole thing was set up by the magician Jasper Maskelyne, who used to have a Christmas show in the Scala Theatre, just near where Alec de Antiquis got killed when he tried to stop a getaway and my friend was topped over it.

Anyway Maskelyne puts on this illusion that the factory's gone up the spout and it's all over the papers. The Huns are well pleased and they tell Eddie to get himself back to Germany where there's wine and women waiting for him and after that it'll be off to the States. What he really wants to do is have a go at killing Hitler but our authorities wouldn't wear it. I don't know why not. So Eddie's put on a boat to Lisbon which is neutral but full of Nazis. He's given a piece of coal and told to go and put it in the coalhole of the ship he's on. The idea is that it was going to blow the ship up when it goes in the boiler but Eddie's handed it over to the captain. The Huns don't suspect anything and he's a bit of a hero with them and they give him the Iron Cross just before he's sent back to England. Same thing happens; he lands, rings up the local police and they tell him he's drunk and should go to bed. The MI5 put him up in Knightsbridge but that was a bit too near to Soho for Eddie and he was forever meeting his pals, so he got dropped out. But he'd more than done his bit.

After the War Eddie wrote his memoirs; they got published in France, so he was done under the Official Secrets Act. He got fined £50, something like that. Eventually they came out over here and they've done very well. There was also that film about him with Christopher Plummer, called *Triple Cross*. By then though, Eddie was well in with Billy and the rest of us. He was a good man to have around. He wasn't a drinker like some of the younger men. But you'd see him in Ginny's in Archer Street from time to time. Until

Aggie Hill opened the New Cabinet, that and Bobby's were the places to be. Well, before Tommy McCarthy opened the Log Cabin.

It was after I was put away for slashing Jack Spot that Billy decided to have him and a few others go to Africa. If I hadn't been away I'd have been with them. I've written about it before but they was going to kidnap some Sultan or other in Madagascar. They never got near. People started quarrelling on the boat and then they got into a fight in Tangier and were thrown out of there. I think the boat went up in flames as well.[1]

In a way Eddie was mixing with a different circle by then. He'd grown away from our life. He'd moved out of Soho and into Knightsbridge and Chelsea. Over the years Eddie put a good bit of money away because he had a sort of health club, funnily enough not far from Hatfield, and he spent a lot of his time trying to get people interested in police corruption but he never really managed it. He knew what was going on with coppers but no one wanted to know. He was in that television programme, *The Underworld*, with me in 1993, and a bit after that he went to the Canaries. I had a drink with him just before he left. He died a few years back. He really was one of the best.

---

[1] *Mad Frank and Friends.*

NEWCASTLE

Fortunately I don't like holidays so I've never been tempted to buy a timeshare. Many people have and some have done well out of them, but my advice would be not to go near most of them. They've often caused a lot of trouble and there's been a lot of problems, particularly down in Tenerife in that resort of Los Cristanos. A lot of big money's been made and lost over timeshares there and a number of big people from the North East had interests. There's also been a lot of stories about bad fights and beatings, and of girls being hung out of the windows by their feet as warnings from rival salesmen and, from what I know, they're more than half right.

That girl, Jackie Ambler, from near Doncaster got 27 years in Tenerife back in 1998. The pros out there said she'd got hold of a couple of men who'd agreed to do in Michael O'Hara, her boyfriend who was a partner in a bar she had in Los Cristanos. In 1995 he'd been beaten over the head with a beer barrel and then had a cloth stuffed down his throat at Stevie's Bar, which was the one he owned with Jackie. The story the pros had was that she offered £54,000 to a fellow, Gary Holmes, and another, Stanley Stewart, to do him in. Now, £54,000 seems a lot to me. You could have probably found a hundred people who'd have done it for a tenth of the price and they wouldn't even have wanted a business class ticket on the plane. Jackie always said she'd nothing to do with it but the trouble was the men had gone and confessed, a bit after they got arrested. That's the difficulty, once you say something, or put it down on paper more particularly, you're in trouble saying how you was made to do it.

When the trial came about, Gary Holmes changed his story and said that he'd killed O'Hara over a drug debt and he'd made things up against Jackie and Stanley Stewart because he thought she'd lollied him over drug dealing. He said that Stanley had just tried to break up the fight. In his statement Stewart had said he'd gone along with things because he was scared of Holmes and the men he worked for. The trouble in their case was they'd not just made the statement to the police; they'd done it before an examining magistrate. The men got 29 years apiece.

There have been some good people up in the North East over the years. In my day a lot of them was doing time for blowing peters. That was their strong coup. They'd worked in the mines and they knew what they was doing. Sometimes they was recruited to help out on a job but generally they kept to themselves. I know Newcastle isn't as far away as Glasgow but in them days it seemed like it was. Eddie and me had a couple of machines up there but it was really a bit far for us to go. We was doing so well in Manchester and Leeds we hadn't expanded further. If Mr Smith's hadn't happened we might have started there but it's history now.

More recently Viv Graham was one of the biggest but it's never been satisfactorily worked out whose side he was on. Like so many towns, Newcastle's had its bouncer wars. There was one back in 1988. People wanted to get their drugs into clubs and the bouncers are often there to make sure only the favoured friends can sell in them. It was reckoned to be a place to make a reputation, an easier place than, say, Manchester or Liverpool. There was big trouble again in 1993 with a lot of shootings and a couple of leading lights disappeared. Things have continued on and off since then even though they've got bouncers licensed now like they have in so many places all over the country.

Viv Graham come from the Winlaton area. The places there were clannish and tough small towns, ruled by such good men as Denny Haig. Graham's father was himself a hardman and Viv did a lot of boxing and bodybuilding. He become a doorman and a protector for many of the winebars and clubs in Newcastle and Gateshead. The police reckoned he was pulling in the region of six figures a year and a lot of it went to support his gambling habit. His right-hand man was Robert Armstrong and he'd been friendly with members of both the Tams and Sayers families. I knew Viv from being in Durham with him. He was quite a big guy physically, well liked and respected. I never saw a lot of him because I was in chokey so much of the time but what I saw I liked. In chokey I'd be in a cage, but I could talk through the wire to the guy in the next one. So I kept up with the news.

Maybe the real Newcastle trouble of the time started in August 1988. That was when Robert Bell was dining in Santino's Restaurant in the Cloth Market with Viv when two men burst in. One of them cut the telephone lines and the pros said the other man went to the table where Bell was sitting and pointed a shotgun at him. Of course there was a ruckus and Viv Graham took the gun off him and smashed it against the wall and told them not to be so stupid. It was after that Bell got stabbed in the heart, but he survived. Graham took on the pair and give one of them a beating. They only found the man Viv had done over and later he got a not guilty for stabbing Bell.

A bit after that, but before the trial, Viv and Rob Armstrong had been shot at when they was outside the Manhattan nightclub in the city, in April 1989. Someone shot out the rear window of their Bluebird Nissan and around 60 pellets was fired into Rob. Viv wasn't hit. There's one version that Viv saw himself as some controlling influence on the clubs, a sort of roving Guardian Angel who went around town late at night stopping trouble, and maybe that's right, but that wasn't the way everybody else saw it. What it was of course was protection one way or another and there was stories a team from Leeds was trying to put things together in the town. Like I say, things on Tyneside weren't as difficult as they were over on Merseyside.

It was all go. A couple of months later a doorman, Mark Stephenson, had his ear bitten off at Idols, a club over in Whitley Bay, and then that good boxer Howard Mills, who was now working as a doorman at Hanrahan's Bar, was shot in the leg which he had to have off.

The next year Viv got three years for wounding Stuart Watson, the doorman of Hobo. You can never really tell what's what and who's who. At the end of the Watson trial the doorman said he was sorry for what had happened and went on to say the coppers had been using him as bait to get Graham and the others. There'd been an undercover bogey posing as a customer when the incident had taken place who had been under orders not to intervene. The briefs for the defence asked whether once he saw a man had got some sort of spike he shouldn't have broke his cover, but he said he was under orders not to.

Along with Viv were members of some of the families. Alan Tams picked up two-and-a-half years and so did Stephen Sayers. David Lancaster and Rob Armstrong also went down as well. It was one of those cases when the police guarded the court. Some of them had been up in court only a few weeks earlier when John Henry Sayers and Stephen Sayers was charged with a variety of things including conspiracy to handle stolen vending machines. Alan Tams was charged with a series of assaults. When it come to it he admitted biting a copper on the arm – he threatened to bite off the man's nose if he come any closer – and he had a bit added to his thirty months. The copper had tried to stop a sort of free-for-all when eggs, flour and ketchup was being thrown at each other. Alan was seen walking from a shop with a tray of eggs whilst the others continued fighting. One of the stories is that it was after he went down for the Watson case Viv went on his own and he fell out with some members of the families.

Viv got the unofficial credit for doing Gazza's knee in September 1991 in Walkers in Newcastle. The coppers could never find witnesses and Gazza, to his credit, said he wanted the whole thing dropped. The troubles had led to a registration scheme for nightclub doormen. It was started in May 1992 by the Northumbria police and it was the first of its kind in the country. Anyone who wanted a licence had to get all their doormen vetted. It's all over the country now but it hasn't got rid of dealing.

It was New Year's Eve 1993 Viv was killed by three shots from a .357 Magnum handgun as he walked to his car in the Wallsend district. It looks like his attackers had been shadowing him for most of the evening. He'd been drinking most the time at a couple of pubs. He crawled thirty yards before collapsing outside a newsagent's shop.

Just about the only unchallenged thing about the killing of Viv is that he's dead. How it happened and who ordered it depends on whether he was a friend. There was all sorts of stories why he'd been topped. One of them was that he was negotiating with the black dealers in Leeds – he was seen in the Hilton there in the summer of 1993 – and there had been attempts by a Yorkshire team to muscle in on the North Eastern trade. Some people have it that he'd upset some of the big North East families and there's a story that goes back to the timeshare business in Tenerife. Then there's people that say that the killers came from suppliers in Liverpool or London, or that the men were Italians brought up from London on contract to do the business. It's really a question of take your pick. If people had been brought up from London it wouldn't have been the first time, but there's plenty of homegrown talent up in the North East.

The timeshare story is related to the death of his arch-rival Andy Winder, who died in Tenerife in 1993. Winder was in charge of the touts for a big firm in the timeshare business in Los Cristanos. Winder'd already got control of the touting in a couple of the other islands, Lanzarote and Gran Canaria, and he wanted control of South Tenerife as well.

The story is there was a bare-knuckle fight between Viv and Winder who needed a lot of work done on his face to make him look respectable again. What he did then was put out a sort of insurance or revenge with a £30,000 contract on Viv, only to be executed after his own death. In fact he got done in late September 1993 which makes the timing about right. You don't do the contract the very next day. You've got to look at things carefully. This time Winder had tried to stab a fellow Teessider who was over in Tenerife and, when some others intervened, he stabbed them as well. That was when someone shot him.

There was all sorts of stories flying around about the contracts out on Viv's life. One man meant to have had an offer was Lee Duffy, from Eston near Middlesborough. He'd already got a slice of the protection in Cleveland and he'd been offered a good slice of Newcastle by one of the families if he could get rid of Viv. Not that he didn't have enemies himself. There'd been three goes or more on him. He'd been shot in the knee and in the foot different times. It seems he'd tried to meet Viv Graham on a number of occasions but Viv hadn't turned up before Duffy got stabbed to death in a fight with David Allison in Middlesborough. Duffy had him on the floor banging his head but Allison managed to stab him and I'm pleased to say he got a not guilty. David, poor man, didn't have much luck in his life. He come home one day and found the girl he'd been living with for years had topped herself.

Then there was the question of whether Graham was really in the rackets. A lot of people thought he was well out of the way and they included some licensees. At the time of his death he was talking with designer drug suppliers in Holland.

The story is that the coppers reckoned Andrew Winder was involved in importing drugs through Teeside and Hartlepool and they linked him with a seemingly straight man who they fancied for laundering the proceeds of major crime, along with the businessman's enforcer. I'm not going to name the hardman, just call him Frank – after me that is.

Frank's employer had gone abroad by now and Frank was working in the construction industry so was able to travel the country legitimate, looking after the man's interests. That was when he was approached by a young man and asked how to deal with Viv. Frank reckoned the best thing was to make an example out of Viv as a warning to other villains, particularly the West End families. The idea was he should be kneecapped and so people could see him being wheeled about for the rest of his life. A car was stolen from Birtley, which is between Newcastle and Durham, and a kid was supplied with a .44 short barrel Magnum which had come from Ulster.

If it was to be just a kneecapping it didn't work out. If you're going to do that sort of thing it's like putting a bullet in the nut. It's got to be done at short range. What went wrong is that Viv just sort of dominated the man and the shot come from too far away. The idea if you're doing it for keeps is you follow up with a second shot to make sure. The story is that the fellow who actually shot Viv went into the nick abroad for credit card thefts and robberies.

I've known Joe Stafford – his real name was Siegenberg – and his son, Dennis, most of my life. Hilly was going to do Dennis Stafford once, but his father rang up and said 'Please don't touch him' and Hilly left him alone. Joe Stafford was a publican and bookmaker. He'd buy a bit of crooked gear here and there and laid a few bets and of course he was a straightener. If you wanted someone to talk to the coppers then Joe was one of the men to get into them for you. Joe could always be relied on to go and talk to someone he knew. Of course he wasn't doing it for nothing.

It's amazing that the really big murder on Tyneside took place as long as 35 years ago now. It's never really been cleared up as to who did it and why and who was behind it, but one of the men involved was Dennis Stafford. He'd already had a bit of a career up there before then.

Dennis was a good-looking boy, a bit flashy when he was younger but that was when we all had brilliantine or Brylcream on our hair. He made his name as a high class con-man and burglar and he was a good escaper as well. He picked up a seven at the Inner London Sessions for breaking and entering and having a firearm back in July 1956 but he didn't stay in long. Four months later on a wet and windy day he escaped over the wall at the Scrubs, along with Tony Hawkes who was another high class con-man. He was doing a six-year sentence for false pretences over a textile fraud. Over the years he'd been a foreign attaché, a cavalry officer, a city businessman and I think he'd even been a foreign butler at one time.

They had help, of course, because they was up in Newcastle within three weeks and by then they was flush enough to set up another long firm in the clothing trade. Dennis was Hutton and Tony was Whelby. They got out just before the creditors and the coppers arrived. They got Tony quick enough in a hotel off the Bayswater Road but there wasn't much sign of Dennis, which wasn't surprising since he was in Trinidad. He'd changed his name again and this time he was Wally Birch which was the name of the close mate of Joe Wilkins. Dennis's real problem was that women was always after him or the other way around and he'd ditched the girl he had up in Newcastle and he'd got a new fiancée. The trouble was the coppers knew who she was and was watching her and so when she sent him a telegram saying she was coming out, so was the police.

Old Dennis was a rascal. Whilst he was in the nick in Port of Spain he wrote his exclusive for the *News of the World* saying how sorry he was he'd let everybody down including his dad, Joe, which was a bit rich really. Now he was going to go straight. Joe played his bit saying it was the War which had led the boy astray and if he'd had a bit of dad's right hand he'd have been a lot better. If Joe'd said that today, the kid would have been removed into care and he'd probably be doing a few weeks himself.

Once he was back Dennis picked up another eighteen months. He was sent down to Dartmoor but he didn't stay long there. He tried to get out twice and failed and it was third time lucky. Just after New Year 1959 he got out with William Day, who was a house and garage breaker and was also doing a seven. They reckoned Dennis was abroad within a few days.

It was a bit of bad luck for Bill though. Unfortunately he didn't get clear. It was driving rain and thick fog as well. That's a good time for an escape, of course. If you've never been on the Moor you don't know how it can blanket things down and you can have rain and fog at the same time. That's when the condensation starts in the cells, everything's damp. Bill was found drowned in a reservoir. It seems like he blundered into the water and Dennis had thrown him a lifebelt but hadn't raised the alarm.

In fact Dennis never got abroad this time. He stuck around in this country and a bit over six weeks later he got picked up in Leicester Square and it was back to solitary for him. I was in Dartmoor by then; on stage which is the special wing, where you got privileges after you'd done four years. Some people didn't think Dennis'd done enough for Bill and there was a bit of bad feeling, but in them situations it's every man for himself. You've got to take your own chance and if you go on an escape you know it. Dennis was allowed out of solitary by the Governor to tell Joe that there wasn't any trouble over Bill. He said that he had not just thrown him a lifebelt but he'd gone in the water after him and grabbed him but had lost hold in the dark.

Then what happens? 'Happy' Sambridge, the man I took a leg off for grassing me down at Brighton Races, makes a statement that he'd planted the gun in Dennis's car. He said he'd been approached by a detective who had the needle to Stafford and wanted him nicked. Sambridge says he'd been given a gun by the copper and he left it on the shelf under the dashboard. He'd got a fiver for this, which shows what an evil bastard he was. Doing something like that for a fiver. Still, I suppose you don't know what hold the copper had on him. It goes all the way up to the Home Office and Joe Stafford says this proves his boy's got too long a sentence for the screwing but, of course, nothing happens.

Dennis is out in March 1961 and it's one of those bright dawns. He's a bit of a celeb really which goes to show that all this lionising of the likes of us didn't just happen in the last ten years. He got a job with a car and a four figure wage which wasn't bad considering you could buy two houses for that in Tottenham and probably four in Newcastle in those days. People was saying how he'd settled down and he'd learned his lesson. But rascals like Dennis and me don't learn our lessons until we've lost the legs to run away. Three months later he's found with a Browning and this time he's called Fielding, so it's back in the nick.

Then when he's out in 1965 he makes what's going to be his most expensive mistake ever. He goes back to Newcastle and starts working for Vince Landa. He was another who'd changed his name. He'd been Vincente Luvaglio, who was the big man with the machines up there and who's also running cabarets. One of the other fellows who was working for Landa was Angus Sibbett.

Sibbett was a big man; had a beard in the days when they wasn't as fashionable. He'd been around. He'd worked with people in London and he'd run a Chinese restaurant of all things. I think he did a twelve-month stretch for receiving before he went up to the North East and teamed up with Vince Landa who'd got the Social Club Services Ltd. It was a bit like Atlantic Machines – put the one-arm bandits in clubs, took the money out and split it with the club owners. Like I've said, there was good money for everyone provided you could make sure the staff wasn't skimming.

Landa'd been a copper in the RAF before he came up to the North East and started putting together the machines and things. He really made it – country house, a villa in Majorca. He'd got a Roller and goodness knows how many other cars. His younger brother Michael worked for him and all.

Sibbett got done at the beginning of January 1967. Some miners was passing on their way to work about five in the morning and there was a Mark X Jaguar parked near a bridge at South Hetton and Angus was dead in it. And so it all started to go wrong for Dennis and Michael. He was the one who'd been driving the Jaguar recently.

Someone had bubbled Dennis about his LF all those years before and they done the same over again. Now ten years later someone told the coppers there was a damaged E-type Jaguar in a garage in Sunderland.

It seems like the whole Luvaglio family and Dennis and his girlfriend had been over to Majorca and everyone had flown back up to Newcastle after the New Year. Everyone that is except Vincent who had stayed in London and then pushed off back to Majorca. It seems he'd given permission for Dennis to use the E type.

It wasn't what you'd call a strong case against them. There's no doubt the E type had been in some sort of a smash with the car Sibbett was found in and they'd been planning to meet Sibbett that night. They said he hadn't turned up at the Bird Cage Club and whilst they was waiting Dennis went outside to get some cigarettes he'd left in the car and that's when he saw it was damaged. He told the club doorman what he'd seen. There was some tyre marks in the snow which looked like someone had driven into the motor and then pushed off.

It was one of those cases where the pros said that even with alibis, and both of them had good ones – one of them was that good singer, Selena Jones – the men could have got out of the club, killed Angus, dumped his body and been back inside three-quarters of an hour. And of course it was like one of those detective stories and the time of Angus's death. Did the cold that night make any difference? Anyway, they said, why should they kill Angus who was their friend? The judge didn't do them no favours, saying that friends could be like Judas or Brutus. The pros never said why they thought he'd been done.

The jury was out three hours before returning a guilty verdict. No one was very happy, least of all Dennis and Michael, of course. The Court of Appeal knocked them back and even when that dodgy Home Secretary Reginald Maudling sent it back for a re-hearing of the appeal that didn't do any good. Of course Maudling was well mixed up with the North East. Michael's parents stuck by him and they got hold of that London brief, David Napley, who always reckoned Michael was innocent.

Joe Stafford did what he could as well. If you read Nipper Read's book you can see he was offering to turn the Krays in if Read could do anything about his boy's conviction. He even tried to see the then Prime Minister, Harold Wilson. It's funny how things go circling round. Just like 'Happy' Sambridge who said he'd been paid to plant the gun which did for Dennis all those years back, in 1967, a North East face, George Shotton, come forwards and said he'd been offered five grand to do Sibbett. He'd been in the Bird Cage when he'd been approached and he thought the man was Italian. George was a car dealer now but he'd got a string of form and the authorities wasn't going to listen to him if they didn't need to. Another geezer come forward and said the same thing but he thought the fellow who put the offer up might have been a bubble.

There was something of a campaign for them and it went back to the courts but the House of Lords give them their final knockback in the October. Both men were paroled in 1979 and that was when Dennis did neither of them a favour. Well, he might have got himself out of a mess short term but it didn't help long term. He went and told a fellow from the papers that he'd done Sibbett. He was said to have got ten grand for the confession.[1] He'd done it whilst Michael was in bed. That really messed things up. He was wanted for a few credit card frauds and was on his toes again. Poor old Michael. He'd done well for himself in the nick and he'd got an Open University degree. Since he come out he's been working with disabled kids.

Dennis tried to get out of the trouble he'd caused by telling another paper he'd only given the interview for the money and it was all cobblers, but then he went and said something about how he was trying to expose the judicial system. The next I heard of him was when I came out from the twenty and someone told me he was in the nick in South Africa over another fraud out there.

The killing did for just about everyone involved. Vince Landa's empire went bust and it turned out that Sibbett had had his forks in the till. He'd been screwing the firm out of around £1,600 a week, which was serious money then and it's not even bad now. Landa had pushed off back to Majorca once more and sort of moved around the Mediterranean for a few years before he showed up in Malta in 1977. He got brought back here and got fined for frauds on working men's clubs which had happened in the Sibbett days. The judge give him credit for the time he'd been in the nick abroad waiting to be brought back which is more than my David got when he got done over drugs a few years ago. The last I heard of Landa was that he was in Florida but that can be wrong.

A bit later Dennis got pulled in for breaking the conditions of his licence. Something to do with a bit of fraud, non-violent anyway. He went back to the courts to get them to say the Home Secretary was wrong but he got blanked off over it. I heard Dennis was out and about a year ago but

---

[1] *News of the World*, 7 September 1980.

I haven't seen him. Then I heard he was trying to get his conviction looked at by the Criminal Review Board. It was about that time that I heard the story that the killing had been done by a London firm and was nothing to do with either Dennis or Michael. I knew the names put up and from what I know it was possible but where I come from you hear stories like this every week.

Over the years there's been some other big murders up in the North East and one of them was one of the early railway murders. Of course, the first murder on the railway was big news. It was back in 1864 when that fellow Franz Muller – they named a hat after him – killed a fellow called Thomas Briggs during a robbery whilst the train was going between Bow and Hackney Wick. He only got away with the man's gold watch and he left his own hat behind, taking his victim's. There was a lot of publicity and a man came forward to say he recognised it. After that it was a bit of a chase with Muller trying to get to America. The coppers went on a faster boat, just like Dew did when he was chasing Crippen and that was that so far as Muller was concerned.

After that come a number of killings. There was Percy Lefroy. He did a fellow called Isaac Gold who was a coin dealer from Brighton, in the early 1880s. He shot him as the train went into the Merstham Tunnel in Kent. Lefroy's story was a load of flannel. He said he'd been knocked out by three men who'd shot Gold. He never could explain how he came to have Gold's coins. They topped him quick enough. Then come a woman who was found dead when the train arrived at Waterloo. Another fellow got done near Wimbledon and the last before the one up near Newcastle was a real mystery. A girl called Sophie Money was killed. Funny, that was also down near Merstham. They could never work out what she was doing on the train in the first place let alone who did her. You'd have to bet on a secret boyfriend though.

Nearly fifty years after the first murder came the case of John Dickman. March 1910 it was. It was a wages robbery and Dickman was said to have done John Nisbett who'd collected about £370 to pay the miners at the colliery he worked at. People said they saw Dickman getting on the train with a man and Mrs Nisbett had seen her husband on the train with a man when she come to give him a wave at the station. She knew Dickman but she never picked him out as the man with her husband. When the train gets to Alnmouth, a porter looks in and there's blood under the seat and Nisbett's been shot five times with two different guns. Remember in those days there wasn't open carriages like there is now. You sat four or five aside facing each other.

The bag, without the money, is found down a mine shaft near Morpeth where Dickman got off. The police never found the guns that was used but they could prove Dickman had one and they could prove he'd got gambling problems. What it amounted to was that Dickman admitted he been on the train and when he was nicked and the house searched there was a pair of bloodstained trousers and £17 in gold sovereigns. He said the blood had come from a nosebleed and, of course, in them days there wasn't the testing there is now. He said the coins was part of his commission from a bookmaker but if that's right it was a lot.

The ticket collector said that when he handed in his ticket at Morpeth, Dickman had kept his other hand out of sight and what he meant was that he was trying to hide the bag. No one ever managed to get over the fact that there'd been two guns used which makes it seem like it was a double handed robbery. In fact it came out later that Dickman sometimes wrapped smaller bullets in paper and that made up for the difference in the bullets.

There's no doubt when the murder went off he owed a few hundred to money lenders. There really wasn't anything but circumstantial evidence but everyone was against him at the start of the trial. By the end, when he was sentenced to swing, people had turned around, saying there wasn't really enough evidence to top him. Five of the jurors asked for a reprieve. The day before he was due, there was handbills all over London but by then it was too late. There was about 1,500 outside the nick to watch the flag go up.

Funnily enough his name was mentioned over a case in Kent in August 1908. There'd been a big unsolved murder down there near Ightham when a woman, Caroline Luard, was found shot dead in a summerhouse. Someone had pulled the rings off of her fingers. There was a bit of evidence Dickman had forged a cheque which she'd sent him in reply to an ad asking for financial help but that was about all. Her husband topped himself soon after – threw himself under a train. It came out later that all the judges who heard Dickman's appeal knew Luard and that case and so did Winston Churchill, who was the Home Secretary and turned down the reprieve.

It was about twenty years later came one of the really big unsolved murders. It was a girl called Evelyn Foster back in 1931. She ran a taxi service with her father and one night in early January a bus driver came across their cab in a place called Wolf's Nick on the road to Otterburn. Their new Hudson was on fire and the girl was laying nearby badly burned. They got her back home and she'd got a funny story saying she'd picked up a fare who wanted to go on to Ponteland where he could pick up the bus to Newcastle. A few miles before they got to Ponteland he tells her to turn back and, when she does so, he throws fluid over her and sets fire to her. Then he puts the car in gear and it runs off the road with her in it. The girl's last words is when she tells her mother she's been murdered. She's also told her she's been assaulted. She said he'd got a bowler hat on and he was a heavy smoker and had a Tyneside accent.

It was a funny old case as I say. It turned out from tests that the car had been carefully driven off the road and then set on fire, not the other way around. There wasn't any evidence she'd been raped either. The inquest comes back with wilful murder but the police said they were convinced the man didn't exist. They thought she'd topped herself and there was a story it was for the insurance, but it's a hard way to collect. You'd have thought she didn't need to set fire to herself if she was going along those lines, but when you're dealing with petrol and the like it's easy enough for the wind to blow back a flame.

Just like when Neville Cream was being topped and he called out 'I'm Jack . . .' and started people thinking he was Jack the Ripper, so a fellow called Ernest Brown started a story that he might have been the man who did for Evelyn. He was a groom who'd shot his employer, a Frederick Morton, and had tried to get rid of the body in a burning garage. Brown had been having it off with Morton's wife. It just shows you shouldn't have it off with the servants. Brown cut the telephone wires whilst Morton was away and terrorised the woman and the maid by shooting outside the house. There's a big explosion about 3.30 the next morning and the garage is on fire. When it cools down enough for people to get near, there's Morton's two cars burned to bits and Morton himself is shot in the chest. The story goes that just as Brown was about to swing he said something like 'Otterburn'. It may have been 'ought to burn' for all anyone knew because they didn't stop and ask him what he meant. But the thing stuck. I don't think there was any evidence against him at all except, as a groom in them days, he wore a bowler hat and he'd been going around the North East going to agricultural shows.

There was a sort of early Craig and Bentley case back in 1940 when a PC Sheill got killed. There's no doubt who was involved and one of the men was Ostler, the son of a copper from Leeds. Him and another kid Appelby was out screwing the local Co-op at Coxhoe, Co. Durham at the end of February 1940 when Sheill saw them. Sometimes it seems that the Co-op was the only place that was screwed back then but, if it was, it was because every place had one and often it was the only shop for miles. Sheill blew his whistle for help and then chased them into Westley Place, where he was shot. The kids got away and he was taken to the local hospital where he said he was finished.

The local justices' clerk was called to take what they called a dying declaration from him. The dying declaration was quite often used in those days when people had respect for religion. Normally if someone said something against you it had to be in your presence before the beak would allow it to be given. It stands to reason. Otherwise it was called hearsay and wouldn't be allowed in. This dying declaration was an exception. People was thought to be so fearful of dying and God that they wouldn't lie about what happened. This time the copper said he'd cornered them and one had pulled a revolver and the other had said, 'Let him have it. He's all alone'; almost the exact words that did for Bentley.

One of the reasons I got an acquittal in that murder trial after Dickie Hart got killed at Mr Smith's was I was alone in the dock. I didn't have to worry about what other briefs was going to say to the court or what the other defendants was going to say. Not that it come to my giving evidence, but I didn't have to worry about what I said harming anyone else either.

The real worry is if you've got too many defendants and they start running what's called a cut-throat defence, putting the blame on someone else in the dock. Very often they cut everyone's throat and their own. That's why the pros likes to have as many in the dock as possible all together. That's what happened this time. Ostler ran an alibi but what happens is Appelby says he was present when Ostler had shot the copper. And he went and gave evidence to that effect. Appelby denied saying 'Let him have it. He is all alone.' What he'd really said was, 'Let's give him a clout.' The judge wasn't having none of it. He reckoned they was both in it and if Appelby hadn't called out then

Ostler might not have shot Sheill. They both swung of course, just like Bentley.

If I had a pound for every time I've heard the story about how the Krays tried to take over Manchester or Leeds or Newcastle or wherever, and the local villains banded together and gave them a beating, or the police put them on the train back to London, I'd not need to write these books. The story's just not true. For a start they always went by car. The stories have become part of those urban legends you read about, like the fellow who goes to bed with a girl and next morning he finds she's gone but she's left a message, 'Welcome to the World of AIDS' in lipstick on his mirror. That would have made him miss his breakfast. There's no doubt the Twins did go up to Newcastle. They took Joe Louis up with them and they met with the top people just as when they came down they've the same hospitality given them, but Ronnie and Reggie wasn't interested in taking things over.

By the middle of the 1980s there were rumours that some of the big families who'd been at war with each other for years was going to come into an alliance. I was away at the time so it was only what I heard as I was being moved about, but if they ever did it come to nothing. They're still at war today from what I hear.

It was just around when I came out for the last time in 1989 that a fellow, Nigel Robinson, stabbed his girlfriend. Up in Billingham it was, near where my friend who I was with in Borstal all them years ago, came from. It turns out at his trial that Robinson's done a previous girlfriend when he was seventeen. He'd only been out six months when he did the second. Sometime you do wonder if the authorities know what they're doing.

It was up in the North East that ramraiding really took hold some years back – stealing big heavy cars like Rovers and

Jaguars and driving them through shop windows so's you can get at the televisions and things. They used to have paving stones in the cars as well so they could chuck them at the police if they was being chased.

There was one blagging a bit ago where the people sealed off a whole town, just like the Wild West. Back in August 1993 it was when a gang took over Rothbury, Berwick on Tweed. What happened was that five men in ski-masks turned up in the village, cut the telephone wires and threatened the residents with crowbars.

Then they took over the main street with a stolen council van and told the residents who were looking out of their windows to go back to bed and stay there. After that they then forced their way into the post office and got away with £15,000 in cash and stuff. For the amount of bird that would have been handed out if they'd been caught it wasn't even worth while. Work it out. Assuming they get even money for the stamps they took, which isn't likely because there're going to have to give a discount unless they want to be sending letters for the rest of their lives, the top clearance is £15,000. Divide that between five and it's three grand each. What are they going to get? Fifteen minimum and that makes it about £200 a year unless they get parole when it makes it £300. I know people don't think like that. We think we're never going to get caught and if we do we won't be convicted, but that's taking a chance for silly money. They got away with it but I still think I'm right for that sort of dough. Funnily enough the year before the village store there had been ramraided.

There's still plenty of trouble up in the North East and it's just the same as everywhere else – drugs. You look at the linens. Drug dealers shot in gardens, another shot in the back at Kirkheaton Showground; it goes on and on. They had a big undercover operation in Blythe in the middle of the 1990s. There'd been something like seventeen drug-related deaths in and around the town and they had a copper, who'd grown up in the Gorbals and knew the Cumbie gang up there, come down and live as an addict. It gave him what people now call street cred. His moody was that he wanted to buy drugs to re-sell in Scotland. He was set up in a flat with an intercom system, a camera hidden in the kitchen cooker and a cupboard with a false bottom in which to hide the drugs. He'd a false passport, bank cards and a car with video equipment in the dashboard. And, of course, he went to meetings wired up. He did well because it ended up with about twenty convictions of dealers. It took it's toll on him though. He'd worked undercover in different cities for three years and he ended up going out of the police for ill-health. He's really a lesson to people. Don't trust anyone you haven't known since your childhood or who has someone vouching for them from the day they was born. It did for poor Charlie Kray and plenty of others, and it'll do for you.

DURHAM

When I'm signing books I often have a laugh with the younger girls. I say 'I knew your father' and they giggle and say 'Did you?' That's when I say I was in Borstal with him. They always look surprised and then I say 'Course I wasn't, I'm only joking.' Anyway James Morton, when he's with me, says it's insulting to them and at my age I ought to say I was with their grandfathers. It turns out he's right. We was in Hammicks in Walthamstow the other Saturday doing *Mad Frank's London* and this young girl comes up for a book to be signed. So I go through the routine and she interrupts and says 'No, it was my Granddad.' So of course I ask his name and she tells me. I say 'From up Northumberland way?' and she says 'Yes, from Workington.' I remember him well. Big man he was physically; in Portland with me, for fighting rather than thieving. I remember he had a good straightener with another kid. I can't have thought of him for fifty years. Just think of the coincidence.

By the time topping was coming to an end Albert Pierrepont, the one I attacked in Wandsworth, reckoned it was ten seconds from the moment he got in the cell to the time the trap opened. It wasn't always like that. When Sir Gilbert Middleton, who was leading a sort of brigands' band, kidnapped the Bishop of Durham on the Great North Road nine miles from Darlington back in 1317, Edward II, who was the king then, devised the punishment himself.

The poor sod had his feet tied beneath a horse and dragged a couple of miles through London to the gallows where they hanged him. They cut him down and beheaded him, tore his heart out and burned it. Then they chopped his body in four and sent one bit to Newcastle, and one to York. The other quarters went to Bristol and Dover. I don't know how they chose them last two.

I missed the riot in Durham Special Wing by about a month. February 1968 it was. Eddie and Charlie Richardson were there but I'd chinned a guard. After the seeing to I got I was put in the hospital and then I was moved to Leicester. That was another time I was asked if I wanted to go back into Broadmoor. It was the same after the Parkhurst riot; Dr Cooper, the doctor who did so much to help us, asked me again.

I wouldn't have been sent to Broadmoor by the courts and so they couldn't have thrown away the key. I had enough people behind me who would have kicked up trouble if necessary. By then you could get the press to take a bit of interest. Jimmy Brindle could have said, 'Nothing wrong with my brother-in-law'. Particularly after the Parkhurst riot which was a bit, but not that much, later, people were beginning to take some sort of interest in prisons.

I can't say I wasn't tempted to go back to Broadmoor. In fact I badly wanted to go. It would have made things much easier for me but Doreen really didn't want me there for Francis' sake. It was bad enough for him at school having me in the nick. Having me in the nut house would have made things that much worse for him. Doreen meant well, don't get me wrong, but that was her big mistake. If I'd gone to Broadmoor from Leicester there wouldn't have been no Parkhurst riot. Not with me in it anyway. No extra five years. I knew how to behave in Broadmoor and it would have been easy bird.

I liked life in the security wing although you was hemmed in. There'd be usually about eight or nine of you but at Durham there was probably about eighteen. We were all high grade trouble makers or escapers. You wouldn't have had someone like Brady. No sex cases at all, just us career criminals. Many prisoners were fighting to get in. It wasn't where you wanted to be if you was applying for parole, however. The mere fact you'd been in one could severely put you back. On the other hand it upped your status for a start.

The parole thing never worried me. I never asked because I knew I'd always get a knockback. If I thought I'd have had a fair chance I'd have gone for it but I never did. I never got any home leave in all them years either. Discipline in the security wings wasn't so fierce. There was more screws than prisoners. You didn't have to work and you did your own cooking. You could get so much a week out of your cash and you could buy food. It was the easiest bit of bird I did but the screws didn't like it. It was killing them seeing you get privileges and so there was always some screw looking to cause trouble, and it wasn't that long before I was down the chokey. I think it was their aim to close down the Security Wings and that's what happened eventually.

Charlie and Eddie and the others did wonders in that Durham riot though. It was all over another set of petty restrictions to make life difficult. The whole wing was taken over by the inmates and they managed to get into the E wing office, looked through their records and rang up the *Daily Mirror*. The records wasn't that accurate. One said that John McVicar was a friend of Charlie and Eddie and I don't think they'd ever even met.

In the end the cons more or less got what they wanted. A man from the Home Office came up to discuss things and it wasn't until then the barricades come down. Even the Home

Secretary, James Callaghan, come up to Durham to see what was going on. There was no taking them outside to the courts. You could get the equivalent of three years anyway so it wasn't worth the aggro to the authorities of giving the cons a chance to be heard. It was only after Parkhurst that they took us out and did me for incitement to murder and a few GBHs. Then when it all came out about the conditions there and how we got a beating after the riot I don't think the authorities ever prosecuted anyone for disturbance again on the outside, certainly not for years. They'd learned their lesson how to keep things buttoned up.

As I say I was in the chokey at Leicester. At first you did chokey on your own wing and so I got all the news but as I became more violent I got taken down the punishment cells beneath the security wing. Even there I could shout out the window and I could get things which the fellows would attach to a bit of string and lower down for me. I had small hands so I could reach through the window and collect it. I was even caught with some tea a couple of times by screws who were patrolling with their dogs whilst I was meant to be on bread and water. But they sort of smiled as if to say 'if that's all he's up to let him do it'. So I won even then.

News travels fast in prison. The grapevine's the thing. Prisoners are always being transferred back and forwards and there's visits from the outside to a brother or a cousin and you can have relatives in more than one nick at a time so there's a constant flow of info going backwards and forwards. Then there'd be cons who was in the officers' mess. A lot of them would be grasses but if you got a stand up man then you'd get a lot of good information about what these screws was thinking of doing. There'd be other cons who worked in offices and were good at reading things upside down. They'd relay it out to a guy in the bathhouse and he'd pass it on. It sounds very melodramatic but it was very effective. As the years went by the screws got wise and they started feeding the grasses false information.

* * *

It was from Durham that John McVicar made his great escape, along with Wally Probyn who was so well thought of until he went down for interfering with kids and lost all respect. The third member was my friend Joey Martin, who did a six for shooting a bird over in Tottenham and wasn't out barely six months before he was lifed off over a blagging at a dairy in Wood Green when the milkman got shot.

No disrespect to John but he was a better escaper than he was a thief. He got something in double figures in a raid with Billy Gentry who got put away later by the first woman grass. But as an escaper John was just about in a class of his own, although his son Russell wasn't that bad either. Even when he'd been in Borstal John had been over the wall and it was 1966 when he got away from Winchester. He was part of a group of cons who was going to give evidence in the trial of a fellow in Parkhurst charged with stabbing. In those days they didn't have a proper courthouse on the island and so they brought everyone over to Winchester and took them on a coach to the court in the middle of the town, just by the cathedral, which I suppose makes it a city really. Anyway the fight in the nick was a get-up and the whole thing was a well thought out long-term escape plan. Funnily enough the fellow who's charged with the stabbing gets a guilty and five years for it.

On the way back to the nick at the end of the trial there's thirteen cons on the coach and nine of them are like John and known to be escape risks. There's seven screws and the cons are handcuffed, three to screws and ten in pairs. Whoever did the search of them before they got on the coach missed three sets of keys and the ten soon unlocked themselves. The authorities must have got word that something was on top but they reckoned it was going to be at the ferry terminal at Portsmouth and they'd got the heavy mob there ready. When it came to it the coach never got to Portsmouth. They was going through a little village, Bishops Waltham, when the cons got hold of the screws and grabs the driver. The coach comes to a halt and they're off on their toes. Some good men got away that day.

Mind you the authorities weren't that foolish. There'd been a police car behind the coach and even though the men had gone in different directions it didn't do them no good. The place was full of dogs and roadblocks within minutes. They got hold of an RAF helicopter and seven was pulled in by the next morning. John was one of two who got clean away. He stayed out about four months when he got nicked on a botched security van job. Like I say, he was a better escaper than he was a thief.

What was lucky for John was that when he was in Durham he'd run into Wally Probyn who, give him credit, was a great escaper as well. They discovered that there was a ventilation shaft under the wing floor. Probyn was very good with his hands and he started digging whilst John distracted the screws by dropping his weights. He was always a big fitness man. Probyn had lifted the equipment from the prison workshop when he pretended the cage he had for his hamster had broken and he needed wire and tools to fix it up.

Joey only turned up the day before they was due to be off. He'd been having a bit of trouble in Leicester and they fancied him as an escaper so they took him up to Durham. They went at the end of October 1968. I know Charlie had wanted to go as well and he was very upset. They got through the hole they'd dug in the shower, into the air-shaft and through a gate and climbed out onto a plastic roof. The trouble was they made a din and half the prison knew they was off before they'd got fifty feet. Poor Joey got grabbed pretty quick but Probyn and John kept going over the roofs and then they separated. Probyn went through a trapdoor and was cornered. He didn't get out until 1974.

John did a lot better. He dropped into the garden of a terraced house and then unfortunately fell over on some waste land and sprained his wrist. He also realised he'd lost a shoe and the screws had the dogs out by now. He swam twenty yards across the River Wear and hid on the other side, listening to the dogs and the crews barking at each other. Then he does this tremendous thing. He decides he's going to swim out of the city. There wasn't any other way but it was midwinter. He's dead fit mind and in he goes. Even he couldn't stand the cold though and he had to get out, so he stayed hidden for three nights in the freezing weather until he managed to get a reverse call through to his wife Shirley and she sent two men up in a car to get him. They did the right thing. Wouldn't take a penny for it. They never even knew him before and they was looking at a five for helping him if they was nicked. That's goodness for you.

It may be that I'm old fashioned but I've never fancied having my greens after another man's had his. But there's plenty who don't mind. There was a couple up in Jarrow, where that famous march started. Robert Upton and Charles Gribben were the men and they shared their housekeeper, a Mrs Burdon. Monday to Wednesday was Gribben's turn and then it was Upton who was getting it for the rest of the week. She moved beds so at least they didn't all have the same sheets. I think they was all three well on the booze. It worked perfectly well for a long time until in the middle of December 1914 Mrs Burdon told them she was fed up with being a buttered bun and was going to go off to live with a third man, Jack Bloy. They was leaving the district because I bet the neighbours was pointing their fingers from behind the curtains.

Gribben didn't mind so much but Upton wouldn't wear it and said if he couldn't have the woman then no one else was going to either. They calmed him down but just before Christmas he went out with his son Joe and with Gribben. During the night he took a razor to his mate and then turned it on himself. The police was called and he said he wanted to die but they wouldn't let him. They had to patch him up for the hangman who topped him about three months later.

Talking of buttered buns there was another case like that a few years later, a woman called Charlotte Bryant, down in Nether Compton in Dorset in 1936. Black Bess she was called and from the pictures of her she was quite a good-looking woman, about six years younger than her husband, Frederick. She was a gypsy from Ireland and she'd met him when he'd been there with the Black and Tans. She used to bring men home and sleep with them in the same bed as Frederick. I don't know if he got his turn or not. She was doing it for money and she was a good little blackmailer as well. She conned some man into paying £25 for an abortion, which was big money in those days, and then brings out a child and tries to get a few shillings a week off of him. Fred must have been in on things. He was warned about living off immoral earnings but he said that £4 a week was better than thirty shillings.

Then she goes and falls for another gypsy, Leonard Parsons, and has a kid by him. It's now she decides the husband's got to go so she can keep a hold on Parsons and get him away from another woman whose also got a few of his kids. So she poisons Fred. She give him arsenic over quite a long period. She was bound to be found out and it all come on top. The doctor wouldn't issue a death certificate and there was an inquest. Then the coppers got hold of a friend of hers and played her off. The woman was nicked and let out when she'd made a statement. Casswell defended Charlotte and he thought she was unlucky to go down. Her hair turned white whilst she was in the condemned cell and she was only 33. She learned to read and write there and made a will in which she left everything she had to be divided between her kids. All she had was less than six shillings. Parsons doesn't seem to have missed her. He was out drinking with his mates when she got topped. Over the years the story is he used to complain that whenever he tried to sell a horse people mentioned the case and it hadn't been good for his business.

Funnily there was a woman who went clinically blind when she was on remand. She was Yvonne Sleightholme and she was done for killing Jayne Smith at a farm at Salton near Malton in Yorkshire. She'd been in love with Jayne's husband and she thought he was going to marry her, but he changed his mind and married Jayne instead. Yvonne said it had been hitmen who'd done Jayne but the jury went against her. Back in 1991 it was. She never got her sight back. Even after Yvonne had done the ten years which the judge said was the tariff, she was still inside. She wouldn't admit her guilt and she was in the trap like so many others who won't do what the authorities want. Until they admit their guilt they aren't likely to get out on licence.

Mind you there's been plenty of people sold their wives over the years, particularly when divorce was so difficult to get. They'd take them down the market and auction them. Then there was a burglar sold his wife to a mate in about 1912 but then he went and shopped him so that wasn't much of a success, and in the 1920s there was a story that a woman had been sold up in South Shields along with the fixtures and fittings when a fellow sold his house. She denied it but she had a kid by the second bloke later.

There was a story about a woman, Nancy Dodds, a bit before my time; she came from Hamersley near Bishop Auckland. Married twice, buried twice and both husbands was hanged was the saying. It worked out that her first husband had committed suicide, hanging himself, and the next one, Matthew, who'd only got one leg and who'd been a miner, killed her in 1908. They'd only been married three years. She'd made a bit of money by then and at first was going to leave him £40 but either he talked her round or she changed her mind, because she told him she'd left him the lot. She only lasted a month after that. At first they thought she'd suffocated when she'd accidentally set fire to herself but there was talk in the village and an exhumation was ordered. That's the buried twice bit. When they did the examination it turned out she'd been strangled. He always maintained he was innocent and the last thing he wrote to his brother was that, 'It seems very hard that I have to suffer when I am quite innocent'. In fact he was the first person ever to go before the Court of Criminal Appeal but they set the trend with him. That was the second hanging.

He was the third person to swing in Durham that year. The first fellow, William Lowman, cut his girlfriend's throat, but they had a double hanging after a robbery at the local Co-op at Windy Nook. There'd been a lot of night time screwing the previous year and so some security guards was brought in. In the November they caught Joe Noble getting through the back door. One of the guards give him a terrible beating and the other, John Patterson, said to lay off him. Noble managed to get a gun and shot Patterson for his troubles. He got away but they found some of the property at his blacksmith's yard. They had a good line in talk that year. He's supposed to have said to the judge, 'You may break my neck but you won't break my heart'. They swung Lowman and Noble together.

There was a killing just like that Craig and Bentley case up in Gateshead years later in 1990. All those years arguing whether Bentley should have been hanged when he was in custody at the moment Christopher Craig shot the copper and it all happened again. This time the kid who got lifed off was only fifteen. People had been drinking and there'd been some trouble up on the Cloverhill estate and this Philip English and Paul Weddle, who was ten years older, became involved in a fight with a copper who'd come to sort things out. The story for the pros was that Philip struck the copper, Sergeant Bill Forth, with a fence post. He ran away and got tackled by other coppers and was in handcuffs a hundred yards away from where the Sergeant and Paul Weddle was having it out. It's then Weddle went and stabbed the copper in the heart. What the pros said was that it was a joint enterprise and that even though the kid had run away and was in custody he hadn't done or said nothing to stop his mate still taking part. I suppose he should have shouted out, 'I don't want nothing more to do with this' or 'Stop it Paul', but seeing he was a hundred yards away it's a bit difficult to know what good that would have done. Philip went down on a ten to two majority and both him and Paul, who got a unanimous, was lifed off; well because he was so young, Philip was detained during Her Majesty's pleasure, which is just another way of putting it. It took three years before the House of Lords let him out.

Over the years there's been a good clear-up rate of murders in Durham. It may have changed a bit now with drug dealers but, I think I'm right in saying, back in the early 1990s the murder of Ann Heron was the only one they'd never cleared up. She'd been done in her garden sunbathing in the village of Middleton St George near Darlington. Whoever had done it cut her throat with a weapon like a Stanley knife and part of her bikini had been removed.

Her husband found her when he came back from work and he put up a five grand reward. The coppers conducted literally thousands of interviews but they never found anyone. Then in 1994 there was a series of anonymous letters written to the police and the editor of the *Northern Echo* which began, 'Hello, editor, It's me, Ann Heron's killer!' It was signed The Killer. I'm not sure the person didn't send some to Mr Heron as well. They thought there might be a lead from that but it may have been a hoax. When it come to it there was still no charges.

GLASGOW

The Glasgow gangleaders in the '20s and '30s were funny
people. A bit of protection not to break the shopkeeper's window was about the biggest thing they did, but
their fights were something else. Of course half the trouble
was it was Catholics and Protestants. The Glasgow boys
didn't take no prisoners; choppers, knives, razors, bayonets
and most of them well, they was just kids. Percy Sillitoe,
who'd cleaned up Sheffield, eventually brought a lot of it to
a halt in the '30s. He never shut it down fully though. By
the 1960s, just before I went away for my twenty, there was
fighting gangs all over the place. A lot of people had been
moved out of the old Gorbals, which was on the south side
of the river as you come in on the train, over to Easterhouse
and they fought all over the place. In his day though, Sillitoe
just had the biggest, roughest coppers organised into what
they called batter squads to go in and beat the daylights out
of them. He did it subtly in a way. The coppers would arrive
and watch the gangs do each other and then go and nick the
winners who was half exhausted and give them a beating as
well. It's the same today with bouncers in clubs. You don't
break up a fight straightaway. You wait till they've

weakened themselves and then you do the winner. You don't do yourself so much damage that way.

Like I say they were a funny lot. There was one Glasgow gangleader would only dance with boys because he thought that people would call him a cissie – Jessie was the word they used – if he was seen on the floor with a girl. The dance halls up there were where it went off a lot of the time. They'd have their girls take in the weapons for them and the police didn't dare search because of the screams they'd make. It caused trouble if the coppers tried to search them because there weren't all that number of women police around then. One of the last to hang was James Smith who stabbed a fellow Martin Malone in the Hibernian Hall on 16 November 1951. That was at Barlinnie, of course. Big L they call it.

They used to call the place they did the topping in Barlinnie, The Hanging Shed. There was only ten of them hanged there altogether. Afterwards the bodies were wrapped in hessian and then put in lime in unconsecrated ground along the outside wall of D Hall. I never saw it but there used to be a row of plaques with the men's names on but I heard even that got taken down.

Before that there'd been other nicks where you could get topped. If you went out to the docks area at Greenock about twenty miles away, there had been the old Nelson Street prison. The last person to hang there was way back in 1891 when a fellow, Frederick Storey, who was a circus manager, killed a girl who worked there when she wouldn't come across for him. He'd stabbed her in Argyle Street. After that they pulled the nick down.

You don't get brothers topped too often. If there'd been the death penalty then of course the Twins would have gone, but as far as I know there was only the Stratton brothers and then the Reubens around the 1900s. Both of them robberies in London. There were the Fowler brothers in Sheffield like I've said elsewhere, and the Rowlands brothers were set to swing in Cardiff, only one of them went mad. But in 1950 there was nearly a pair of brothers hanged in the Shed. If one of them hadn't done the decent thing they'd both have swung. This time it was the Harris brothers, Paul and Claude, and they went round to Neptune Street in Govan. They were with a man called Drennan and they were going to sort out someone who'd beaten up his sister. Her kids had had to get out of a window otherwise they'd have got a piece of it too. The fight seems to have spread out into the yard and, just like with Paddy Carraher, it was a man called Martin Dunleavy who was just there who copped it – got a broken bottle in his neck. Good man, when the coppers questioned him he said he knew who it was and he'd deal with it himself. Then he started bleeding again and that was it. The charge of murder against Drennan was dropped but both the brothers got a guilty and although the jury recommended mercy the Scottish Office wasn't having it.

The likes of us never knows what exactly goes on behind the scenes but when there was the death penalty there was definitely all sorts of comings and goings. When Ruth Ellis was due to swing, the day before she was going to be topped her solicitor got some info which might have helped her and they tannoyed a Home Office official who was at Ascot Races to sort it out. It seems like this time the Scottish Office would have worn a confession from one of the brothers and reprieved the other, but at first the brothers weren't having it and so they thought both could swing.

They were both in the same death cell and then when they got the news there was no reprieve, Claude says to Paul that he could have saved him if he'd told the truth. That's when Paul sent for the priest and got him to help write a confession. Claude thought it would be too late but they held his topping back a week and then gave him life imprisonment. He did eight but he didn't last long on the outside. He died of drink.

They say that Paul took it very well. The papers had it in for him though. One of them said there should be no sympathy for him and 'Let other back-land bravos be warned. The mood in Glasgow is to meet toughness with toughness.' Nice.

As I've said before there hasn't been too many people acquitted of murder in this country that goes and gets done again for it. There was my pal Jimmy Essex of course. He got chucked twice of the murder but got put away for manslaughter both times. First was over a fight at a coffee stall near the Elephant and the second time was over a fight in the clothing shop at Armley. Another was Patrick Carraher who wasn't so lucky the second time. He got done both times in Glasgow. He was a hardman in the days when people in Glasgow was really hard. I know we didn't have much in the way of luxury in Waterloo when I grew up there but you wouldn't even say the word luxury in the Gorbals district then. No one would understand what you was talking about.

The first time he was done was August 1938 when he stabbed a soldier, James Shaw, who got involved in a dispute between Carry, as he was known, and a pimp called James Drurie. Carry wanted the girl and she didn't want to go with him. The soldier tried to intervene and his jugular vein got slashed.

Carry just got one of those Scottish verdicts of culpable homicide, which is what we'd call manslaughter, and three years' penal servitude that time. Then again he was lucky because Glasgow juries of them days weren't keen on people being topped and they'd do what they could not to bring in a murder verdict. That and he had a brilliant brief by all accounts. When he come out it didn't half help his reputation on the streets. After that he was known as Killer and he liked that.

He never learned though that knives could be dangerous, not only to the people that got cut but the people who used them as well. He was back in the nick for a slashing in 1943. He got another three years for that. Then the second murder charge was in November 1945 with his brother-in-law. They were a good pair of street fighters but Dan was on his own when he ran into some brothers called Bonnar. He got away and went and found Carry and they went looking for the brothers. What they did though was pick the wrong man completely. It was another soldier, John Gordon. Carraher stabbed him in the neck thinking he was one of the brothers. This time he wasn't so lucky and he got sentenced to death. With his form there was no question of a reprieve and they topped him at Barlinnie in April 1946. My friend Paddy Meehan told me Carraher fought all the way to the gallows.

By then juries in Glasgow had got over trying not to send people to the gallows. John Lyon had been topped in the February that year, also at Barlinnie. He was the first person they topped in Glasgow for eighteen years. He'd stabbed a kid with a bayonet in one of their gang fights. The topping before him had been back in 1928 of a fellow called James McKay, who cut his mother to pieces and put bits of her in the coal bunker at their home and other bits on the banks of the Clyde. You might think he'd have been found insane but you'd be wrong. He was topped at the old Duke Street prison. The other that year was the last person to have swung at the prison and that was George Reynolds who killed one of his workmates. He thought the man was after his job and he did him with a shovel after they'd been out drinking.

Another one of the top men was Danny Cronin who was a big man in the 1930s and 1940s, and then a rival put glass in his booze. Well, that's the story. The police didn't do anything about it so he may have died of natural causes. It was no big deal. This would be in the late '40s. I met him a couple of times when I went to Glasgow to do some work for Arthur Thompson. You hear of the glass trick quite often. I've tried it myself but it's never worked. Once was in Manchester when I was doing it as a contract. The man must have had a cast iron stomach; never so much as a murmur.

If I went on a contract like that it would be for a good friend. I'd be doing it out of friendship really although, of course, there'd be a few quid in it. You wouldn't do it for any Tom, Dick or Harry. Only if they're a friend of yours and even then you'd be dubious. If it came back to them they could collapse and shop you.

It was the same with cutting someone. If you did it for Arthur Thompson or Manuel Morris well, then it was for a friend and there'd be no question of a fee or even exes. But if Arthur had, say, a businessman who wanted someone done, well then that was different and the fee could be £500 which was a lot of dough then. Remember you could buy a small house for that money in London in the 1950s. You could probably buy a whole row in some parts of Glasgow.

You might have to go up there twice; once to have a look at him and then for the job. Arthur or Morris would make sure they were well away when it went off. You'd do it out in the open and you'd want a motor standing by if you could. In a bar or a club there'd be witnesses, and not all of them would be crooked people. You're not up there to knock on a door and go to prison. Provided you took care it was almost literally impossible to get caught. There was none of the stuff you get in films either. No 'This is from Michael Corleone'. If you were topping them, well that's one thing, but if it was just a cut, then you don't want to open your mouth. They'd know full well who it was from anyway and if they didn't, that was a bit more trouble for them to worry about. Later Morris or Arthur would let it be known. It would be rubbed in. As for the mug going to the coppers, there was not much chance of that; 100–1 on he'd be a hooky man himself.

We had a good relationship with Scotland, funnily much more than with Wales or even Manchester or Leeds. It worked both ways. There'd be people to be hidden, like Andy Anderson when he got out from Wandsworth by mistake with Ronnie Biggs. There'd been a plan to spring Biggsie and Andy and another geezer took advantage. When the rope was lowered for Biggsie, Andy takes the opportunity and he's up and off. They didn't know what to do with him when he lands in the lorry so they give him a few quid. He knows where I am from when he was in the nick with me and so he makes his way across London. Like I've said, he just turned up blind at Atlantic Machines which I had off Tottenham Court Road with Eddie Richardson. I got him to my mother's and then rang up Arthur and he agreed to have him up in Glasgow straight away. No payment, no questions. That was friendship. I drove up with him myself.

There'd be jobs to be done as well. If I went up for one for Arthur Thompson I'd stay in his flat in the Gorbals on the sofa in the front room. It would be a couple of times a year. A lot of the stuff we wanted the Scots for was safeblowing.

As I've said the biggest man in my day was Arthur Thompson. He took over from Manuel Morris when Manny was getting out. Manny taught him just about everything he knew about city life. Arthur really came good when he beat up a hardman, Alec Earch, who reckoned he was top of the pile at the end of the 1940s. Earch never recovered from the humiliation and he fell further and further away and ended up a meths drinker. Arthur went on from strength to strength. A big, hard man but respectful with it. He didn't take advantage of people.

I've written a lot about Arthur over the years, but it's been sad to see how the empire he built has just faded away. Firstly, there was his son the Fat Boy, who was killed and then there was his boy Billy, who fancied he could take over, started sampling what he was selling and become a heroin addict. By the end he was begging a few quid off of people and two men done him really bad one night in 2000. He'd tried to blag three quid off them and they wasn't having it. They just kicked him and trod on his skull. It seems like for the fun of it. I read that the doctors said they'd crushed it like it was an eggshell. He lived but apparently he can only follow really simple instructions. The people who did it got an eight and a five.

Poor old Arthur's wife, Margaret, died last year. I hadn't seen her since Arthur's funeral and it seems like she'd been in a poor way both health and money wise so the papers said. Glasgow's a funny place. When you're on top you're on top. If you're not they're lining up. She'd had a hard life. First her mother got blown up when someone put a bomb under Arthur's car. That was back in 1967. Then in 1989 her daughter Margaret died after a heroin overdose. And then there's her two boys. But what a woman. She was like a mother to so many people. She could easily have said 'No' to having Andy Anderson coming to stay with her. After all if he was found there it was straight inside for both her and Arthur but she never thought twice.

Funnily a namesake of mine got topped in Glasgow; Alfred James Fraser, same spelling but he was no relation that I know of. He was an Australian deserter from the First World War. He was working with an Irishman, James Rollins, rolling people with a girl as the decoy. It was the old, old story. She picked up a fellow Henry Senior and said they should go for a walk in Queen's Park. Once she'd got him in there they knocked him down, give him a beating and stole his money and some of his clothes. Then they hopped it to Ireland. They were found in Belfast the next week and the girl gave evidence against them. She went and said that she'd left them giving him a seeing to and had said they shouldn't be too hard on him. They put in a plea of culpable homicide, which would have meant they wouldn't have been topped if it had gone right, but the jury wouldn't wear it and they both swung.

Once you was a deserter it was like being on the run from prison, you'd nearly always got to thieve to keep yourself alive. It wasn't quite the same thing with Percy Barrett and George Cardwell. They'd deserted but they'd managed to work at a colliery and they was staying with Cardwell's sister. They was only nineteen and 22. They'd been out three months or so and things was working out quite well. Then what do they do? They change back into their uniforms and do an elderly widow, Rhoda Walker, who's got a jeweller's shop in Pontefract. They give her a very bad beating and she dies the next day. So it's down to London, where they stayed with Barrett's girlfriend. When the coppers eventually come round there's a lot of rings found from the blagging. They blamed each other at the trial and they was hanged together in the December. Funnily Cardwell had been a good soldier and that was how they come to him. He'd been wounded five times, gassed and put up for medals. He'd got six 'wound' stripes sewed on his uniform and that was what was noticed by a fellow who saw them hanging around Mrs Walker's shop.

Another good man in Glasgow was Sammy McKay – they called him Dandy. He'd be a couple of years younger than me if he's still alive. He had some bad luck. Once he got nicked after a robbery and whilst the coppers were questioning him he took out a fountain pen. The coppers had him unscrew it and inside was the cloakroom ticket for where he'd put the gear.

He was a big man in the nightclubs and he was a good gambler as well. There was one in Paisley he liked, the Cuba I think it was called. Manuel Morris owned it. Then he was the manager of the Gordon Bridge Club which Morris also had. That was a bit like the Mayfair Bridge Club in Mount Street where Scotch Jack Buggy was done. Bridge was about the only game not played in either of them. He got out of Barlinnie in 1959 and went off to the States where he blew the better part of forty grand he'd made in a blagging in the Clydesdale Bank in Shettleston Road. He'd managed to get himself in the prison hospital and did a bit of sawing and was out over the wall. He had help, of course, and there was a car waiting for him. His wife and kids were at Butlins at the time and they left. Asked to, I expect, but they got their dough back. There was all sorts of stories flying about, how he'd had plastic surgery and how he was smuggling himself back on a liner. Usually most of them is rubbish but not in his case.

He did go down to London and have a nose job. It cost him £61 and £25 for the hospital bed, which is a bit less than nowadays. You wouldn't get much more than a bandage and a few aspirin for that today. Then he went to the States and stayed on the East Coast. He come back to London in the November and drove up to Glasgow, picked up his wife and kids and came down south again. That's where he made his mistake. If you think you're going to stay away for ever, like Ronnie Biggs, you've got to be ruthless about losing touch with your family. The wife and kids is going to be the weak link; the way they can get to you. Then it was over to Ireland where he rented a house in Dublin and then bought one in Killiney. They picked him up in the June. Like so many he opened the door in his pyjamas and that was it.

They'd had the trial of the others the previous year and Alex Gray got a ten. Sammy's brother John got three years for re-set, which is what we call receiving or dishonest handling, and a kid who'd worked in the bank and had arranged to let out the keys got a three. Alex had had the keys cut by a man in Manchester. The boy from the bank gave evidence against Sammy. It was ten as well for Sammy, including a couple for escaping. The judge said he shouldn't think escaping was part of the game. Sammy had that crooked brief Jimmy Latta as his solicitor. Latta was big in Glasgow in them days. He defended an awful lot of people but he liked mixing with the likes of us too much; called the villains up there his boys. He went down in a big way himself. He's dead now. The week Sammy went down was when that Victor Terry pushed off to Glasgow after shooting the bank clerk down in Worthing.

Whilst Sammy was back in Barlinnie doing his bird someone tried to push gelignite through the ventilator of his cell but there was an explosion on the outside. After that he must have made his peace with the others and he was left alone. He'd given evidence against that Peter Manuel the previous year. Of course with a dog like that the usual rules about grassing don't apply.

Peter Manuel was about five years younger than me and he'd been in trouble since about the same age as when I started, but by the time he was fifteen he'd got a con for indecent assault, and by the time he was twenty he'd got eight years for rape. For that he went up to Peterhead. Before then he'd done a bit of work in London but he wasn't regarded as reliable. Couldn't shut his trap. He got out in 1953 and started going out with a bus conductress. But he couldn't stop himself. He says he's bought her a decent engagement ring and he tweedles it, giving her a fake. Then she gets a note saying his real father had been topped in America and that he had spied in Russia for the British Secret Service and, sensible girl, she calls it off. She must have looked back a thousand times and thought what a decision she made. Some people seem to think he sent her the note himself. The day he was due to marry he defends himself against another indecency and gets an acquittal.

In December 1957 there's a whole lot of killings. It starts off in Carrick Drive in the suburb of Mount Vernon which is a nice area. Just after Christmas, a young girl, Isabelle Cooke, doesn't turn up to go to a dance with a bloke. The parents started looking for her just after midnight and by next morning there's a full search. They found a cosmetic pouch under a railway bridge but it wasn't for a fortnight that they found her buried in a field on a farm.

There was another killing on New Year's day when the Smart family – Peter and Doris and their eleven-year-old son Michael – were done in their home at Uddingston. Their bodies weren't found for nearly a week. They were the last victims, but another couple, John McMunn and his wife, was lucky to escape. Mind you it shows what you can do if you think quick enough. McMunn had woken and found a man at the bedroom door and he'd pretended he'd had a gun, which got rid of the fellow.

Manuel got picked up a bit before 7 a.m. a week after that. He'd been kipping on a chair in his parents' place in Birkenshaw. If the coppers came in those days it was usually a bit before seven. You was still half asleep and there wasn't always the chance to get hold of a brief. They could take you to any nick they fancied. 'All right, Mrs Fraser, we're taking Frank to Paddington. He'll be there in half an hour', and they could have you half way across the country. Your wife would have the brief ring up Paddington and he'd get the reply, 'No, he's not here. Never heard of him. We haven't got a DI Smith here.' And of course they was right. I remember Terry Dewsnap, who was related to my mate Joe Wilkins, saying how he'd been swagged up to Stoke or somewhere like that when he'd been nicked over a robbery in Dunstable. Things have changed now.

One reason they picked Manuel up was because he wasn't sensible. There'd just been a change of colour on some Scots' banknotes and he was flashing some around. Peter Smart had picked up a load from the bank just before he was killed and it wasn't Brain of Scotland at least to have a look at Manuel. Then again they'd fancied him for a lot of things including the killing of a young girl the year before, but he'd put in an alibi which held. The coppers had also got a mate of his to give them the SP on what he was up to.

They lifted Manuel's father for receiving some of the stuff which had been nicked from another house in Mount Vernon just before Christmas. Then people picked Manuel out on an ID as the man who'd been paying for drinks with the new notes. He went and said he'd been given them by Dandy McKay and that's how he come into the case. Dandy wasn't pleased at all and he told the coppers how Manuel had had a Beretta.

Give Manuel a bit of credit. He tried to row his parents out of it and he wrote the senior copper a couple of letters starting to say what he'd done. But the coppers was crafty, they must have sensed he couldn't wait to tell them everything – just like he couldn't stop blabbing when he was down South – and they said no. All they had to do was wait a bit and he spilled his guts. During the evening he showed the police where he buried Isabelle Cooke's body and then he showed them where he'd put the iron he'd battered another girl, Anne Knielands, with. That was the one he'd put up an alibi for. Nowadays DNA would have done him for that much earlier. Meanwhile he's written a long confession. Of course he tries to get round that at the trial, saying he only did it to get his Dad released.

When it came to it he went down for a whole raft of killings. Apart from Isabelle Cooke and the Smarts there was the Watt family who'd been found by the daily help in September 1956. Now I know I've said look for the husband but this was a case where the coppers did just that and they was wrong. They had him locked up in Barlinnie for the better part of three months before they offered no evidence. Then, worse for the poor man, Manuel lodges an impeachment against him. In Scots law if you say someone else did the crime it's sort of like an alibi. You have to name the name and give particulars. So poor Watt has to go through the torment again.

Manuel always liked defending himself. There's often an edge in that. You get a bit of leeway from the judge when your brief wouldn't. You can try and get in bits which are technically inadmissible and then say sorry you didn't know. The judge is always a bit afraid of you. He's got in the back of his mind that if he comes on too strong the jury's going to say, 'Poor Mr Fraser, the judge didn't give him a chance', and they'll bring in a not guilty. Alfie Hinds was good at it and Manuel had done it when he got the eight for rape; half-way through this trial he sacks his brief and takes over himself. When it came to it nothing was going to help him; he got a guilty on seven murders but not on the one of Anne Knielands. He got topped at Barlinnie in the July. I was in Rochester with Manuel's brother, who we all called John. He was a good man but I never saw him again.

What was interesting was what come out after he'd been topped. Apparently he'd done a taxi driver from Newcastle, cut his throat and a couple of women in Glasgow. He also said he'd done the brass 'Red' Helen Carlin in Pimlico, a couple of years earlier.

It's not often you get a father and son who've both gone down for separate murders but Robert Mone and his son, who was called that as well, both did in their day. I suppose this time the son was more famous and his father tried to live up to him. It was a bit confusing because it was the father who was known as Sonny. Robert jnr started things off when he took a whole needlework class hostage at St John's Secondary High School, Dundee for a couple of hours in November 1968. A nurse who knew him tried to persuade him to give himself up but that didn't do any good and he attacked a couple of the girls and killed the teacher before the police dogs was let loose on him. He wasn't fit to plead and he got sent to the Carstairs State Mental Institute. He met up with another fellow, Thomas McCullough, in the place and they began to plan an escape. McCullough had had an argument with a chef over some sandwiches and had gone home, made a tape recording about what he was going to do, and then gone back and shot at the man and his wife.

It's wonderful what you can do if you really try. McCullough made a whole lot of weapons including a sword in the prison workshop, along with a ladder. They also got hold of a map of the area, a torch and £25 as well as some moody ID.

They got out at the end of November 1976 when they killed a nurse and a patient and got the nurse's keys. That's when they picked up a large fire axe and it was out over the wall. They was gone half an hour before anyone noticed they was missing They was now wearing nurses' caps and they flagged down a driver saying there's been an accident. It's almost unbelievable the coincidence, but just as the man got out of his car up comes a police van. McCullough cuts the throat of one of the officers and starts on the other. The driver of the other car gets away and goes to the hospital to tell what's happened; at first people don't believe him. It was heavy snow and Mone and McCullough got off with the police car and then crashed it about ten miles down the road. The blue light was flashing and when a couple of men stopped to help they was attacked as well. They drove off in the men's van and got to a farmhouse where they took an Austin Maxi. But the farmer's young daughter managed to phone the coppers whilst the pair was arguing with her father.

After that they made a dash for England with the police after them, and they got as far as the M6 where they crashed again. This time four young people got out of their car to help but just as the pair was about to do another hi-jack, the police turned up and recaptured them. They both picked up life imprisonment this time. McCullough said it was mostly his fault but no one was taking another chance with either of them. It's interesting that they was insane when they broke out, but by the time they was caught and had killed three people three hours later they was sane. It's as if you get a shot in the mental hospital and if you blow it that's it, sane or not it's off to prison. Just like Straffen. It seems like they don't want people in psychiatric hospitals who are a bit tasty. They say they've got a personality disorder and are untreatable.

Anyway next it was dad's turn. He kept saying there was nothing better he wanted than to be inside with his boy and he did three women in Dundee in 1979. When it come to it though he said he'd been in the house with them but he'd not done them. He'd had a five back in the 1960s. Then whilst he was in the Aberdeen nick he went and insulted a fellow, Anthony Currie, known as Cyclops and he was killed in January 1983. Cyclops got eight years for what the

Scots call justifiable homicide. The Mones was a bit of a violent family because Robert Mone jnr's sister, Rose, did three years for attacking a fifteen-year-old girl with a bottle and knife. She said she'd just been standing up for her dad.

As far as I know Robert Mone jnr and McCullough are still in their nicks and they don't look likely to be coming out. McCullough got put away in a special cell where he's got a couple of rooms, really, and three warders with him night and day. He makes a lot of toys for local kids' charities and I heard recently he's getting a bit of association with other prisoners. Robert Mone's been in the prison normal.

One of the big teams up in Glasgow was the one known as Norval's Criminal Syndicate run by Walter Norval. He was the king of the armed robbers up there at the time until he was put away by his henchman, Phillip Henry. In November 1977 the North Court was set alight just before Norval's trial commenced. No one could say exactly who'd done it. His daughter was charged but I'm glad to say the case against her was chucked. His son-in-law picked up a five for threatening a witness and Henry, who was meant to be in solitary for his safety, had boiling water tipped on him. John McDuff, who was then 22, received 21 years. Joe Polding had eighteen. When it came to it Norval only got a fourteen. I suppose that was because he wasn't involved in as many robberies even though he was reckoned to be the Daddy. It wasn't bad when you consider the bird that had got handed out to the Workers' Party of Scotland a few years before. Maybe they was regarded as more of a threat because they was a sort of political organisation.

Walter went down in the November of 1977, six months after his stepfather Joe 'The Pole' Kotarba was stabbed to death in the April at his home in Maryhill, by one of the brasses he ran. He'd been beating her and Joe Beltrami got her acquitted.

* * *

When I'm giving talks, people say they think I shouldn't be making money out of crime. What I say is that people remember me and Charlie and Eddie and the Twins but there's plenty of others like coppers who've done dreadful things and their names are never mentioned. Take that Glasgow copper James Robertson, for example. What a wicked thing he done.

July 1950 it was when they found the body of a woman laying on Prospecthill Road in the Mount Florida district. It looked like a car had driven over her, the body had become trapped and then the driver had reversed again. It turned out it was a girl called Catherine McCluskey. What happened was a woman who was looking after her kids come forward to say she hadn't collected them. Catherine had told her that the father of one of them was this copper from the Glasgow Southern Division.

It was the usual story – a copper goes off the rails, but people turn a blind eye and try to cover up for him out of loyalty. It seems like he'd been a non-drinking, non-smoking family man who was up for promotion. Then he'd fallen off the wagon and he hadn't been turning up on his beat in the Gorbals. Not that I'd blame him for that. He'd also been seen driving a large black Austin car. He could never have afforded it but he said he'd borrowed it from a friend.

When they checked it out he hadn't been on his beat the night Catherine was done. When he said he didn't know her he was put on an ID and was picked out by her friend. By the time he got to court there was not only the murder but breaking into a car showroom and stealing a radio and registration books, and stealing a car another time. What he'd done to her was to batter her with his truncheon and then driven the car, which had false plates, over her to make it look like an accident. I don't understand it. Here he is a copper. Why does he think a doctor can't tell between a blow with a truncheon and being knocked down by a car?

It was quite a long trial for those days. He went in the box and said he did know the girl. He'd met her when he was called to a disturbance. He said he'd found the car. He thought it was abandoned and he'd begun to use it. I don't know who he thought he'd convince. You don't find too many large smart cars abandoned nowadays, and you certainly didn't not long after the War.

As for doing the girl, it had all been a terrible accident. He'd been down to meet her and they'd gone for a drive. She'd asked him to take her to see a friend some fourteen miles away. He said he was still on duty and couldn't and told her to get out of the car when she began to cry. Then he says he changed his mind. He slowly reversed about a hundred yards and that's when he heard a sort of jarring, and when he got out to look he'd run over the girl. He tried to get her free and when he couldn't, he'd panicked, reversing the car and then driving forward. After a few minutes he succeeded and he pushed off. He wasn't the copper who'd been paying money to her for the child and he hadn't hit her with a truncheon.

Of course no one believed him for five minutes. Well, certainly not for an hour because the jury was back in that time with a majority verdict of murder. You can do that in Scotland. Fifteen on the jury and it could be eight to seven one way or the other. Of course there was always that non-proven which saved a lot of people. Robertson lodged an appeal, which rightly got blanked, and people say it was only in the last few days before he was topped at Barlinnie a bit before Christmas 1960 that he realised what was coming to him.

A couple of my friends went down over a raid in Glasgow. Just before Christmas 1973 it was. A team went up from London and a guard at what was British Rail's St Rollex Works was killed. Robert Marley put it together and the team included Siddy Draper, who later got out of Leicester in a helicopter, and Steve Doran whose brother, Ian, picked up 25 in that Scottish Workers' Party case. The job seemed fairly simply but Jim Kennedy, the security guard, had a go and was shot. They didn't half get some bird – 183 years between them.

One of the team was Billy Murray, whose dad had been with me at school. He was the last of them to get nicked. Down in Brighton it was, funnily enough. He was staying in a boarding house when the police burst in about five one morning. Someone had grassed him. He did get to the stage in his bird where he got out on leave but then he didn't come back and they nicked him again. He's still in the warehouse as far as I know.

The other, Alan Brown, was also a friend of the Twins. By March 1999 Alan had got himself in the situation where he was working outside the prison. He'd had a bad time in his early years. In 1985 he'd taken some staff hostage, he'd been involved in a riot and he'd tried to escape twice. When Marilyn and me went up for Arthur Thompson's funeral we went over and saw Alan. Now in 1999 he was on day release at a church-run Undercroft Café in George Street in Edinburgh. He'd just had another knockback on his application for release on licence and he'd been told he would not be eligible to appear before the Board for another review for four years. He was due to return to the prison at 3.30 but he just disappeared from the café around lunchtime. I don't think anyone thought too much about it until he didn't show. I hoped he'd gone abroad but it turned out he hadn't. As I've said, he was found in Brighton with a load of drugs, so the coppers said.

Of course not all robberies which went wrong was professional jobs. Take that Charles Templeman Brown. A bit before Christmas 1945 he decides he's going to do a single-handed raid at the Pollockshields East station in the evening. There were three staff on duty and he shot all three of them – William Wright, Anne Withers and a fifteen-year-old kid, Robert Gough. The kid and the woman didn't survive but Wright was able to give an ID of Brown.

You'd think that in a case like that the authorities would be keen to put up a reward, get the grasses nibbling so to speak, but when it was said it was coming from the police fund the Lord Advocate said no it wasn't and the Secretary of State said it had to come from the council. In the end a newspaper put up a grand. That was good money back then. Still, no one come forward for about ten months, then in the October the police makes a move on Brown's mother's place.

He was in regular work, very respectable, and the next day he goes up to a copper and asks him to telephone the Glasgow police and tells him he did the Pollockshields job. He went and handed in a gun, a Luger it was, and another thirteen bullets he had. Whilst he was waiting for the coppers he wrote a note to a friend saying he hoped that the man wouldn't think too badly of him and how he'd tried to top himself anyway. When the coppers questioned him he said he'd only fired because the kid had tried to dive for the gun. In fact the boy had been trying to shield the woman.

Of course there was no defence to the killing. The only thing left was to show he was mental but he got found guilty. It's funny how things turn out. When that Victor Terry told the trick cyclists that he was being controlled by Legs Diamond they wouldn't listen, but Brown does a whole lot better. He probably was a bit simple. He wore spotted bow ties as a tribute to Frank Sinatra, he said, and a white whipcord jacket of which he was so proud he wore it to collect his wages. The doctors said he was 'addicted to swing music' which, in them days, was a sure sign he was off his trolley; he got a reprieve and he only served about a ten. Then he was released and went back to work as a travelling salesman. Just under three years later he's killed when his car hit a wall near Dunblane. That's where the massacre was a few years ago. Some nutter goes into a school and starts shooting the kids. It was after that handguns got banned. Tribute to the kids, the politicians said. Of course it didn't do any good at all. I was reading in the papers that there's more handguns around now than there was before the ban. The going price in London was £200.

Back when I was working it wasn't that easy to get a gun. There's guns and guns, however. It depended on what sort you wanted. Of course shotguns were no trouble. After all, they were more or less legal and you could do a bit of work on them yourselves. As for a revolver, that was more difficult. The trouble was you had to be very careful where you got them and who you got them off. The man might not be able to keep his box of tricks shut one hundred per cent. Then there was no telling who'd used them first and I've always liked a clean knife and fork. If you weren't going to use it yourself, only wave it about, well that might not be too bad unless you were caught with it. Then the police might start checking up to see if it had been fired before. The price would depend on how quick you wanted it. It was always best not to buy but get it from someone you trusted and on condition that if, when it came to it, you didn't use it you'd return it and if you had to then you'd get rid of it and pay him. You could get a good clean gun in 24 hours.

The big dance hall in Glasgow was Barrowlands, named after a part of the city and just off Gallowgate North, east of the city centre. I think it's big still but back in the '50s and '60s, you could hardly get in at the weekends. Pick up place it was. It wasn't my sort of place at all. It was a place the women took their wedding rings off and what you thought was Miss Right turned out to be Mrs Wrong. Same applied to the men. That was where that serial killer they called Bible John did three girls. That was a big case back in 1969. He used to hang around the dance floor, pick up women and then, when he went off with them after the dance, strangle them. The first one had been in the February and no one thought too much about it, not as a serial killer that is. Then the next one come in the August and the last in the November. All of the women were raped and they was all on at the time it happened. There was a bit of ID because Jeannie Williams, the sister of the last of the girls,

Helen Puttock, went in a taxi with this Bible John and Helen when he was spouting off the scriptures. She was dropped off and he continued with her sister. He was quoting the Bible and called Barrowlands a den of iniquity, which is how he got his name. She told the coppers that he had sandy hair and he was well spoken. They had more than ninety ID parades but nothing came of it. The murder at the end of the year was the last but the case kept coming up over the years. They had Jeannie up on an ID parade within three days of the death of her sister but she never picked out John McInnis who they fancied for the jobs.

Anyway, like I said, the killings stopped and McInnis topped himself in April 1980. What the police had done was keep a semen stain off of Helen Puttock's tights and when DNA come in they decided to exhume McInnis and check it out. The coppers said they was pretty sure but five months later they said it wasn't a match. Apart from anything else the fellow had bitten Helen Puttock and the bite showed he had a deformed tooth, and McInnis didn't. The last I heard there was a fellow written in saying he thought it was his cousin who was still alive and living in England. But that was a couple of years ago and I don't think anything's come of it.

I never really knew James Griffiths. I met him in the nick after he got that four for robbery back in 1963 but he'd walked out of Parkhurst before I got there. He was, I think I'm right in saying, the only man ever to get off the Island. If there was others they were very rare. It wasn't as if people hadn't tried, and with three nicks on the Island, Camp Hill, Albany and Parkhurst, it wasn't as if there wasn't plenty of punters, but it was like Alcatraz in San Francisco Bay, the currents was such that you couldn't swim or row away. Also it was easy for the authorities once they knew someone was loose to shut down the exits. After all there was only the ferry and from time to time a hover back in those days. So it had to be pretty organised. Someone had to have a boat lined up or a plane and they didn't come all that easy. You could stay out on the Island and people would put food and clothes out for you, just the same as they did on the Moor, but really if you couldn't get off it was only a matter of time.

James just walked away from an outside work party in December 1965. He had a few coins on him and he got on a bus to Ryde where the ferry goes and got a ticket for a £1 note. The man in the booking office never even looked up. At Portsmouth he sees there's a lot of coppers so he gets a cab to the Town station instead of getting on the train at the harbour, and he shares a compartment with a prison officer and his wife. Apparently he got some funny looks from the man because he was still wearing overalls, but the screw said nothing. He made his way up to Scunthorpe where he was put up by a fellow, Wally Gow, and he started courting Wally's sister. Of course he had to continue screwing to make a living and the story was that once when he was hiding out waiting to do the owner of a scrapyard, he sees a figure and gives it a bashing with some wood he's got. It turns out it's just a kid come for his bike and he makes the boy hand over all he's got on him.

It couldn't last of course, and in March 1966 he got another four and was sent back to Parkhurst, which is where he met Paddy Meehan. In July 1969 there was one of Scotland's biggest cases, certainly of the time, although I suppose the Ice Cream Wars case has been bigger since. An old girl was the victim of a tie-up at her place near Racecourse Road, Ayr. Her husband was hit with an iron bar and stabbed. One of the men knelt on her chest and she later died in hospital. Her husband said he'd heard the men call each other Pat and Jim. That was enough for the coppers to start a lookout for Paddy Meehan and Jimmy Griffiths. They'd been in the area and a couple of young girls ID'd them as being given a lift by them. Meehan told the coppers where they could find Jimmy and they went looking.

Jimmy had always said he'd never be taken alive again and he wasn't. He sort of went on a rampage. The coppers come with a warrant to his place in Hollywood Crescent and when the door was opened there was Jimmy firing at them. One of the coppers was shot and by the time the rest of them got out the way he was firing at more or less anything that moved. All in all he shot five coppers in the space of a few minutes. Then there's silence and it's clear he's somehow got out the back. He got in a car and crashed at the Round Toll, so he goes into the Round Toll Bar at Possill Road tells them he'll shoot if someone moves, and puts a couple of bullets in the ceiling. Then some man goes to put down his glass of beer and Jim shoots him and all. It's funny how some people act in circumstances. The barman just goes to Jimmy and pushes him out the place. Jim fired a few shots at him after that but he missed and he made his way back to Kay Street, where he holes up and fires at another couple of people. That's where the coppers caught up with him. One of them opens the letter box and there's Jim pointing a gun at him, so the bogey fires and kills him. The whole thing lasted an hour-and-a-half. Possill is where tourists go and buy clothing nowadays.

There was a bit of a stink even after he died. A TV producer wanted to do a reconstruction of the case. It's all the rage now but it wasn't then. The man found himself hauled up in front of the Sheriff when he had actors firing blanks and bashing a window in Hollywood Crescent, and someone in camouflage rush into the Round Toll. Fined £50 I think he was. The authorities said he was breaching public order.

It wasn't the first time someone had shot it out with the coppers in Glasgow and I'm sure it wasn't the last. One a few years earlier had been a bit of a funny case altogether. There was this kid, Edwin Finlay, who nicked around £900 from the British Linen Bank where he worked. He was only eighteen and it didn't seem a problem to arrest him. A couple of coppers saw him in Hyndland Road early one morning where he'd gone round in the hope of seeing a girl he knew. When they approached him he just opened fire. He killed John Macleod and wounded another and then he turned the gun on himself. What was amazing was the kid had got three guns on him including a Walther and a Derringer. He'd also got a wrist bandolier as well as a body one. It seems he'd been over to Ireland the previous week and he'd smuggled them back in. Back in September 1952 that was.

As for Paddy, the Griffiths shoot out didn't do him no good at all. You can see how public opinion wasn't going to be on his side. First, an old lady's been killed and second it looks like from what Jim's done they got the right man.

Paddy went down on a majority verdict but there was soon rumours that a couple of different hardmen, Ian Waddell and Tank McGuinness, were the real blaggers. There was all sorts of appeals and petitions for Paddy. McGuinness kept visiting Joe Beltrami, the top lawyer, and dropping hints, but he never come outright and say anything concrete, and anyway a lawyer can't betray a client's secrets without permission. Just like a priest.

In March 1976 McGuinness was done over close to the Celtic football ground down Parkhead way in the East End and he never recovered consciousness before he died a couple of weeks later. Not that he'd have said who did it. Although it was never proved it was put about that Tank had been killed over his involvement in the murder. Then it turned out Waddell's alibi was false and he'd been pushing a good bit of dough about after the blagging. So what happens? Paddy gets pardoned two months after McGuinness is killed and Waddell's put on trial for the Ross murder. That didn't do any good. Just like Manuel he put in a special defence saying 'It wasn't me. It was Meehan and Griffiths.' Jury was only out an hour before they give him a not guilty.

It was all change. A few years later Waddell's murdered in Blackthorn Street in Springburn in the north of the city by his mate, Andy Gentle, who was lifed off. Then there's an inquiry into the Ross case and it comes up with the theory that all four, Paddy and Jim, Tank and Waddell, was involved. If you want a lawyer on your side, that Beltrami was a man to have. He worked and worked for Paddy and eventually he got him over fifty grand compensation, but Paddy wasn't that grateful. He slagged Beltrami off for not trying hard enough and wrote another book himself which he'd peddle at the railway station saying it was an MI5 conspiracy. Eventually it all died down and he died in Swansea a few years back. He'd got throat cancer.

That's a thing with people who get a long stretch of bird. Eventually they convince themselves it was all their brief's fault. Either the man didn't try hard enough or he actually sold him to the pros. It's never their own fault. It stands to reason. You sit in the peter day in and night out and you go over things in your mind. It's like being in a car accident. You readjust things. Even if you come out of a side turning and bang into a car on the main road, well he was going too fast and he should have seen you. Of course, sometimes it does happen and the brief has gone bent on you. The next thing is they'll turn on the man who found the brief for them. He's in league as well. In fairness, I've never thought that about any of the cases I've had. Briefs have always done what they can for me, but there's plenty about who reckon they should never have gone down.

Sometimes you get an unsolved murder which you think should be easy to solve and the coppers just can't do it. There was one up in Inverness back in 1976 when a woman, Renee Macrae, and her little boy Andrew just disappeared. Mid-November that year she was going away with her boyfriend, William Macdowell, who was the kid's father and that was the last she was seen of. In fact he'd worked for the company her old man owned. She'd been driving a BMW and it was found about ten miles away in a lay-by on the A9 near Dalmagarry. It was big stuff. They had

Canberra bombers with heat-seeking devices flying over the place and of course there was divers and frogmen, but they never found the bodies. Macdowell agreed he'd arranged to meet her but he'd had a touch of seconds and never turned up. Later, he went on to say he'd no intention of leaving his wife. A few years later Macdowell picked up thirty months for fraud. And that was about it.

When I was young I use to read those Peter Cheyney detective books. They cost about 1/6d. He was a right old fascist, supported Mosley, but they was good stories. They was always about men in dinner jackets eating chicken sandwiches and drinking scotch and soda in clubs in the West End after the War, and women in silk dresses who were accused of doing their husbands in for the insurance. The detective was called Slim Callaghan, I think, and he always sorted it out so's it was the brother-in-law. I saw one again the other day on a stall in a market; £2 it was, so someone made a profit. It reminded me there was a case up on Deeside a few years back when a woman did her husband in and claimed the estate. That was another thing in those books, under English law you couldn't benefit from the estate if you murdered someone and that was always a reason to frame the girl.

Anyway, back in 1994 this lady, Daphne Pertwee, just walked out of the living room leaving her friends, shot her husband and then their three-month-old son point blank, and I mean point blank, something less than a foot, and then she come back saying what she'd done and that she'd got bad depression. I should think she had. She got popped in a mental hospital once she'd admitted the topping. The little boy had survived his father for a few seconds and so he inherited. Once he was dead it should have gone to the husband's family. What she said was that under Scottish law the judge should make an exception and let her have a share at least, but before it come to a hearing it was all settled out of court. It never happened like that in the books.

WALES AND THE BORDER COUNTRY

I never did a lot of heavy work in Wales. I did a fair bit of work for that Welsh family who stood by me all the years I was in the nick but overall it was really just as I went away that things were getting started. What had happened was there were new trunk roads and motorways and you could get about a lot faster; remember there was no speed restrictions on motorways then. Go as fast as you could. In a way that was what made crime national; that and putting people from different areas in prisons. Of course that led to trouble for us. You didn't know the people and while you got on well with them in the nick you couldn't necessarily get anyone to vouch for them if they come up with a bit of work after you was both out. So you took a chance and a lot of people come a tumble finding out they was wrong 'uns, or lacked bottle or technique.

It's always hard when you get a Dear John in the nick – you know the kind of thing 'Dear John, I have met this man and I am having his baby ...' Some people just can't take getting a Dear John. I've seen really mentally strong men just broken up by them and turned into shambling wrecks.

They're devastated. They change from being very level people getting on with their bird to a mixture of everything – disruptive, depressed, violent. Pride comes into it of course and, particularly in the old days, it was the feeling of frustration. You couldn't do anything about things on the outside. People say prison's got easy but it's the being locked up that does it. There's a story – I don't know how true it is – of the con who yells at the judge 'You stupid cunt' just after he gets five years. The judge has him back and says 'Listen. When I leave here about four o'clock I'm going to drive home in my new car and I'll probably have tea with my wife and sit by the swimming pool. Then around six o'clock I'll have a glass of wine and then we'll have dinner, something like salmon and salad and some strawberries. Then I may have a cigar and perhaps a brandy. You are going to go from here in a van which stinks and is hot and you'll be sweating by the time you get to the prison. There you're going to be searched with people looking up your backside. Then you'll get clothes that don't fit you and you'll be put in a cell with two others and in the morning you'll have to go and empty your chamber pot and you'll do this for five years. Now, who do you think is the stupid cunt?' And whether it's true or not, in a way he's right.

There was no such thing as compassionate leave or even a letter, let alone a telephone call which would have helped people keep in touch. Remember, you could send out a letter but if one come in from a person you hadn't written to, it was put in your property and when you was released you'd get a bundle of letters in your hand. So if a friend wrote saying there was a bit of trouble at home there was maybe no way of you knowing. Letters could just go missing. 'Proof of posting is not proof of delivery, Fraser', and so every letter Doreen sent for twenty years was recorded.

There really wasn't any welfare before 1948. There was the bag of yeast (priest) might come round. He did when my grandmother died in 1947 but there wasn't any possibility of my going to the funeral. Things did change for the better after April 1949 when the Criminal Justice Act come into force.

Back in the '40s and earlier the Chaplain was really the only outside influence – but there again, if a priest or a vicar come round back then, the screws would often say, 'Don't go near Fraser, he's in a bad mood' whether I was or I wasn't and they'd listen to them. Don't forget very often the C of E Chaplain had a house next to the governor. One or two did raise the question of beatings of prisoners but they was very much in the minority.

I never went to the chapel of a Sunday though there was plenty who did it to get out of their cells. When you first went into prison at reception it was 'Religion?' and if you said 'No religion', they'd hammer on at you. You had to have some sort of religion put down and atheism didn't count. You had to go through it a bit at first. There'd be some bread and water for having no religion but eventually you won through. It wasn't my style, even to get out of my cell for an hour.

You could hear them of a Sunday. The screws would come round unlocking people and the cons would be ringing their bell and banging on the door in case they was missed. 'All right, we ain't forgot you.' There was no talking in chapel. There's stories about how people sang questions and answers to the lines of hymns but I doubt it really. It may have happened, I can't say because I wasn't there, but the number of prisoners nicked for talking in chapel, I wish I had a £1 note for every one. I'd have a nice few quid. Really you had to be daft to go. You could always end up sitting next to a mug, 'Got any 'bacco? Got tinder?' because there wasn't matches in them days. You had a sort of flint. Both of you would be nicked even if you never replied. And there was plenty of people nicked just to make up numbers just like in the workshop.

The chance of a Dear John never worried me. Me and Kathleen had more or less finished before I went in for the

Bedford job when I was nicked on the way back, but then Eva heard she'd been larking about and she told me to forget her and she marked her card and all. That was one of the best bits of luck I had. I've never seen her from that day to this.

The last time I saw my three boys as kids, the eldest ones that is, was when I went off to do that job in Bedford. Then it wasn't until the 1960s, when I'd finished the seven over Spot, that I saw Frank again. He'd have been nineteen then and already a good thief at the heavy work and all. I think he got three years and I went to see him in Maidstone. He'd been working with sons of the guys I worked with.

When I went to Broadmoor from Durham during that stretch I told them that Kathleen and me was finished. In them days it was different. If they thought you was married or had a girlfriend and there was bad feeling, that could hold you back on your release. Since you was mad they didn't want you going round topping your ex the moment you was out and them getting the blame. Anyway, I was sensible. First chance I had I explained things and Eva and my mother went and saw the doctors.

It was a good job we all did. I was well in my sentence and I hadn't heard from Kathleen when, blow me, she turns up with the three boys at Broadmoor out of the blue. Never says she's coming. Then one afternoon she's just there. I turned down seeing her straight away and I've never seen her from that day to this. I did hear of her a few years back when she wrote in some paper about me, but I haven't clapped eyes on her. She's six years older than me so that'll put her in her mid '80s now. Over the years when I was away Eva kept in touch with the boys.

As for Doreen, she was a one-off. Twenty years she trailed round prisons with Eva. Visits were terrible with me being brought up from the punishment, aggressive screws, not allowed to touch. People may say why didn't I tell her not to come and to go and find someone else but I wouldn't have insulted her by even mentioning it. That was the amazing thing about her, her loyalty, even though she didn't come from a criminal family.

Often it's the ones who've been violent to the girls in the first place who react the worst when they're told it's all over. Take that Phillip Manning. His marriage broke up in the early 1990s and he did his ex, Margaret, then. He picked up four-and-a-half years for attempted murder. He did just two and got parole. Then, when he comes out he tries to get her back but things have moved on. So, Christmas 1994 he lays in wait for her. She comes home just after midnight with her new bloke to her house in Abertillery and he shoots both of them. He got her in the jaw and she died straight away. The new bloke lived but he had to have a plate in his skull. Then Phillip goes off to London where they find him in a pub. He's got a nail bomb strapped around him. He got lifed off of course. It'll be a long time before they let him out. That's what the judge said anyway.

There've been some good murders in Wales over the years. By that I mean ones which never got solved for one reason or another. One of the problems for the coppers is that they call in Scotland Yard and the local people don't take to them. Clannish. The copper who was meant to be the great detective of his time, Reginald Spooner, come a cropper with two of them, and he did his level best to have one fellow swing and all.

The first was when Ernest Melville, who was a known top of the roof, was found by some children near the Full Moon pub on waste ground near Croft Street in the Swansea dock in January 1949. Someone had done him around the head. In fairness it wasn't a promising case. Even round the docks people weren't that tolerant of irons. It might be all right on board when it was rum, bum and concertina, but on shore it was wine, women and song.

Melville wasn't a big man, came from a family of six and he'd always been regarded as a bit iffy. That evening he'd been importuning men and he'd tried to touch up at least one bloke. Then he'd been seen with two seamen and it looks like he must have pushed his luck once too often for someone had squeezed his balls and then throttled him. After that he'd been knocked about. The police checked the men on the ships which had recently docked but when they did no good there, they called in the Yard and Spooner.

The locals weren't going to tell him anything. They might have helped the Welsh police but they were certainly not going to assist people they reckoned were intruders. Spooner stuck it out but he got nowhere. He wasn't the only one. It seems no one else had cleared up a murder on the docks either.

Even if he had they could probably have got away with what was called the Portsmouth Defence in them days. If a top of the roof come up to you, you give him a good beating and took his watch. Then when you was prossed you said it was because of his outrageous behaviour. It wouldn't work now but it did often enough then. The Swansea Defence it would be in Wales.

The other Spooner case down there was in January 1953 when an old girl, Elizabeth Thomas, who was a retired schoolmistress, got done. A man who was passing heard screams and went for the local law. She'd been beaten and stabbed and although she lived to the next day she never regained consciousness. If they was after money they didn't get it because there was £200 under her mattress. You could buy a cottage in Wales for that money in them days, possibly two.

They could never find the knife, and it was one of those cases where the whole village was out looking and went and trod all over the place so the coppers didn't have much to go on.

The man they fancied was a 46-year-old odd-job man, George Roberts, who lived in the village. He had everything going for him. He was illiterate and he was Mutt and Jeff as well. The only way he could talk, as it were, was by sign language and he couldn't do much of that. That was when they called in Spooner. So far as he could work out Roberts had been seen by another of Elizabeth Thomas's neighbours, a Miss Lewis. At about 4.30 p.m. Roberts had called round to show her a pair of gloves he had bought and an hour later he had been seen by the local grocer standing on the pavement near his shop. Other people said they saw Roberts near Miss Thomas's cottage up to a quarter to six. They said he was wearing a mackintosh and cap at the time.

With the help of his uncle, Roberts made a statement that he had come home about 4.45 p.m. and then later that he had come home at 5.30 p.m. The next day, with a deaf and dumb interpreter he made a statement that at about 4.15 he had seen Miss Thomas on her doorstep and had waved to her. He said he had not been out after 5 p.m. It shows how they did things in them days. He stayed in the station for the next four days. The coppers' version of events was that he was told he could go home but just stayed there. Just like anyone would. You'd have thought they'd have got his uncle to take him home.

Next Spooner got hold of him, without an interpreter, and by the time he'd finished he reckoned Roberts had killed the old girl and thrown the knife into the sea. After that they brought in another couple of interpreters and it seems like Roberts confessed again. That was what the pros said anyway. The brief he had said he didn't think anyone could make Roberts understand anything but the simplest of things. So off he was slung to the Assizes.

The first thing was, was he fit to plead? Because if he wasn't it was off to the asylum and he wouldn't have got out of there in a hurry. The jury was told no one had heard him speak for 29 years and they found he was mute by visitation of God. So then the case got transferred to a new jury in Cardiff. But he was lucky he had that judge Devlin who threw out the confession, which was a big thing to do in them days. Normally if the coppers said the man had said something, he had. After that the pros chucked its hand in. Roberts drew two pictures after his not guilty. One was of a spade and the other of a man in a boat. The interpreter said it meant he was going fishing and then going back to work, but I suppose Spooner could have said it meant he was going to bury her at sea.

In fact, all the time it's looked as though Roberts didn't do it. Before they got Roberts to confess they thought a witness had heard the old girl call out something like Harry and as for Roberts's confession, all he may have been doing is trying to tell what he saw. He may just as easily have been recounting in his own way what he saw the actual killer do. Later there was a story that she'd been done by another local man, Ronald Harries, who was topped at Swansea jail in April 1954 for killing his aunt and uncle.

When you're dead you get the blame for everything. You can't sue people so they can say what they like. Take my friend Jimmy Moody who got out of Brixton and just vanished for years. Once he was dead he was blamed for just about anything which had happened up and down the country that hadn't been cleared up. A sort of one-man crime spree with nothing like evidence to back it up. He was even said to have done in a middle-aged couple, Peter and Gwenda Dixon, who vanished whilst they was out walking in Wales in the summer of 1959. The man's credit cards got used a few days after they was last heard of, and their bodies were found on a cliff top a bit after that. There was all sorts of stories and since Jimmy had escaped with an IRA man it was put about they might have stumbled on an IRA cache of arms and Jim had done them in on behalf of the Republicans. Or it could have been Father Christmas. When he finally turned up was when he was shot in the Royal Oak down the East End. No one was ever found for that. A lot of us knew it was coming on top for Jim but there was nothing we could do about it. I made sure I was well out of the way. I was staying with Jack Trickett at that nice hotel he has in Stockport but no one ever questioned me when it came to it.

There's a case in Wales which is meant to have been a legal precedent, but it wasn't really. It was the idea that you had to have a body before someone could be found guilty of murder. The idea went way back to the 1660s when a fellow disappeared and a man confessed, saying him and his mother and brother had done it. Since she was meant to be the local witch there wasn't a lot of support for her when she said it wasn't right. Anyway they strung them all up and as they did in them days, they left the bodies in sort of cages as a warning to others. That was when the missing man turned up. Anyway after that the rule was clear. No body, no murder.

As things happen though the rule gets watered down and there's an idea that if the body disappeared at sea, well, that's different. That case was when the steward pushed a woman he'd been having it off with through the porthole. But there had to be a body if there was a case on land. That's how it was thought to be when a couple of Poles started farming in Wales after the war and one of them, Stanislaw Sykut, was last seen alive a bit before Christmas 1953 when he took a cob to be shod by the local blacksmith at Cefn Hendre near Llandilo. He'd been the working partner of a fellow called Michail Onufreczyk, who'd been a major in the Polish army, and now they farmed something like 120 acres in the valley.

Onufreczyk didn't get on well with people and Sykut was his third partner in four years. Eventually Sykut had complained to the police about bullying and had a solicitor draw up a notice to dissolve the partnership. The idea was that if Onufreczyk didn't buy him out, then the farm would be put up for auction. New Year's Eve, when the local police officer paid a routine visit to the farm, he was told Sykut had gone to London for a fortnight. The police did things like that then, come round to check people was all right. Sykut still hadn't come back a few weeks later and this time Onufreczyk said that around 8 p.m. one evening a bit before the holiday, three Polish men had come to the farm in a car and, after Sykut had sold his share for a down payment of £450 with the balance in May, he had driven off with them. Onufreczyk produced the receipt, apparently witnessed by a man called Jablonski. He'd borrowed the money from a Polish lady in Holloway, North London, a Mrs Pokora, but she said it was a moody.

Sykut never collected his mail and he never drew off of his post office account and the police did start making serious enquiries. Onufreczyk said his partner must have gone to rejoin his wife behind the Iron Curtain. When the police began a search of the farmhouse they discovered something like 2,000 tiny blood specks on the walls and ceilings and a tiny bit of bone. There was also a large bloodstain on the Welsh dresser. They couldn't find Sykut though. I should think the pigs had had him for an early Christmas dinner.

They still went ahead against Onufreczyk and it was reckoned the first conviction in modern times of murder on land in which there was no body. There was an appeal, of course, and it come up in front of Goddard, who set out the rules for making sure there couldn't be any other explanation.

When it come to it though Onufreczyk was reprieved. It seems like the Home Secretary was afraid that if he had allowed the topping to go ahead there might be someone from behind the Iron Curtain who would come forward and claim to be Sykut. There was always that joke that at the end of the trial, the brief would say, 'I call my final witness; step forward Mr Sykut.'

Onufreczyk didn't speak much English, but he was a good chess player and he taught a lot of people in the nick. He was allowed out in 1965 and went to the Polish community in Bradford. That's where he was killed the next year in a car accident.

In fact it wasn't the first no body case in England in modern times. Before the war a fellow called Thomas

Davidson had been done in 1934 over his eight-year-old kid. He'd made a number of confessions that he'd drowned the boy in a canal and then dumped him on a blazing refuse tip in Yiewsley in Middlesex. He went down and the Court of Appeal said 'Quite Right', but he got a reprieve as well.

There was some tragic cases though. Take that Somali seaman Mahmood Mattan. He was hanged at Cardiff prison in the September of 1952 for the murder in March of a Jewish shop owner, Lily Volpert. She'd got an outfitters in Bute Street in the Tiger Bay district. Mattan was really unlucky. The killing took place not long after there had been anti-black rioting in the area. He'd got a Welsh wife, Laura, and she'd been targeted by the neighbours, calling her stuff like a black man's whore.

There wasn't much against him, and it was based on a bit of circumstantial evidence. The coppers had also got a grass who came forward when there was a sniff of a £200 reward. She said she had seen Mattan with a roll of money shortly after the killing in which £100 was nicked. The other key witness claimed that Mattan had been seen coming out of Miss Volpert's shop around the time of the murder. This witness, who'd got form for violence himself, said a number of other black men were near the shop at the time. Mattan called an alibi that he was with his wife a mile away from the shop at the time. It didn't do him no good at all.

What was so evil is that there'd been a witness all the time. She'd seen a black man with a moustache go into Miss Volpert's shop at the time of the murder. There hadn't been an ID parade but a straight confrontation with Mattan, which is usually a good way of getting an ID. She had said that he was not the man she had seen. The pros didn't think that was going to help their case and they never told the defence. Although they was meant to it didn't always happen. It was the first case the Criminal Review Commission sent back to the Court of Appeal and it was a stone certainty. Not that it did poor Mattan any good. It must have been a bit of comfort to the family but I couldn't ever forgive if I'd been them.

Another terrible case was that of the boy, Harold Jones, who was said to have done a little girl in February 1921. She'd come into the shop where he worked and he'd taken her to a shed down the road and killed her. Well, that's what the pros said. The jury wouldn't have it and gave him a not guilty. The boy returns to a triumph in Abertillery where he lived. It was like a boxer winning the world title. There was a charabanc with flowers all over it and he gave a speech to the crowd from the balcony of the local hotel.

A few months later he does another little girl. This time he cut her throat. It was all up and he confessed he'd done the first as well. The judge said that if there hadn't been such a fuss made of him after the first case he might not have done it again but I think that's rubbish. He'd got it in him from the start.

There's not too many solicitors get done for murder, nor barristers neither. In fact if one of them hadn't been acquitted for doing his wife just after the First World War I don't suppose the second brief would have even tried. He comes in my second class of murderers, those that think they'll never be caught. Funnily both of them took place a few miles from one another. The first one to go was Mabel Greenwood whose husband Harold worked in Kidwelly, Herefordshire. She died in June 1919 and the pros said Greenwood had poisoned her. He seems to have done everything he should; called the doctor when she said she'd got pains and he sent for a district nurse. The doctor was in and out their place all night but she didn't last.

Greenwood wasn't popular. People can be very clannish in Border country, particularly back then and he wasn't a local. He wasn't making money out of the law but she came from the Bowaters, the paper family, and he stood to pick up a bundle when she died. Then there was stories he was a ladies' man and the doctor's sister had been seen on his knee in a railway carriage. People soon added it up and made five or even six. Then what does he do? He goes and remarries, only four months later. Not the doctor's sister but a girl, Gladys Jones, who's nearly twenty years younger than him. That's it then. They dig up Mrs Greenwood and it's not the gooseberry pie which did for her but a whole load of arsenic, so it's off to the Assizes where he has Marshall Hall defend him.

The pros said it wasn't the gooseberry pie he'd put the arsenic in but weedkiller was in the bottle of burgundy they'd drunk. What saved him was their daughter Irene said she'd drunk some of the burgundy and it hadn't made her ill.

Even so Greenwood was ruined. He was another they made a waxwork out of and he got £150 damages for it. His practice was finished and he applied to be clerk of the local council and got a knock back. He ended up reporting the trial of the second brief, Herbert Armstrong, for a magazine. Maybe Greenwood's getting chucked had nothing to do with Armstrong. He must have been mad because he almost certainly had a go at another local solicitor, Oswald Martin. He had him round for tea and give him a buttered scone saying, 'Excuse fingers' and the poor man near enough died. He wasn't the only one. It turned out that, before he come to Hay, Armstrong had been a brief in Plymouth and one of the men there had been taken ill after going for tea with him. Then there was another fellow in Hay was taken bad after having eaten a chocolate which had been sent to Martin.

Armstrong had a practice in Hay in Brecknock and he was the clerk of local justices as well. People rather liked him because his wife, Katherine, was a nagger and he never did anything but smile. In June 1920 he got her to make a will in his favour and next month he got her committed to the local bin. She was back in January 1921 but she didn't last a month. He ran the defence she'd committed suicide but the pros said it was him. Armstrong agreed he'd got arsenic in his pocket when he was nicked but it was for killing off dandelions. Still the local bookies fancied him for a not guilty, but they was wrong and he was topped at Gloucester. After the trial, one of the jury gives an interview to a paper about what went on and the court was real fierce about it. There's some people who think that Darling, who was the judge, went in too strong and there's a brief who's recently written a book showing how Armstrong was really innocent. All my eye and Oswald Martin.

Just one last thing. When I was in Shrewsbury after the War they was still using gas to light the cells. There was a bit of thick glass in the wall and behind it was the gas light so you couldn't get to it. The screws would come round and turn the gas off individually. You had to do your mailbags of an evening in the cell of course, eight stitches to the inch and punishment if you only did six or seven stitches. There wasn't much in the way of rehabilitation for your eyesight in them days.

There's always been a saying, 'It was the butler who done it', and over the years there's been a few of them that has.

When I was a kid there was Charles Houghton. He'd been the butler to the Woodhouses, a couple of middle-aged spinsters who lived in Burghill Court near Hereford. He'd been there twenty years or more but as the years went on he started lifting his elbow instead of the serving trays and they reckoned he had to go. In September 1929 the older one, Elinor, give him 24 hours notice and two months wages to go along with it. That was her mistake; she should have had someone come and put him out straightaway. He turns up at family prayers the next morning and then, whilst she's in the kitchen talking about lunch with the cook, he comes in with a gun and shoots her. A couple of minutes later he does the younger sister May. Then he goes upstairs and tries to cut his throat. There was some story that he had fits but it wasn't enough to save him. You can't have the servants behaving like that and not make an example of them. It's bad for discipline. They topped him a bit before Christmas.

I suppose the most famous of the butler killers was that Archibald Hall and, in a way, I suppose he was a bit unlucky at the beginning. He'd been taken around the place to good hotels and stuff as a youth by an older woman. A toy boy they'd call it today. Then she dropped him and he started embezzling. They put him away as mentally unstable during the War, but once he was out he got sent to the nick for a string of stuff, theft, a bit more embezzlement, that sort of thing. Then he got himself a job as a butler to a couple up in Scotland in Stirlingshire. That was all right for a good while but he just can't stop dreaming of the good life he had with this woman. One day, whilst the couple are on holiday, there's an invite to a royal garden party in Edinburgh in the post, which he's taken to opening. He rents himself out a morning suit, borrows the Bentley and he's off. The trouble is he goes back and robs the fellow who gave him the monkey suit. The coppers are called and of course they tell the employers. Give them credit they say he can stay but there's local gossip and this is when he starts his real career.

He does a series of jobs and ends up with thirty years PD. His father dies and he's let out for the funeral without an escort and he's back on time. Next it's proper parole after seven and he's back to being a butler, nicking the guests' jewels and changing the diamonds for glass which he's had cut by his friends. I think he even worked for the millionnaire Charles Clore for a few days. In fact Charlie Clore didn't have too much luck with his butlers because he employed an old screwsman, Roy Fontaine, at one time. He ended up in Parkhurst as well. Anyway once he's got the sack from Clore, Hall's really into jewellery theft and he winds up with a ten in Blundeston. He got out of there with another couple of cons and he took up with an Irish girl. He was out for about two years before he was nicked and got a five on top of the ten. They let him out after he'd done seven and he took up with another Irish woman, Mary Coggle. He was at a few more jobs and he went back inside in 1973 for another four years.

When he comes out in 1977 he gets another job as a butler to a Lady Hudson up in Waterbeck in Dumfriesshire. He really seems to have settled down, but what he does is have one of his old mates David Wright come up and do a few jobs around the place. That's when Wright nicked some jewellery and silver. Hall managed to get a ring back from Wright's girlfriend but soon after that Wright comes in at night and shoots the bedhead where Hall's sleeping. Hall gets him to quieten down and promises to turn the place over with him. Next day he takes Wright out rabbit shooting and Wright's the rabbit. He buried the body near a stream and covered it with rocks. It's quiet after that but then in the autumn the coppers tell Lady H. that her butler's got form and she gives him the shove.

It's back to London and he gets a job with an ex MP, Walter Scott-Ellis, and his wife in Richmond Court, Sloane Street. It doesn't take him long to work out that they're really rich and here's the chance for one last job and retirement. Well, that's what he said. I'm not sure any of us retire until our nerve or our legs give out. Mind you he was in his fifties by then. Then, who does he bump into but Mary Coggle, who's got a new man Michael Kitto who's just done a pub at the Oval. The idea is that Kitto should screw the place and Hall would stay on and do a bigger fraud.

They thought that Mrs Scott-Ellis was in a nursing home and her husband was a solid sleeper so they start to screw her room but there's the old girl. Hall must have panicked and they shoved a pillow over her face. A few seconds later they realise she's dead. The old man wakes up and they tell him Mrs Scott-Ellis has had a nightmare. He's fairly ga-ga and now they have Mary Coggle in to impersonate the old girl and give him sleeping pills.

That night they drove him up to Scotland with the old boy still thinking Mary Coggle was his wife and the real one in the boot and spent the night in Cumberland. They buried the old girl in Perthshire and took him to Glen Afric where they tried to strangle him. Eventually they hit him over the head with a spade and buried him and all. The idea was to get hold of the couple's bank accounts, but then it was a case of thieves falling out. Mary wanted the old girl's mink coat but they wouldn't give it her. She was the next to go. She got hit with a poker and her head put in a plastic bag. Her body got chucked in a stream, on the Glasgow–Carlisle Road. Then the pair came back down South and sold off the Scott-Ellis' possessions.

The trouble was that Hall's brother Donald, who he didn't like, came over. He started asking about how they had so much money and they gets a bit worried. Still they all went up to Cumberland together where Hall had rented another cottage. This time it's Donald who goes. What he does is say he knows how to tie people up with six inches of string and he'll let them practice on him. Well, that's too good to miss. He's there with his thumbs tied behind his back and they chloroform him and drown him in the bath. The trouble is that the ground's frozen and they can't bury him, so they book into a local hotel and start charging their booze to their rooms. The governor thinks they might be trying to stiff him of the bill and he gets the local police to run a check on them. That's when it goes all on top. The police find they've rung the plates on their Ford Granada and it's down the nick. Hall gets out through a window but he's only out a few hours on his way to Dunbar. By the time they get him back to the nick the coppers have opened the boot and that's it. He got lifed off and Kitto got a fifteen. Hall's just a few years younger than me if he's still alive. I haven't heard he's dead.

DUBLIN

Dublin always had an appeal for a good thief. Once you were successful and back across the Irish Sea that was really end of story. Once you'd made it the Irish police had to be in touch with the Yard, and they might come round and touch you for a few quid and call it a day. The Dublin police more or less had to give up. It was the same if you did a job in the sticks; if the local police left it to the Yard to investigate then it come to nothing for them. That's why they had to come down themselves if they wanted anything to happen. Even then they was supposed to go and check in with the local coppers before they could move. Very often they didn't because someone at the local nick would have got out the word out double time.

The other thing with Dublin was that provided you was able to get across the border into Northern Ireland you was safe there as well. In my day there wasn't all that amount of co-operation.

I remember Jackie O'Connell, small curly-haired fellow, doing a job over there. I never knew him well because he didn't do a lot of bird. Lucky Jackie you could call him, until someone blew his leg off and then he didn't half suffer.

I did know his cousin Frank well though. He was with me a lot. He picked up a fifteen in around 1966 so we was often together. Anyway Jackie and two others and a girl blows a betting shop in Dublin and the other men and the girl got lifted by the Gardai. Jackie, like Billy Hill did years earlier, just walks away. In them days you had to put up cash for bail over there and like a good 'un that's what Jackie did. Got the girl out and then the men one after another. It was big stuff I believe. Five or ten grand each when five or ten grand meant something. Anyway, there's an adjournment and, of course, they have to go over for it so that costs; then there's another adjournment and then another. Finally one of the fellows dies and the other picks up a long stretch over here and the police don't think it's worth having him back, so they offer no evidence against the girl and Jackie sends his brief over to collect all his money. It was the shop's money really.

As for Billy Hill, he just walked out of a jewellers and away whilst poor old Bimbo Smith walked out into the arms of the coppers. They've screwed the place and then they find they're surrounded. Billy manages to brazen it out but poor Bimbo got a twelve I think. He was a good man. He was the type who could have been to Haileybury. He was a good all-rounder. You could have him act the crooked copper who stumbles on something and will take a bit of money off the mug to let him go. He came from around Chelsea way and he was a cut above the rest of us. In the end he just faded away. It must have been just before Mr Smith's club I saw him for the last time.

In recent years there's been a big campaign against the drug dealers in Ireland. It's not all that long ago – 1996, I think – that a crowd beat Joseph Dwyer to death with baseball bats in the Dolphin's Barn area. They reckoned he'd been flogging drugs and he'd done a four over it. The people chased him and another man, and gave them a beating near the ice rink they have there, not far from the Guinness brewery. After that it was another bashing at Basin Lane and he went and died.

It was one of the ploys that they used against Ronnie and Reggie when they sent Nipper Read over to Dublin. He'd just been brought to the Murder Squad and the high-ups reckoned when the Twins heard about it, which they was bound to do within about five minutes, they'd know he was on to them again. So they sent Read over to Dublin to do a case there as a sort of camouflage. The coppers thought a British officer had gone and killed a brass over there and Read had to take him back from England and then later go back for the case. She'd been strangled and left on the beach at Sandycove Point. When it came to it the man got a not guilty but it looked to Ronnie and Reggie that Read was not on their backs. It was at Shannon Airport that the hit man who Ronnie and Reggie had in mind to do Read and had brought over from America was nicked and turned back.

I was watching a television programme the other night and it made me think about that big case they had in Dublin after the War. An abortion went wrong and the woman was done for murder. The programme was about those girls who got knocked up in villages in Ireland either by their boyfriends or often enough their brothers and fathers, and got put in sort of asylums. There was one in Co. Cork but there was others. They didn't even have to be in the club. If the family thought the girl was a bit lively in she went, and it seems like many of them didn't come out until the family signed them out and they weren't too quick to do that. The nuns were pretty severe by all accounts. No question of sparing the rod and spoiling the child. Their wickedness got beat out of them. The places were called Magdalene Asylums and the girls was known as Maggies, nothing to do with the matrons in our Borstals. You'd think maybe that happened in the nineteenth century or at the beginning of the twentieth, but it looks like it continued right up to the 1960s and maybe later. No wonder girls with a bit of money come to Dublin to get an abortion or get rid of the kid to an adopter. There wasn't proper adoption in Ireland till well after the War and so there was a good trade in baby farming. Of course some girls came over to England for the abortion but it was still illegal here, and that cost even more money. There's a big movement now to try and get some money for the girls who was treated so unfairly over the years.

The woman who got done for murder had made a good living out of everything for years. Her name was Marie Ann Cadden and she was known as Mamie. I think she was originally American and she was a good-looking blonde by all accounts. When she was younger she drove around Dublin in a red sports car, which wasn't that usual for women. From the start she was an abortionist working out of a place on Rathmines Road but she also had a line in disposing of unwanted kids. For a fee of £50, which was big money when you think the average weekly wage for a girl then was well under four quid, she'd agree to place the kid for adoption. What she did was take the poor thing into another local authority's area and dump it. When the kid was found then that authority had to take care of it, so it was pure profit, except for the petrol, and she'd have already taken a good few quid from the girl over the birth. She got twelve months when she was seen dumping a kid in Rosetown, in Co. Meath. She said she'd just been out for a drive with her boyfriend but she wouldn't give his name. She also got struck off the Roll of Midwives; not that that stopped her. She just carried on doing abortions. Of course she wasn't the only one. There was a doctor in Merrion Square, who was a bit more upmarket by all accounts.

Mamie Cadden was done a second time in 1945. She'd moved to Upper Pembroke Street by now and she did a roaring trade there. It was the usual story, one of the jobs went wrong and the girl ended up in hospital where they got the story out of her. This time it was five years, which was quite strong but then the authorities there haven't ever been keen on abortionists. Even less than over here.

When she came out she dyed her hair and she was probably going a bit off her head. She started a quarrel with the Revenue over tax and then she threatened to shoot her landlord when he wanted the rent. If you're going to be in the sort of business she was you want to keep your head down, not make yourself known all over the place. It all come on top in June 1951 when a girl who used to dance at the Olympia got herself in the club and went to see 'Nurse'. She ended up bleeding to death on the street, but for once Cadden kept her trap shut and there wasn't enough evidence to pin her down. Of course, by now the coppers were just waiting for her. Had to wait a bit because it wasn't until April 1956 another girl's found dead near St Stephens Green by a milkman. He goes and gets help from the Hume Street Hospital and once the Gardai started searching the place they found Mamie Cadden had a flat nearby. She was reckoning to be an adviser on hair loss and constipation. This time she couldn't keep her trap shut. When they found a couple of specula and asked her what they was for she said it was to save you using your hands to have an Auntie Ciss on a cold morning.

It was funny, the girl she's done was Helen O'Reilly, whose husband was a sort of minor Lord Haw Haw, making broadcasts in favour of the Germans, but that didn't cut any ice with the jury. Mamie's brief didn't dare call her, but he made a six-hour speech for her. It didn't do her no good. She must have been seriously going off her trolley because when the judge asked if she'd anything to say before he passed the death sentence she said she was going to report him to the President of the United States. Of course she got a reprieve and it was off to the Dundrum Central Criminal Lunatic Asylum. She only lasted a year there before she died.

You don't get too many cases nolle prossed; that's where the Attorney General says he's not going to go on with the case. Even if the judge don't agree he can't do anything about it. It's what happened in the case of a fellow called Michael Pratley on a murder charge in Northern Ireland. In March

1924 he went on a wages snatch at a factory in Belfast and one of the employees, Nelson Leech, had a go. He was shot in the back. By this time the local peelers, which is what they call them in Northern Ireland, was on their way and Pratley tried to shoot one of them but his pistol jammed. When he come up for trial he said it was one of the others who shot the fellow, but there was a lot to say he was the one and he was topped.

How the nolly came about was that he'd been charged with another murder from 1922 but once they'd convicted him over Leech they didn't bother a second time. They just brought him up in the dock and took him down again. They went on against the other fellow, a James Woods who was an officer in the Irish Free State Army though. The claim was they'd shot a William Waddell who was an MP in the new Ulster Parliament. One of the men involved in the shooting of Waddell had a limp and so did Pratley. That and the fact he was in the Irish Free State Army had been enough to put him in the frame. Woods got a not guilty but he got interned afterwards.

Over the years I've been in the nick with a lot of IRA men, and good men they've been as well. As a rule they've kept their politics to themselves and got along with the other prisoners. I never saw them get stick from the others; from the screws yes. They've been careful though, making sure which cons they could trust. The ones I was in Bristol with back in 1975 was really good men. I was losing a terrible amount of remission over trouble with the screws; 700 days it was. That's almost exactly two years. They wanted to give evidence for me in front of the Visiting Magistrates but I said no. It was bad enough for them as it was. They didn't need any more aggravation from being seen speaking up for me.

It was through the wire mesh in the punishment cells in Durham I first spoke to Eddie Butler who was in that siege in Balcombe Street. I asked him why have a siege when they must have known they was going to get taken and he told me it was to give other people time to get out. If they'd just been nicked then the alert wouldn't necessarily have gone round. As it was, with all the publicity this was a warning for the others. Good man. I was also in the nick with Billy Armstrong who was doing around 25. After we'd both come out he invited me to his wedding in Dublin, and I went over with Marilyn and her Mum and Dad because Tommy Wisbey was in the nick with him as well. Billy married a lovely girl who helped the families of IRA prisoners. After that we went up to Belfast where there was another do in a social club on the Falls Road. It was terrific. They had a band and Marilyn sung at both of them.

Later I went back and did about ten shows in Dublin at the Abbey Lane Theatre and a lot of the people I'd been in with came to see me. Whilst I was there I went on the Gay Byrne television show. I wasn't that keen. People was telling me he might have a right go at me and it would be hard to hold my own, but he was a smashing fellow, never took advantage of me. We had a drink together afterwards.

POSTSCRIPT

GOODBYE

London's changed so much, even in recent years. I was in Old Compton Street a month or so before last Christmas and it was packed, but it wasn't packed with the faces as we know them that you used to find there. We was in an Indian restaurant up the Charing Cross Road end and we had a table in the window looking out. There was cars parked all along and black guys were sitting doing their business with drugs. It was beyond belief. Two or three cars with black guys in them. People jumped in, bought and jumped out. There wasn't a copper in sight. If the police had come up there was no way the dealers could have driven away. It's like the police have give up. If I was wanted I think that's where I'd go in future. A wanted man could stay there all night and not see a copper.

If I had to say I regretted something in my life it would be that I never saw my boy, Francis, play football for Brighton. He was seven when I went away for the twenty years and by the time I come out his career was over. I could see even at the age of seven he was shaping up. We'd play at the front of my house in Hove, him attacking the garage doors. I was always careful to play that way around so he didn't run into the road if the ball got past him. I made sure it never did.

He's got two boys now, just coming up to their teens. They'll never be in any trouble. Of course, they mix with their cousins; some's got form even at their ages but there's no question of their corrupting them. My other sons never corrupted Francis and they were all into heavy work. The more I think about it the only thing that makes people into criminals long term is if they want to be. When I think of all the research I done on the ground over the years I reckon my guess is as good as anyone's.

I wrote the words above a few years back and I had one of the best days of my life recently. I went down to Brighton's new ground this last Autumn to see my grandson Tom – named after Tom Shillingford his great-grandfather – play on the wing in the Championship. He's only seventeen but he's a real neat player. My other grandson James, named after my father, is also with the club but since he's only fifteen he's a bit of a way to go. I was so proud watching Tom and people knew who I was, kept coming up all evening to shake my hand. It brought back all the memories of me captaining the school side and even playing for that team of crooks the Soho Rangers.

It's always sad when people die in prison. Billy Blythe, who was with me in the Jack Spot slashing, died just a few months into his sentence in Liverpool. His wife Dot was the sister of Harry Barham, the bookmaker. Harry was kidnapped in Red Lion Street, Holborn a few years back and his body was found on Hackney marshes. No one was ever nicked for it. Poor Billy, even before he went away he'd a duodenal ulcer. People didn't think nothing of them then – a bit of stomach ache was all. He'd complained a bit and kept drinking milk. The guy who had a pub in Shoreditch took him to see someone in Harley Street and the fellow said Bill was all right but he wasn't.

I was at Gartree at the time Freddy Sansom died. He was a lovely man, very popular. He give evidence for us at the riot trial. He'd been playing football at Albany and just collapsed. We had a collection round the prison. People who had money in their property applied to send it to his widow and those that didn't made arrangement for people at home to send stuff. It was a tribute to Freddie but also it was to get up authority's nose. 'I'd like to have it sent out to Mrs Sansom'. 'Why do you want it sent out Fraser?' 'I just want it, sir'. And they couldn't do nothing. They'd dock you the cost of registering it but that was all.

Some people kept a lot of money in their property. It would either be money they'd had at the time they was nicked or the family would sent it in or there'd be a bit from the wages. I never kept above £25 but there was some who'd have as much as two or three grand. Of course the governor would try and make them put it in a bank account where at least it could have a bit of interest but some fellows thought it give them a gee to have so much laying around doing nothing.

When I think the risks they've taken, it's surprising more wheelmen haven't been killed but there again many of them was so good they could have been racing drivers themselves. Look at Roy James and Danny Allpress, both of them had a go round Brands Hatch and places like that. Roy nearly made it to the big time before the Train. But as for the people that have been killed, there was Jack Rosa who's meant to have said 'I wasn't driving' because he'd had his licence taken away from him when the coppers come and found him laying by the roadside. Then there was 'Cadillac' Frank Copley, died in a smash during a chase over Tower Bridge. My friend Adgie Pitts was another. He was killed on the road down to Brighton. There was also another fellow – I can't remember his name now – he was a driver, got killed a few months after his got a not guilty on a bank robbery. The other fellow in the accident was to blame and the man's widow sued, claiming loss of his robbery earnings. That went down big, I can tell you.

I was really sad to see George Francis, the boxing trainer who got Frank Bruno a world title, had hanged himself last April. I'd known him years. He was a little bit younger than me and he was part of the Camden Town mob which ran around with Billy Hill. He'd been a bit wild in his youth but then every kid from a poor family in Camden Town was a bit wild. He wasn't that old in the war when he went to Bedfordshire, evacuated like so many and he ran a black market in tinned corned beef. They had to send him back to London and that's when he become involved in boxing. He was a porter in Covent Garden and I knew him when he was with the amateurs at St Pancras. The last time I saw him was at Waterstones in Finchley just before Christmas last year when I was doing a signing and he come in and had a chat and bought a book. People say bad things about boxing but it's taken many a kid off the streets and out of trouble. What George was good with was handling black fighters at a time when there wasn't many who would. He got Bunny Sterling a British title and also a European one back in the early '70s and of course he trained John Conteh to his world title. He was a lovely man. He was the last person I'd have thought would have killed himself.

Funnily, the man he come in the shop with was Leslie McCarthy, from the Atlantic Machine days. I've kept in touch with him over the years and he's put my website together. When you think the average age of a website is around six weeks mine's been going nearer six years. What was really good is that the site was chosen by *The Guardian* as their website of the month for March 2002. I'm really pleased for Leslie. It give him a great gee.

Because I've lasted so long there's many people, good men and women I've known, who've died. The Twins and their brother Charlie, of course. I went to the funeral of Charlie and Eddie Richardson's mother a few years back. She was a lovely woman. There was quite a few faces there I knew. Bobby Welsh from the Train was there. He's lost a leg and he was on sticks; Jimmy Hussey was there as well. We give him a lift home. Tommy Wisbey, he's still about and I hear he's writing a book so good luck to him. But there's a lot from that job who aren't. There's Charlie Wilson, Roy James, Billy Boal, Lennie Field – all gone. Poor Ronnie Biggs is still inside and in a very poor way at the time I'm writing.

If they'd wanted a hostage sort of thing I'd have done a few years for him. It may sound daft but I would have. They are getting their pound of flesh now. He's had a few strokes, can hardly get out of bed and I hear he has to point to an alphabet if he wants to talk. What's the point of keeping him in Belmarsh now? Think of they money they're having to spend on him.

There's plenty of people been let out because they authorities think they're going to die on them and they've surprised everyone and lived a few years so what would it matter if Biggsie did?

Others like Roger Cordery have dropped away and Gordon Goody's in Spain. He's been there years. I heard Clifford Saxe went this Spring. He'd been in Spain ever since the Security Express job Johnny Knight did. They'd been trying to extradite him but he beat them in the end. His friend Ronnie Everett's been brought back and done over some drugs in Leeds. He's got an eight. He'd been in Spain for years as well.

Most of the men I worked with have passed away – Jimmy Robson's one of them – but I ran into one of them the other day. The man who actually nicked the World Cup back in 1966, not the one who was done for it. He and I had done a bit of thieving years back and he just come up to me in the Walworth Road, threw his arms round me and said, 'Hello Frank'.

The nicking of the World Cup was a right coup. It was on view at an exhibition in Westminster Hall and my friend took the screws from the plates of the padlocked double doors and the lock off the glass cabinet and that was that. That World Cup was a good job. The trouble was just like nicking a famous painting, unless you've got someone who'll keep it in their cellar there's not a lot you can do with it except try and negotiate with the insurance. I don't know exactly what happened because I was in Wandsworth at the time but eventually the cup was dumped and a fellow out with his dog in Streatham found it. The dog got all the credit and it become a right hero. A year's supply from a dog food manufacturer and a medal from a dog's society. I think it even starred in a film. The story is it didn't last too long. It strangled itself on its lead chasing a rabbit, but I don't know if that's true.

Most of the old quarrels have been patched up. I seen Billy Hayward from Mr Smith's a bit before his death and we had a few drinks and quite often I've seen his brother, Harry. He's not been well. When you think what that evening cost me and the rest of us. Like I said Henry Bottoms who grassed me that night is dead and good riddance; shot at his front door. Nothing to do with me I'm sorry to say. On the other hand Jimmy Moody, that good man who helped me after the fight, has been gone over ten years now; shot down the East End.

It's funny, the Twins could have learned so much from us going down but they never did. There was never any need to spring Frank Mitchell as a weapon against me. I was locked up and going nowhere. They'd managed to get away with the Cornell shooting. They was the masters of London after we went away but they never learned.

Marilyn is doing well now. She and I split up a few years ago but we still see each other. Apart from the flower stall in Covent Garden her family's got a souvenir stall at the top of St James's and she does a bit to help out there. That and she's gone back to college. She's studying interior decorating so when she's got a bit of experience she can come over and do my place up.

It's easy to make mock when we say things were different when Billy Hill and Jack Spot and Reggie and Ronnie – and Charlie and Eddie for that matter – were about but women were safer on the streets in those days. I can't say there weren't fights in dancehalls but we didn't go into places and just fire into the crowd or hold them all up as some of the Yardies have been doing. And we certainly didn't go into restaurants and pull rings off women's fingers as they was having their meals, like happened in Knightsbridge recently.

I don't suppose ever again there'll be as big gangland funerals as there were for Ronnie, Charlie and then Reggie. They were the ones in the limelight, even thirty years later, no matter what Melford Stevenson, the judge, had said about everyone being tired of them.

I can't think how many funerals I've been to in the last few years. And there's plenty I've missed through being away. Billy Blythe – God rest his Soul – who died in the nick after he was sent down with me over the Jack Spot slashing, was one. That was big. And, of course, I missed Billy's himself although that was a quiet one. He was as clever as he always was. Didn't want any publicity or anything.

No one really ever heard when Spot died. In fact I was in a taxi three or four years back and the driver told me he knew he was still alive. He wasn't. James Morton went and spent a few hours at the Deaths Registry and turned him up. He died in March 1995. He'd been a home in Isleworth. I heard some of his ashes were sent to Israel to be scattered there. More's the pity all of them weren't. Rita had gone years before in September 1988. I still don't understand why he ever let her give evidence against us like that.

Buster Edwards and Charlie Wilson from the Train are in the cemetery in Streatham and, like I've said, Tony Ash is in Camberwell New Cemetery. So is Freddie Mills and George Cornell.. Jimmy Moody is in the cemetery down in Manor Park. Tommy Smithson, who got shot after he was leaning on some Maltese, is buried in there as well. The Twins and Charlie are all in Chingford Mount. Albert's over in Bromley.

I've often said that if I'd had had an Uncle Jim who'd done some bird he's have shown me the ropes and I wouldn't have got in the trouble I did in the nick.

Nowadays what with decent food, two hour face to face visits every fortnight or so and the box in your cell I don't think I'd have got in the trouble I did. There's too many carrots with too many perks in the nick nowadays to want to cause trouble. How often do you hear of prison riots nowadays? Mind you there'll always be a rogue screw who'll still try and upset you and, of course, there's all them drugs swilling around the nicks, not that that would worry me.

The downside of visits is actually getting in. There's so much searching and waiting. It's not as if its really worth while. If you're going to get something into a nick you don't take it in yourself. You do it through a crooked screw. There's always going to be one or two of them about – hundreds if you believe the linens. Thank God for that.

Looking back I've had a bit of luck in my life. The pros putting me up on my own for the murder of Dickie Hart was one. If there's two or three of you charged, which is what the pros likes then there's always the chance you'll cut each others throats – no even intentionally like; just your defence cuts across theirs. The death penalty was still around if I'd been found guilty but I don't think I'd have swung. After all I'd been in Broadmoor twice and they couldn't hang a man who's been insane, could they?

Then there was the luck I had at Parkhurst. The judge was meant to be Lawton whose father I'd tried to hang and who I'd had a run in at Victoria Station before he took the Torture Trial and put me away for ten years. If he'd been the judge I don't know what would have happened. There again I was lucky – we all were – that they held the trial on the Island. That was only because of security fears. John McVicar and a whole lot of others had escaped when they was meant to be giving evidence at a trial at Winchester and the authorities weren't having it again. What was good about it being on the Island was that the jury knew what went on in the nicks there. They knew it wasn't all one way on our part. So did the judge. That's why I got such a reasonable sentence. Mind you after I'd got a Not Guilty on the incitement nothing was going to be too bad.

But the best luck I had in my life was my sister Eva. She's been passed away a few years now. She'd been in poor health after her husband Jimmy went and then her daughter Shirley. She sort of faded away The way she stood up for me in all those years I was in the nick, trailing round the country in all sorts of weather to see me, only to be told that I'd been transferred a couple of hours before she arrived – and she'd booked the visit. All those registered letters she had to send to make sure I got them. She was the best pal in the world to me. That was my best luck to have such a terrific sister.

There was a tragedy also with my nephew Jimmy. He sold the Tin Pan, his club off the Charing Cross Road and took his family to Disneyland. Gives them a few dollars for a hamburger and says he'll see them in half an hour. He doesn't turn up and when they get back to the hotel there's the coppers. Jimmy's been knocked down and killed crossing the road. Another face who's gone now is Bobby Oakes, one of the Elephant Chaps, all of them the business.

These must be about the most dangerous times ever that I've lived in. Worse than before 1939. Everyone then knew something serious was going to happen and it's like that now. Today's climate is even worse than it was seventy years ago. America's looking to stem in. It's like war amongst gangsters. Whoever had the gamest, the biggest, strongest on their side – not frightened of dying or going to prison was going to come out on top. And that's exactly the same with nations. People, even people like us, had codes and they didn't overstep them. There aren't codes today.

I don't think a lot about death. I'm a practical person; you know it's going to happen, especially at my age. When it does, it does. Despite all the headaches I've enjoyed my life. I'm quite satisfied I wouldn't have wanted to be a straight person. I don't frown on people who are; it's just me. I don't think of death. It could happen anytime. I accept it. I'm fit but I could get an illness and not have the strength to fight it off as I could have done when I was younger. Years ago I'd have dreaded death but not now. I've had a decent innings, a good innings for my lifestyle. I can't grumble.

I don't think there's any chance I'll go back to the Roman Catholic Church. It breaks my heart to say it but you've got to be practical. I might turn people against me by saying this but when I was a kid Heaven was a big thing up in the clouds you sort of got to by an invisible ladder. Now it's becoming conclusively clear that there isn't anything up there. The Church doesn't talk as much about a real Heaven nowadays . It's all Spirit. If there is a down there, I'll have the chief stoker's job.

As for me. I don't want a big funeral at all. Otherwise genuine people who may not have a lot of dough at the time may think they've got to send expensive flowers or take half a day off work to come. I'd want to be cremated; end of story. After all I'm not going to be alive to enjoy it. It's not going to bring me back just by having a big funeral. But those who are left may say different.

BIBLIOGRAPHY

More about a number of the cases and people mentioned by Frank Fraser can be found in his previous books *Mad Frank* and *Mad Frank's Friends* (Warner Books) and *Mad Frank's Diary* (Virgin Publishing). There is an overview of crime in London in the last century and more particularly in East London in James Morton's *Gangland* and *East End Gangland* (Warner Books). Duncan Campbell provides an overall survey in *The Underworld* (BBC Books).

Duncan Webb's exposures of London's vice, the Messinas and their successors which first appeared in the *Sunday People* can be found in *Line Up for Crime* (Frederick Muller). There are any number of books on the Kray twins, including several by themselves and their brother Charlie. The most comprehensive is John Pearson's *The Profession of Violence* (Penguin Books). Tony Parker wrote an account of the Richardsons in *Rough Justice* (Fontana).

A number of police officers mentioned by Frank Fraser published their memoirs. They include Edward Greeno, *War on the Underworld* (John Long), Leonard Read, *Nipper* (Little, Brown) and John DuRose who deals particularly with the Jack the Stripper or the Towpath murders in *Murder was my Business* (W. H. Allen).

Even before the current fashion for the memoirs of former criminals, Billy Hill wrote *Boss of Britain's Underworld* (the

Naldrett Press) and the American pulp writer Hank Jansen wrote his rival's memoirs, *Jack Spot – Man of a Thousand Cuts* (Alexander Moring). Both are extremely difficult to find. Ruby Sparks produced *Burglar to the Nobility* (Arthur Barker). More recently, Peter Scott wrote *Gentleman Thief* (Harper Collins).

There are detailed accounts of some cases including Robert Hancock, *Ruth Ellis* (Weidenfeld Paperbacks). In 1974 Brian McConnell wrote *Found Naked and Dead* (New English Library), also about the Towpath Murders. Leonard Read also deals with the investigation into the death of Freddie Mills. Jack Birtley wrote the biography *Freddie Mills* (New English Library) and Tony Van den Bergh offers a novel suggestion about his death in *Who Killed Freddie Mills?* (New English Library). Paul Foot's *Who Killed Hanratty?* (Jonathan Cape) is the definitive account of the case, whilst Bob Woffinden provides an excellent summary in *Miscarriages of Justice* (Hodder & Stoughton) and also deals with the case of Bobby Maynard and Reggie Dudley. This case is not mentioned by Bert Wickstead in his *Gangbuster* (Macdonalds) but he does deal with the Pen Club case.

The jewel theft from Hatton Garden to which Fraser refers can be found in Christmas Humphrey's *The Great Pearl Robbery of 1913* (Heinemann). For those really interested, the papers on the case and Grizzard's activities generally are stored in the Public Records Office in Kew under reference MEPO 3 236 B. Valerio Viccei wrote his own account of the safe deposit and other raids in *Knightsbridge: The Robbery of the Century* (Blake).

The story of Harold Davidson, the Rector of Stiffkey – pronounced Stukey which rather spoils things – can be found in Christine Keeler's *Sex Scandals*, which quotes extensively from Tom Cullen's fuller version *The Prostitute's Padre*. Shirley Green wrote *Rachman* (Michael Joseph).

As for prison escapes generally, J. P. Bean has most of the more interesting ones in his *Over the Wall* (Headline) and

Martin Randle and Pat Pottle retell their involvement in *The Blake Escape* (Harrap).

For those interested in the debate over the abolition of the death penalty, Fenton Bresler's *Reprieve* (Harrap) looks at how the decisions were made, both generally and in some individual cases, beginning with that of Florence Maybrick. Terence Morris and Louis Blom-Cooper provide an analysis of cases from 1959 to 1964 in which a reprieve was or was not granted in *A Calendar of Murder* (Michael Joseph). Elwyn Jones deals with the case of Peter Allen and Gwynne Jones in *The Last Two to Hang* (Macmillan).

As for the thieves and robbers, the legendary country house burglar George Smithson wrote *Raffles in Real Life* (Hutchinson) and his some-time partner, George Ingram, wrote *Hells Kitchen* (Herbert Jenkins). In the latter's book Smithson is referred to as The Other Bird. Ruby Sparks wrote *Burglar to the Nobility*.

Eddie Chapman wrote two books, *The Eddie Chapman Story* (Wingate) and its sequel, *Free Agent* (Wingate). Billy Hill writes about Chapman in *Boss of Britain's Underworld* (Naldrett Press). In Ted Greeno's *War on the Underworld* (John Long) Chapman is referred to as Mike S.

There are a number of books about Sir Edward Marshall Hall and his famous cases. Perhaps the best is by Edward Majoribanks, *The Life of Sir Edward Marshall Hall K.C.* (Victor Gollancz). It includes detailed accounts of the Holt-Breaks and Bennett cases. J. D. Casswell, who defended so many people accused of murder including Neville Heath, wrote his memoirs, *A Lance for Liberty* (George G. Harrap & Co). There are many judicial memoirs and biographies of judges, including *Lord Goddard* (Harrap) by Fenton Bresler.

After her release from prison Florence Maybrick wrote her memoirs, as did John Lee after his. Alfie Hinds wrote his version of the case with Herbert Sparkes in *Contempt of Court* (The Bodley Head). Herbert Sparkes' version of events is covered in *Iron Man* (John Long). There have been two books about Archibald Hall. Norman Lucas's *Monster Butler* and the second by Hall himself (Blake). Stephen Richards has written a trilogy of life and crime in the North East centred around the death of Viv Graham. The first of these is *Viv (Graham) Simply the Best* (Mirage Publishing). John Allen, the so-called Mad Parson, wrote about life in Broadmoor at the time of the Second World War and his escape, in *Inside Broadmoor* (W. H. Allen).

There are many books on the case of the Stratton brothers and the development of fingerprinting. One is James Morton's *Manhunt* (Ebury Press). J. P. Bean has the story of the pitch and toss wars which led to the execution of the Fowlers in his book *The Sheffield Gang Wars* (D & D Publications). His other book about North Country crime, *Crime in Sheffield* (Sheffield City Libraries), contains an account of the life of Charles Peace. There is a good deal about the Sabini brothers in James Morton's *East End Gangland* (Warner Books), and there is a fictionalised and entertaining, if not wholly accurate, account in Edward T. Hart's *Britain's Godfather* (True Crime Library). A W. Brian Simpson wrote a history of internment in Britain in the Second World War, *In the Highest Degree Odious* (Oxford). For those interested in the experiences of women who marry prisoners serving lengthy sentences, Angela Devlin has written *Cell Mates/Soul Mates* (Waterside Press).

There have been numerous books and accounts of the Wallace case arguing his guilt or innocence. The most recent contains new research which provides a possible motive. Similarly there have been dozens of accounts of the Gilchrist murder in Glasgow. Perhaps the definitive one is Richard Whittington Egan's *Oscar Slater*. Peter Manuel's story appears in Murder Casebook No. 26, *Glasgow's Multiple Killer*, and John Gray Wilson wrote *The Trial of Peter Manuel* (Secker and Warburg). Ludovic Kennedy examined the case for and against Patrick Meehan in *A Presumption of Innocence* (Gollancz) and Meehan himself wrote *Innocent Villain* (Pan). Meehan's lawyer, Joe Beltrami, wrote an account of his attempts to have his client released in *A Deadly Innocence* (Mainstream Publishing). Chester Lewis and Peter Hughman collaborated on *Most Unnatural* (Penguin), a study of the Stafford-Luvaglio case.

The Scottish Records Office has details of the confession of Paul Harris and the circumstances of the reprieve of his brother, Claude. The cases of Ernest Melville and George Roberts are covered by Iain Adamson in his life of Reg Spooner, *The Great Detective* (Frederick Muller). There is also a file at the Public Records Office, Kew, on the Melville case, PRO/MEPO/3/3125, in which he bemoans his lack of progress, saying he believes the locals are sheltering someone. Unlike many police officers of his generation, Frederick Balmer did not publish his memoirs in book form. They appeared in the *Liverpool Echo* on his retirement in 1967.

Douglas C. Browne and T. Tullett also look at the Melville case in *Bernard Spilsbury* (Harrap), a biography of the forensic pathologist. For other views of the great man see the memoirs of pathologists Sidney Smith, *Mostly Murder* (Granada) and Keith Simpson, *Forty Years of Murder* (Panther), neither of whom were wholly enamoured with him.